Population, Poverty, Policy

Population, Poverty, Policy

Essential Essays from Nicholas Eberstadt

Nicholas Eberstadt

VOLUME 1

THE AEI PRESS

Publisher for the American Enterprise Institute
WASHINGTON, DC

ISBN-13: 978-0-8447-5012-5

Dedication

To Henry Wendt III

*With admiration, affection,
and deep appreciation*

Contents

List of Illustrations ix

Foreword xiii
    Christopher DeMuth

I. Population and Policy 1
  1. "Population Change and National Security," *Foreign Affairs,*
     Summer 1991 2
  2. "Too Many People?" International Policy Network, July 11, 2007 18
  3. "The Demographic Future," *Foreign Affairs*, November/
     December 2010 51
  4. "The Human Population Unbound," *Current History*,
     January 2014 65

II. The Politics of Hunger 73
  5. "Hunger and Ideology," *Commentary,* July 1981 74
  6. "Famine, Development, and Foreign Aid," *Commentary*,
     March 1985 95
  7. "Starved for Ideas," World Food Summit in Rome, November 15,
     1996 111

III. Demographic Destinies 125
  8. "Mortality and the Fate of Communist States," *Prosperous Paupers
     and Other Population Problems*, 2000 126
  9. "Growing Old the Hard Way: China, Russia, India," *Policy Review*,
     May 2006 157
  10. "Hastening Korean Reunification," *Foreign Affairs*,
     March/April 1997 187

IV. Human Imperatives 195

11. "The Global Poverty Paradox," *Commentary*, October 2010 197
12. "Haiti in Extremis," *The Weekly Standard*, October 9, 2006.............. 211
13. "The Global War Against Baby Girls," *The New Atlantis*,
    January 12, 2012..222
14. "Bring Them Home," *The Weekly Standard*, June 6, 2005................. 238

V. O My America 251

15. "America's Infant Mortality Puzzle," *The Public Interest,* Fall 1991 253
16. "The Mismeasure of Poverty," *Policy Review,*
    August/September 2006.. 271
17. "Demographic Exceptionalism in the United States: Tendencies
    and Implications," *Agir*, 2007.. 310
18. "American Exceptionalism and the Entitlement State,"
    National Affairs, January 5, 2015 326

Afterword 340
    Arthur C. Brooks

Index... 343

Acknowlegments.. 371

About the Author... 373

List of Illustrations

FIGURES

2-1 Population Density vs. GDP per Capita...22

2-2 Population Density vs. GDP per Capita, PPP....................................23

2-3 Arable Land vs. GDP per Capita...24

2-4 Arable Land vs. GDP per Capita, PPP...25

2-5 Estimated GDP per Capita...30

2-6 Estimated Global GDP...31

2-7 World Population vs. Prices of Wheat, Maize, and Rice, 1900–2003. 32

2-8 World GNP vs. Relative Primary Commodity Prices 33

2-9 Total Fertility Rates vs. GDP per Capita, 1960 40

2-10 Total Fertility Rates vs. GDP per Capita, 2005 41

2-11 Estimated Total Fertility Rates vs. GDP per Capita 42

2-12 Estimated Total Fertility Rates vs. Illiteracy Rates 42

2-13 Per Capita Caloric Availability 43

9-1 Percentage of the Population Aged 65+ vs. GDP per Capita:
    Developing Countries 1950–2000 vs. Emerging Economies 2000 .. 161

9-2 Estimated and Projected Population Structure of China:
    2000 vs. 2025...164

9-3 Male Survival Schedule, Ages 20–65: Russia vs. Switzerland, 1999. 170

9-4 Age and Education Pyramid for Kerala, India: 2001 and 2026........176

9-5 Age and Education Pyramid for Bihar, India: 2001 and 2026..........177

13-1 Reported Sex Ratio in China by Province, 2005...............................224

13-2 Reported Child (0–4) Sex Ratio in China by Country, 2000 225

13-3 China: Reported Sex Ratios at Birth by Birth Order (parity),
    1982–2005...227

13-4 Sex Ratios at Birth Reported in East Asia: 1980–2005 229

13-5 Reported Child (0–6) Sex Ratio, India, Re-aggregated
    Sub-Districts, 2001...230

16-1 No Progress for Three Decades? U.S. Poverty Rate, 1973–2004 279

16-2 Long-Term Probability of Staying in Poverty, by Age 1996–99 293

16-3 Absolute Annual Income Variability, 1970–2000:
Medium-Income Families...296

16-4 Poverty Rates vs. Infant Mortality Rates: USA, White Children
1959–2001 303

16-5 Percent of Children Under 18 Years Without a Reported Health
Care Visit in the Past Year, by Percent of Poverty Threshold 305

17-1 US "Demographic Exceptionalism": TFRs, Canada vs. USA,
1975–2004... 314

17-2 TFRs, Europe vs. "Anglo" USA: 2000.. 316

17-3 Population Structure, 2025:Western Europe vs. USA (US Census
Bureau Projections) 322

TABLES

2-1 Estimated Life Expectancy at Birth (Both Sexes) 28

2-2 Estimated Infant Mortality at Birth (Both Sexes) 28

2-3 Estimated Illiteracy Rate (Both Sexes, Aged 15 and Over) 44

2-4 Estimated Educational Attainment by Sex (Population Age 15
and Over 45

8-1 Expectation of Life at Age One and Age 30: Warsaw Pact Region,
c. 1965–c. 1989 131

8-2 Changes in Age Specific Death Rates for Cohorts Aged 30–69:
Warsaw Pact Region, c. 1965–c. 1989 (percent)............................. 132

8-3 CIA Estimates of Changes in Per Capita GNP vs. WHO Estimates
of Changes in Age-Standardized Male Mortality: Selected Warsaw
Pact and Western European Countries, c. 1965–c. 1989 140

8-4 CIA Estimates of Per Capita GNP vs. WHO Estimates of Total
Age-Standardized Mortality: Warsaw Pact Countries and Selected
Latin American Countries, c. 1989... 141

8-5 Officially Claimed or Independently Reconstructed Changes in
Life Expectancy at Birth: Surviving Communist Regimes,
c. 1965–c.1989 143

8-6 Mortality Differentials in Germany, 1989: Eastern German
Death Rates as a Ratio of Western German Death Rates 148

8-7 After "Die Wende": Reported Changes in Age-Specific Death Rates . 149

8-8 "After the Revolution": Age-Standardized Mortality in
        Eastern Europe, 1989–1990.. 150
9-1 Population Aging in Developed Economies Today vs. Emerging
        Market Economies Tomorrow 162
13-1 The Rise of Gender Imbalance in China.. 224
13-2 Selected Countries with Populations over 1 Million Reporting
        Sex Ratios at Birth over 107 in a Recent Year (and Near-Complete
        Viral Registration).. 232
13-3 Selected Countries with Populations over 1 Million Reporting
        Child (0–4) Sex Ratios Above 107 in a Recent Population Census .. 232
15-1 Estimated Proportion of Low-Birth-Weight Babies: Single Live
        Births, 1982, by Selected Maternal Characteristics........................... 259
15-2 Infant-Mortality Rates by Race, Education, and Marital Status
        for Woman Age Twenty Years or Older: Eight Pilot States,
        United States, 1982 Birth Cohort (per 1,000 Live Births) 261
15-3 Infant-Mortality Rates by Race of Mother and Number of
        Prenatal Visits: United States, 1986 Birth Cohort
        (Deaths per 1,000 Live Births)... 263
15-4 Characteristics of Children, Families, and Persons in States
        with Highest and Lowest Reported Black Infant-Mortality Rates
        c. 1980 267
15-5 Average Number of Physician Contacts for American Children
        Under Eighteen Years of Age by Selected Characteristics:
        1985–1987.. 268
15-6 Patterns of Consumer Expenditure by Reported Household
        Income and Age of Head of Household (1988 U.S. Dollars)........... 270
16-1 Poverty Rate and Other Possible Indicators of Progress Against
        Poverty: 1973 vs. 2001... 281
16-2 Consumer Expenditure Patterns for Low-Income Americans:
        1960/61–2002... 287
16-3 Selected Housing Characteristics, Poor and Other Households,
        USA: 1970–2001... 301
17-1 TFR by Ethnicity: USA, 2004 315
18-1 Entitlement Dependence in America, 1983 v. 2012 331

Foreword

The papers collected in this volume recount a 40-year struggle between scholarship and illusion on matters of great importance. They do much more than that: They present a matchless course of instruction in the demographics of poverty and prosperity, hardship and health, and progress and decline, and they paint a vivid, pointillist portrait of the circumstances of modern humanity. But readers should be alert to the underlying drama and seek to learn from it, too.

Here Nick Eberstadt, armed only with data and patient study, debunks Al Gore, Jared Diamond, and Planned Parenthood on population growth and population control; then demolishes a phalanx of ideologues on world hunger and famine; then shreds Jeffrey Sachs and UN officialdom on economic growth and international aid programs. And then dares all of us to confront humanitarian catastrophes that many prefer to ignore, such as enforced immiserization in North Korea and the now-extensive global practice of selective abortion of females.

The reader may be tempted to judge these contests as one-sided. That, as our author would say, would be a fallacy of construction. On the page and at the podium, the essential Nick Eberstadt reigns supreme. His learning, mastery of data, and sophisticated interpretations will win over many skeptics and edify every careful student. The wider world, however, is governed by more than reason. Problems of mass poverty, depravation, and disease, viewed at a distance from societies grown rich and comfortable, stir our deepest emotions, as well they should. But they are also fertile ground for sentimental thinking and abstract moralizing—and for political ideologies and government projects that are highly resistant to logic and evidence.

There is much good news in this volume. Thought and action on problems of world poverty have become more practical and results-oriented in the decades since Eberstadt first entered the fray (and he is due a share of credit). The period of economic and political liberalization running from the late

1980s to the early 2000s produced stupendous improvements in economic welfare and health among the inhabitants of nations previously drenched in misery and not infrequently in blood—China, India, and others.

Nevertheless, wishful thinking and counterproductive programs continue to enjoy great prestige and ample funding, and many of Eberstadt's excellent recommendations have yet to be adopted. In recent years, many authoritarian, autarkic governments and movements have sprung up, while America has lost confidence in itself as a liberalizing force. In this environment, progress has stopped and indeed regressed in many regions—notably within the "weak states" of sub-Saharan Africa and parts of East Asia and Latin America, within Russia and the Central European nations formerly ruled by the Soviet Union, and in the effectively stateless nation of Haiti.

So the arguments of this book still have much work to do. We can be grateful that its author is as energetic and persistent as ever, as his most recent essays demonstrate; this collection is just a first installment.

Nicholas Eberstadt majored in economics at Harvard College and earned his Ph.D. in political economy and government at the Kennedy School of Government. Along the way he determined to study questions of social welfare and public policy through the lens of demographics. This surprising choice is a key to the quality and influence of his work. Which takes a some explaining.

Demography is the measurement of the size of large populations, usually national populations, and their composition by age, sex, region, ethnicity, and other subgroups. At this basic level, demographics is not a social science at all but rather a practical art, concerned with the mechanics of counting noses, organizing the results, and calculating trends and comparisons. The tabulations serve many immediate purposes—designing election districts, distributing government funds, and guiding business investments and marketing programs.

But demography also serves an explanatory function. It aims to project future population trends and assess their implications for social welfare, economic growth, and politics within and among nations. On these matters it must borrow from economics, sociology, history, and other disciplines. It needs them to answer such questions as how higher incomes affect fertility and longevity, and how changes in population size and composition affect health, welfare, and economic performance.

Some of these questions can be addressed in a scientific spirit—theory, hypothesis, and empirical testing, leading to rejection or acceptance with more or less confidence for the time being. As a field, however, explanatory demography is loose, atheoretical, and open to improvisation. This is because it is universal and accessible—demographics is democratic in method as well as subject.

First, the size and composition of populations are the most elementary and universal of social data. They are of interest to numerous disciplines, each with its own methods and purposes. But the vast variety of human circumstance and endeavor limits the range of every disciplinary explanation and every attempt at scientific parsimony. No general proposition is more firmly established, for example, than that couples with higher incomes tend to have fewer children. Yet even here there are numerous qualifications, elaborations, and uncertainties—Eberstadt would point us to wealthy Mormons with large families and poor Burmese with small families. It is true and illuminating that wealthy modern urban couples have higher opportunity costs and lower immediate benefits of childrearing; but it is not the whole story.

Second, population numbers are uniquely accessible. They are official government statistics, reported as news; they quantify social developments that everyone knows something about through personal experience; they invite interpretation without need for specialized background or technical assumptions; and they seem to be associated in some way with a host of important issues—pollution, immigration, pensions, health care, crime, national defense, the electoral prospects of political parties. Explanatory demographics is therefore a popular sport open to every pundit, politician, promoter, and prophet of ruin or salvation. So we are awash in population propositions. Some of them are sensible and reasonable, but many, on examination, are partial and incomplete, or confuse cause for effect, or are self-contradictory. Worst of all, many are efforts to make policy causes seem apodictic—an imperative response to an inexorable trend rather than a debatable political choice.

I surmise from Eberstadt's writings that it was these qualities of universality and accessibility that attracted him to demographics. He wanted to work on the largest questions of human wellbeing and saw demography as a suitable canvas. But he was appalled by the chasm between the seriousness of the problems demographics revealed and the unseriousness of much that was being said and done about those problems. The field's unstructured, democratic character was an opportunity for a man of ambition. He would use his knowledge of economics, political science, and history to sort out truth, error, and claptrap, inject rigor into desultory debates, and point the way to better policies. He would employ direct appeals to fact, logic, and experience that required special talent to formulate but no special training to understand. In this manner, he would address himself not only to other academics but also to politicians and policy officials, journalists and activists, and the demographic worker bees who do the practical work of designing and conducting government censuses and surveys.

I have more to go on than his writings, because Eberstadt and I were colleagues at the American Enterprise Institute for twenty-five years. When I arrived as AEI's new president in 1986, the young researcher walked me through an intellectual to-do list, filling many pages of foolscap, that was astonishing in its range and audacity. He was intent on invading many territories that were uncharted and, it seemed to me at the time, unrelated—puzzlingly high infant mortality in the United States, preposterously high industrialization in sub-Saharan Africa, impossibly high economic growth in Communist nations. Fortunately for both of us, I was too inexperienced to advise him to narrow his focus and be a good career specialist. I could only respond that his agenda would take decades to accomplish so he'd better get on with it; I was right, and that list is now the table of contents of this collection (at least in part—it will take a second volume to complete the list).

And over time, as our friendship and collaborations deepened, I saw firsthand his determination to penetrate to the realities behind the numbers in government reports and academic papers. Presiding at policy conferences in exotic foreign locales, I noticed that when the formal sessions were in recess most conferees turned to recreation and sightseeing (the leisure of the theory class). Not Eberstadt—who would instead disappear for long afternoons in obscure government office buildings with statisticians and census-takers and health experts, and long evenings in slum neighborhoods where few academics or bureaucrats would dare to tread.

My interpretation of Eberstadt the interloper demographer is confirmed by the originality and excellence of the papers collected here, and by several striking features of his approach to understanding and persuasion:

- He employs simple logic to demolish many entrenched, lazy assumptions. That large numbers of people are poor does not mean that the large numbers cause the poverty. The "graying" of a population is much more a function of falling birthrates than of lengthening lifespans (arithmetic says so).

- He is cautious of broad generalizations but can construct powerful ones of his own. If rapid population growth causes poverty, how does one explain the twentieth century, which saw enormous concurrent increases in both population and in incomes and wealth? That century's population explosion occurred not because people began breeding like rabbits but rather because they stopped dying like flies. And the health improvements were notably egalitarian, dramatically reducing the differential lifespans of rich and poor.

- He would never say that demography is destiny, but he can show where it constrains destiny. Official Western estimates of steady economic growth in the Soviet bloc nations during the 1970s and 1980s were implausible given the steadily worsening health of their inhabitants. Communist regimes collapsed in nations with worsening health and mortality—and survived where mortality, at least, was improving. China's central problem today is that its population (unlike Japan's) is going to grow old before it grows rich; China's fertility collapse, and radical imbalance of males to females, makes the fashionable long-term extrapolation of its recent rapid economic growth unlikely in the extreme.

- He is unafraid of hard facts without confident explanations. In Russia and some other Soviet bloc nations, mortality, longevity, and other measures of health status significantly worsened after the fall of Communism. The deterioration was beyond that in any other time or place other than in times of war or plague. Eberstadt identified and documented this terrible development although he could not explain its cause, other than that the ravages of totalitarianism may have been worse than we knew.

- He insists on the importance of local culture and attitudes, political norms, and government structure—factors that have become off-limits to most demographers and development specialists, and that are largely (not entirely) unquantifiable. One of his most striking propositions (based on research by Lant Pritchett) is this: The best predictor of the fertility level in a population, which operates independently of the availability of birth-control technology, is the number of children its women say they would like to have. Another: The worst and most persistent conditions of poverty and depravation are in nations whose governments are highly corrupt, incompetent, and incapable of providing basic levels of personal safety, never mind potable water.

Eberstadt teaches that, broadly speaking, economic development and poverty reduction are functions of "Western values"—a modicum of economic liberty as a prerequisite to growth, a modicum of democracy to protect against state corruption and indifference to citizens' welfare, and a modicum of optimism and progressive spirit to encourage individuals to act with a view toward the future. In his latest papers, he worries that these values are at risk in America itself because of the growth of a comprehensive welfare state. He is concerned about this because America is his country, but also for another reason. America's foreign aid programs, he has long observed, promote unproductive government-directed development strategies that are the opposite of those it promotes at home and among its allies in the developed world. That inconsistency may now be ending—but not in the manner he would recommend.

There is a deceptively simple passage in the first paper in this collection that could have served as the epigraph for the entire volume: "Demography is the study of human numbers, but it is the human characteristics of those numbers that define world events." I said at the outset that these papers tell of a struggle between scholarship and illusion. The reader may conclude that they tell of something more—of a victory of morally informed scholarship over materialist ideologies of every sort.

—Christopher DeMuth
May 2016

PART I

Population and Policy

Demography is the study of human numbers, but it is the human characteristics of those numbers that define world events. What is called a demographic problem may better be described as a moral and intellectual problem that takes demographic form.
– From "Population Change and National Security"

In our era, neo-Malthusian ideology—the notion that people are a sort of plague—has been embraced by many as a truth of nature. Ever since my first published forays in demographics, I have spoken out against the folly of this worldview. Human resources are intrinsically an asset, not a liability, as even the most elementary examination of basic trends in modern economic development should underscore. Unlike fruit flies or red deer, human beings possess human agency, and through that very agency they—unlike other animals—can deliberately transform and augment the resource base that sustains them. Neo-Malthusianism proposes to reduce human poverty simply by reducing the number of children that the poor are encouraged or allowed to bear—a mindset that inescapably draws its adherents toward the inhumanity of "population control." As I attempt to demonstrate with empirical evidence in the following chapters, the relationship between population change on the one hand and human prosperity and well-being on the other is actually far more complex—and also much more promising—than population ideologues and activists understand.

1

1

Population Change and National Security

Foreign Affairs, Summer 1991

For better or worse, ours is a time of rapid and pronounced demographic change. For hundreds, if not thousands, of years before the Industrial Revolution, the pace of global population change was negligible. By some estimates population grew by roughly 14 percent per century between the years 1000 and 1750. At current rates the same proportionate growth is achieved in less than eight years.

Over the past few generations demographic change has not only radically altered human numbers but has profoundly affected their composition and global distribution. While the role of population in world affairs may seem self-evident, its relevance to state power and national security is often far from obvious.

Demographic change is but one factor limiting a state's ability to impose its will abroad or maintain itself at home. It might be—but need not be—a major consideration. Indeed, the impact of demographic change is often difficult to gauge. Demographic forces do not typically exert a single pressure on a society or state. Furthermore some demographic projections have proved famously wrong, and there is little reason to believe that new predictions will turn out much better.

Regardless of their exact calibrations, virtually all current population projections anticipate comparatively slow population growth in today's more developed regions (Europe, the Soviet Union, Japan, North America and Oceania) and comparatively rapid growth for the less developed regions (the rest of the world). With variations, these projections point to a continuation of trends evident since the end of World War II. If these trends continue for another generation or two, the implications for the international political order and the balance of world power could be enormous.

II

Perhaps no demographic trend in the postwar era has aroused as much public concern as the acceleration of population growth in low-income countries. Between 1950 and 1985, according to the most recent estimates of the United Nations' Population Division, the population of the more developed regions grew by about 41 percent. During that same period the population of the less developed regions increased by about 119 percent, or almost three times as fast. Although the tempo of growth varied by country and year, this "population explosion" has affected virtually every society in Africa, Asia and Latin America. The total population of these areas was thought to be growing by over 80 million annually in the late 1980s, and the rate of growth may have risen slightly in recent years.

Western policy circles often view rapid population growth in the Third World as a serious problem, sometimes a pressing one. Rapid growth of poor populations, by these arguments, can only speed the spread of poverty. Population growth, moreover, is envisioned as "eating away" at economic growth in poor countries, reducing or altogether canceling potential improvements in living standards and aggravating such conditions as poor health, malnutrition, illiteracy and unemployment.

The political implications of such trends are often described as ominous. By some assessments rapid population growth threatens to destabilize governments in low-income countries—through food shortages, for example, or by overwhelming the state with social service demands or by creating an unmanageable and volatile crush in urban areas. Some suggest rapid population growth increases the risks of a general confrontation between "haves" and "have nots" by contributing to a widening gap between rich and poor countries. Finally, it is sometimes said, by creating major new demands for global resources, rapid population growth in low-income countries pushes humanity toward an era of scarcity—perhaps toward an unsustainable overshoot of the environment's carrying capacity.

The vision of a population explosion consuming the world evokes powerful emotions. Because discussions of rapid population growth in less developed countries seem at times to be governed by fervor of faith, it is often difficult to persuade the convinced through reasoning or empirical evidence. Yet recent experience suggests the consequences of rapid population growth are significantly different from those commonly supposed.

Take the notion that rapid population growth has prevented economic progress in low-income countries. The Development Research Center at the Organization for Economic Cooperation and Development (OECD) has recently published estimates of economic growth rates for a sample of 32 countries, whose populations comprise about three-fourths of the current world total. This sample includes such countries as China, India, Indonesia, Brazil, Bangladesh, Pakistan and Mexico (although, for want of reliable data, it excludes all of sub-Saharan Africa).

Estimated per-capita output for this sample rose by a factor of more than four between 1900 and 1987. Though the populations of the nine Asian countries in the sample more than tripled during this period, and the population of the six Latin American countries rose by a factor of nearly seven, per-capita output is estimated to have risen dramatically as well—by a factor of more than three for the Asian group and by nearly five for the Latin American group. Moreover, despite Latin America's highly publicized economic problems, per-capita income in the sampled Latin American countries—nations accounting for roughly three-quarters of the total population for Central and South America and the Caribbean—more than doubled between 1950 and 1987. Evidently, rapid population growth has not prevented major improvements in productivity in many of the societies most directly transformed by it.

These figures indicate per-capita growth accelerated sharply in most of the poor countries in this sample in the period after 1950—in other words, after the advent of the population explosion. But correlation does not imply causation. Some observers will be surprised that these two trends broadly coincided in the Third World. Their surprise derives in part from a misperception of the causes of the recent rapid rates of population growth in low-income countries.

The population explosion in low-income countries has been driven by a revolution in health. Between the early 1950s and the early 1980s infant mortality rates in the less developed regions fell by half, and life expectancy at birth rose by more than 16 years. By this particular, hardly unimportant measure, the "gap" between rich and poor countries narrowed appreciably in recent decades. Even in perennially troubled Africa, health progress appears substantial.

In itself health progress constitutes an improvement in living standards and may speak as well to conditions bearing upon health, such as nutrition, education and housing. Improvements in health may also directly affect a population's economic potential. Human capital, to be sure, corresponds with economic potential, not actual achievement. Like other sorts of capital it need not be used; it might be depleted through injurious policies. Be that as it may, the same forces driving population growth in poor countries appear to have increased the potential for widespread and continual material advance.

Such a cautiously optimistic conclusion might seem to be challenged by the current example of sub-Saharan Africa, where troubles abound and population growth rates—already the world's highest—have been accelerating. Many observers attribute the social, economic and political ills of the region directly to its rapid population growth. They may fail to consider other obvious factors central to the region's misfortunes.

Sub-Saharan Africa is currently characterized by what might be described as pervasive misrule. Ethnic animosities are widespread and sometimes incorporated into government policy by the dominant group. State involvement in the local economy is often far-reaching, and more often than not mismanagement and misappropriation are the norm. Some governments have set about systematically uprooting their subjects and overturning their livelihoods, even when such groups are on the barest edge of subsistence. Under such circumstances societies would be expected to experience serious economic problems, irrespective of any contribution from population growth. A population problem that proves independent of a society's actual demographic conditions is a problem misdefined.

What of the concern that continued population growth will place a devastating burden on the global environment, endangering the well-being of all? When public opinions are as strong and popular emotions as inflamed as they seem to be over global environmental degradation, a few words will unlikely change many minds. Yet concerns about impending resource exhaustion and environmental catastrophe have been voiced for more than a century. While the inaccuracy of past predictions (e.g., the prophesied English coal shortage of the nineteenth century or the U.S. "timber famine" of the early twentieth) does not invalidate current concerns, it should raise questions about why such dire forecasts have been so recurringly amiss.

Perhaps such assessments have paid inadequate attention to the economic process, which generated demand for resources. Between 1900 and 1987, by U.N. estimates, the world's population more than tripled, and its level of economic output, to generalize from the OECD's sample, may have increased more than a dozen times. Despite such growth of demand the inflation-adjusted prices of many primary products—ore, farm goods and the like—are lower today than at the turn of the century. By the information that prices are meant to convey, many resources would appear to be less scarce today than they were at the turn of the century.

How could this be? Quite simply, because the economic process prompts responses to shortage and scarcity. To over simplify, the price mechanism identifies scarcity through higher prices, thereby encouraging substitution and rewarding innovation within the limits of human preference. Previously worthless materials are brought into use (bauxite, petroleum); previously plentiful resources are more likely to be husbanded (German forests).

Much remains unknown about the workings of the global environment; considerably more may be understood about the general workings of the economic exchange process. Uncertainties about the environment may call for prudence—but it is not clear in which direction prudence points. Until we better understand our surroundings it may be unwise to ignore the possibility that forceful initiatives to "save the environment" could have a more adverse impact on human populations and existing political systems than would the trends they fear.

III

At the national level population change is propelled by three demographic forces: fertility, mortality and migration.

The mathematics of demography can easily demonstrate fertility's tendency to dominate other demographic forces in the shaping of "closed" populations. In a world where the scope for migration is limited, and where mortality levels are relatively stable, fertility can be expected to act as the decisive force: driving changes in the local composition and global distribution of population. Yet, under all but the most catastrophic circumstances, neither wartime losses nor mass movements of people will have as much impact on a population's size and structure as will ordinary shifts and fluctuations in fertility.

On occasion a country's absolute level of fertility may motivate a government to adopt unexpected policies. Contemporary examples would include China's on-going campaign of population control and Japan's long-standing trade surpluses (which are indirectly related to the nation's low fertility level). For the most part, however, it is relative differences in fertility among groups within a country that give rise to events of political consequence. In some societies differential fertility may have contributed directly to the collapse of the state.

Consider the case of Lebanon. An unwritten 1943 agreement, later known as the National Pact, stipulated that political authority be shared among the country's "confessional" or religious groups in accordance with their strength in the national population. Top ministers were to be divided in a six-to-five ratio between Christians and Muslims (including the Druze sect), corresponding to the breakdown reported in the country's 1932 population census. Subsequent surveys, however, underscored a pronounced difference between Christian and Muslim fertility.

In the early 1970s the Christian community was estimated to have a total fertility rate of less than four children per woman, as compared with an estimated fertility rate of nearly six children per woman for the Muslim community. By 1975 Lebanon is widely believed to have become a Muslim-majority country.

The permanent refugee Palestinian population in the south of the country, great-power ambitions evidenced by its Syrian neighbor and evolving Israeli security measures all posed threats to the integrity of the Lebanese state. Nevertheless the Lebanese government's chances of persevering might have been greater if a changing population balance had not simultaneously undermined the rationale for the existing order.

Israel is another Middle Eastern country facing fertility driven security pressures. Though vastly outnumbered by its Arab neighbor states Israel has succeeded in preserving, even enhancing, its security since its establishment over four decades ago. Israel occupied the territories of Gaza and the West Bank during the Six Day War of 1967 and has maintained administrative control of these areas ever since—a policy still viewed as essential to Israel's security prospects by both major blocs in Israel's Knesset, or parliament.

Though above replacement, and indeed higher than rates for almost all other contemporary Western populations, the fertility level of Israel's Jews has been distinctly lower than that of Israel's Arabs. Fertility rates for Palestinians in the occupied or administered territories are higher still. Even with stepped-up Jewish immigration from abroad and rapid fertility decline among Palestinians in the West Bank and Gaza, Jews could become a minority population in "Greater Israel" within a few decades.

Lebanon was, and Israel remains, a mass democracy. But even under governments that do not accord each adult a vote, the weight of numbers can affect the state's ability to augment and deploy power. The Republic of South Africa offers a case in point.

In 1951, as the laws and practices of "Grand Apartheid" were being formalized, South Africa's whites accounted for slightly more than one-fifth of the country's enumerated population. By the early 1980s whites accounted for less than a seventh of the population within the country's 1951 boundaries. By 2020, according to official government projections, the white population would amount to no more than a ninth of the total population, barring massive net migration of whites from abroad. Adjusting the projections to 1951 borders, whites might comprise less than one-eleventh of the country's total. South Africa's current liberalizations may not have been motivated by these trends, but they are surely informed by them.

Even more than South Africa, the Soviet Union can be viewed as a tangle of demographic problems. There, perhaps more than any other large country, trends in differential fertility bear directly on the government's prospects for projecting power and even maintaining authority.

Ethnic Russians accounted for barely half (50.8 percent) of the enumerated population in the U.S.S.R.'s 1989 census. Like South Africa, the Soviet Union assigns each citizen a state determined race or ethnicity (in Soviet parlance, "nationality"). More than one hundred nationalities were recognized in the country's 1989 census. By that same census less than half of the U.S.S.R.'s non-Russian population reported itself to have a command of the Russian language; the proportion was somewhat lower than in the previous census. The Russian population is separated by language from the life of other Soviet nationalities, but not by language alone. Fertility differences are also evident, for example, between the U.S.S.R.'s Russian population and its populations of Muslim heritage.

Between 1959 and 1989 the U.S.S.R.'s Russian population rose by about 27 percent, but its nominal Muslim population grew by about 125 percent. This reduced the ratio of Russians to Muslims to 2.6-to-1. By early 1989 the U.S.S.R.'s population of persons of Muslim heritage may have exceeded 55 million. If these people are to be counted as Muslims (there is some debate about this), the Soviet Union would today contain the world's fifth largest Muslim population—outnumbering the populations of Egypt, Turkey or Iran.

Within the U.S.S.R.'s multiethnic configuration Russians have been the dominant element. As in the imperial order that preceded it, Russians have provided the Soviet Union with its official language and have supplied the overwhelming majority of political personalities within the country's ruling circle. Fertility change will directly challenge prevailing assumptions about the administration of Soviet power. Russians no longer constitute a majority of Soviet men of military age (18–25). Within a decade they will no longer form the majority of the working-age population, and by then may account for less than two-fifths of the country's children. Such changes have implications for Soviet military, labor and language policies. If the Russian Republic substantially underwrites living standards in Central Asian republics, as some analysts in the Soviet Union and the West believe, these changes will have major budgetary implications as well.

Fertility differentials in the Soviet Union do not consign the country to domestic disorder or reduced international stature. The impending shift in Soviet population composition will be gradual and therefore unlikely to set immediate constraints on the day-to-day options for the Soviet leadership. Over time, however, it may just as surely alter the boundaries of the possible. Today, when central authority in the Soviet Union seems to be relatively weak, centrifugal ethnic passions have come to the fore. Such forces are likely to be accelerated by the current momentum of differential fertility.

IV

The twentieth century has witnessed a revolution in health. Very possibly, three-quarters of the improvement in life expectancy has occurred since 1900. So powerful have been the forces promoting improved health that even the advent of total war has been incapable of counterbalancing them. Despite terrible loss of life and attendant devastation, life expectancy was higher in post-World War I France than in the prewar period; higher in Spain after the Spanish Civil War than before; and higher in Japan and West Germany in 1950 than before World War II.

The recent histories of West Germany, Japan and South Korea, among others, demonstrate that the loss of significant portions of the working-age population—and the debilitation or episodic starvation of some considerable fraction of surviving cohorts—does not preclude rapid restoration of prewar levels of output or a rapid subsequent pace for material advance. Moreover, despite the severe privations its people suffered during and immediately after World War II, Japan currently has the longest life expectancy rates (and generally the lowest age-specific mortality rates) of any country—arguably suggesting that the Japanese are today the world's healthiest people.

In the future health progress might be halted by some cataclysm. Imaginably a plague or pestilence against which human populations could not develop immunity might strike. (Some current commentators believe the AIDS epidemic to be just such an affliction.) One need not look to a hypothetical future, however, for instances of interruption and even reversals of health progress in national populations. The Soviet Union and eastern Europe provide contemporary examples.

In the 1950s the Soviet Union enjoyed a rapid drop in overall mortality and a corresponding increase in life expectancy. So dramatic was this health progress that the United Nations Population Fund estimated life expectancy to be slightly higher in the Soviet Union than in the United States in the early 1960s; before World War II the American level is thought to have been about a decade and a half higher. In the mid-1960s, however, Soviet mortality reductions came to an abrupt halt, and death rates for men in certain age groups began to rise. As the 1960s and 1970s progressed, death rates registered a rise for virtually all adults, male and female. Mortality rates apparently also began to rise for Soviet infants. Though the immediate official reaction was to withhold data on these trends, glasnost has provided evidence on their scope. Between 1969–70 and 1984–85, for example, Soviet death rates for persons in their late forties are now reported to have risen by over a fifth; for those in their late fifties, by over a fourth. Between the mid-1960s and the mid-1980s Soviet life expectancy at birth is now reported to have fallen by almost three years and to have declined for both adult women and men.

Although the Soviet Union was apparently the first industrial society to suffer a general and prolonged deterioration of public health during peacetime, it is no longer unique. Similar, though less extreme, tendencies have been reported in eastern Europe over the past generation. Between the mid-1960s and the mid-1980s life expectancy at one year of age fell by an average of slightly less than a year for the European members of the Warsaw Pact; for men at 30 years of age, life expectancy dropped by an average of over two years during the same period. According to the most recent estimates of the World Health Organization, by the late 1980s total age-standardized death rates (adjusted to the who's "European Model" population) were higher for the Soviet Union and the countries of the Warsaw Pact than for such nations as Argentina, Chile, Mexico or Venezuela.

A significant and pervasive rise in the number of deaths attributed to cardiovascular deaths figures prominently in these overall trends. Smoking patterns, drinking patterns and health care policies all played their part. Recent evidence suggests that severe environmental problems played a greater role than previously appreciated. Intangible and intrinsically immeasurable factors, such as attitude and outlook, may also have been involved.

Whatever the etiological origins of these trends, their implications for state power are unmistakably adverse. Rising adult mortality rates reduce the potential size of a country's work force. Between 1977 and 1988 the U.S. Census Bureau reduced its projection for turn-of-the-century population aged 25–64 in eastern Europe by about two million persons, or three percent. Insofar as the cohort had been born by 1977, and migration was negligible, the revision basically reflected a reassessment of the impact of health trends. With deteriorating health, moreover, the economic potential of surviving groups might be constrained. To the extent that attitude and outlook factor in the decline, far-reaching problems of popular morale may be indicated.

There is nothing immutable about the U.S.S.R. and eastern Europe's unfavorable mortality trends. To the contrary: at a time of generally improving health potential, it would almost seem to require special effort to prevent health progress. Evidently, these states were up to the task. At the very least, they have proved to be unwilling or incapable of embracing the sorts of policies that would have forestalled such declines. One may wonder whether acquiescence in such long-term attrition does not in itself speak to a brittleness or decay in presiding polities, and thus directly to political prospects for the states in question.

V

Paradoxically, even as economic development has been increasing the scope for, and role of, human mobility in material advance, the demographic significance of international migration has decidedly diminished. The Age of Exploration is finished; the territories of the globe are now divided among standing governments, virtually all of which limit the absorption of new citizens from abroad in some fashion. Many presume to regulate even the right to travel.

At the turn of the century gross emigration from continental Europe was averaging over eight million persons per decade, or a rate equal to roughly two percent of the area's population. In absolute terms the flow is much smaller today; in proportional terms, all the more so.

Opportunities for voluntary migration for most Third World inhabitants remain limited, given the reluctance of most foreign governments to welcome them as citizens. Increasingly, therefore, twentieth-century emigration has become a response to catastrophe—the *Aussiedlung* of millions of ethnic German refugees during and after 1946 into what became West Germany, or the movement of Jewish refugees into what became the state of Israel. Upheavals and turmoil have also given rise to a distinctly new form of "migration"—the long-term refugee, housed for decades in a country not his own. Millions of such people are found today in such places as Lebanon (Palestinians), Pakistan (Afghans) and Thailand (Cambodians). Modern waves of migration have often served as an unhappy barometer of instability and tensions in the emigrant's native land.

Though overall flows of migration have been small by comparison with world population, or even with global births and deaths, they have nevertheless been significant in particular areas. In the 1880s, for example, about 670,000 Scandinavian immigrants entered the United States; that relatively small figure accounted for roughly seven percent of the total population for the countries of origin and perhaps an even greater portion of the working-age population. The political consequences of even seemingly modest streams of migration can be profound. Between 1948 and 1967 net Jewish migration into Israel averaged under 50,000 persons per year. That inflow, however, was consonant with the emergence of Israel as the region's major military power.

For a country accepting migrants national security may be affected greatly by the manner in which the state encourages newcomers to involve themselves in local economic and political life. Saudi Arabia and other gulf states have inducted a total of several million foreigners to man and operate their oil-based economies; in some of these places, mercenaries from abroad hold important positions in the security forces. Showing little interest in bringing guest workers of Palestinian, Pakistani or Korean extraction into the social fabric, the governments of these countries must engage in a complex balancing game to assure national power is augmented more by the foreign workers' presence than domestic stability is compromised.

By contrast, the United States has taken a markedly different approach to immigrants. Exceptions noted (most significantly, the years of slavery), it may be fair to describe the traditional American attitude toward immigrants as universalist: predicated on the assumption that one can "become American" by developing a particular set of political, social and economic values. Without ignoring the problems of assimilation, the American experience appears to have been remarkably successful. Since its founding, more than 50 million persons have voluntarily emigrated to the United States. Though initially a product of an English-speaking population and Anglo-Saxon political theory, the American system proved capable of absorbing large numbers of persons from Ireland, Germanic cultures and successively more remote south and east European cultures.

More recently, non-European groups have figured prominently in the flow of persons adopting a new American identity. The ability to absorb and assimilate immigrants from diverse cultures has been at the core of American strength at home. And to no small degree, the United States' international power and security can be traced to its approach to immigration.

Inability to solve problems of migration or mobility, for its part, can constrain power and limit security of standing governments. Once again the Soviet Union can be used to make the point. For decades Soviet planners have attempted to move labor into western Siberia and the Soviet Far East, areas rich in exploitable natural resources. Today, however, Soviet planners can no longer take "surplus laborers" for granted. Soviet rates of labor force participation are unusually high (regardless of how well employees actually work). Moreover growth in the Soviet "European" population of working age is negligible today. The fastest-growing working-age population, found among predominantly Muslim Central Asian nationalities, has proved remarkably unwilling to leave rural communities, even in the face of considerable financial incentive. So pronounced is this aversion that two Central Asian republics, Tadzhikistan and Turkmenia, registered lower levels of urbanization in 1986 than in 1970. As long as Muslim populations are unwilling to move and work according to state plan, state power in the Soviet Union will suffer.

VI

Demography is the study of human numbers, but it is the human characteristics of those numbers that define world events. What is called a demographic problem may better be described as a moral and intellectual problem that takes demographic form. Indeed, divorced from an understanding of the people behind the data, population studies can provide little insight for statesmen, diplomats or generals contemplating an uncertain future.

Current population trends are redistributing global population and moving it away from today's industrial democracies. In 1950 two of the top five, and seven of the top 20, countries by population could be described as industrial democracies. Their combined populations accounted for nearly a quarter of this big-country total. By 1985 industrial democracies accounted for only one of the top five, and six of the top 20; they comprised less than a sixth of the group's total population. In the year 2025 only one of today's industrial democracies—the United States—is projected to rank among the top five, and only two—Japan and the United States—among the top 20.

In this future world today's industrial democracies would account for less than one-fourteenth of the total population of the big countries. Yet they would rank among the top in the world's population of geriatrics. By one recent U.S. Census Bureau projection, for example, today's industrial democracies would account for eight of the top 18 national populations of persons aged 80 and older by the year 2025.

Whatever their ultimate accuracy, current U.N. projections for the year 2025 depict an American population slightly smaller than Nigeria's, an Iranian population almost as large as Japan's and an Ethiopian population nearly twice that of France. Today's industrial democracies would almost all be "little countries." Canada, one of the Big Seven industrial democracies today (alongside the United States, Germany, Japan, Britain, France and Italy), would have a smaller population than such countries as Madagascar, Nepal and Syria.

In aggregate the population of today's industrial democracies would account for a progressively diminishing share of the world population. Whereas they comprised more than a fifth in 1950, they were only a sixth by 1985 and prospectively stand to be less than a tenth some thirty years hence. By U.N. projections the total population of today's Western countries would be considerably smaller than those of either India or sub-Saharan Africa in 2025 and would not be much greater than those of the Latin American and Caribbean grouping.

Projected shifts in birth totals are perhaps even more striking. Though these projections posit a slight rise in fertility in more developed regions, and a steady drop in less developed regions to near net-replacement levels, women in today's Western countries are projected to bear fewer children in total than mothers in the expanse from Casablanca to Tehran by the year 2020. They are projected to be bearing a third fewer children than mothers in Latin America and the Caribbean; less than half as many as mothers in India and less than a third as many as those from sub-Saharan Africa.

By these projections a very different world would seem to be emerging. Such trends speak to pressures for a systematically diminished role and status for today's industrial democracies. Even with relatively unfavorable assumptions about Third World economic growth, the share of global economic output of today's industrial democracies could decline. With a generalized and progressive industrialization of current low-income areas, the Western diminution would be all the more rapid. Thus, one can easily envision a world more unreceptive, and ultimately more threatening, to the interests of the United States and its allies.

The population and economic-growth trends described could create an international environment even more menacing to the security prospects of the Western alliance than was the Cold War for the past generation. Even without the rise of new blocs or alignments, one can envision a fractious, contentious and inhumane international order: liberal precepts could have steadily less impact on international action and belief in human rights could prove a progressively weaker constraint on the exercise of force.

Imagine a world, indeed, very much like the United Nations today, but with rhetoric in the General Assembly informing policy on a global scale, directing actions affecting the lives of millions of people on a daily basis. Even without an aggressive or hostile Soviet bloc, or the invention of new weapons, this world could be a very dangerous and confused place.

In our day the proximate guarantor of global security has been American force of arms, around which various security alliances have been forged. Security, however, is a matter not only of power but of the ends for which— and means by which—power is exercised. American power has been guided by a distinctive set of principles, broadly shared by all the governments and populations in today's Western countries. They include respect for individual rights and private property; adherence to genuine rule of law; affirmation of the propriety of limited government and a belief in the universal relevance of these principles.

These values and precepts are not necessarily shared, or are only intermittently acknowledged, by the states presiding over the great majority of the world's population. The distinction, in large part, defines our security problem today—and points to our security problems tomorrow.

How to increase the share of the world's population living under such "Western" values? Some writers have endorsed the notion of pronatalist policies for the United States and other industrial countries. Imaginative as such proposals may be, their results are likely to be of little consequence. To date pronatal efforts in Europe and elsewhere have proven expensive (as might be expected when the state gets into the business of "buying" children for their parents), punitive or both, and have had only a marginal long-term impact on fertility. (Under communism, Romania's Ceauéescu regime implemented forceful and harsh pronatalist policies, but these were unable to keep the country's fertility rates from dropping below replacement by the 1980s.) A government reflecting the will of the people, moreover, is unlikely to implement measures that would actually transform popular behavior in such an intimate and important realm as family formation.

A narrow focus on pronatalism also neglects and perhaps even undercuts the greatest strength of Western values—their universal relevance and potential benefit for humanity. Rather than devise means to raise birth rates in societies already subscribing to these values, the leading democracies might better contemplate how such precepts can spread in societies where they are still fundamentally alien.

It is often argued that these values—the notion of a liberal and open order—are culturally specific and therefore cannot or should not be promoted among non-European populations. Such a view, of course, is widely endorsed by governments hostile to these notions in principle, or unwilling to be constrained by them in practice. However these political values are not decisively limited to populations of European culture and heritage. Postwar Japan demonstrates this (although, to be sure, some specialists challenge the degree to which Japan is an open and liberal society).

Will future security prospects depend on the West's success in seeing two, three or many Japans emerge from the present day Third World? The security of the United States and its allies need not be diminished by the economic and demographic rise of countries sharing, and defending, common political principles. To contemplate the Japanese example, however, is to appreciate the enormity of the task. Japan's present order emerged from highly specific and arguably unique conditions. Modern Japan's political system, after all, was erected under American bayonets in an occupied country after unconditional surrender. Whatever else may be said about the contemporary international scene, no world wars seem to beckon.

Even within Europe the transition to a liberal order remains far from complete. The diverse soundings from eastern Europe suggest that prospects for such a transition for the region as a whole are not imminent.

How to effect such a transition in current low-income regions of Latin America, Asia and Africa? Demographers are unlikely to provide penetrating answers to the question. To contemplate the question, however, is to consider the nature of the West's ultimate security challenge—a challenge that will be all the more pressing by current and prospective demographic trends.

2

Too Many People?[1]

International Policy Network, July 11, 2007

The Imperative of "Stabilizing World Population": A Widely Accepted Notion

A demographic specter is haunting authoritative and influential circles in both the United States and the international community. This specter is the supposed imperative to "stabilize human population".

The quest to "stabilize human population" (or to "stabilize world population", or sometimes just "stabilize population") was formally launched on the global stage in 1994 by the United Nations at its Cairo Conference on Population and Development, whose "Programme of Action" intoned that "intensified efforts" to this end were "crucial" given the "contribution that early stabilization of the world population would make towards the achievement of sustainable development".[2] That objective is today embraced by a panoply of subsidiary institutions within the "UN family", including the United Nations Environmental Program (UNEP), the United Nations Children's Fund (UNICEF), and the United Nations Population Fund (UNFPA), which explicitly declared its mission in 2002 to be the promotion of the "universally accepted aim of stabilizing world population".[3]

Closer to home, the goal of "stabilizing human population" is championed by a broad network of population and environmental advocacy groups, including most prominently Planned Parenthood and the Sierra Club (the latter of which has established "stabilizing world population" as goal #4 of its "21st Century agenda".[4] The objective, however, is not merely proclaimed by an activist fringe; to the contrary, it is broadly shared by many elements of what might be called the American "establishment". "Stabilizing world population", for example, is now a programmatic effort for most of the prestigious multi-billion dollar American philanthropic organizations that commit their resources to "international population activities". This list includes—but is not limited to—the Ford Foundation, the Hewlett Foundation, the MacArthur Foundation, the Packard Foundation, and the Rockefeller Foundation.

Further, "stabilizing world population" is a prospect that has been welcomed and financially supported by many of America's most prominent and successful captains of industry: among them, self-made multi-billionaires Ted Turner, Warren Buffet, and Bill Gates. The propriety—or necessity—of "stabilizing global population" has been expounded by a wide array of respected writers, spokespersons, and commentators in the US media. Politically, the goal of "stabilizing world population" is officially approved by USAID (America's foreign aid apparatus). And the quest to "stabilize world population" is championed in the United States by political figures who are both influential and widely popular: one of America's most passionate and outspoken exponents of "world population stabilization", former Vice President Al Gore, very nearly won the presidency in the closely contested 2000 election.

What, exactly, does "stabilizing human population" actually mean? Though the objective is widely championed today, the banner itself is somewhat misleading, for advocates of "stabilizing population" are in fact not concerned with stabilizing human numbers.

If they were, one would expect champions of "population stabilization" to turn their attention to the outlook for Europe and Japan, where populations are currently projected to drop significantly over the next half century.[5] On a more immediate front, human numbers have entered into an abrupt and as yet unchecked decline in the Russian Federation over the past decade: in 2006 alone, that country suffered almost 700,000 more deaths than births.[6] Yet virtually no supporters of "population stabilization" have agitated for coordinated measures to lower Russia's death rate, raise its birth rate, and staunch its ongoing demographic losses.

The reason for such seemingly curious insouciance about demographic decline by self-avowed population "stabilizers" is that their chosen standard does not quite describe their true quest. For exponents of "stabilizing human population" do not simply look for population stabilization: rather, as the former Executive Director of the UNFPA framed the goal, they strive "for stabilization of world population at the lowest possible level, within the shortest period of time".[7]

Upon inspection it is apparent that "stabilizing human population" is really code language: a new name for an old and familiar project. Today's call for "stabilizing human population" is actually a rallying cry for anti-natalism. After all: its envisioned means of achieving "stabilization" is through limiting the prevalence and reducing the level of childbearing around the world, especially in the Third World: implementing policies to reduce births, and thereby depressing fertility in various venues around the globe (and particularly where fertility levels are deemed to be "unacceptably" high).

The ongoing anti-natal population crusade couches its arguments in the language of social science and invokes the findings of science to bolster its authority—but it cannot withstand the process of empirical review that lies at the heart of the rational scientific method. Whether they realize it or not, advocates of "world population stabilization" are devotees to a doctrine, not followers of facts.

The Premises of "World Population Stabilization"

Reduced to its essence, the case for action to "stabilize world population" rests upon four specific premises.

The first quite simply holds that we are manifestly in the midst of a world population crisis: a crisis defined by rapid population growth, which in turn is exacerbating "overpopulation". Former Vice President Gore nicely illustrated this tenet of thinking in his best-selling book, *Earth in the Balance*, and elsewhere, when he stated that in today's global population trends, "the absolute numbers are staggering"[8]; and that, "we can't acquiesce in the continuation of a situation that adds another . . . China's worth of people every decade".[9] Jared Diamond, author of *Collapse—How Societies Choose to Fail or Succeed*, reiterates a similar argument: "The statement about our ability to absorb current rates of population growth indefinitely is not to be taken seriously . . . because that would mean 10 people per square yard in the year 2779".[10]

The second premise underpinning the "population stabilization" project is that current rates of world population growth are not only unsustainable over the long term, but have direct and immediate adverse repercussions upon living standards, resource availability and even political stability today.

In the estimate of the Planned Parenthood Federation of America, for example, "Slowing population growth helps poorer countries develop politically and economically".[11] Jared Diamond is more vivid: he enumerates the consequences of population growth as "food shortages, starvation, wars among too many people, fighting for too few resources and overthrows of governing elites by disillusioned masses".[12] He lists overpopulation as the key cause for the "collapse" of past societies, such as the Mayas, as well as for recent civil wars and mass violence in countries such as Haiti and Rwanda.[13]

The third premise implicit in the agenda of "stabilizing human population" is that reduced birth rates constitute the solution to the population problems adduced by premises one and two. The fourth and final premise bolstering this agenda is the presumption that well-placed decision-makers can effectively and expeditiously engineer the desired changes in worldwide population patterns through deliberate policy interventions. Once again, Al Gore may have represented this presumption best: in his words, "we know how to stabilize world population",[14] because "population specialists know".[15]

Unfortunately, all of these premises are highly problematic. None of them are self-evidently true. To the extent that any of these separate premises are testable, it would appear that they are demonstrably false.

"Overpopulation": A Problem Misdefined

Consider the first premise: that the world faces a crisis of being burdened by simply too many people. If that premise is offered as an aesthetic judgment, it is irrefutable. (By their very nature, subjective opinions are not falsifiable.) But how does it fare if treated as a testable proposition?

Jared Diamond associates overpopulation with "more deforestation, more toxic chemicals, more demand for wild fish, etc",[16] while Gore writes that an "overcrowded world is inevitably a polluted one"[17]—a verdict that many of those worried about world population growth would accept without reservation. But "overcrowding" is not as easily established as some might suppose.

Population density, for example, might seem to be a reasonable criterion for overcrowding. By that criterion, Haiti, India, and Rwanda (each with over six times the world's average population density) would surely qualify as "overcrowded", and Bangladesh—with almost twenty times the inhabited

Figure 2-1. Population Density vs. GDP per Capita

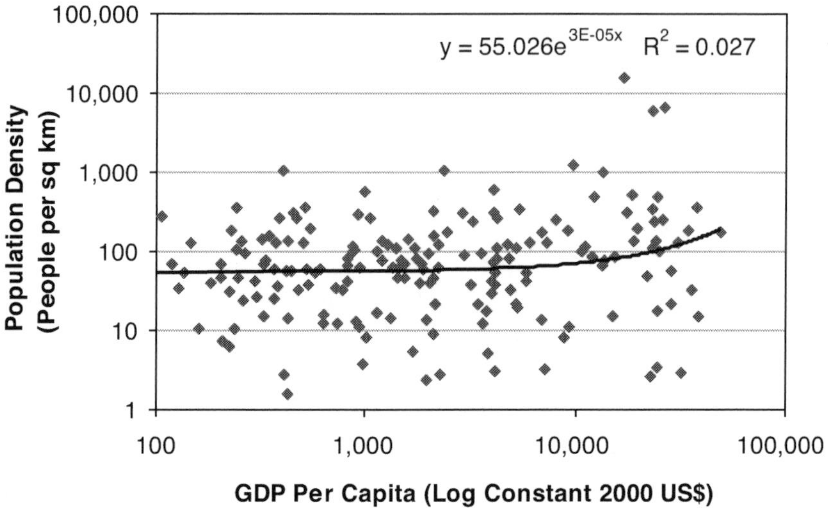

$$y = 55.026e^{3E-05x} \quad R^2 = 0.027$$

Source: World Development Indicators 2007.

globe's average density—would be manifestly "overcrowded". By that same criterion, however, Belgium (2000 population density per square kilometer: 336) would be distinctly more "overcrowded" than Rwanda (2000 population density per square kilometer: 289). Similarly, the Netherlands would be more "overcrowded" than Haiti, Bermuda would be more "overcrowded" than Bangladesh, and oil-rich Bahrain would be three times as "overcrowded" as India. But the most "overcrowded" country in the world would be Monaco: with a dire 33,268 persons per square kilometer in 2000, it suffers a population density almost forty times that of Bangladesh, and over seven hundred times the world average.[18] Yet as we all know, population activists do not agitate themselves about the "overcrowding" problem in Monaco—or in Bermuda, or in Bahrain.

Moreover, it is hardly self-evident that there is any association at the international level between population density and economic performance (see Figures 2-1 through 2-4, which are specifically drawn from data compiled by the World Bank in its compendium of *World Development Indicators*; although other databases could be used to much the same effect.)

Figure 2-2. Population Density vs. GDP per Capita, PPP

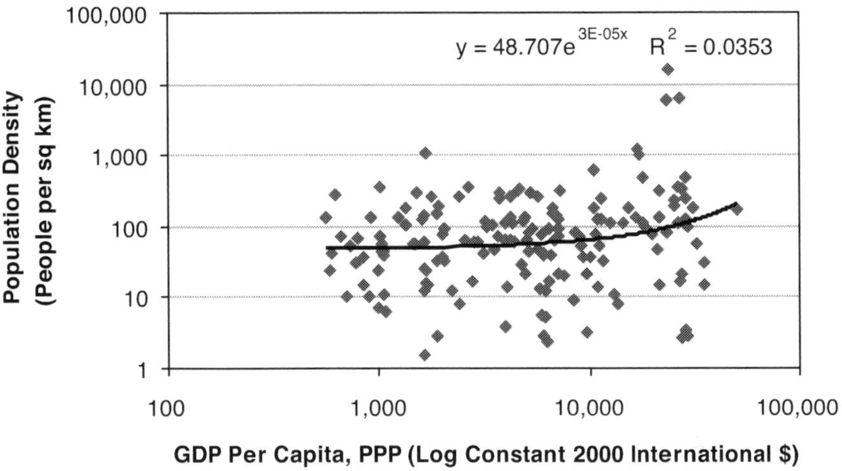

$$y = 48.707e^{3E-05x} \quad R^2 = 0.0353$$

Population Density (People per sq km)

GDP Per Capita, PPP (Log Constant 2000 International $)

Source: World Development Indicators 2007.

As Figures 2-1 and 2-2 attest, there was no discernable international relationship between overall national population density and a country's per capita GDP in the year 2003 (the most recent year for which such data are currently available), regardless of whether one measured per capita output on an exchange-rate basis or in terms of "purchasing power parity" (i.e., "international" dollars). The same holds true for the density of population with respect to arable land: by the data in Figures 2-3 and 2-4, it is impossible to distinguish any meaningful association—positive or negative—between a country's per hectare output level and the number of people "supported" by each local hectare of farm—or pasture—land. Surprising as it may sound to those convinced that the world is beset by "overpopulation", the fact is that in our era, *population density provides us with no information whatsoever for predicting a country's level of economic development or economic performance.*

Do other demographic measures provide a better reading of the population problem that so many take to be so very obvious today? Perhaps we might look at rates of population growth. At the dawn of the 21st century, sub-Saharan Africa was estimated to have the world's very highest rate of population growth—the United Nations Population Division put its pace at

Figure 2-3. Arable Land vs. GDP per Capita

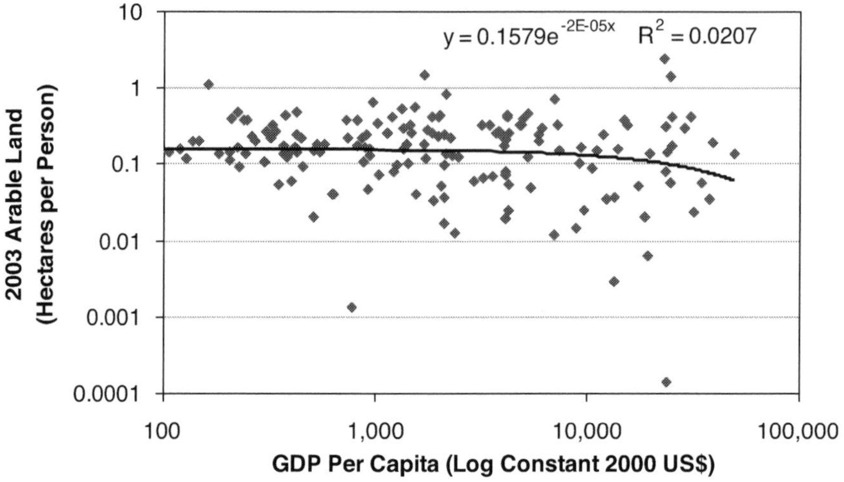

$$y = 0.1579e^{-2E-05x} \quad R^2 = 0.0207$$

Source: World Development Indicators 2007.

just under 2.5 per cent a year for the period 2000/2005[19]—and sub-Saharan Africa is clearly a most troubled area these days. However, if we look back in history, we will discover that the United States had an even higher rate of population growth at the end of the 18th century: in the decade 1790–1800, in fact, the U.S. pace of population growth was 3.0 per cent a year.[20] Some today may believe that sub-Saharan Africa has too many people—but would they say the same about early frontier America?

Fertility rates are hardly more illuminating. In *Earth in the Balance*, Gore expressly mentions Egypt, Kenya, and Nigeria as candidates for places with too many people (either today or in the decades immediately ahead).[21] All three countries are thought to experience fertility levels above the current world average. According to the latest (August 2006) projections by the U.S. Census Bureau, as of 2007 the total fertility rate (births per woman per lifetime under prevailing childbearing schedules) for the world as a whole was about 2.6, as against 2.8 in Egypt, 4.8 in Kenya, and 5.5 in Nigeria.[22] But once again: fertility levels were far higher in the United States in the early years of the Republic than in any of these places today. Around 1800, according to estimates by the demographer Michael Haines, the total fertility rate for white Americans was just over

Figure 2-4. Arable Land vs. GDP per Capita, PPP

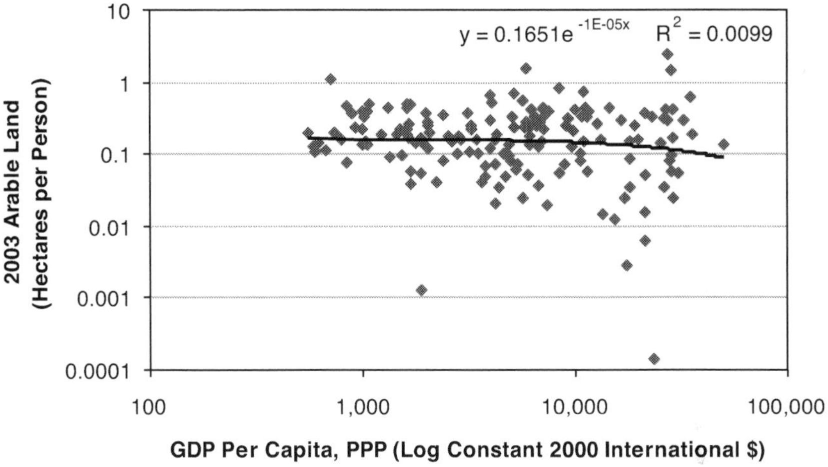

Figure showing scatter plot with trend line. Equation shown: $y = 0.1651e^{-1E-05x}$ $R^2 = 0.0099$

Y-axis: 2003 Arable Land (Hectares per Person), values 10, 1, 0.1, 0.01, 0.001, 0.0001

X-axis: GDP Per Capita, PPP (Log Constant 2000 International $), values 100, 1,000, 10,000, 100,000

Source: World Development Indicators 2007.

seven births per woman per lifetime[23]—yet Thomas Jefferson's America is not today widely regarded as a society in the throes of a population crisis.

We could continue combing for demographic measures that might help to clarify the nature, and pinpoint the epicenters, of the population crisis that Al Gore, Jared Diamond and so many others envision. But as our exercise should already indicate, that would be a fruitless task. Additional demographic criteria will confront the same problem of obvious misidentification of presumptive regions suffering from "too many people" because *demographic criteria cannot by themselves unambiguously describe "overpopulation"*. This is a basic fact, recognized by every trained demographer. And that basic fact raises correspondingly basic questions about the concept of "overpopulation".

The "population crisis" that advocates of "world population stabilization" wish to resolve is impossible to define in demographic terms because it is a problem that has been mis-defined. In most people's minds, the notions of "overpopulation", "overcrowding", or "too many people" are associated with images of hungry children, unchecked disease, squalid living conditions, and awful slums. Those problems, sad to say, are all too real in the contemporary world—but the proper name for those conditions is *human poverty*.

And the correspondence between human poverty and demographic trends, as we shall see in a moment, is by no means as causal and clear-cut as some would suppose.

If we are to make inroads against the problems of humanity, it is important that we begin by calling those problems by their proper names. The problem of global poverty, in and of itself, cannot in an empirical sense be defined as a "world population crisis"—unless one means it is a crisis that so many people today should be suffering from poverty. But it is a fundamental lapse in logic to assume that poverty is a "population problem" simply because it is manifest today in large numbers of human beings. The proper name for that logical error is "the fallacy of composition".

Population Growth, Development, and Political Stability

Let us now consider the second premise of "world population stabilization": that rapid population growth and high fertility levels cause or exacerbate poverty, resource scarcity, and political instability. If we wish to treat this premise as an empirically testable proposition (rather than an unchallengeable tenet of faith), we will recognize immediately the complexity of the processes we propose to observe. The relationships between population change and economic or political change encompass an extraordinarily broad and complicated set of interactions with an array of multi-directional influences, and consequential second-, third- and even higher-order impacts.

Describing these interactions comprehensively and accurately is a tremendous and subtle challenge. And researchers who have approached this challenge with care and objectivity have typically described the economic impact of demographic changes in nuanced and qualified terms. Typical of such work are the findings of econometrician Dennis Ahlburg, who concludes that "it is not clear whether population growth causes poverty in the long run or not, [although] high fertility leading to rapidly growing population will increase the number of people in poverty in the short run".[24] Development economist Robert Cassen accurately describes the state of current research when he notes "the issue of whether per capita economic growth is reduced by population growth remains unsettled. Attempts to demonstrate such an effect empirically have produced no significant and reliable results . . ."[25]

Even so: we need not rely upon the judgments of experts, or attempt to replicate their efforts at model-building, to appreciate the flaws inherent in this premise.

We can begin by recalling the reason for the 20th century's "population explosion". Between 1900 and 2000, human numbers almost quadrupled, leaping from around 1.6 billion to over 6 billion;[26] in pace and magnitude, nothing like that surge had ever previously taken place. But why exactly did we experience a world population explosion in the 20th century? It was not because people suddenly started breeding like rabbits—rather, it was because they finally stopped dying like flies.

Between 1900 and the end of the 20th century, the human life span likely doubled: from a planetary life expectancy at birth of perhaps thirty years[27] to one of well over sixty years.[28] By this measure, the overwhelming preponderance of the health progress in all of human history took place during the past hundred years.

Over the past half-century, worldwide progress in reducing death rates has been especially dramatic. Tables 2-1 and 2-2 underscore this important fact. Between the early 1950s and the first years of the 21st century, according to estimates by the United Nations Population Division (UNPD—not to be confused with UNFPA), the planetary expectation of life at birth jumped by almost 20 years, or over two-fifths: from about 46 years to 65 years. For the low income regions, the leap was even more dramatic: taken together, estimated life expectancy in these "developing countries" surged up by 23 years, a rise of nearly three-fifths. Even troubled sub-Saharan Africa—despite its protracted post-independence-era political and economic turmoil and the advent of a catastrophic HIV/AIDS epidemic—is thought to have enjoyed an increase in local life expectancy of roughly a third. (Practically the only countries to register no appreciable improvements in life expectancy over this period were the handful of "European" territories within what was once the Soviet Union; in the Russian Federation in particular, gains over these five decades were negligible.)

Among the most important proximate reasons for the global surge in life expectancy was the worldwide drop in infant mortality rates. In the early 1950s, according again to UNPD estimates, 153 out of every 1000 children born around the world did not survive their first year of life; by the start of the new century, that toll was down to 54 per 1000. In "developed"

Table 2-1. Estimated Life Expectancy at Birth (Both Sexes)

	1950/1955	2000/2005	Absolute change (years)	% change
World	46.4	66.0	19.6	42%
Developed Countries	66.1	75.6	9.5	14%
Developing Countries	40.8	64.1	23.3	57%
Latin America and Caribbean	51.4	72.0	20.6	40%
Asia	41.0	67.5	26.5	65%
Sub Saharan Africa	36.7	48.8	12.1	33%
Memorandum items:				
Russia	64.5	64.8	0.3	0%

Source: UN World Population Prospects, 2006 revision.

Table 2-2. Estimated Infant Mortality at Birth (Both Sexes)
Deaths per 1,000 live births

	1950/1955	2000/2005	Absolute change (years)	% change
World	153.1	53.9	− 99.2	− 65%
Developed Countries	59.1	7.5	− 51.6	− 87%
Developing Countries	175.0	59.0	− 116.0	− 66%
Latin America and Caribbean	126.2	25.4	− 100.8	− 80%
Asia	176.0	48.6	− 127.4	− 72%
Sub Saharan Africa	177.4	99.8	− 77.6	− 44%
Memorandum items:				
Russia	97.5	17.2	−80.3	−82%

Source: UN World Population Prospects, 2006 revision.

countries, infant mortality is thought to have fallen by seven-eighths during those decades, and by almost two-thirds in the collectivity of "developing" countries. Even in troubled regions, great advances in infant survival were achieved: in sub-Saharan Africa, for example, the infant mortality rate is thought to have declined by over two-fifths, and Russia's infant mortality rate may have declined by over 80 per cent.

These sweeping and radical declines in mortality are entirely responsible for the increase in human numbers over the course of the 20th century: the "population explosion", in other words, was really a "health explosion".

Now, with respect to economic development, the implications of a health explosion—of any health explosion—are, on their face, hardly negative. Quite the contrary: a healthier population is clearly going to be a population with greater productive potential. Healthier people are able to learn better, work harder, and engage in gainful employment longer and contribute more to economic activity than unhealthy, short-lived counterparts. Whether that potential actually translates into tangible economic results will naturally depend on other factors, such as social and legal institutions, or the business and policy climate. Nevertheless: the health explosion that propelled the 20th century's population explosion was an economically auspicious phenomenon rather than a troubling trend.

All other things being equal, one would have expected the health explosion to contribute to the acceleration of economic growth, the increase of incomes, and the spread of wealth. And as it happens, the 20th century witnessed not only a population explosion, and a health explosion, but also a "prosperity explosion". Estimates by the economic historian Angus Maddison, who has produced perhaps the most authoritative reconstruction of long-term global economic trends presently available, demonstrate this (Figure 2-5).[29]

Between 1900 and 2003, by Maddison's reckoning, global GDP per capita (in internationally adjusted 1990 dollars) more than quintupled. Gains in productivity were globally uneven: in both relative and absolute terms, today's OECD states enjoyed disproportionate improvements. Nonetheless, every region of the planet became richer. Africa's economic performance, according to Maddison, was the most dismal of any major global region over the course of the 20th century: yet even there, per capita GDP was approximated to be over two and a half times higher in 2003 than it had been in 1900.[30]

Suffice it then to say that the 20th century's population explosion did not forestall the most dramatic and widespread improvement in output, incomes, and living standards that humanity had ever experienced. Though severe poverty still endures in much of the world, there can be no doubt that its incidence has been markedly curtailed over the past hundred years, despite a near-quadrupling of human numbers.

Figure 2-5. Estimated GDP per Capita

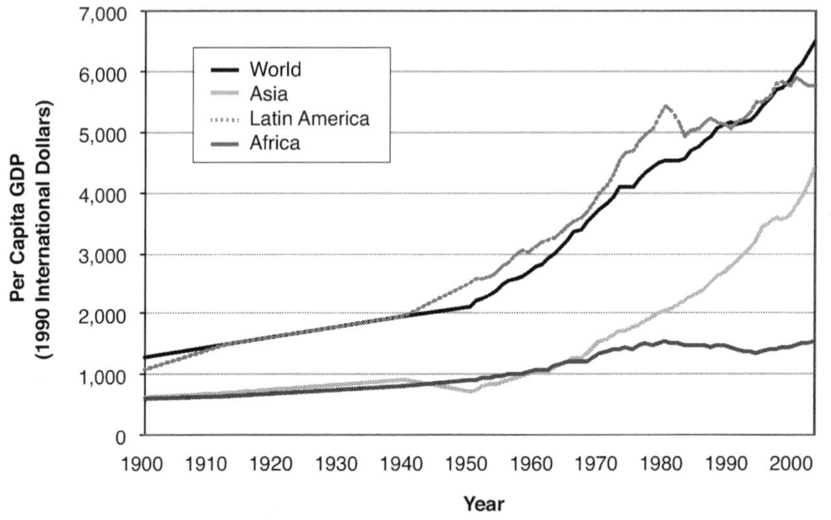

Source: Angus Maddison, "Historical Statistics for the World Economy, 1–2003 AD," Table 3: Per Capita GDP, available at http://www.ggdc.net/maddison/, accessed May 8, 2007.

Maddison's estimates of global economic growth highlight another empirical problem with the second premise of the "population stabilization" project. With a near-quadrupling of the human population over the course of the 20th century, and a more than four-fold increase in human GDP per capita over those same years, global economic output has taken an absolutely amazing leap: Maddison's own figures suggest world GDP might have been over 18 times higher in 2000 than it was in 1900, and over 20 times higher by 2003 (Figure 2-6). But GDP is a measure of economic output—and for the world as a whole economic output and economic demand must be identical. If the demand for goods and services multiplied nearly twenty-fold during the 20th century, humanity's demand for, and consumption of, natural resources has also rocketed upward. But despite humanity's tremendous new pressures on planetary resources the relative prices of virtually all primary commodities have fallen over the course of the 20th century—for many of them, quite substantially.

Despite the tremendous expansion of the international grain trade over the past century, for example, the inflation-adjusted, dollar-denominated

Figure 2-6. Estimated Global GDP

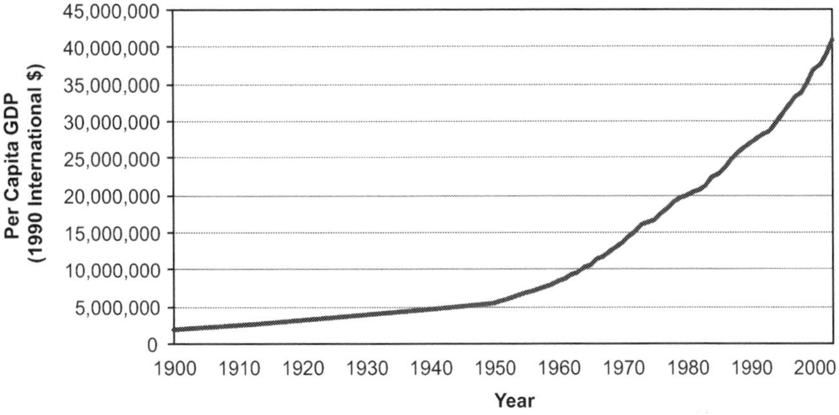

Source: Angus Maddison, "Historical Statistics for the World Economy, 1–2003 AD," Table 3: Per Capita GDP, available at http://www.ggdc.net/maddison/, accessed May 8, 2007.

international price of each of the major cereals—corn, wheat and rice—fell by over 70 per cent between 1900 and 2000 (Figure 2-7).[31] Over the course of the entire 20th century, the long-term trend in real prices for each of these cereals was a decline averaging over one percentage point per year. By the same token: *The Economist* magazine's "commodity-price index"—a weighted composite for 14 internationally-traded metals and non-food agricultural commodities[32]—registered a decline in inflation-adjusted dollars of almost 80 per cent between 1900 and the very end of 1999.[33] Perhaps the most comprehensive index of long-term real primary commodity prices was the one constructed by Enzo Grilli and Maw Cheng Yang in 1988, and subsequently updated and extended by Stephan Pfaffenzeller and colleagues in 2007.[34] This series encompassed 24 internationally-traded non-fuel primary commodities. Grilli and Yang's initial calculations extend from 1900 only up to 1986, but their results were nevertheless arresting. For that 86-year period, Grilli and Yang found that real prices (deflated by the value of manufactured products) of non-fuel primary commodities—renewable resources like cereals, and non-renewable resources such as metals—fell substantially, trending downward by an average of 0.6 per cent per year. When the series is extended to the beginning of the 21st century,

Figure 2-7. World Population vs. Prices of Wheat, Maize, and Rice, 1900–2003

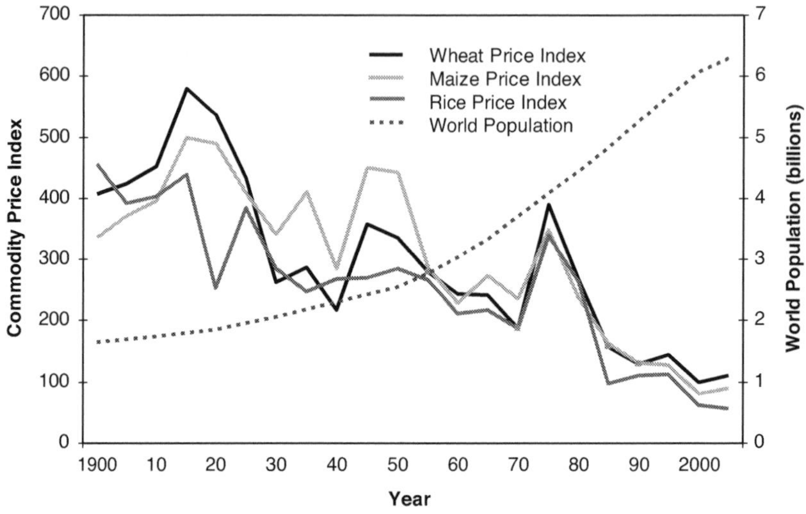

Sources: Commodity Price Indices: 1900–1984 compiled from World Bank data by Enzo R. Grilli and Maw Cheng Yang, World Bank; data for 1985–2003 compiled form World Bank data by Stephan Pfaffenzeller, University of Nottingham. (Adjusted for CPI inflation.) The author thanks Stephan Pfaffenzeller for providing this data. World population: U.S. Bureau of the Census.

Pfaffenzeller and his colleagues found, the long-term rate of decline in commodity prices accelerated somewhat, to around 0.8 per cent a year. Suffice it to say that the Grilli-Yang commodity price index entered the 21st century nearly 60 per cent lower than the level it recorded for the year 1900 (see Figure 2-8).[35]

The paradox of exploding demand for resources and simultaneous pronounced declines in real resource prices will appear curious and compelling to any observer, but it should be especially arresting to those with essentially Malthusian sensibilities. In the most fundamental sense, after all, price data are meant to convey information about scarcity—and by the sorts of information that they convey, they would seem to be indicating that the resources used by humanity have been growing less scarce over the course of the 20th century. There are, to be sure, explanations for this paradox—but the "stabilization" project's second premise, which holds that population growth must result in resource scarcity, is hardly able to provide it.

Figure 2-8. World GNP vs. Relative Primary Commodity Prices

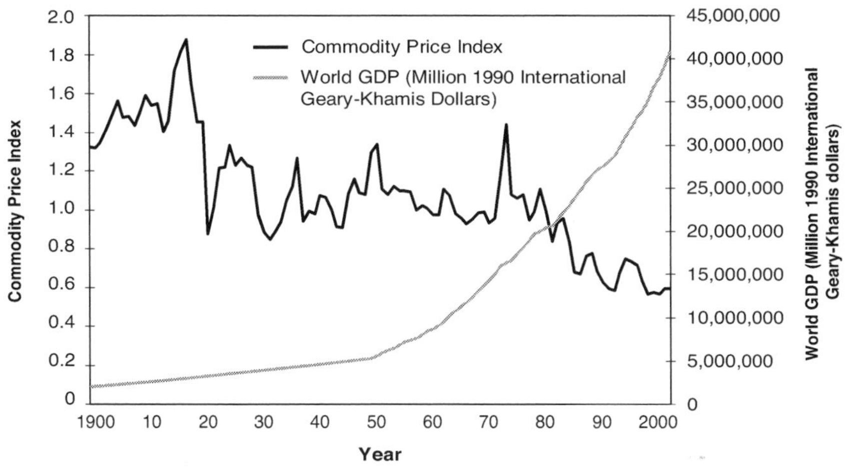

Sources: Commodity Price Index: Stephan Pfaffenzeller, "Supplementary Data," Grilli and Yang Data, http://www.stephan-pfaffenzeller.com (accessed June 22, 2007). Angus Maddison, "Historical Statistics for the World Economy, 1–2003 AD," Table 2: GDP, http://www.ggdc.net/maddison/ (accessed June 21, 2007).

The dilemma can be stated even more starkly: if the presumptions incorporated in that premise regarding the interplay between population growth, living standards and resource scarcity were valid, the 20th century should not have occurred.

What about the supposed relationship between rapid population growth and political strife? The hypothesis that population growth could affect political stability is certainly worth entertaining. It is plausible, after all, to conjecture that instability is more of a risk for governments that do not cope well with change—and population growth, whatever else it may be, is also inescapably a form of social change.

The vision of the link between rapid population growth and political de-stabilization, however, is sometimes undercut by the very evidence adduced to support it. Take Gore's aforementioned attribution of the carnage in the former Yugoslavia in the early 1990s to rapid population growth. The problem with the argument is that the former Yugoslavia was characterized neither by especially rapid rates of population growth nor by particularly high levels of fertility.

Consider Bosnia and Herzegovina, which suffered war, horrific "ethnic cleansing" and other atrocities in the early 1990s. Over the three decades before pandemonium erupted (i.e., 1961–91), Bosnia-Herzegovina recorded a population growth rate of about 1 per cent a year—slower than the United States' 1.1 percent per annum rate over the same period, and barely half the average worldwide pace of 1.9 per cent during those years. Moreover, in 1991—on the eve of its descent into chaos—Bosnia's estimated total fertility rate was 1.7 births per woman per lifetime—well below the replacement level. Estimates by the United Nations Population Division suggest that Bosnia-Herzegovina's fertility levels had been below replacement throughout the 1980s as well. The situation is little different in the other fragments of the former Yugoslavia. Fertility levels and population growth rates were even lower than Bosnia's in Croatia and Slovenia, and only marginally higher in Macedonia; Serbia's fertility level was slightly higher, but its rate of population growth was slightly lower.[36] (Today, incidentally, all the countries carved out of the former Yugoslavia report fertility levels far below the replacement.)[37]

One can only wonder: if the former Yugoslavia is an example of a region wrought by demographically-driven political turmoil, exactly how low are population growth rates supposed to fall, and birth rates to sink, before a region is safe from this purported menace? It is perfectly true that political conflict cannot take place without human populations—but it does not follow that the surest and soundest way of preventing political conflict is simply to prevent the existence of people in the first place.[38]

"World Population Stabilization" Through Scientific Population Policies?

The third premise of "world population stabilization"—that birth rates must be lowered to alleviate the world population crisis and to mitigate the adverse economic, resource, and political consequences of rapid population growth—requires absolutely no substantiation if one is a true believer in the anti-natalist creed. To the anti-natalist way of thinking, the purposeful reduction of birth rates (and especially birth rates in poorer regions) is an incontestably worthy policy objective—for to this way of thinking it is axiomatic that fewer births translates directly into benefits for present and future generations. For those who must be convinced that a problem exists before consenting to the public action proposed to redress it, that premise rests on their first two premises—and for the empirically inclined, as we have seen, those are shaky foundations indeed.

But even if we were convinced of the pressing need to take public action to lower global birth rates, it would not necessarily follow that the desired result could be achieved—or achieved at an acceptable cost—or achieved voluntarily. Here lies the pivotal importance of the fourth premise of "world population stabilization": for this tenet maintains that it is an established fact that "population specialists" know how international birth rates can be lowered, and that these specialists can consequently provide policymakers with reliable advice about the precise interventions that will bring about fertility declines.

But once again, the final premise underpinning the quest for "stabilizing world population" is badly flawed. The plain fact is that students of contemporary and historical child-bearing patterns have not uncovered the magic formula that explains why fertility changes occurred in the past—much less identified the special levers that can determine how these trends will unfold in the future.

The trouble with the mission to identify universal and reliable determinants of fertility decline goes back literally to the origins of the phenomenon. "Secular fertility decline"—the sustained, long-term shift from big families to small ones—commenced for the first time in Europe, about two hundred years ago. But it did not begin in England and Wales—then perhaps the most open, literate, and industrialised part of the continent, if not the world. Instead it began in France: a country then impoverished, overwhelmingly rural, predominantly illiterate—and, not to put too fine a point on it, Catholic. Clearly, the "modernisation" model does not plausibly explain the advent of fertility decline in the modern world. And unfortunately, alternative models do not really fare much better. Reviewing the theories of fertility decline in Western Europe and the evidence adduced to support them, the historian Charles Tilly wrote that "The problem is that we have too many explanations which are plausible in general terms, which contradict each other to some degree and which fail to fit some significant part of the facts".[39] But what was true for Western Europe at the onset of this process holds equally for the rest of the world today.

Al Gore's bestseller *Earth In The Balance* exemplifies the thinking of many current proponents of "world population stabilisation" in describing the factors that he holds to be instrumental in achieving sustained fertility reductions:

> High literacy rates and education levels *are important, especially for women; once they are empowered intellectually and socially they make decisions about the number of children they wish to have. Low infant mortality rates give parents a sense of confidence that even with a small family, some of their children will grow to maturity . . . and provide physical security when they are old. Nearly ubiquitous access to a variety of affordable birth control techniques gives parents the power to choose when and whether to have children.*[40] [emphasis in the original]

Each of these three *desiderata* may qualify as a social objective in its own right, entirely irrespective of its influence on demographic trends. As purported "determinants" of fertility change, however, the explanatory and predictive properties of these three factors leave something to be desired.

Data from the *2007 WDI* underscore the problem. According to the World Bank's figures, the adult literacy rate in 2006 was almost 15 percentage points higher in Malawi than Morocco (54 per cent vs. 40 per cent)—but the fertility level in Malawi was also over twice as high in 2005 (5.8 births vs. 2.4 births). Kenya and Iran were said to have almost identical rates of adult literacy in 2006 (70 per cent), yet Iran's 2005 fertility level is put at just over replacement (2.1) while Kenya's is almost two and a half times higher (5.0). Iran's total fertility rate, incidentally, is said to have plummeted by nearly 70 per cent—from 6.7 to 2.1—between 1980 and 2006. But presumably the Iranian revolution was not quite what Gore had in mind in arguing that intellectual and social empowerment of women would lead to smaller families.

Infant mortality provides scarcely more information about fertility levels or fertility change. By the UN Population Division's projections, for example, the 2000/2005 infant mortality rate for Armenia was somewhat higher than for the "Occupied Palestinian Territory" of West Bank and Gaza

(30 per 1000 vs. 21 per 1000)—but while Armenia's estimated fertility level at that time was far below replacement (1.35 births per woman), the level for the West Bank and Gaza was put at 5.63 births per woman per lifetime, over four times as high! By the same token, although infant mortality rates were said to be similar in Bangladesh and Yemen in the early years of the new century, Yemen's total fertility rate at that time was almost twice as high as Bangladesh's (6.02 vs. 3.22).[41] Historically, the onset of sustained fertility decline in France took place during a period (1780–1820) when the country suffered an estimated average of almost 200 infant deaths for every 1000 births.[42] No country in the contemporary world suffers from such a brutally high infant mortality rate—but a number of present-day countries with considerably lower infant mortality rates than prevailed in Napoleonic France evidently have yet to enter into fertility decline (among them: Afghanistan, the Democratic Republic of the Congo, East Timor, and Liberia). Conversely, literally dozens of contemporary low-income countries with much more favorable infant and child survival schedules than prevailed in that of bygone France have yet to report fertility levels as low as the 4 births per woman per lifetime estimated for French society around 1800.[43]

As for the relationship between fertility and the availability of modern contraceptives (or national programs to subsidize or encourage their use), inconvenient facts must once again be faced. To start with, the utilization rates for modern contraceptive methods are not an especially reliable indicator of a society's fertility level. According to World Bank figures, among married women aged 15–49, the rate of modern contraceptive utilization was higher in the West Bank and Gaza in 2004 than in Bulgaria in 1998 (51 per cent vs. 42 per cent)—yet the total fertility rate was over four times higher in the former than the latter. In the first years of the new century, contraceptive prevalence rates were all but identical in Japan and Jordan (70 per cent)—but Jordan's fertility level was said to be two and a half times higher than Japan's (3.5 births vs. 1.4 births). Contraceptive prevalence in Bangladesh in 2004 was reportedly higher than in Austria in 1996 (58 per cent vs. 51 per cent)—and fertility levels were also well over twice as high.[44] There are many more such examples.

For another thing, the independent influence of national population programs on national birth rates appears to be very much more limited than enthusiasts are willing to recognize. A comparison of Mexico and

Brazil, Latin America's two most populous countries, illustrates the point. Since 1974, the Mexican government has sponsored a national family planning program expressly committed to reducing the country's rate of population growth. Brazil, by contrast, has never implemented a national family planning program. In the quarter century after the introduction of Mexico's national population program, Mexican fertility levels fell by an estimated 56 per cent. In Brazil, during the same period, fertility is estimated to have declined by 54 per cent—an almost identical proportion. And despite the absence of a national family planning program, Brazil's fertility levels today remain lower than Mexico's.[45]

In the final analysis, the single best international predictor of fertility levels turns out to be *desired* fertility levels: the number of children that women say they would like to have.[46] Perhaps this should not be surprising: parents tend to have strong opinions about important matters pertaining to their family; parents tend to act on the basis of those opinions; and even in the Third World, parents do not believe that babies are found under cabbages. The primacy of desired fertility explains why birth rates can be higher in regions where contraceptive utilization rates are also higher: for it is parents, not pills, that make the final choice about family size.

For advocates of "stabilizing world population", the predominance of parental preferences in the determination of national and international birth rates poses an awkward dilemma. If parental preferences really rule, and a government sets official population targets for a truly voluntary family planning program, those targets are not likely to be achieved. Indeed: if parents are genuinely permitted to pursue the family size they personally desire, national population programs can only meet pre-established official demographic targets by complete and utter chance.

On the other hand, if a government sets population targets and wishes to stand a reasonable chance of achieving them, the mischievous independence of parental preferences means that wholly voluntary population programs cannot be relied upon. If states, rather than the parents, are to determine a society's preferred childbearing patterns, governments must be able to force parents to adhere to the officially approved parameters.

Despite previously denouncing coercive and violent population control techniques, Jared Diamond still goes on to praise the Chinese government's courage to "restrict the traditional freedom of individual reproductive choice

. . ." It is this type of population control—coerced restrictions, forced abortion, infanticide—that apparently "contributes to [his] hope" and "may inspire modern First World citizens" to follow a similar path.[47]

Whether they recognize it or not, every advocate of anti-natal population programs must make a fateful choice. They must either opt for voluntarism, in which case their population targets will be meaningless. Or else they must opt for attempting to meet their population targets—in which case they must embrace coercive measures. There is no third way.

Prospects for World Population Growth in the 21st Century

Advocates of the project to "stabilize human population" typically regard the phenomenon of natural increase as an inexorable and almost uncontrollable phenomenon. (The purportedly all-but-irrepressible nature of human population growth, in turn, helps to explain why anti-natalists view the process as inherently fraught with terrifying consequence.) Some of these advocates have warned that the human population will double, or more than double, over the course of the coming century unless the comprehensive program of population action that they prefer is rigorously implemented. Thus Alex Marshall, a spokesperson for the UNFPA, speaks ominously of a near-doubling of global population in the next half century: without "promised cash for family planning in developing countries", he reportedly explained, world population is likely to hit 11 billion—a prospect he likened to "looking over a cliff".[48] Likewise, Al Gore justifies his call for a "Global Marshall Plan"—the first of whose four points is "stabilizing world population"—with the assertion that experts "say the [world population] total could reach 14 billion or even higher before leveling off" at the end of the 21st century.[49]

As we have already seen, the grim and inescapable connection between population growth and mounting economic problems that is posited by today's anti-natal doctrine is hardly faithful to the actual record of global demographic and economic development over the past century. But the apparent anxiety that some proponents of "stabilizing world population" experience in contemplating a future with 11 billion, 14 billion, or more human inhabitants of our planet may also be misplaced for a more prosaic reason: to judge by current trends, such levels may never be achieved.

Figure 2-9. Total Fertility Rates vs. GDP per Capita, 1960

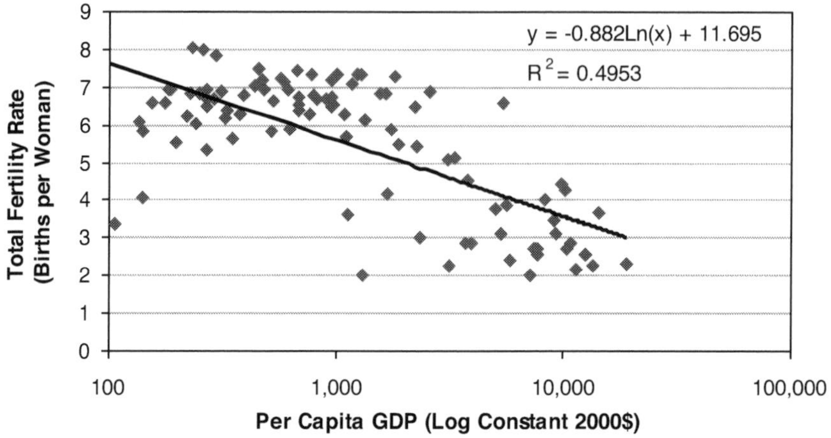

$$y = -0.882Ln(x) + 11.695$$
$$R^2 = 0.4953$$

Source: World Development Indicators 2007.

To be sure: long-term population projections are extraordinarily problematic. No robust scientific basis exists for anticipating desired parental fertility in any locale—much less for the world as a whole—very far in advance. Since it is fertility levels that largely determine future population trajectories, this is more than an incidental inconvenience. The experience of the past four decades, however, is worth bearing in mind. In the four decades since the early 1960s, global fertility levels are thought to have dropped by almost half: from a "total fertility rate" (TFR, or births per woman per lifetime) of around 5 in 1960/65 to one of about 2.6 in 2000/2005. Over that same period, the average TFR for "developing countries" is thought to have dropped by over half, from 6 to under 3.[50] Although there is a well-known and general correspondence between increasing affluence and lower fertility, material progress alone does not account for this tremendous decline in birth rates in low-income countries. Equally important has been the largely overlooked fact that parents still caught in *Third World poverty have been choosing to have ever-smaller families.*

Figures 2-10 to 2-13 illustrate the point. They draw upon World Bank data on fertility levels, per capita income levels, and adult female illiteracy

Figure 2-10. Total Fertility Rates vs. GDP per Capita, 2005

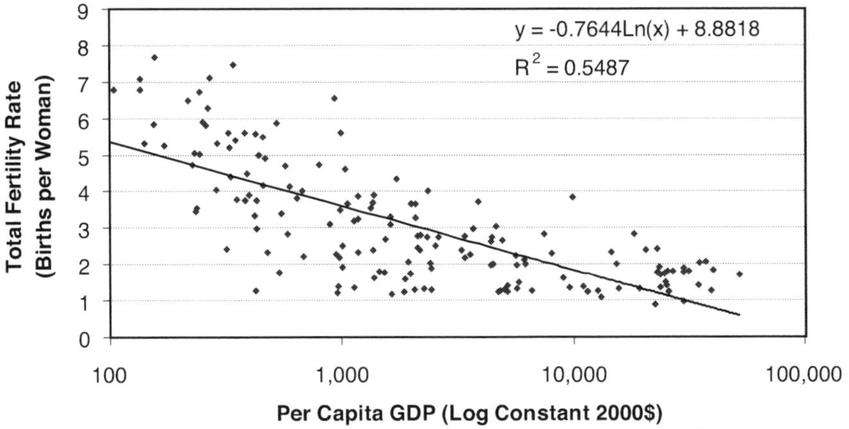

$y = -0.7644Ln(x) + 8.8818$

$R^2 = 0.5487$

Source: World Development Indicators 2007.

levels for almost 200 countries over the period 1960–2005. In 1960, the international association between per capita GDP (calculated on the basis of exchange rates) and TFRs was relatively strong (although by no means mechanistic)—and the same was true in 2005 (Figures 2-9 and 2-10). But over the intervening four decades, the particulars of that association had shifted quite dramatically: the income-fertility curves of 1960 and 2005 look quite different (Figure 2-11). In 1960, a country with a per capita GDP of $1000 (on exchange-rate basis) would have a TFR of about 6. In 2005, a country with that same income level would have been predicted to have a TFR of about 3.3 births per woman per lifetime fewer. At any given income level—including even very low income levels—parents around the world have generally been opting for fewer children over the past four and a half decades.

The World Bank databases do not offer estimates of illiteracy rates for women for 1960 or 2005, but they do make possible comparison of the illiteracy-fertility situation in 1980 and 1999 (Figure 2-12).[51] Once again, it appears that even in settings where female illiteracy levels happen to be very high, fertility levels are in general substantially lower than they would have been in the past.Few people would choose to be poor or illiterate. Yet poor and illiterate people have demonstrated, over the past generation and a half that

Figure 2-11. Estimated Total Fertility Rates vs. GDP per Capita

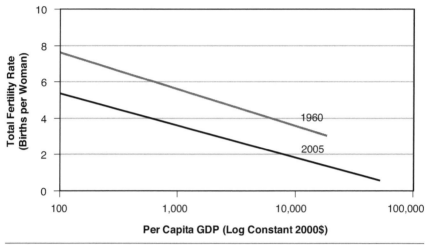

Source: World Development Indicators 2007.

Figure 2-12. Estimated Total Fertility Rates vs. Illiteracy Rates

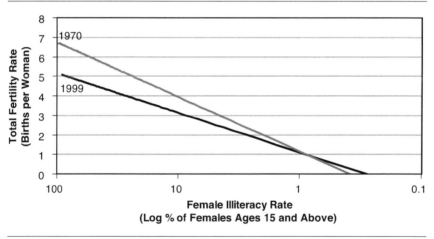

Source: World Development Indicators 2007.

they too can make family planning choices—and they have increasingly chosen post-traditional fertility regimens. Quite clearly, neither low income levels nor the lack of education among young women constitute the sort

Figure 2-13. Per Capita Caloric Availability

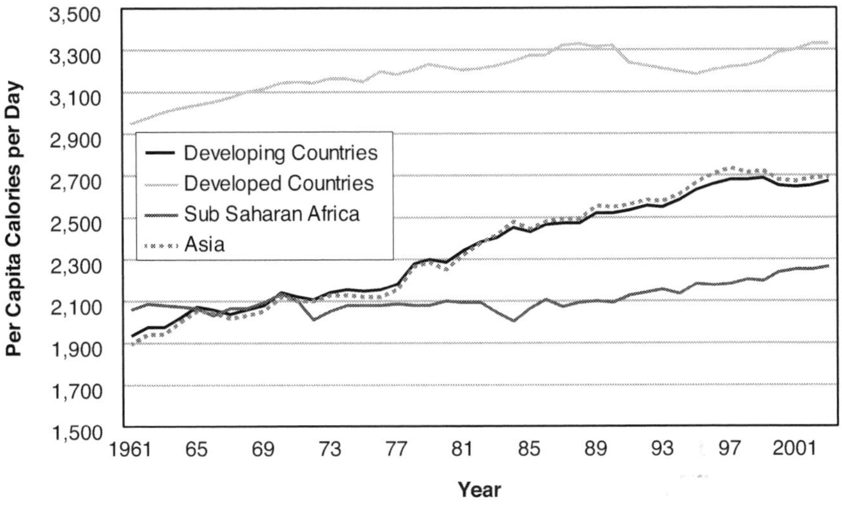

Source: Food and Agricultural Organization of the United Nations, http://apps.fao.org.

of "structural" barrier against fertility decline that many population activists have heretofore supposed.

Expert demographic opinion is today catching up with revealed reality. Thus, in August 2001, a study in *Nature* by researchers with IIASA (International Institute for Applied Systems Analysis) spoke of "the end of world population growth", contending that "there is around an 85 per cent chance that the world's population will stop growing before the end of the century . . . [and] a 60 per cent probability that the world's population will not exceed 10 billion people".[52] In March 2002, in a major shift from its previous practices, the United Nations Population Division (UNPD) announced that the 2002 revision of its *World Population Prospects* would presume sub-replacement fertility levels for 80 per cent of the world by the middle of the 21st century, hypothesizing further that "below replacement fertility will lead first to the slowing of population growth rates and then to slow reductions in the size of world population".[53] With the 2006 revision of *World Population Prospects*, moreover, UNPD's "medium variant" projections posit that global fertility will fall below the net replacement level in

Table 2-3. Estimated Illiteracy Rate (Both Sexes, Aged 15 and Over)

	1970	1980	1990	1995	2000
World	37.0	30.6	24.8	22.7	20.6
Developed Countries	5.7	3.4	1.9	1.4	1.1
Developing Countries	51.9	41.8	32.6	29.5	26.3
Least Developed Countries	73.2	66.0	57.7	53.7	49.3
Latin American and Caribbean	26.1	20.3	14.9	13.3	11.7
Asia	49.1	39.4	30.5	27.7	24.9
Sub Saharan Africa	71.6	61.7	50.7	45.2	39.7

Source: UNESCO Institute for Statistics, http://unesco.org/en/stats/stats0.htm.

2025/30—that is to say, about two decades from now.[54] (For a decade now, incidentally, the UNPD's *World Population Prospects* series has offered a "low variant" projection for global population that envisions a peaking of human numbers around the year 2040, and an indefinite decline thereafter.)

All these population projections are, of course, based on the same fragile theoretical foundations as the earlier projections they supersede; there is no reason to accord them special and unparalleled authority. The simple fact of the matter, however, is that even poor people can choose to have small families, and that increasing numbers of poor couples around the world are doing just that. If poor people in low income countries reveal a preference for smaller families in the decades to come, world population totals will be distinctly lower than proponents of "world population stabilization" have heretofore imagined—and those lower totals would have been reached without the emergency worldwide population programs that many activists today advocate.

Natural Resources, Human Resources, and Development

Fortunately for our perennially troubled planet, humanity's population demographic and development prospects appear to be seriously misconstrued by the pessimistic doctrine of "world population stabilization".

While the prevalence of poverty across the globe is unacceptably great today—and will continue be so in the future (after all: what level of

Table 2-4. Estimated Educational Attainment by Sex (Population Age 15 and Over)

	Average school year	Gender ratio (female/male %)	
		Females	Males
World			
	1960	4.31	4.98	86.7
	1970	4.74	5.59	84.7
	1980	5.42	6.43	84.3
	1990	5.93	6.94	85.5
	1995	5.94	6.95	85.4
	2000	6.13	7.19	85.3
All developing			
	1960	1.46	2.63	55.7
	1970	1.94	3.38	57.2
	1980	2.74	4.37	62.5
	1990	3.61	5.21	69.3
	1995	3.99	5.56	71.8
	2000	4.33	5.92	73.2
Middle East/North America			
	1960	0.83	1.63	51.0
	1970	1.39	2.75	50.5
	1980	2.41	4.15	58.0
	1990	3.57	5.17	69.1
	1995	4.21	5.74	73.3
	2000	4.69	6.17	76.0
Sub-Saharan Africa			
	1960	1.34	2.17	61.8
	1970	1.56	2.60	60.1
	1980	1.91	2.89	66.0
	1990	2.49	3.83	65.0
	1995	2.82	3.98	70.8
	2000	3.01	4.04	74.4
Latin America/Caribbean			
	1960	3.24	3.36	96.3
	1970	3.52	4.14	85.0
	1980	4.29	4.57	93.7
	1990	5.24	5.41	96.8
	1995	5.58	5.91	94.4
	2000	5.81	6.3	92.2

Source: Barro, Robert J. and Jong-Wha Lee, International Data on Educational Attainment: Updates and Implications, CID Working Paper No. 42, Harvard University, April 2000.

poverty should be *acceptable*?)—humanity has enjoyed unprecedented and extraordinary improvements in material living standards over the past century, and over the past few decades in particular. Those improvements are represented in the worldwide increases in life expectancy and per capita income levels that we have already reviewed.

The tremendous and continuing spread of health and prosperity around the planet betokens a powerful and historically new dynamic that anti-natalists today only dimly apprehend. This is the shift on a global scale from the reliance on "natural resources" to the reliance on "human resources" as fuel for economic growth. The worldwide surge in health levels has not been an isolated phenomenon. To the contrary: it has been accompanied by, and is inextricably linked to, pervasive and dramatic (albeit highly uneven) increases in nutrition levels, literacy levels, and levels of general educational attainment (Figure 2-13, Tables 2-3 and 2-4). These interlocked trends speak to a profound and continuing worldwide augmentation of what some have called "human capital" and others term "human resources"—the human potential to generate a prosperity based upon knowledge, skills, organization and other innately human capabilities.

In a physical sense, the natural resources of the planet are clearly finite and therefore limited. But the planet is now experiencing a monumental expansion of a different type of resource: human resources. Unlike natural resources, human resources are in practice always renewable and in theory entirely inexhaustible—indeed, it is not at all self-evident that there are any "natural" limits to the build-up of such potentially productive human-based capabilities.

It is in ignoring these very human resources that so many contemporary surveyors of the global prospect have so signally misjudged the demographic and environmental constraints upon development today—and equally misjudged the possibilities for tomorrow.

Notes

1. This essay is a revised and updated version of a chapter originally prepared for a Competitive Enterprise Institute volume edited by Ronald Bailey. Special thanks go to Ms. Megan Davy of AEI for her superb data analysis, and to Ms. Caroline Boin of IPN for acute editorial comments and suggestions. Thanks are also due Professor Stephan Pfaffenzeller of the University of Liverpool for generously sharing his research on long-term

commodity price trends. The usual caveats apply.

2. UN Cairo Conference on Population and Development, Programme of Action, Preamble, Paragraph 1.11, available electronically at http://www.unfpa.org/icpd/icpd_poa.htm#ch1, accessed June 20, 2007.

3. UNFPA Annual Report 2002, available electronically at http://www.unfpa.org/about/report/2002/1ch1pg.htm, Accessed July 2006.

4. Sierra Club, "Ecoregions: Strategy", available electronically at http://www.sierra-club.org/ecoregions/strategy.asp, accessed July 2006.

5. The U.S. Census Bureau's most recent (May 2000) projections, for example, envision a decline in the population of continent of Europe from 727 million in 2007 to 640 million in 2050. For Japan, the corresponding figures are 127 million in 2007 and a projected 100 million in 2050. Data available electronically from the U.S. Census Bureau website at http://www.census.gov/ipc/www/idbagg.html, accessed June 20, 2007.

6. For 1999, Russia reported 2.166 million deaths and 1.476 million births. "Federal Statistics Service: Russia's Population was an estimated 142.2 million on January 1, 2007", Russia and CIS Statistics Service, May 3, 2007.

7. Jaya Dalal, "Population: U.N. Agency Projects Record Income for 1996", Inter Press Service, November 7, 1995.

8. Al Gore, *Earth in the Balance: Ecology and the Human Spirit*, (New York: Houghton-Mifflin, 2000), p. 309.

9. Al Gore on *Nightline* (ABC News), Transcript # 3467, September 6, 1994

10. Jared Diamond, Collapse—*How Societies Choose to Fail or Succeed* (London: Allen Lane), p. 511.

11. Planned Parenthood Federation of America, "Fact Sheet", available electronically at http://www.plannedparenthood.org/library/FAMILYPLANNINGISSUES/fpworldofdifference_fact.htm, accessed July 2006.

12. Jared Diamond, *ibid.* p. 6

13. Jared Diamond, *ibid.* p. 176

14. Former Vice President Gore in "Beyond the Numbers", loc. cit.

15. Al Gore, p. 310.

16. Jared Diamond, *ibid*, p. 496.

17. Al Gore, p. xxi.

18. All data in this paragraph taken from United Nations, *Demographic Yearbook 2000*, (New York: United Nations, 2000), Table 3. Estimates of population density are for 2000, and the estimate of global population density excludes uninhabited territory (e.g. Antarctica).

19. Population Division of the Department of Economic and Social Affairs of the United Nations Secretariat, *World Population Prospects: The 2006 Revision*, http://esa.un.org/unpp, Thursday, June 14, 2007; 5:50:35 AM.

20. Michael R. Haines, "The Population of The United States, 1790–1920", in Stanley Engerman and Robert E. Gallman, *The Cambridge Economic History of the United States, Volume 2*, (New York: Cambridge University Press, 2000), Table 1.

21. Al Gore, p. 309.

22. Projections available electronically from U.S. Census Bureau International Data Base at http://www.census.gov/ipc/www/idbagg.html; accessed June 21, 2007.

23. "The Population of The United States, 1790–1920", loc. cit., Table 3.

24. Dennis A. Ahlburg, "Population Growth and Poverty", in Robert Cassen and contributors, *Population and Development: Old Debates, New Conclusions*, (New Brunswick, NJ: Transaction Publishers, 1994), p. 143.

25. Robert Cassen with Lisa M. Bates, *Population Policy: A New Consensus* (Washington, DC: Overseas Development Council, 1994), p. 15.

26. U. S. Bureau of the Census, "Historical Estimates of World Population" available electronically at http://www.census.gov/ipc/www/worldhis.html; and *idem.*, International Data Base, available electronically at http://www.census.gov/ipc/www/idbagg.html, accessed September 27, 2001.

27. Samuel H. Preston, *Mortality Patterns in National Populations*, (New York: Academic Press, 1976), p. ix.

28. The U.S. Census Bureau's August 2006 projections put global life expectancy at birth for the year 2000 at 63.7 years. (U.S. Census Bureau International Data Base, available electronically at http://www.census.gov/ipc/www/idbagg.html, accessed June 21, 2007.) The projections of the United Nations Population Division are similar: for 1995/2000, that estimate of planetary life expectancy at birth is 65.2. http://esa.un.org/unpp/, accessed June 21, 2007.

29. Angus Maddison, *Monitoring the World Economy: 1820–1992*, (Paris: OECD, 1995); *The World Economy: A Millennial Perspective*, (Paris: OECD, 2001); *The World Economy: Historical Statistics*, (Paris: OECD, 2003), and "World Population GDP and Per Capita GDP 1-2003" (March 2007), available online at http://www.ggdc.net/maddison/Historical_Statistics/horizontal-file_03-2007.xls, accessed June 21, 2007. Though specialists may quibble over particular figures in Maddison's detailed long-term series, the overall economic picture that his calculations paint, and the general trends they outline, are not matters of dispute among serious students of economic history today.

30. *Monitoring the World Economy*, Tables E-1, E-3; *The World Economy: A Millennial Perspective*, Tables A-a, B-21, A4-c.

31. Nominal prices for corn, wheat and rice for 1900–1984 compiled from World Bank sources by Enzo R. Grilli and Maw Cheng Yang, World Bank; 1985–98 series compiled from World Bank data by Stephan Pfaffenzeller, University of Nottingham. Nominal prices adjusted by US CPI (consumer price index). The author thanks Mr. Stephan Pfaffenzeller for generously sharing his research.

32. Aluminum, copper, nickel, zinc, tin, lead, cotton, timber, hides, rubber, wool 64s, wool 48s, palm oil, and coconut oil. The makeup and weighting of the index is outlined in Bjorn Lomborg, *The Skeptical Environmentalist: Measuring the Real State of the World*, (New York: Cambridge University Press, 2001), p. 382, fn. 1006.

33. "Indicators—Millennium Issue: Commodity Price Index", Economist, December 31, 1999, p. 139. Note that an updated and re-based *Economist* commodity-price index, now covering 25 primary commodities (but excluding oil and precious metals) was released in 2005; for the 1900–2000 period, the revised index reports a real decline in the commodities it covers of over 70%. See "The Economist's commodity-price index: 160 years on", Economist, February 12, 2005.

34. Enzo R. Grilli and Maw Cheng Yang, "Primary Commodity Prices, Manufactured Goods Prices, and the Terms of Trade of Developing Countries: What the Long Run

Shows", *World Bank Economic Review*, Volume 2, Number 1 (January 1988), p. 1–48; Stephan Pfaffenzeller, Paul Newbold, and Anthony Rayner, A Short Note on Updating the Grilli and Yang Commodity Price Index, The World Bank Economic Review 2007 vol. 21, no. 1 (January 2007), pp.151–163.

35. Note that neither the Grilli-Yang index nor the Pfaffenzeller et al updates include energy products—an arguably quite serious omission. In one computation, however, Grilli and Yang added coal and oil to their 24 commodity trade-weighted series. The introduction of fuels altered the picture, but only slightly: with energy included in their primary commodity index, real prices still fell at a pace of 0.5 percent per annum from 1900 through 1986, a trajectory that would imply a drop of about 40 percent if continued over the course of a century.

36. Data utilised in the preceding paragraph are drawn from *World Population Prospects: The 2006, loc.cit.* and from the Census Bureau's International Data Base, available electronically at http://www.census.gov/ipc/www/idbagg.html, accessed July 2006.

37. Serbia's most recently reported total fertility rate (2005), for example, was 1.18; Bosnia-Herzegovina's (2005), 1.29; Macedonia's (2005), 1.47; Croatia's (2005), 1.33; Slovenia's (2005), 1.21. (Data available from Institut National d'Études Démographiques website at http://www.ined.fr/population-en-chiffres/pays-deelopes/indefcon.htm; accessed July 2006.) A total fertility rate of roughly 2.1 is necessary for long-term population stability.

38. Some might object that other settings have seen political instability or conflict driven by high rates of population growth or increasing population density: contemporary Haiti or Rwanda might be adduced as examples here. It is true that in both of these societies—unlike the former Yugoslavia—fertility levels were above replacement in their eras of upheaval and breakdown. This fact in itself, however, does not establish demography as the causative factor in their political travails—or even necessarily a significant contributor, .Suffice it to say that until the role of such factors as quality of governance, soundness of policy regimens, and security of property rights and rule of law, etc. are carefully assessed in relation to these political breakdowns, the presumption that population was the driving force behind the plunge into political chaos or catastrophe remains at best premature.

39. Charles Tilly, "Introduction", in Charles Tilly, ed., *Historical Studies of Changing Fertility*, (Princeton, NJ: Princeton University Press, 1978), p. 3.

40. Al Gore, p. 311.

41. Data for the preceding analysis drawn from *World Population Projections: The 2006 Revision, loc. cit.*

42. Michael W. Flinn, *The European Demographic System, 1500–1820*, (Baltimore, MD: Johns Hopkins University Press, 1981), p. 94.

43. For France's 1800 total fertility rate, see Ansley J. Coale, "The Decline of Fertility in Europe Since the Eighteenth Century as a Chapter in Human Demographic History", in Ansley J. Coale and Susan Cotts Watkins, eds., *The Decline of Fertility in Europe*, (Princeton, NJ: Princeton University Press, 1986), p. 27.

44. Data derived from WDI 2007.

45. For more information, see David P. Lindstrom, "The role of contraceptive supply and demand in Mexican fertility decline: Evidence from a microdemographic study",

Population Studies, vol. 52, no. 3 (November 1998), pp. 252–274; George Martine, "Brazil's fertility decline, 1965–95: a fresh look at key factors", *Population and Development Review*, vol. 22, no. 1 (March 196), pp. 47–75, and U.S. Census Bureau International Data Base, available electronically at http://www.census.gov/ipc/www/idbagg.html.

46. For data and analysis, see Lant Pritchett, "Desired fertility and the impact of population policies", *Population and Development Review*, vol. 20, no. 1 (March 1994), pp. 1–55.

47. Jared Diamond, *ibid*, p. 524.

48. Jude Sheerin, "Population Crisis Looms Because of Failed Promises—UN", *Press Association Limited*, November 7, 2001.

49. Al Gore, p. 308.

50. *World Population Prospects: The 2006 Revision, loc. cit.*

51. Data drawn from WDI 2002.

52. Wolfgang Lutz, Warren Sanderson, and Sergei Scherbov, "The end of world population growth", Nature, vol. 42, pp. 543–545 (August 2, 2001).

53. UNPD, "The Future of Fertility in Intermediate-Fertility Countries", *Expert Group Meeting on Completing the Fertility Transition*, UNPD, New York, March 11–13 2002, available electronically at http://www.un.org/esa/population/publications/completingfertility/RevisedPEPSPOPDIVpaper.PDF , accessed July 2006.

54. "World Population Prospects: The 2006 Revisions", *loc. cit.*

3

The Demographic Future

Foreign Affairs, November/December 2010

It is already possible to draw a reasonably reliable profile of the world's population in 2030. This is, of course, because the overwhelming majority of those who will inhabit the world 20 years from now are already alive. As a result, one can make some fairly confident estimates of important demographic trends, including manpower availability, the growth in the number of senior citizens, and the resulting support burden on workers.

Overall, it is apparent that the future global economy will not be able to rely on the kind of demographic inputs that helped fuel growth in the era before the current global recession. For today's affluent Western economies, the coming demographic challenge of stagnant and aging populations combined with mounting health and pension claims on a shrinking pool of prospective workers is already generating concern, especially in Europe and Japan. But at the same time, demographic constraints in the rising economies that are expected to fuel future global growth are more serious and intractable than generally recognized.

When the current painful and protracted economic crisis is eventually resolved, the global economy will likely embark again on a path of sustained long-term growth but at a slower pace, because of new demographic realities. These demographic pressures can be substantially offset only if both rich and poor countries undertake profound and far-reaching changes in working arrangements, lifestyles, business practices, and government policies.

More Health, Fewer Babies

The twentieth century was an era of unprecedented population growth. Between 1900 and 2000, the world's population almost quadrupled, from about 1.6 billion people to around 6.1 billion. This huge expansion did not occur because people suddenly began reproducing at higher rates; instead, population surged because humans finally stopped dying like flies. Over the course of the twentieth century, global life expectancy at birth more than doubled, soaring from about 30 years in 1900 to about 65 years in 2000. This global population explosion was, in reality, a health explosion: the entirety of the enormous increase in human population over the past several generations was due to dramatic declines in mortality and improvements in general health conditions.

If the twentieth century's revolutionary demographic trend was a health explosion, the twenty-first century's hallmark trend appears to be a fertility implosion. A dramatic, far-reaching, and, as yet, unremitting global reduction in childbearing and birthrates is now under way. Sustained and deliberate reductions in family size through birth control began to lower national fertility levels in certain European countries long ago. But sustained fertility decline only became a worldwide phenomenon after the end of World War II. Over the past half century, according to the United Nations Population Division (UNDP) and the U.S. Census Bureau, the number of births per woman dropped by almost half, from 4.9 in the early 1960s to an estimated 2.5 today, with the steepest decline occurring in less developed countries.

Close to half of the world's population now lives in countries with fertility rates below the replacement level, which, as a rough rule of thumb, is 2.1 births per woman. In these states absent steady compensatory immigration current childbearing patterns will lead to an eventual and indefinite depopulation. Almost all of the world's developed countries have sub-replacement fertility, with overall birthrates more than 20 percent below the level required for long-term population stability. But developed countries account for less than a fifth of the world's population; the great majority of the world's populations with sub-replacement fertility in fact reside in low-income societies.

China is one such low-income society with sub-replacement fertility. It may seem exceptional, given Beijing's one-child policy. Yet sub-replacement fertility is also the norm today in many low-income countries without coercive population controls. Strikingly, some of these are countries with predominantly rural populations where educational opportunities for women remain limited and health conditions are still poor. One such case may be Myanmar (also called Burma), an impoverished and isolated country where, according to the UNDP, birth levels have fallen below the replacement rate.

The U.S. Census Bureau and the UNDP both estimate that sub-replacement fertility is the norm in every East Asian country and in much of Southeast Asia, including Vietnam and Thailand; in most of the Caribbean islands; and, increasingly, throughout Latin America. What is no less striking, sub-replacement fertility has also come to parts of the great Islamic expanse that stretches from northern Africa through the Middle East and into Asia.

Much remains unexplained about the continuing march toward ever-lower levels of fertility. For example, there are few socioeconomic preconditions for rapid and pronounced fertility decline or even for slides into sub-replacement fertility, as the case of Myanmar underscores. Furthermore, it is not known how long a society that has entered into sub-replacement fertility mode will stay there: Japan, for example, began reporting sub-replacement fertility in the 1950s and has had uninterrupted sub-replacement fertility since the early 1970s. Demographers, it should be emphasized, still have no reliable techniques for making accurate long-term fertility forecasts. Nevertheless, some specialists argue that ultralow fertility rates may be but a harbinger of future—and currently unimaginable fertility declines.

Although little is conclusively known about the underlying causes of the fertility revolution, some of its consequences are discernable. First, pronounced fertility declines today imply a slowdown in the growth of the working-age population tomorrow. Second, low fertility today leads to population aging tomorrow—a process that becomes turbocharged if sub-replacement birthrates are sustained over time.

Men at Work

On a global level, returning to pre-crisis economic growth rates will be complicated by the impending and inalterable—trends in worldwide manpower availability. Between now and 2030, the global supply of potential workers is set to grow much more slowly than in the previous two decades. According to U.S. Census Bureau projections, the absolute increase in the world's working-age (between 15 and 64) population between 2010 and 2030 will be around 900 million people, 400 million fewer than over the past two decades. The projected average rate of global manpower growth for the coming decades is 0.9 percent per year, only half the rate for the period between 1990 and 2010.

Complicating matters still further is the prospective regional distribution of the coming growth in global manpower. Over the past 20 years, the two greatest centers of manpower growth have been China and India, which also happened to be two of the world's most rapidly growing economies. Over the next 20 years, however, the largest share of growth in the world's working-age population well over a third of the total will take place in sub-Saharan Africa, the region with the worst record of long-term economic performance. Bangladesh and Pakistan will account for nearly another eighth of the world's manpower growth. In other words, over the next two decades, sub-Saharan Africa, Bangladesh, and Pakistan will generate nearly half the growth in the world's working-age population.

At the same time, most of the current advanced economies of the Organization for Economic Cooperation and Development (OECD) and many promising emerging economies are set to experience shrinkage in their working-age populations. This group includes China, Japan, the countries of eastern and western Europe, and the former Soviet states.

The prospect of shrinking manpower does not look any better when broken down into subsidiary age-group components. Younger workers are important for growth, because they typically have higher levels of education and better knowledge of the latest technology. But over the next 20 years, growth in the worldwide pool of young manpower will undergo a severe deceleration. According to U.S. Census Bureau projections, total young manpower defined here as men and women between the ages of 15 and 29 will increase by just four percent, or 70 million people, between today and 2030, representing barely a fifth of the increase over the past two decades. Only the countries of sub-Saharan Africa will see appreciable growth in young manpower. Japan and the states of western Europe are on course for significant prospective drops in this key manpower pool over the next 20 years (in the case of Japan, by almost 25 percent). But by far the most massive falloff in young manpower is set to take place in China: over the next 20 years, this working-age group will fall in China by around 100 million people, or about 30 percent.

Yet as young manpower grows relatively scarcer, older manpower is becoming increasingly abundant. Over the next 20 years, the oldest segment of the conventionally defined working-age population men and women between 50 and 64 years of age is projected to account for nearly half of all global manpower growth, nearly twice the share for the period between 1990 and 2010. China will face a particularly huge increase in older manpower; the working-age population will also age in many other emerging markets, as well as in all the developed Western economies. Older workers do bring some particular skills, based on experience, but they also tend to be less educated and less healthy than younger workers. Furthermore, labor-force participation rates for older workers tend to be lower, and in some affluent societies, much lower.

The prospective global work force of 2030 is on track to being more educated and healthier than previous generations of workers, which should increase overall labor productivity. But the economic potential of such prospective benefits should not be exaggerated. Projections by the International Institute for Applied Systems Analysis, in Austria, and the Vienna Institute of Demography suggest that improvements in educational levels for the world's working-age population stand to be slower over the next 20 years than they were over the past 20 years. For example, the proportion of global manpower with no education at all is projected to drop by less than five percentage points, compared to an eight-point drop in the past 20 years. And the share of the working-age population with secondary schooling or better is estimated to increase by ten points, three points fewer than in the previous two decades.

Taken as a whole, these manpower trends point to mounting demographic pressures and, quite possibly, a slowdown in the rate of long-term economic growth. All other factors being equal, these trends also suggest a slowdown in consumer spending, which could perhaps lead to a slowdown in business profits, as well.

Aging Ungracefully?

The economic performance of the world's six major economies will largely determine growth patterns for the world as a whole over the next 20 years. China, India, Japan, Russia, western Europe, and the United States account for over half of the world's current population and over 70 percent of the world's GDP, adjusted for purchasing power parity. And over the decade before the current financial crisis, they accounted for about 70 percent of global economic growth.

No major economy has more radiant prospects for the coming decades than China. Its economic transformation has been nothing less than dazzling according to World Bank estimates, in the three decades following Deng Xiaoping's 1978 moves toward systemic reform, China's GDP grew by almost ten percent a year. (Other sources suggest a slightly slower rate of growth but still one that is historically unprecedented.) Beijing officially forecasts annual growth rates of roughly seven percent per year between now and 2030. But this rosy prognosis does not take into account China's looming demographic tempests. Population specialists believe that China became a sub-replacement fertility society about two decades ago and that since then, birthrates have fallen far below the replacement level. For example, the U.S. Census Bureau puts China's total fertility rate at about 1.5 children per woman, or 30 percent below the level required for long-term population stability.

Persistent, and now extreme, sub-replacement fertility is the demographic driver shaping the China of tomorrow. Given current trends, U.S. Census Bureau projections anticipate fewer people under the age of 50 in China in 2030 than today and many fewer Chinese in their 20s and early 30s. These same projections foresee many more elderly Chinese in their 60s, 70s, and 80s. China's older workers are much less educated than their youthful successors—nearly half of today's working-age population between the ages of 50 and 64 has not completed primary school. Educational levels for older workers will improve in the decades ahead but will still lag behind Chinese national averages. And China will be experiencing a population explosion of senior citizens over the next 20 years; they are the progeny of the pre-population-control era. In 2010, about 115 million people in China were 65 or older. By 2030, this number is projected to approach 240 million people meaning that China's cohort of senior citizens would be soaring at an average rate of 3.7 percent per year.

How Beijing will support this coming tsunami of senior citizens remains an unanswered question. As yet, China has no national public pension system and only the most rudimentary provisions for rural health care. Meeting the needs of its rapidly growing elderly population will place economic and social pressures on China that no country of a comparable income level has ever had to confront.

Moreover, in the decades ahead, China will face a growing number of young men who will never marry due to the country's one-child policy, which has resulted in a reported birth ratio of almost 120 boys for every 100 girls (most societies report the births of 103 to 105 boys for every 100 girls). This imbalance is setting the stage for a "marriage squeeze" of monumental proportions. By 2030, projections suggest that more than 25 percent of Chinese men in their late 30s will never have married. The coming marriage squeeze will likely be even more acute in the Chinese countryside, since the poor, uneducated, and rural population will be more likely to lose out in the competition for brides. Beijing will have to determine how it will cope with a growing demographic of unmarried, underprivileged, and, quite possibly, deeply discontented young men.

China still has potential sources for enhancing productivity, including the migration of rural workers to more productive urban jobs, the wider application of currently underutilized technical know-how, improved financial intermediation for the country's high savings rates, and broader institutional and policy reforms to enhance efficiency. Such untapped potential can fuel future growth, but nevertheless, China's serious demographic challenges could slow economic growth more than is currently expected.

Russia is another emerging-market country widely regarded as holding immense economic promise, not least by the leaders in the Kremlin. Despite the current economic downturn, official Russian plans envision economic growth of six percent a year through 2020 and continuing rapid growth thereafter. But these ambitious visions seem to ignore the fact that the country has been in the grip of a protracted demographic crisis since the end of communist rule. Since 1992, Russia's deaths have outnumbered births by roughly 50 percent, or about 13 million, and official figures suggest that the country's population has shrunk by about five percent nearly seven million people from 148.6 million in 1993 to 141.9 million today. Immigration has helped slow the country's population decline but has not been able to prevent it. The outlook is for further depopulation: medium variant projections by the Kremlin's official statistical service envision ten million more deaths than births over the next two decades.

Even more troubling for Russia is the country's disastrous public health situation. In 2009, as hard as it may be to believe, Russia's overall life expectancy was a bit lower than it had been in 1961, almost half a century earlier.

To make matters worse, at least from an economic standpoint, Russia's health crisis is concentrated in its working-age population. Over the 40 years between 1965 and 2005, for example, the death rates for men between their late 20s and their mid-50s virtually doubled. Death rates for women in that same age group generally rose by about 50 percent. Public health experts do not entirely understand the reasons for this death spiral although poor diet, smoking, sedentary lifestyles, and, above all, Russia's deadly romance with vodka can explain much of the deterioration, the actual decline is worse than what these risk factors alone would suggest. In some respects, contemporary health levels for Russian adults are akin to those for adults in the world's most impoverished states. According to estimates by the World Health Organiza-tion, life expectancy for a 15-year-old man in 2008 would have been lower in Russia than in Cambodia, Eritrea, or Haiti. Between now and 2030, the U.S. Census Bureau projects that Russia's working-age population will fall by nearly 20 percent, and Russia's work force will almost surely suffer more ill health than its counterparts in the OECD and than the work forces of the other BRIC countries (Brazil, India, and China). In 2008, according to World Health Organization estimates, mortality levels for Russia's working-age pop-ulation were 25 percent higher than those for India's.

Urban centers are typically the hubs of economic growth, but Russia's urban population is smaller today than it was at the end of the communist era, and the UN projects that there will be even fewer inhabitants in Russia's cities 20 years from now. In addition, Russia's old-age burden will be steadily increasing—whereas 13 percent of the Russian population today is 65 or older, the projected proportion for 2030 is 21 percent. Taking all the above into account, it is difficult to see how Russia can hope to generate sustained and rapid economic growth on the basis of its human resources. Natural resources may offer the country economic opportunities in the years ahead, but these opportunities should not be exaggerated. Despite all of Russia's energy and mineral wealth, its annual export earnings have never exceeded those of Belgium, not even at the height of the pre-crisis oil boom.

India's GDP growth has averaged an impressive 6.5 percent a year since the economic reforms that began in 1991. Recently, the economy has been humming along at eight percent growth per year. Not a few observers think the best may be yet to come. In just one example, a member of India's Plan-ning Commission suggested in 2008 that India's economy would be growing at eight to nine percent a year for the next quarter century. In the same time frame, India's total population is set to grow by just over one percent per year, and about five-sixths of that growth will be in its working-age population. Thanks to the disproportionate growth of India's manpower pool, the country's dependency ratio (the ratio of children under 15 and persons over 65 to the working-age population) will be falling, and the society will remain relatively youthful. Such changes in population structure could facilitate higher levels of national savings and investment and, thus, economic growth. In short, India appears to be a poster child for a potential demographic dividend.

But India has striking regional disparities in population profiles. India is bisected by a great north-south fertility divide: in much of the north, including parts of the Ganges river belt and some of the country's westernmost districts, fertility levels remain quite high, at four, five, or more children per woman; in much of the Indian south, however, fertility levels are at, or already below, the replacement level. In effect, this means that two very different Indias are being born today—a youthful, rapidly growing northern India whose future population structure will be akin to that of a traditional Third World society and a southern India whose population growth will be slowing or ceasing, where manpower growth will be coming to an end, and where pronounced population aging will be taking hold.

This demographic divergence could make sustaining rapid economic growth a trickier proposition than it might seem at first. India's engines of economic growth are mainly its sub-replacement fertility areas, which include much of the south and practically all its major urban centers: Bangalore, Chennai, Kolkata, and Mumbai. But its demographics mean that the country's future workers will increasingly come from the high-fertility areas of the north. This reveals a fundamental mismatch: India's continued economic growth requires workers who are relatively well educated, but India's mostly rural high-fertility areas are producing a rising generation with woefully low levels of schooling.

India, it is true, can boast of a cadre of millions of highly trained engineers, scientists, researchers, and professionals. But in a country of well over a billion people, these specialists compose only a tiny fraction of its overall manpower. In the country as a whole, educational levels are still remarkably limited, and remedial efforts will take generations to achieve substantial improvement. Currently, about a third of India's working-age population has no education at all; 20 years from now, a sixth of the country's work force may still be totally unschooled. These educational shortfalls place material constraints on the prospects for sustaining rapid rates of economic growth.

Broadly speaking, all the developed economies will face demographic slow-downs and population aging in the coming decades, but Japan stands to be the most heavily burdened by the looming trends. It has had the steepest and longest fertility falloff in modern history. In 2008, the country recorded around 40 percent as many births as it had 60 years earlier. Japanese childbearing is currently estimated to be nearly 35 percent below the replacement level. But Japan has also enjoyed rapid and continuing improvements in public health since the end of World War II. The Japanese have an average life expectancy of 83 years, higher than any other country in the world. Taken together, the country's fertility, migration, and mortality trends are propelling Japan into demographic decline, and into a degree of aging thus far contemplated only in science fiction.

Over the next two decades, according to U.S. Census Bureau estimates, the surfeit of deaths as compared to births is expected to drive Japan's total population down from 127 million to 114 million, a ten percent decrease. The relative decline in the working-age population is projected to be even steeper, from 81 million to 67 million, or a 17 percent decrease. All the while, the number of Japanese senior citizens would be rising and by 2030, the country's median age will be above 52 years, with 30 percent of the total population 65 or older. The economic implications of these impending changes are far from positive. Even with healthy aging and later retirement, these trends suggest a marked contraction in the country's labor supply. Moreover, the social and economic strains from Japan's looming old-age boom could further complicate efforts to maintain even the country's current sluggish rates of economic growth.

Western Europe, for its part, can expect population stagnation, according to the U.S. Census Bureau its population may grow by just three percent over the next two decades, with near-zero growth projected by 2030. Germany and Italy are expected to experience population decline. A stagnating Europe will also be a graying Europe. The U.S. Census Bureau estimates that western Europe's median age would rise from 42 years today to nearly 46 years by 2030. Despite overall population stagnation, western Europe's 65-and-older population is set to rise by nearly 40 percent, while its manpower pool is slated to shrink by 12 million people. And these projections are premised on a net inflow of approximately 20 million immigrants, mainly of working age.

Two unanswered demographic questions loom over the future of the western European economy. First, can the countries in the region succeed in attracting and incorporating the foreign workers their economies will need in the coming decades? Thus far, western Europe's record on the social inclusion of immigrants may have been somewhat better than many appreciate; however, there have been increasing assimilation problems, which, if left unattended, could impinge on economic growth, as well as social cohesion. Second, can the countries of western Europe translate public health improvements into longer working lives for progressively aging populations? At the moment, overall life expectancy at birth in western Europe is about two years higher than in the United States (80 years compared to 78 years). But the average retirement age in western Europe is lower than it is in the United States, even despite recent increases in the labor-force participation of older workers in northern Europe. This summer's public protests in France against a proposed increase in the French retirement age from 60 to 62 shows how tough it may be to achieve political consensus.

The Demographic Exception

The United States will avoid the demographic stagnation and decline that faces most other OECD countries. The U.S. population, according to U.S. Census Bureau projections, is set to grow by 20 percent, or over 60 million people (from 310 million to 374 million), between 2010 and 2030. By such projections, the United States' population growth rate will nearly match India's. According to these calculations, the United States' rate of population growth approximates that of the world's average, meaning that the U.S. share of global population is not set to shrink. Virtually every age group in the United States is set to increase in size over the next 20 years. Unlike all other affluent countries, the United States can expect a growing pool of working-age people (a moderate but steady rise averaging 0.5 percent per year over the next 20 years), and it can expect a slower pace of population aging than virtually any other state in the OECD.

The United States' demographic exceptionalism is explained by the country's relatively high fertility rate and its continuing influx of immigrants. Over the past generation and a half, while fertility rates in most other Western countries were plunging, the fertility rate in the United States was actually increasing, and unlike that of any other large rich country, its rate has been hovering just around the replacement level for the past generation. If fertility and immigration in the United States remain more or less at their current rates, as U.S. Census Bureau projections assume they will, the United States will enjoy a surplus of births over deaths of nearly 35 million and will tally a net inflow of almost 30 million immigrants over the next 20 years. Both factors would keep the nation growing and relatively young, shaping a distinctly more auspicious outlook for economic growth in the United States than exists for Japan or western Europe.

Nevertheless, there are also clouds on the U.S. demographic horizon, all of them regarding the quality of future U.S. human resources. The United States has a relatively good record when it comes to assimilating immigrants as productive newcomers, but resistance to continued immigration, or unexpected new problems in absorbing immigrant inflows, could limit future success. Furthermore, the United States' primary and secondary public education system produces uneven results that are mediocre in comparison to other affluent societies. The percentage of Americans graduating from high school has been slowing and could possibly plateau in the years ahead. And advances in health in the United States do not compare well with those under way in other affluent states. Education and health will be key to enhancing the productivity and wealth of the U.S. population in the decades ahead, which means there are few grounds for complacency when contemplating these challenges.

Despite the particular differences in their demographic outlooks, Japan, western Europe, and the United States share a common fiscal problem: the relationship between population aging and public-debt obligations. Over the past two decades, a striking feature has emerged in the macro-economies of the OECD countries. The gross burden of public debt as a proportion of GDP has come to correspond with the proportion of the population that is 65 or older. Very roughly speaking (as my colleague Hans Groth and I have shown), costs associated with population aging are estimated to account for about half the public-debt run-up of the OECD economies over the past

20 years. In the next two decades, the increase in the 65-and-older population will be about twice as great as it was in the decades just past. Coping with the fiscal and public-debt implications of the pressures that population aging places on macroeconomic performance may not be an entirely new challenge for affluent societies, but it promises to become an ever more salient one over the next 20 years.

Humanity's Secret Weapons

Left unattended, the global demographic trends outlined above suggest serious and gradually mounting pressures on global economic development and may lead to downward revisions of worldwide material expectations. But feasible options do exist to alleviate some of these pressures and to capitalize on new demographic opportunities that may arise. Addressing these new demographic challenges will require deliberate, concerted, and sustained efforts. Such an approach must focus on augmenting human capital by expanding education, improving health conditions, and creating an economic environment in which greater returns can be generated by the world's precious human resources.

Improving educational opportunity and quality in low-income areas, for example, should figure centrally in enhancing prospects for local and global growth. Better-educated workers tend to be not only more productive but also healthier and better placed to lead longer working lives. Simply put, populations in developing countries cannot hope to generate First World income levels with Third World educational profiles. Improving health status should also be a central objective, since health advances could prove critical to maintaining or increasing long-term economic growth rates in an ever-grayer world.

For affluent, graying societies, taking economic advantage of healthy aging will become ever more crucial to the quest for higher national income levels. This suggests that the existing disincentives in so many rich countries to continuing to work at older ages should be reexamined and ultimately eliminated. At the same time, governments should consider careful incentives for the voluntary extension of working life. More generally, in both rich and poor countries, governments should enact business and economic policies that enhance the efficiency of manpower resources, thereby eliciting higher productivity and faster economic growth.

Humanity has one additional "secret weapon" in accelerating growth in the years ahead: knowledge production and technological innovation. The revolutions of the past generation in health and life sciences, information technology, and materials science point to the sorts of opportunities that may lie ahead for improving productivity. More than ever before, research and development must be incentivized to reward risk takers.

For the sake of the world's future prosperity, reforms and innovations must be pursued with urgency. Demographic changes unfold slowly from month to month, but the cumulative impact can be staggering. It is not alarmist to warn that there is no time to lose in recognizing and adapting to the enormity of the world's unavoidable demographic challenges.

4

The Human Population Unbound

Current History, January 2014

Over the past hundred years, global demographic changes have been more than just historic—they have been so sweeping and profound as to rank almost on the scale of an evolutionary leap. What we have witnessed is nothing less than a departure from the demographic rhythms that previously characterized human existence. Across the world we have seen humanity unshackled from practically all the patterns and limits that bound us before, save for reproduction and death itself.

Humans since 1914 have undergone a global population explosion, a health explosion, a fertility revolution, and an urbanization revolution—with further, equally monumental changes currently in the works, promising to transform the world's population profile in likewise previously unimaginable respects over the century to come.

By very approximate orders of magnitude, it is believed that around 100 billion people have ever been born, with around 90 billion of these souls born before 1914. For that first 90 billion, life was almost always rural—and very short. Until the outbreak of World War I, global population growth was perilously contingent—the race between deaths and births, desperately close. From the dawn of our species until the twentieth century, human numbers increased painfully slowly. Although uncertainty is obviously inherent in such calculations, we can nonetheless suggest that human numbers could not have grown on average by more than three one-hundredths of one percent per century over the 50,000 years preceding 1900. For almost all of history—and pre-history—"population balance" was enforced by recurrent and disastrous setbacks, including the regular disappearance of clans, nations, and even entire civilizations.

Then, over the course of the twentieth century, the human population suddenly quadrupled—from very roughly 1.5–1.6 billion around 1900 to about

6.1 billion in 2000 (a much more solid figure, given the universality of population censuses nowadays). During the century, the tempo of world population growth accelerated by something like two orders of magnitude over the previous epochal pace, and human numbers virtually everywhere surged on an unprecedented scale.

Life Chances

How could this have happened? Arithmetically, the answer is clear. This did not take place because people suddenly started breeding like rabbits. Rather, it happened because they finally stopped dying like flies. Simply put, the twentieth century saw an unprecedented revolution in life chances. Around 1900, the global expectation of life span at birth was roughly 30 years—not so different from Neolithic or even Paleolithic times. By 2000, according to estimates from the United Nations Population Division (UNPD), worldwide life expectancy surpassed 65 years.

In every region of the world, mortality fell— and fell dramatically. In both relative and absolute terms, the gains in longevity tended to be greater in the world's poorest regions. In 1900, the female life expectancy in New Zealand—around 60 years at birth—was likely the highest yet achieved. By 2000, a female life expectancy of 60 was characteristic of countries like Haiti: places now among the least healthy on the planet. In 1950, according to the UNPD, the gap in life expectancy between what the UN terms "more developed regions" and "less developed regions" was about 23 years; by 2000, it was down to 10 years, and it is continuing to diminish. Strictly speaking, the twentieth century's "population explosion" was in reality a health explosion: Improvements in survival prospects accounted for every bit of the global population increase.

From the beginning, more or less all the planet's non-human species have been consigned to a grim cycle of population surges followed by die-offs, as they predictably breed beyond the fixed resource bases sustaining them. Past theories of human population dynamics, most famously Thomas Robert Malthus's 1798 "Essay on the Principle of Population," held that people were subject to these same immutable biological laws. But just as the twentieth century reset the limits for world life expectancy, it also reset the limits on resource availability, and along with this, the limits to living standards that the human masses might enjoy.

The great economic historian Angus Maddison estimated that worldwide per capita output nearly quintupled over the course of the twentieth century—rising unevenly, to be sure, but rising everywhere. Suffice it therefore to say that the greatest population explosion in history did not prevent the greatest jump in per capita income levels ever recorded.

No less remarkable, during the very century when the global demand for goods and services soared nearly twenty-fold, inflation-adjusted prices plunged for the whole market basket of commodities that people consume. Indeed, international prices for the main cereals—rice, wheat, and corn—fell in real terms by about 70 percent over the century. Prices are meant to convey information about economic scarcity—so this tremendous decline in commodity prices implied that these resources were becoming less scarce even as people demanded ever more of them.

Human Resources

The paradox of increasing plenty in an ever more populous world is explained by the momentous new role of human resources in economic production. The global health explosion was accompanied by a worldwide literacy and education explosion (to say nothing of the related explosion in international scientific knowledge and technological innovation). A hundred years ago, the overwhelming majority of adult men and women on earth were illiterate, as in all previous times. Yet by midcentury, in the estimate of the UN Education, Scientific, and Cultural Organization (UNESCO), a slight majority of the planet's adults possessed the rudimentary skills of reading and writing.[1] And by 2011 (UNESCO's latest figures) the global literacy rate was about 84 percent: five out of six adults.[2]

By 2010, according to the World Bank, nine out of ten primary school–age children were in fact in primary school. Educational attainment has been expanding as well. In 1970, according to researchers at Austria's International Institute of Applied Systems Analysis, the global average for women 15 and older was just 1.3 years of schooling. By 2010, it was estimated at 4.6 years,[3] and is on track to reach about 9 years by 2050[4]—roughly the level of Austria today.[5]

"Human capital" has become an ever more important element in the economic process: In our time, it has arguably emerged as the indispensable element. Unlike various natural resources, which in theory could be exhausted, there is no obvious limit to human resources—not to scientific discoveries, not to schooling, perhaps not even to health.

With progressively greater health, education, and productive knowledge, the global population, not surprisingly, also has become increasingly mobile. The past hundred years have witnessed an extraordinary relocation of people from the countryside to cities. By the UNPD's reckoning, the world was still overwhelmingly rural in 1950: Over 70 percent of the globe's population lived in the countryside, including nearly half of those inhabiting the more developed regions. By 2010, the world's population had become majority-urban—with over three fourths of people in the more developed regions living in cities, and the less developed regions on track for their own urban majority before 2020.

In earlier ages, the growth of cities was severely limited by both demographics and economics. Before modern sanitation and medicines, cities were epidemiological playgrounds of infection and contagion: Death rates were typically higher than in the countryside, indeed so high that urban concentrations were only sustained by continuing influxes from the hinterlands. Furthermore, for much of history the wealth of cities actually amounted to surplus extracted from the countryside—an arrangement that perforce conduced to small urban populations. All this changed over the course of a hundred years. Almost everywhere today, urban populations are both better educated and longer-lived than their rural counterparts—and urban agglomerations now increase per capita income, even after taking health and education into account.

Below Replacement

Another radical departure from past demographic trends is the ongoing, worldwide decline in childbearing. As the twentieth century's population totals shot up, fertility levels around the globe began to plunge—first in rich countries, then in much poorer ones. Before 1900, communities that did not maintain high birth rates had been doomed to demographic decline, or eventual disappearance. (When female life expectancy was around 30 years, nearly five births per woman were necessary just for population replacement.)

Sustained reductions in family size under non-catastrophic conditions (what demographers call "secular fertility decline") seem to have begun in France in the late eighteenth century. From this initial foothold, the tendency gradually spread through the more developed regions, so that by the middle of the twentieth century, during the 1950s "baby booms," the total fertility rate (TFR, or births per woman per lifetime) in Europe, North America, Australia, New Zealand, and Japan had fallen collectively to an average of about 2.8.

For the less developed regions, TFRs averaged about 6 births in the 1950s—a level possibly higher than a generation or two earlier, thanks to intervening health improvements. But in the 1960s fertility declines in these regions commenced in earnest, first in East and Southeast Asia, then Latin America, South Asia, the Middle East, and southern Africa. At this writing, western and eastern Africa are the only reaches of the earth that have not yet been fully inducted into secular fertility decline.

The scale and pace of global fertility decline over the past half-century have been breathtaking. For the world as a whole, TFRs dropped by half between 1960 and 2010—and by well over half in the less developed regions (from 6.1 in 1960/65 to 2.7 in 2005/10, according to the UNPD). Thus fertility levels for the less developed regions are lower now than they were for the more developed regions just 50 years earlier.

While myriad factors are at play in the modern era's momentous birth rate drops—including socioeconomic advances and the spread of new contraceptive methods—these changing fertility patterns necessarily reflect drastic changes in the demand for children, and thus in familial ideals and parental mentalities. We have no way of guessing how much further mindsets will shift—or how low birth rates will ultimately go. So far, however, we have seen no obvious limits to the "lowest-low" fertility under conditions of orderly progress.

In the early 1950s, Luxembourg was the world's least fertile society, with a TFR of just under 2.0. By the late 1990s, Hong Kong was registering a TFR of less than 0.9—which if continued would result in a shrinkage of each successive generation by more than 50 percent.

Given the seemingly relentless worldwide march toward lower and lower fertility, humanity must now contend with an extraordinary new mass phenomenon: voluntary sub-replacement childbearing, the proliferation of societies with TFRs sufficiently low as to portend indefinite population decline in the absence of compensating immigration. In the early 1950s, only a handful of spots on the map—all in northern or eastern Europe, accounting for maybe 3 percent of the world's population—were registering below-replacement fertility. By the late 1970s, the more developed regions as a whole had gone sub-replacement. By the late 2000s, about 80 countries and territories were sub-replacement, accounting for just about half the total world population.

The great majority of people living in sub-replacement societies are now found in the less developed regions, including not only China with its forcible population control policy, but also countries like Brazil and Thailand, and an increasing number of surprises, such as Myanmar and Iran.

Paradoxical Prospects

Looking ahead, it is fairly clear that the current century will not be a demographic repeat of the one just completed. We can reasonably expect some of the twentieth century's big new demographic trends—improvements in health, mass education, mass urbanization—to continue, of course. But human numbers are not about to undergo another quadrupling. At this writing, the world population totals about 7.1 billion, and is growing by roughly 80 million persons a year. Growth rates for world population peaked in the late 1960s, at over 2 percent per annum; they are just over 1 percent per annum today. Even absolute annual world population increments are lower today than in the recent past—those peaked in the late 1980s.

If current trends continue (an immense "if," since we lack any reliable method for forecasting births), many more countries stand to join the worldwide sub-replacement club. Current UNPD "medium variant" projections hypothesize that more than 120 countries and territories will be at sub-replacement by 2025/30, encompassing nearly three quarters of the global population less than a decade and a half from now. Already some large countries—Germany and Japan—are in the midst of what we might call voluntary depopulation. It is entirely possible that the current century could see a peaking of global population numbers, and a gradual voluntary depopulation thereafter, as healthy, educated, and increasingly prosperous populations opt not to replace their ranks through children. But obviously this is only one of the possible trajectories that lie ahead.

Along with orderly depopulation, several other still largely unfamiliar trends stand to define and transform the global demography of tomorrow. The first of these is the graying of humanity, since low birth rates are an engine that generates more elderly population structures. All around the world, the fastest growing age group today is senior citizens. Although projections to 2100 are admittedly somewhat fantastical, the UNPD produces them, and for what they are worth, their "medium variant" depicts a global population in 2100 with a higher median age and a greater share of people 65 and older than for the more developed regions in the late 2000s.

A second trend is the "flight from marriage," already well under way in the more developed regions, but also in East Asia, and now evident in much of the Arab Middle East. In all its regional variants, this trend has been attended by a sharp rise in childlessness and a growing share of lone adults: men and women divorced, separated, or never married in the first place. On current trendlines, according to some Japanese demographers, fewer than half of the women born in Japan in 1990 will get married and stay married to age 50; count on more of this in the world to come.

Finally, we can expect much more "demographic convergence" in the decades ahead.

In many respects—for example, the gaps in life expectancy, family size, and median population age—the countries of the world have never been so differentiated as they were in the second half of the twentieth century. But these gaps are starting to close. The global distribution of life expectancy is more even today than at any time in recorded memory. Fertility levels and population structures are likewise on track to become more similar in the generations ahead.

Healthier, but also more elderly; more prosperous, but increasingly faced with demographic decline; more alike, but also more alone. Barring an environmental catastrophe or some other manmade global calamity, these could be the paradoxes of the demographic prospect that we and our descendants face in the twenty-first century.

Notes

1. World Illiteracy at Mid-Century: A Statistical Study, (Paris, France: UNESCO, 1957).

2. UNESCO, "Adult and youth literacy: UIS Fact Sheet," (fact sheet No. 26: UNESCO, September 2013).

3. Wolfgang Lutz et al., "Reconstruction of populations by age, sex, and level of educational attainment for 120 countries for 1970-2000," *Vienna Yearbook of Population Research* (2007): 193-235.

4. Samir KC et al., "Projection of populations by level of educational attainment, age, and sex for 120 countries for 2005-2050," *Demographic Research* 22, no. 15 (2010): 383-472.

5. Robert Barro and Jong-Wha Lee, "A new data set of educational attainment in the world, 1950-2010," *Journal of Development Economics* 104, pp. 184-198.

PART II

The Politics of Hunger

One may also make the case that economic liberty is especially important to the poor, the vulnerable and the marginalized, the groups, in other words, least capable of fending for themselves in an economic and political system that is neither regular nor just.

— From "Starved for Ideas"

Why does the specter of starvation—and even mass famine—continue to haunt our era, despite the huge surge of food production and explosive increases in global wealth that we have witnessed in modern times? Neo-Malthusians and neo-Marxists each claim to have the answer to this terrible question. To the former, the problem is reproduction itself, especially by the world's poorest; to the latter, the problem is an exploitive global capitalist system that generates immiseration. The facts, however, speak otherwise. Despite the twentieth century's extraordinary population explosion, humanity was incontestably healthier and better fed at the end of the 1900s than at its beginning. And it was under Marxist-Leninist governments—not "capitalist" regimes—that the threat of famine was always greatest. Indeed, anyone who died of famine during the twentieth century most likely lived under communism. Nowadays killer states are the main cause of famines. As I attempt to demonstrate in these chapters, the solution to the global hunger is to be found in good politics: more specifically, economic liberty; rule of law; and accountable governance.

5

Hunger and Ideology
Commentary, July 1981

World hunger is not only a material problem, but an intellectual problem as well. To an extent we do not fully recognize, the hunger which stalks millions of wretched families and homeless drifters is related to a lack of understanding and a want of ingenuity.

These are not failings of the poor themselves. Quite the contrary: anyone who has spent time in the villages of Asia can testify that the world's greatest economists are the illiterate women, for somehow they manage to keep their families fed on what seem like impossibly small budgets. The problem lies at precisely the opposite end of the social spectrum: with the well-educated, well-paid, and well-meaning functionaries who are meant to attend to world poverty and the desperate hunger it causes. These men and women do not lack the funds with which to make greater inroads against severe want, nor do they lack the good will of the world's free and affluent peoples. What they lack, quite simply, is understanding. Their misinterpretations of the world food situation are frequently so fundamental as to impede significantly the effort to eliminate malnutrition.

To be sure, there are some valid reasons for the confusion which surrounds this subject. Much of the information we must work with is inadequate. There are for example discrepancies of nearly fifteen million tons—about as much as Bangladesh uses to feed itself—between U.S. Department of Agriculture (USDA) and UN Food and Agriculture Organization (FAO) estimates on food-grain exports from developed countries—and those are estimates that are relatively easy to compile and relatively error-free. Evaluations of the severity of hunger are likewise dogged by ambiguity: depending on the assumptions, one can "prove" that the average Bengali needs nearly 2,400 calories a day, or only 1,600.

Most of our confusion, however, arises not from inexactitudes like these but from ideological argumentation and *idées fixes*. To a distressing degree, those charged with helping the world's poor do their work without regard for readily available information which would challenge their approach and their conclusions. Needless to say, the hungry suffer from this.

In the welter of common misperceptions about the world's food situation, four myths are particularly injurious. These are the myths of widespread and growing hunger; of increasing agricultural scarcity; of an ominous turn away from self-sufficiency and toward a reliance on foreign grain; and of the superiority of "socialist" economics in food production.

Widespread and Growing Hunger

With few exceptions, authorities in the fight against world hunger depict the situation as almost unimaginably bad. FAO figures suggest that about half-a-billion people in the less developed countries (excluding China) suffer from a malnutrition so acute that they would probably be hospitalized if they lived in Europe or the United States. The World Bank estimates that about three-fifths of the families in poor non-Communist nations—nearly one-and-a-half-billion people—do not get enough food to fill their caloric needs. Robert McNamara, the Bank's president, has stated that 30 million children die of starvation each year. Tens of millions who survive, moreover, are said to be permanently crippled by irreversible, hunger-induced brain damage. As far as these experts can tell, the situation is getting no better; in fact, despite thirty years of relief programs backed up by relatively rapid economic growth, the poor world may be getting even hungrier.

Such shocking assessments may be consistent with the politics of budgetary requests within the hunger industry. They are certainly consistent with the apocalyptic preaching of those who claim the world is currently unable to feed itself, and who place the blame on anything from the incontinence of the poor to the irredeemable rottenness of capitalism. But they are quite simply inconsistent with the most basic and readily obtainable facts on the world's food situation.

McNamara's assertion, for example, is flatly wrong. Demographic figures are subject to considerable uncertainty, but no serious estimate of the annual number of child deaths would be higher than 17 million, and a more reasonable figure would probably be 15 million.[1] This would include deaths from all causes: accidents, trauma, maternal neglect, bad sanitary conditions, and lack of medical care. Even if hunger were completely eliminated, many—perhaps more than half—of these tragic deaths would continue. McNamara's claim, then, is something like four times too high.

Likewise, the lament that countless numbers of unfortunates in the poor world are mentally deficient is a rhetorical convenience. For better or worse, human beings are not nearly so frail as doctors, social planners, and other concerned administrators sometimes assume. As Lewis Thomas once wrote, "Far from being ineptly put together, we are amazingly tough, durable organisms, full of health, ready for most contingencies." Rather than collapsing at the first sign of adversity, the human body protects itself from environmental insult, and protects especially the two systems most necessary for survival, the organs of reproduction and of thought. John Bongaarts has shown that women's fertility is basically unaffected by nutrition until the point where they are beset by starvation, when they would not be able to provide for their newborn. As for mental activity, Rose Frisch once demonstrated that every important experiment "proving" the connection between mild or moderate malnutrition and human brain damage is embarrassingly flawed in construction or interpretation. Subsequent analyses support her conclusions. In reality, if one is so starved that one's brain will be seriously and irreversibly damaged one is not likely to live to tell about it.[2]

Authoritative estimates of the prevalence of hunger may be numbingly grim, but when we bring ourselves to look at them squarely we learn that they are superficial and deceptive. Take the World Bank's count. With the Bank's "Reutlinger-Selowsky" malnutrition methodology, one comes to the chilling conclusion that something like three-fifths of the people in low-income countries live under the shadow of "caloric deficits." On inspection, however, the numbers this formula churns out prove meaningless. In Taiwan, for example caloric deprivation would be ascribed to 48 percent of the population; in Hong Kong, to 46 percent. This sounds serious indeed, until one learns that life expectancy in both places is over seventy-two—about the same, in fact, as in Finland or Austria.

As this might suggest, the World Bank method is unable to assess the incidence of hunger in a useful way. This formula, and others which imitate it implicitly insists that anyone eating less than some fixed nutritional average must be underfed. Forgotten is the obvious fact that human needs vary. This is a simple mistake, and it is not a new one. In the depth of the Depression, Sir Arthur Bowley announced that the United Kingdom was in the midst of a nutritional emergency: according to his figures, about half the country was ingesting less than the average caloric requirement. The government politely rejected his report, pointing out that about half the country would probably need less than the average caloric requirement by definition. This may have been obvious in the 1930's, but it seems to escape most of our hunger experts today.

FAO figures are no better. In 1950, the FAO's director, Lord Boyd-Orr, wrote that two-thirds of mankind lived with the threat of hunger. His report apparently based its conclusion on a simple computational error, a transposition of columns. Though the mistake was pointed out, it was never corrected, or even officially acknowledged. In the more than thirty years since that gaffe the FAO has not done much to improve its reputation for attention to detail and respect for accuracy. Most of the data and calculations in its first three World Food Surveys, the last of them released in 1963, are still not available for outside inspection. In 1974 an unexplained revision in methodology raised the FAO estimate of the incidence of serious hunger from 360 million to 434 million—or from exactly 20 percent to exactly 25 percent of the Third World—just in time for the World Food Conference. Currently the FAO computes its hunger figures with a modified version of the World Bank Reutlinger-Selowsky formula.[3]

Hunger, it seems, is not as easy to measure as we might have thought. It is difficult to find out how much the poor actually eat, for one of the hallmarks of poverty is social invisibility. If we did know how much the poor were eating, though, we still might not know how hungry they were. Food needs vary from person to person, often by 50 percent, not infrequently by 100 percent. Food needs also vary for any given person over time, depending on whether or not he is sick: intestinal bacteria, for example, may eat as much as 10 percent of any Bengali child's meal. And food needs vary with the availability of food. The body can metabolize what it consumes with greater or lesser efficiency, depending on need: we seldom use or store as much as 40 percent of the food energy in the things we eat.

If we wanted to get a meaningful impression of the extent of hunger, we might start by looking at the results of eating patterns. What nutritionists all "anthropometric" tests, such as weight-for-age and weight-for-height readings or measurements of arm and head circumference can tell us important things about the nutritional well-being of a population. By the time they are five, for example, Guatemalan Indian children are shorter and lighter than the children of Central African Pygmies (although what is called "catch-up growth" eliminates this difference later on).

Unfortunately, anthropometric data can be easily misinterpreted. If Asian boys and girls are measured against an American or Swedish ideal, the findings will probably be meaningless. One recent AID study painted a sorry picture of Sri Lanka: by American height and weight references, 42 percent of the nation's children were moderately or severely malnourished; less than 10 percent were "normal." If these researchers had bothered to measure life spans, however, they would have found that the average Sri Lankan can expect to live nearly seventy years, or about as long as the average Belgian in 1968. At that time the Belgians were the most abundantly fed people on earth, with only a few thousand derelicts and vagrants among them thought to be hungry.

Evidently, it is possible to be "small but healthy," to borrow a phrase from David Seckler. Most nutritionists do not seem to appreciate this. A recent study by the Pan American Health Organization concluded that more than 49 percent of the populations of Barbados, Costa Rica, Guyana, Jamaica, and Panama suffered from some degree of malnutrition. Yet none of these countries has a life expectancy under seventy.

A proper examination of serious hunger might relate such things as height and weight to death rates—which has hardly ever been done. In this connection the findings of Lincoln Chen and his colleagues at the Cholera Research Laboratory in Bangladesh are instructive.[4] In the district of Matlab Bazaar, death rates for children typed as "normal," "mildly malnourished," and "moderately malnourished" were all about the same—in fact, "normal" children died slightly more frequently than did their smaller and lighter playmates. But children who were "severely malnourished"—those 40 percent or more below their "reference weight"—died in droves: their mortality rates were four to six times higher than for all other boys and girls the same age. This would certainly suggest that attention be concentrated first on the fraction of the world's population that is severely underfed.

How large would that fraction be? According to a World Health Organization survey a decade back, almost ten million children under five were "seriously malnourished" by anthropometric criteria. Obviously, that number vastly understates the full extent of serious hunger: some children will always be misclassified: at any point the number dangerously hungry will be lower than for the year as a whole, moving to the rhythm of the harvest and the vagaries of parental fortune; boys and girls do not develop an immunity to hunger on their fifth birthday. To correct for these biases, and to take account of China, Indochina, and North Korea, which are usually excluded from such studies, we should probably multiply this figure by an order of magnitude, and put the world's desperately hungry population at something like 100 million.

Attending to about 100 million people spread across perhaps ninety or a hundred countries would be an enormous task, but a *manageable* one. Concerted international action could conceivably eliminate the most horrifying manifestations of hunger in a matter of years. By reciting inflated figures which have already lost their shock value, hunger experts risk making the problem seem hopelessly large.

Of course, simply preventing the desperately needy from succumbing to death by starvation can in no sense be construed as a fully satisfactory solution to the hunger problem. There is a world of difference between being kept alive and living; checking deadly hunger is only a first step. Many tens of millions of families who do not show up in the rosters of stark malnutrition would choose to eat more if only they had the money. In this sense, the hunger problem will not be resolved until involuntary hunger of all degrees is eliminated—though even then nutritional troubles can be expected to persist, if of an entirely different nature and severity.

Three final points should be made about serious hunger. First, while we think of it as an Asian problem, the incidence of severe malnutrition is highest in black Africa. This is reflected, if imperfectly, by a consistent and alarmingly high incidence of acute nutritional deprivation as revealed by anthropometric testing, and by a life expectancy which for black Africa as a whole falls about six years below India's. Whatever India's problems may be, its peoples can rely on a highly sophisticated government apparatus which has both the ability and the inclination to deal with sudden hunger. Few Africans are so fortunate.

Second, severe hunger is a greater problem for the countryside than for the city, both in absolute and relative terms. To be sure, urban hunger is more visible, more dangerous politically, and more immediately influenced by the limited tools available to poor governments. Throughout the poor world, however, it is villagers who are the more needy. The hunger which Western visitors encounter in the big cities of the poor world is shocking enough, but the fact of the matter is that children grow more slowly, and end up smaller and lighter, in the countryside. They also die earlier: in India, for example, a person born into the comparatively easy routine of city life can expect to live about ten years longer than one who must work and eat in the country.

Finally, prognostications notwithstanding, the world hunger situation does seem to be improving. If 100 million is about the right figure for those threatened with dangerous hunger, this would be slightly more than 2 percent of the world's population: a lower fraction, in all likelihood, than for any previous generation in man's recorded history. In the past thirty years, life expectancy in the less developed countries, excluding China, has risen by more than a third (and China's may be up by 50 percent). In the past twenty years in these same nations, death rates for one-to-four-year-olds, the age group most vulnerable to nutritional setback, have dropped by nearly half.

This does not mean that hunger and ill health have disappeared from the poor world: the nearly twenty-year gap in life expectancies between the rich and the poor nations is grim testimony that they have not. The fact that much remains to be done, however, should not blind us to the progress that has been made or to the very real possibility that we are now within striking distance of eliminating the most extreme forms of hunger.

Growing an Inevitable Scarcity

To solve a problem we must understand its causes. Several of the important "schools of thought" concerning the hunger problem deter us from doing this.

Take the Malthusian position, recently embraced by no less prestigious a document than the *Global 2000* report prepared for President Carter. In its strictest construction, this argument holds that since there are too few goods and resources to go around, poverty and hunger are inevitable. Man's insatiable appetites, in this view, have outstripped the capacities of our fragile ecosystem to sustain them; if disaster is to be avoided we must ruthlessly cut back the wealth of the rich world and the fertility of the poor.

The case against this position is so thorough that it is hard to know where to begin. Perhaps a good place would be the current global availability of food. Let us disregard for a moment such things as tubers, vegetables, fruit, nuts, legumes, sugars, food oils, fish, and range-sized livestock. Even without these, food-grain production by *itself* could satisfy not only the caloric needs of the entire world population, but of a billion people beyond. This is a *conservative* estimate.

Moreover, as the worldwide decline in mortality might suggest, food is not becoming scarcer. Since 1950 worldwide per-capita food production has risen by about 40 percent, according to the USDA. Even the FAO admits the situation has improved dramatically, although by its count the rise is less than 30 percent. Since consumers prefer meat, vegetables, and sweet foods to cereals and root crops, this means that man's diet has also improved in quality and digestibility.

The benefits of progress, however, are never evenly spread. By conventional measure, poor nations have profited less than rich ones from die postwar prosperity. Even so, the poor world seems to be on a course toward greater abundance. Over the past twenty-five years, grain production per person in the less developed world (again excluding China) rose by about 13 percent.

This figure significantly understates the increase in overall availability, for in that same period the trade position of the less developed nations shifted from one of rough self-sufficiency to a heavy reliance on food imports. Whatever else this may have done, it necessarily increased the amount of food available for consumption. If FAO and USDA figures can be relied on, caloric intake, to say nothing of diet quality, has improved in each major region of the poor world over each decade—except perhaps for China. When caloric need is measured in terms of functional requirements rather than aesthetic ideals, the only nation whose food supplies unquestionably fall short is Cambodia, whose leaders deliberately induced agricultural disaster. Hunger in the poor nations, then, would seem to be neither necessary nor inevitable.

Contrary to Malthusian doctrine, there is no measurable evidence that global agricultural production is pushing against environmentally determined limits. While it is true that poorly managed farms and pastures are degrading the soil in Nepal, the Sahel, and elsewhere, there is nothing inevitable about this deterioration: improved cultivation and conservation practices could restore them, as agronomists at the Rockefeller Foundation and elsewhere have shown. If anything, agricultural resources are becoming less scarce. Between 1950 and 1980, thanks to the persistent and careful work of farmers, the world's arable area—that fraction fit for cultivation—grew by more than 20 percent, and at an even more rapid rate in the poor countries as a whole. In the decade ending in 1977, the world's irrigated acreage shot up more than 25 percent.

As for fertilizer, pesticide, seeds, and simple machinery, perhaps the best measure of scarcity is price (after all, prices in some sense are meant to indicate relative scarcity). Adjusting for inflation, we find that such prices have dropped meaningfully in the past thirty years, often by more than 50 percent. Only energy is more expensive today than it was thirty years ago, and this is a commodity for which a scarcity has been deliberately contrived.

A final measure of scarcity in world agriculture might seem to be the export prices of American wheat and corn, which underpin the international food market. Adjusting for inflation, we find that these cost less now than in the early 1960's—or in any earlier period, for that matter. And this is not because American farmers have been marginalized; last year per-capita income for U.S. agricultural workers surpassed that for non-agricultural workers.

What Malthusians always forget is that social and economic systems are not static and inflexible. Ours is an age of innovation, and innovations tend to find uses for materials which were previously valueless: sand, bauxite, petroleum. Innovations also tend to occur precisely in response to shortages. We should not conclude that innovation offers us the panacea that proponents of technological utopias sometimes claim: new ideas and inventions do not appear on request; technological change has a social cost, which can be very high; and innovation is a long-term process, while many of man's most troublesome problems press him in the short term. Nevertheless, given the flexibility and creativity of the modern economy, ours may actually prove to be an age of increasing availability of resources. As Julian Simon has pointed out, the "ultimate resource" is human talent, and this is a resource which grows through being used. Praetorian sterilization programs or forced reductions in living standards are not the means to encourage its utilization.

Ominous Food Deficits

To many development experts, the increasing reliance on foreign grain in the poor world is cause for alarm. Last year the net imports of the less developed countries (including China) totaled nearly 70 million tons, up from about 20 million tons in 1960; this group had been essentially self-sufficient in the early 1950's, and had exported a net of about 10 million tons in the 1930's. Sterling Wortman and Ralph Cummings, authors of the otherwise sober *To Feed This World,* term this a trend of "ominous food deficits," and a report of the International Food Policy Research Institute concludes, with a mixture of horror and disbelief, that if trends continue the poor regions, exclusive of China, might import as much as 120 million tons of grain by 1990. Implicit is the notion that imports by themselves are proof that a nation can no longer feed itself, or that it has lost its race against population.

The economists and agronomists who urge the less developed countries to restore their import in dependence view the reliance on outside food both as a sign of hunger and as a hindrance to development. But their analysis is fundamentally flawed. It confuses biological need with economic demand, two things which have nothing to do with each other. Purchases reflect the choices of those who have money to spend; they do not necessarily signify the satisfaction of an irreducible minimum of needs. Taiwan's 18 million people purchase more American food than Africa's 400 million; this is not because they are more hungry. Conversely, the current net export positions of Burundi, Burma, and India should not be taken to mean that these nations have finally eliminated malnutrition.

By the same token, a nation's dependence on foreign food tells us nothing by itself about its development prospects. Rising food deficits did not prevent Israel and Japan from achieving spectacular rates of economic growth. On the other hand, a rising volume of food exports has not stopped Argentina from sliding back in to the Third World.

It would be a mistake to assume that food imports cripple less developed countries financially. The so-called "developing market economies"—the poor world minus OPEC, China, and the smaller Communist states—sold more than $250 billion of goods and services last year. Their net food-grain bill amounted to about $10 billion, or something like 4 percent of their exports. For the poorest nations within this configuration, the food-grain burden was higher, but even they could pay for their purchases with less than 10 percent of their exports. (At the height of the 1972–74 food crisis, grain purchases absorbed less than 15 percent of the poorest nations' merchandise earnings.)

Despite their growing reliance on overseas food, poor nations have been able to cover their purchases with an ever shrinking fraction of their own overseas earnings. In 1960, food—a category in which grain is a relatively small component—was 15 percent of the import bill of the "middle-income countries," and 22 percent of the bill of "low-income countries." By 1977 the proportions were 12 percent and 16 percent respectively. To be sure, less developed countries face some serious financial problems, but it does seem that the poor world could afford to finance even more "ominous" food deficits than it presently does, if it were so inclined.

But why has food production in the poor world lagged behind articulated demand? The answer has little to do with an absolute inability to produce. Nor do "alarmingly high rates of population growth bear much responsibility for this. It can be explained, rather, in terms of a specific set of choices made by almost every regime in the poor world in the period of decolonization and national self-assertion.

The nationalist leaders who came to power after World War II through the break-up of the old empires differed remarkably in their ideologies— one need only compare Nehru, say, with Sukarno or Ho Chi Minh—but on one point they were united: they did not wish to remain weak appendages of the powerful states which had controlled them. Their common ambition was to build powerful, "modern" state apparatuses which would allow their nations, or at least their national elites, to deal on equal terms with their former masters. They would of course provide themselves with all the trappings of national power: airports, sports arenas, presidential palaces. But they would also build up an industrial base, even if rapid industrialization were not economically wise.

Huge discrepancies in rates of return did not prevent the national elites from sanctioning a massive build-up of the "modern" sector at the expanse of the vast majority of the population who lived in the countryside and worked on the land. Agricultural research was neglected, and prices and taxes skewed against the farmer to hasten the growth of cities and factories.

As a result, a peculiar system of comparative advantage has arisen. In poor nations where wages are low and the large majority of the labor force works in the fields, farmers cannot produce food as cheaply as their counterparts in North America. The Indian agricultural sector, for example, uses as much energy as the American, but it produces only a third as much food; it now costs a farmer about 40 percent more to grow a ton of wheat in the Punjab than in Kansas. On the other hand, with new, state-of-the-art factories, cheap work forces, hidden subsidies, and frequently insufficient domestic markets, it is in the interests of the poor nations to export processed goods: India, for example, can forge a ton of steel for half as much as the Ruhr. Thus it makes sense for poor nations to trade their finished products for cheap Western food.[5]

Today's policies, which favor the city over the village and the factory over the field, are likely to impede the elimination of malnutrition. In succumbing to what Michael Lipton has termed "urban bias," politicians and professors in the poor world have skewed income distribution by financing the comfort of teamsters and physicists at the expense of blacksmiths and plowmen. By misallocating investments, they slow down economic growth. Other things being equal, this means the poor will be hungrier. The few poor countries which have refused to favor their urban minorities at the expense of the rural majority—Taiwan, South Korea, Malawi, the Ivory Coast—are all in better economic and nutritional shape than neighbors who have so favored their cities—The Philippines, North Korea, Tanzania, Ghana.

Eliminating the disadvantages under which agriculture in the less developed countries must operate would no doubt narrow income differences and speed economic growth, although hunger might not be reduced as substantially as we might first assume. By virtue of such reforms a nation's grain trade deficit might well decline. If hunger on earth were effectively eliminated, some regions of today's poor world would undoubtedly revert to self-sufficiency, and others would even generate a net food surplus. But many countries could and would undoubtedly accumulate an even larger grain-trade deficit than they have today. And there would be nothing new about such an arrangement. In many of today's rich nations, elimination of hunger was facilitated by reliance on food surpluses from other lands, for this permitted an acceleration of economic growth through an escape from the bind of agricultural self-sufficiency.

The Superiority of the "Socialist" System

Still another current belief is that "capitalism" is an inferior tool in the fight against hunger, while "socialism" is an effective one.[6] According to this argument, capitalism is crippled by an inherently exploitative system of relations which tends to cause growing inequalities, and to produce either nutritional stagnation or hunger crises in the less developed countries. By contrast, "socialism" is said to be more rational, more efficient, oriented toward human development rather than profit, and grounded in the security of central planning. For these reasons, the argument continues, the "socialist strategy" has made strides against desperate want which "capitalist" nations have been unable to match.

Although this argument is Marxist in conception, it has won respectability among a wide range of thinkers and policy-makers who do not consider themselves radicals or even men of the Left. By 1975, for example, no less a figure than McGeorge Bundy was arguing that the success of the Chinese and Cuban experiments should make us rethink our old notions about economic development.

Rather than arguing about the theoretical merits of "socialism" versus "capitalism," let us com pare the nutritional records of Communist and non-Communist nations. Evaluating Communist efforts to eliminate hunger is not a straightforward exercise. Communist states oppose the free flow of information under the best of circumstances; they should not be expected to promote discussions of their system's shortcomings. Measuring Communist and non-Communist nations against each other, moreover, is complicated by the fact that some of the nations we would wish to compare were never really comparable. (Against whom do we judge the Mongolian People's Republic, for example? Turkey? Nepal? South Korea?) Nevertheless, state-sanctioned statistics, refugee accounts, and reports from those few invited visitors with sharp eyes and open minds do permit a telling if imperfect reconstruction of the Communist nations' performance on the hunger front.

A brief summary will suffice. Before the first Five Year Plan in the late 1920's Soviet Russia could be ranked as a peer of Finland or Japan by some agricultural and nutritional measures; by a few it was even ahead. Today it lags embarrassingly behind: its agricultural sector is stricken by chronic and continuous failure; its consumers suffer perennial shortages not just of meat, fruit, and vegetables, but of such "luxury" goods as lard; its infant-mortality rate, unlike any in the Western world, is rising, thanks in no small part to diseases of nutritional deficiency like rickets.

Before World War II, Spain, Greece, and Italy's *mezzogiorno* were all hungrier than Czechoslavakia or Hungary; thirty-five years in to the Eastern European experiment in "people's democracy," they are healthier. When Korea was partitioned, the North was richer and better fed: it possessed about 95 percent of the peninsula's industry, and had just been unburdened by the flight of 5 million citizens to the already impoverished South. After a generation of "socialist development," it is clearly now the South Koreans who are richer and better fed. As one might expect of a nation of a billion people, China's performance differs from one region to the next. Today, however, even mainlanders refer to Taiwan as "China's leading province": it has set the pace in all areas of material progress, including the reduction of hunger.

Over the past generation Thailand has come close to solving its hunger problem; by all accounts neighboring Laos, which was much poorer at the time of its "liberation," has become even hungrier since then. "Unified" Vietnam seems to have dealt its hunger problem by casting its extra mouths into the sea. The nutritional plight of Cambodia is too familiar to require any description.

The performance of Marxist-Leninist regimes in Africa is difficult to judge for a number of reasons, including the fact that total control over their economies and societies has yet to be established, but at first blush Africa's hungry and neglected peoples do not seem to have fared better under the would-be totalitarians than under any of the less ambitious forms of government on that continent.

Of all the "socialist experiments," only two provide evidence of nutritional results noticeably better than their nonCommunist neighbors: Soviet Central Asia and Cuba.[7] Whether total colonization by a European power would have provided Afghanistan or Iran with material results comparable to those produced by total Russian colonization in Turkmenia, Uzbekistan, or the ill-fated Kazakh Republic, we cannot say: nothing like that was ever attempted. As for Cuba, the underpinnings of its success are artificial. Aside from Cambodia and the Yemen People's Democratic Republic, Cuba is the only nation in the world with a smaller percapita GNP today than thirty years ago. It could not possibly survive, let alone function, without enormous annual subsidies from the Soviet Union. The USSR's current grant to its Cuban showpiece is thought to be half as large as Cuba's internally generated GNP.

Socialist regimes have good reason to want their people healthy and well fed: a debilitated labor force, after all, can only impede the attainment of economic targets or political and military objectives. Total command over economy and society, moreover, can indeed be used to produce impressive and immediate material results. Under the aegis of the totalitarian state, land can be redistributed quickly and without legal obstacle; staples can be rationed, and their prices set artificially low; workers can be mobilized, and employment created, by fiat. In the People's Republic of China in the early 1950's such policies contributed to a substantial rise in living standards for the poorest half of the population. But if we can believe China's current leaders, over the next quarter-century living standards rose only slightly and erratically.

Total control over economy and society cuts both ways. In and of itself, it does not serve to augment resources. Instead, it concentrates power, and most frequently this impedes rather than expedites the augmentation of resources. If it can make land reform or rationing easier, it always makes it more difficult to promote technological innovation, accelerate worker productivity, or encourage flexible, creative, and efficient responses to unforeseen problems. The poor and the hungry may benefit from this tradeoff, but only on occasion, and seldom in the long run.

But the dangers of total power are not merely measured in forgone opportunities for progress. There is another aspect to "socialist policy" which nutritionists and development experts seldom confront directly.

Over the course of the 20th century there has been a noticeable and distinctly unpleasant change in the character of severe hunger. In the past, famines were usually the result of bad harvests or economic crisis; increasingly, they can be traced to deliberate acts of government.

With the rise in power and sophistication of the modern state apparatus, governments can now save their peoples from desperate hunger in a way which was impossible in the 19th century. When India's harvests failed in the mid-1960's, for example, a concerted Indian-American relief effort prevented a famine which all observers agree would have caused tens of millions of deaths. Thanks to these joint relief actions, in fact, there was no statistically observable rise in death rates in the drought-afflicted provinces.

A powerful and sophisticated state apparatus, however, can also use hunger as a weapon of assault against its enemies. There have been at least six such massive famines in the last fifty years. The hunger generated by the Soviet collectivization drive killed at least 6 million people; the starvation attendant on the Nazi atrocities, perhaps the same number; the man-made famine in Bengal in 1943, perhaps 3 million; the Biafran famine, at least 1 million; the ongoing Cambodian famine, as many as 2 million from a total population of 7 or 8 million; and China's "Three Lean Years," the aftermath of the Great Leap Forward, may have taken a toll running into the tens of millions.

Each of these famines was government-sponsored; some were even officially planned. The scale of the cruelty involved is perhaps suggested by comparison with the Sahelian famine in West Africa in the early 1970's, which was a "natural" disaster. While authoritative analyses of this tragedy tell us that the death toll from the drought will never be known precisely, they also suggest that its cost in terms of human life should be measured in thousands, not hundreds of thousands.[8]

It is a fact of modern life that governments across the spectrum of political inclination have inflicted starvation on their peoples by design. But the regimes which have made the most consistent practice of this call themselves "socialist." Moreover, these are the only regimes to do so *on principle.* Armed with a philosophy which can turn even their most enthusiastic supporters into "enemies of the people," and which can then justify their elimination by whatever means necessary, and lacking the internal checks which might at least moderate officially sanctioned acts of cruelty, the "socialist" states have pioneered in inflicting needless hunger on helpless populations.

More complicated than a comparison of Communist and non-Communist regimes would be a comparison of the results of "socialist"—i.e., Fabian-economic policy in the poor world with "capitalism." Sri Lanka, for example, pursued Fabian policies until quite recently; economically these may have failed, yet just as clearly they should be credited with social success. With a per-capita income which appears no greater than India's, Sri Lankans have a life expectancy about fifteen years longer. By contrast, Michael Manley's variant of "socialism" in Jamaica appears to have retarded both economic and social progress.

As for laissez-faire capitalism, this has worked well-publicized wonders in Hong Kong over the past generation, yet its results have been far less impressive in neighboring Macao. By the same token, the three black African nations which have strayed least from orthodox capitalism—Botswana, Malawi, and the Ivory Coast—have all outperformed their neighbors, but by seemingly rather different margins.

The comparative strengths of "socialist" democracy and a more rigorously defined "capitalism" in the fight against hunger is perhaps a subject which has received too little attention. Too much attention, however, has been given to Communist anti poverty strategies. The notion that encouraging, or even acquiescing in, the growth of totalitarian governance in the poor nations will help eradicate hunger is a chimera. Everything we have learned in the past ten years suggests that Communist states are consistently, and perhaps necessarily, worse at feeding their peoples than their "capitalist" competitors.

If we were to shake off our blinders on the subject of world hunger, we would see three important things about it.

First, despite the blunders, caprices, and ruinous plans of so many of their leaders, the people of the poor nations are eating better today than ever before. Controlling the worst manifestations of hunger, at least in the non-Communist world, is no longer an impossible undertaking.

Second, where desperate poverty and want have been eradicated, it has not been through population control, artificially enforced food self-sufficiency of "socialist strategies," but through the hard work of millions of men and women scattered on tiny farms, in dull villages, in dirty metropolises and suburban shantytowns, who are determined to improve their own lives and whose governments have given them the wherewithal to do so.

Finally, the United States is in a unique position to facilitate the global escape from poverty and to hasten the day when desperate hunger is eliminated. There are, in fact, a number of things we could be doing today which would measurably improve the world's nutritional status. We have not undertaken any of them, perhaps for want of the idea.

What would these be? I will list seven of them here:

1. **Promoting rural industry.** The Japanese, Taiwanese, and South Koreans can attest to the crucial role that rural industrialization plays in the acceleration of economic growth and the elimination of hunger. In most of Asia and much of Latin America and Africa, population

density places a limit on what can be expected from agriculture alone. A sound and balanced program of rural industry would provide not only the products farmers need to increase their productivity, but jobs and income for the landless laborers and displaced artisans who so frequently rank among the underfed. (A sound program of rural industry would also help stem the rush to the cities, since it would make possible the decent living which migrants leave home to find.)

Much of the technology which would be needed would be simple, inexpensive, and amenable to local repair: "rotoweeders," which roll through a rice paddy like a lawnmower; "biogas converters," which catalyze compost into usable energy; low horsepower pumps which could tap into a locally available energy source; and so forth. Paradoxically, many of these devices are too inexpensive for international industry to develop, for their very simplicity would imperil licensing and royalty arrangements.

2. **Extension training.** We have already helped establish a remarkable network of international agricultural-research centers which have brought the world new, high-yielding strains of wheat and rice and improved cultivation techniques for many other crops. In many parts of the poor world, this knowledge is not reaching the farmer. There are many reasons for this; one of them is a lack of extension agents" capable of passing it on, and then serving as intellectual middlemen between scientists and small growers.

3. **Grain insurance.** Man cannot average his appetite across years or even seasons. In the parlance of economists, the "demand schedule" is highly "inelastic." People have to have food to stay alive, and will pay for it what they can; thus, even a relatively modest shortfall in supply can trigger explosive increases in prices. (During the "world food crisis" of the early 1970's, for example, production never fell more than 3 percent below trend, and yet the cost of grain more than doubled in the international marketplace.) When prices go mad, food is bid out of the mouths of the hungry in much of the poor world. With America's predominance over the world grain economy, the United States could easily champion an international grain-insurance program which

would be well within the range of self-finance for the poor nations and whose benefits, both economic and humanitarian, would be substantial and demonstrable.

4. **Trade reform.** Reducing tariffs and otherwise liberalizing access to the enormous American market would increase exports, hence jobs, income, and presumably nutritional status in the less developed countries. At the same time, it would lower the cost of goods for the American consumer and provide our industries with much needed and potentially vitalizing competition.

5. **Regulating infant foods.** Many children in poor nations suffer from a syndrome which Derrick Jelliffe has labeled "commerciogenic malnutrition." Mothers' milk may be the best food for infants, but for a variety of reasons growing numbers of women in poor nations are choosing to feed their babies store-bought, processed formula. Many women who buy this cannot really afford to prepare it in adequate quantities and are unable to keep it hygienic; their children suffer for this. Our government could initiate an informal, international arrangement with infant food merchandisers to protect the poor and the ignorant against the misuse of such products. In the wake of our vote against the World Health Organization infant-formula proposals, we should have a special interest in doing so.

6. **Lobbying for development.** Obviously, the actions of governments in poor countries will be the primary constraint on the pace at which poverty and hunger are reduced. The United States has no ultimate say over price-support systems, educational strategies, investment policies, land-tenure arrangements, or patterns of administration in independent and sovereign nations. But we should not underestimate the positive influence we may exert through the instruments at our disposal. AID, the World Bank, and the International Monetary Fund can all create incentives for sound and honest governance, liberalized trade, rural development, and technological diffusion, and these are things which will help the poor and the hungry.

7. **Moral pressure.** Through various forums and international channels we should be castigating, embarrassing, isolating, and punishing governments which choose to starve their people. We should ask our allies to help us in doing this. And we should ask why "humanitarian" international organizations, upon which we lavish hundreds of millions of dollars, have been so silent about such abuses. The Food and Agriculture Organization, for example, sounded no alarms about Ethiopia's deliberate neglect of its famine-stricken provinces, or Indonesia's campaign of hunger against the Timorese, or the Khmer Rouge and Vietnamese annihilation of Cambodia. Nor does this organization, which is charged with improving nutrition for the whole of mankind, seem to have any contingency plan for trying to feed the World's hungriest strata. Should it not be shamed for this delinquency?

The list could be continued, but the point should be clear by now. While only a fraction of the many problems of the poor world may be solved by well-meaning Westerners, and while most of the things the West can offer require time to manifest themselves; important, even crucial, opportunities to accelerate the elimination of hunger do exist. They will not be seized so long as we remain in thrall to hallucinatory ideas about the causes of hunger.

Notes

1. See Davidson R. Gwatkin, "How Many Die? A Set of Demographic Estimates of the Annual Number of Infant Deaths in the World," *American Journal of Public Health*, December 1980.

2. This does not mean that we can afford to be complacent about the plight of the wretched and the dispossessed. Rather, it means that there is still hope for the tens of millions whose lives are dominated by desperate poverty. In 1950 nutritional and economic levels in South Korea and what is now Bangladesh were about the same. This did not prevent the South Koreans from learning skills which were to facilitate one of the quickest and most dramatic escapes from poverty in the history of nations.

3. See Thomas T. Poleman, *Quantifying the Nutritional Situation in Developing Countries*, Cornell University Agricultural Staff Paper, 1979.

4. Lincoln C. Chen et al., "Anthropometric Assessment of Energy-Protein Malnutrition and Subsequent Risk of Mortality Among Preschool-aged Children." *American Journal of Clinical Nutrition*, August 1980.

5. Industrialization seems to have played less of a role in this transformation in Africa

than in either Latin America or Asia. In Africa, the unhappy results described below seem to have more to do with the growth of a class of parasitic bureaucrats and the inappropriate extension of cash-cropping. Michael Lofchie addresses the latter problem in his "Origins of African Hunger," *Journal of Modern African Studies*, November 1915.

6. Honest meaning was long ago beaten out of both of these terms. In standard usage the second now seems to be shorthand for "the current practices of Marxist-Leninist regimes," while the first can seemingly be applied to non-Communist systems as different as Morocco and Sweden.

7. Soviet Central Asia's progress is charted, if uncritically, in Charles K. Wilker's *The Soviet Model and the underdeveloped Countries* (University of North Carolina Press, 1969) and in A.R. Khan and Dharam Ghai, "Collective Agriculture in Soviet Central Asia," World Development, April/May 1979. For some reflections on Cuba's performance, see David Morawetz's "Some Lessons from Small Socialist Countries," *World Development*, May/June 1980. The nearest equivalent in the Western experience to the Soviet episode in Central Asia would probably be South Africa. Despite the obvious and enormous differences between these two colonial histories, there may be lessons to be learned from a comparison. On the one hand, the USSR's Central Asians are healthier and better educated than South Africa's blacks; presumably this means that they are better fed as well. On the other hand, the differentials between the living standard for blacks in South Africa and those of adjoining countries may be greater than the differentials in Central Asia: South Africa, after all, has a problem controlling the flow of illegal black immigrants, while Kirgizia is not thought to have an equivalent difficulty. South Africa's neglect and exploitation of its blacks, moreover, may be contrasted with the even more brutal subjection of the nomadic peoples of Central Asia, at least part of which was accomplished through Stalin's policy of deliberately inducing famine. Finally, certain statistical differences between South Africa and the Soviet Union remain difficult to explain: South African blacks, for example, have twice as high a rate of car ownership as the citizens of the USSR.

8. See in particular John C. Caldwell, *The Sahelian Drought and Its Demographic Implications* (Overseas Educational Institute, 1975). In Caldwell's words, "Better roads, greater commercialization of the whole region, more awareness of what was happening . . . and massive international relief efforts all helped the people's own efforts and reduced a potentially murderous period into a very painful one."

6

Famine, Development, and Foreign Aid

Commentary, March 1985

In recent years, American foreign-aid policies have been shaped increasingly by the argument that the many different problems facing the poor nations are inextricably interconnected, woven together into an all-encompassing "seamless fabric." However pleasing this notion may seem to theoreticians, its practical implications are dangerously wrong. The problems facing poor nations can be distinguished from each other and treated separately—and must be. It is no act of charity to suspend the rules of policy analysis and problem-solving at the borders of the Third World.

Although current American policies often fail to distinguish among them, three separate purposes underlie our foreign-aid programs. The first is the humanitarian purpose of alleviating suffering and minimizing loss of life from the upheavals following sudden, unexpected catastrophe. The second is the developmental purpose of encouraging poor nations to find their best path to economic health, self-sustaining growth, and general prosperity. The third purpose is to promote the security of the United States and the Western order through military aid or security assistance to a foreign government.

Military aid to less developed countries is but a part of a larger, global American defense strategy. The aid the United States extends to nations which happen to be poor, moreover, is only a tiny fraction of the money it expends to preserve the security of Allied nations that are already rich—such as Japan and the NATO countries. Military aid to less developed countries, then, is not in any meaningful sense a Third World policy, even though it involves transfers of money and resources to nations in the Third World.

Humanitarian aid and development aid are quite different. These address, respectively, short-term exigencies and long-term prospects of poor nations, and are governed by an attention to poverty. To understand the best use of these different forms of aid, we must appreciate the problems each must address. Let us examine them separately.

II

Much of mankind continues to live under the shadow of life-imperiling disasters and upheavals. Floods, earthquakes, and storms still endanger millions of people every year, and the human cost of famine is even greater. Since the end of World War II it is believed that tens of millions of people have perished from famine in Asia alone.

To deal effectively with today's natural disasters, we must begin by recognizing that there is very little that is natural about them. Acts of God cannot be prevented, but the quotient of human risk and suffering they exact can be vastly and systematically reduced. Current events underline the point. The United States and Japan happen to be more subject than most regions of the earth to sudden natural disturbances. The Japanese archipelago, after all, is an earthquake zone, buffeted by tropical storms and exposed to *tsunami* (tidal waves). The U.S. land mass is threatened by earthquakes, tropical storms, and tornadoes, and the country, in addition, has more active volcanoes than any other. Nevertheless, very few people in Japan or America die from these natural perils.

The African continent, by contrast, would appear to be comparatively well protected against sudden disasters. It is exposed only slightly to tropical storms and tidal waves, has only a small earthquake belt, few active volcanoes, and it experiences tornadoes only in South Africa. Despite these natural advantages, however, sub-Saharan Africa has been stricken by perennial disaster in the decade since decolonization was effectively completed. These disasters are believed to have cost hundreds of thousands of lives.

Western peoples have not always enjoyed their present protection against adverse acts of nature. In the first ten years of the 20th century, over 8,000 Americans died in hurricanes,[1] as opposed to the 100 who died over the past ten years. What accounts for this almost 99-percent drop, despite a doubling of the population and a steady urbanization of the coasts where hurricanes most often strike? Affluence, as manifested in safer dwellings, explains part of the change; even more, however, is explained by those handmaidens of affluence, technical advance and government competence. Improvements in communications, transportation, weather tracking, emergency management, rescue operations, and relief capabilities have made it possible to reduce dramatically the human price exacted by even the worst hurricanes in the most populated areas. Purposeful private and governmental action can now substantially cut the toll from other natural disasters as well, even in the poorest nations.

Not all governments, however, work at minimizing the havoc which sudden disasters wreak upon their people—as the two most costly sudden disasters of the 1970's attest. In 1970, East Pakistan, as it was then known, was devastated by a typhoon. The Pakistani government—seated in and dominated by West Pakistan—responded to the extreme distress in its Bengal territory with what might at best be described as reserve. As many as 100,000 Bengalis are thought to have perished in the aftermath of that typhoon.

In 1976, the city of Tangshan in China was flattened by an earthquake. One of the Chinese government's first responses to the disaster was to announce it would refuse all international offers of aid for the victims. Details about the actual rescue operations which China itself undertook remain obscure to this day. One of the few accounts of the disaster permitted in the Chinese press at the time was a front-page feature in the *People's Daily* praising a peasant who let his own two children die as he rescued instead an aged party cadre; local and foreign readers came to their own conclusions about what this carefully placed article was intended to suggest. Since the rise of Deng Xiaoping, China's media have severely criticized his predecessors' handling of the Tangshan affair; they now state that almost a quarter-of-a-million people died in the disaster.

—⁂—

If government action can be consequential in limiting the suffering caused by sudden upheavals, it can be even more important in controlling or preventing famine. In the past, famines were typically related to regionalized crop failure. It is now possible to cushion the impact of crop failure in even the poorest regions of the earth. Concerned governments can monitor the progress of their nations' harvests by following local markets, by direct on-site inspection, and by studying the data from worldwide aerial and meteorological surveillance services.

These early-warning systems can give governments valuable months in which to prepare against food shortfalls. Food grain may be purchased from the world market, which trades and transports over 200-million tons each year. If for some reason a government cannot finance its emergency food-grain needs, it may draw upon the 7-million ton reserve of concessional food aid which Western governments set aside each year. If a government lacks the administrative capacity to manage a far-reaching relief effort, it may request free assistance from the many impartial international organizations which have proved they can both supervise and staff effective relief operations on short notice and under difficult conditions. Almost twenty years ago, concerted American-Indian cooperation after a series of harvest failures saved millions of Indians from starvation, and even seems to have prevented death rates from rising in the afflicted provinces. Since then, the capabilities of both the world food system and international relief organizations have grown steadily. They now present even the most modest and least sophisticated government with an opportunity to control famine within its borders—if it wants to do so.

The terrible truth, however, is that many governments in the world today have demonstrated that they are not interested in seeing their people fed. Some have deliberately ignored signs of incipient crisis. Others have interfered with international relief for their stricken groups. Still others have actually created famine conditions through premeditated action. In every recent instance where a potential food shortfall has developed into a mass famine, the hand of the state has been prominently involved.

Consider the great famines that have gripped the poor regions over the past quarter-century. In China, the Three Lean Years lasted from 1959 to 1962. Chinese officials now say that millions of people died during this famine, and Western demographers have recently suggested that "excess mortality" during this period may have been as much as thirty million. The Three Lean Years were a direct consequence of the Great Leap Forward, an awesomely ambitious social and economic experiment which resulted in a nationwide collapse of agriculture and a brief but virtually total destruction of the national food system. Even as their policies were causing millions of their citizens to starve, China's leaders denied there was a crisis, refused all offers of international aid, and exported food.

In Nigeria, where perhaps a million ethnic Ibos died of famine in the late 1960's and early 1970's, the federal government deliberately encouraged starvation in that province, which had proclaimed its independence, in the hope that this would hasten its reconquest. In Ethiopia in the early 1970's, the Haile Selassie regime consciously concealed a famine which was ravaging its minority peoples; it is now said that several hundred thousand people lost their lives as a result of this deception, although the exact cost will never be known. In the mid-1970's, the Indonesian government attacked, occupied, and annexed the territory of East Timor; it used hunger as a weapon of conquest. It is believed by outside observers that over 100,000 Timorese starved to death before Indonesia allowed the island to be fed; in all, as much as a quarter of the Timorese population may have perished from famine. In the late 1970's as many as two million Cambodians may have died as a result of hunger; they did so only because the Khmer Rouge government made the mass extermination of whole segments of the national population its official policy.

—₥—

Once again there is famine in Ethiopia. Though its ultimate toll is yet to be determined, its causes are already apparent. After seizing power in 1974, Ethiopia's Marxist-Leninist *Dergue* (Armed Forces Coordinating Committee) launched a campaign against "capitalism" in the countryside, restricting and ultimately prohibiting the private sale and marketing of farm produce and agricultural implements. At the same time, a newly formed secret police executed thousands of students and skilled workers in this predominantly illiterate nation, imprisoned tens of thousands more, and caused even greater numbers to flee their homeland. With the encouragement of Soviet and Cuban advisers, the government used its foreign aid to underwrite military buildup and war.

In a country like Ethiopia, which has always been subject to drought, such policies insured that widespread famine would be only a matter of time. When famine finally did strike, moreover, the *Dergue* gave little priority to relief efforts. Although millions of its citizens were said to be directly affected by the food shortage, the regime concentrated on commemorating its tenth anniversary in power—in a celebration which is said to have cost the equivalent of over $100 million.

Relief operations do not seem to have begun in earnest until after an outcry in the West over the plight of the famine victims. Even then, the Ethiopian government continued to obstruct international efforts to alleviate its people's distress. Instead of helping rescue workers reach famine victims in Tigre and Wollo—stricken regions where the *Dergue* is especially unpopular—the government began a program of mass deportations; 2.4 million of those areas' most able-bodied (thus least endangered) people were scheduled for eventual removal. And in contravention of the two basic principles of humanitarian relief—impartiality and nondiscrimination—the *Dergue* forbade all relief for the territory of Eritrea. Half-a-million people were reported to be starving in Eritrea, but this did not stop the Ethiopian armed forces from attacking convoys suspected of bringing relief supplies into the afflicted region.

Ethiopia is not the only government currently contriving to foment mass starvation. The ongoing efforts of the Soviet Union in Afghanistan, for example, are often forgotten. Since the 1979 invasion, Soviet forces have carefully destroyed the food system in many resisting regions. In so doing, they have turned literally millions of Afghans into destitute refugees, no longer able to feed themselves in their own nation. Over two million of these people subsist today in refugee camps in Pakistan. They are kept alive by charity from the West.

—⁂—

The American architects of the postwar international order did not anticipate such problems. In 1943, as President Franklin D. Roosevelt laid the foundations for the broadest and most successful relief effort the world had ever seen, he explained that the new United Nations Relief and Rehabilitation Agency (UNRRA) would be operating only in "liberated areas." He assured "liberated peoples" that "in victory or defeat, the United Nations have never deviated from adherence to the basic principles of freedom, tolerance, independence, and security." President Roosevelt believed that preventing famine would be an eminently manageable task under governments which respected the sanctity of human life and upheld Western values, and he was right. With the spread in membership in the United Nations, moreover, it seemed that enlightened governance might eventually prevail across the entire globe. Today, however, only a handful of countries beyond the borders of the West embrace the values codified in the United Nations' Charter and its Universal Declaration of Human Rights. Many member states now disregard these codes when they prove inconvenient. Others reject them out of principle, since they are inconsistent with their regimes' totalitarian or anti-Western ideologies.

It is now almost forty years since our victory in World War II. Even so, very few of the world's poorest and most vulnerable peoples live in what President Roosevelt would have considered "liberated areas." It is this fact and not any other which accounts for the persistence of famine in the modern world. Nations can always share the West's technical capacities to save people stricken by catastrophe, but regimes that do not share the West's values cannot be counted on to put these capacities to use.

III

According to many leaders in the Third World and to some development organizations in the West, the principal obstacle to accelerating the pace of material progress in low-income nations today is the insufficiency of concessionary aid from Western countries. It is striking, and inadvertently revealing, that such criticisms of Western giving often neglect to discuss either the quality of the aid received or the ends that it achieves. Such thinking is worse than illogical. By dissociating development aid from measurable results, it reduces Western assistance from a practical policy to an aesthetic, possibly only a symbolic, gesture. To advocate massive new aid programs irrespective of their impact on the economic health of recipient nations would be expensive for the West, but could prove far more costly to the world's poor.

Few people in the West appreciate the magnitude of current resource flows from Western societies to the Third World. Such flows are, in fact, extremely difficult to measure, not only because of the inevitable delays between commitments and disbursals, but because of the complexities of tracking and accounting for funds in a world financial system which is at once open and closed. Nevertheless, the Organization for Economic Cooperation and Development (OECD) attempts to measure these flows, and its computations are instructive.[2] In 1982, the most recent year for which OECD has made estimates, the net total for what it labels "overseas development assistance" provided directly by Western nations to Third World countries was about $18 billion.

But there was more. Multilateral development banks and multilateral development agencies, underwritten overwhelmingly by Western donations, provided an additional sum whose 1982 net OECD put at about $8 billion. And there was still more. Western nations were also providing finance capital to less developed countries under a variety of arrangements, including bank lending, government-to-government loans, export credits, and direct private investment. All told, OECD placed the total net transfer of financial resources from Western nations to Third World countries at almost $80 billion in 1982. This, it must be emphasized, is supposed to be the net total: the residual after financial withdrawals, profit repatriation, and loan repayments have been taken into account.

Of course, 1982 is but a single year. OECD estimates of financial flows to developing countries extend back to 1956. According to these computations, the net transfer of financial resources (both concessional and commercial) from Western nations to less developed countries between 1956 and 1982 exceeded $670 billion. This figure, however, seriously understates the true magnitude of the transfer, since it is denominated in current rather than inflation-adjusted dollars. Adjusting for intervening inflation, we find that the OECD estimate would be valued today at over $1,500 billion—that is, over $1.5 *trillion.*

Even this figure, however, understates the total postwar transfer of resources from the West to the Third World. It does not, for example, seem to measure either concessional grants or commercial loans for military matters, even though these play a prominent role in the finances of many developing countries. And it obviously cannot measure the net flow of resources in either the first half of the 1950's or the years since 1982. Taking everything into account, it seems quite possible that the total net transfer of capital from the West to the Third World since the beginning of the postwar international order may have already exceeded $2 trillion at today's prices. Although the complexities of international financial accounting and the unavoidable inexactitudes of adjusting for inflation and international fluctuations in exchange rates prevent us from arriving at a more precise figure, $2 trillion will probably do as the nearest round number to describe the magnitude of the net financial transfer from the West to the poor nations in the postwar era.

Large figures tend to seem abstract, and $2 trillion is an especially large figure. One way to appreciate its size is to consider what it could buy. Think of the entire U.S. farm system. Now think of all the industries listed on the New York Stock Exchange. At their current market values, $2 trillion would pay for *both*.

—⁓—

What has been the impact on the societies which have received this extraordinary transfer of Western wealth? The answer is obviously different in every case. Even so, broad and unmistakable patterns arise, some of which can be glimpsed in the composition of the transfers themselves. Less than one-quarter of the inflation-adjusted total for the years 1956 to 1982, for example, appears to have accrued from direct (and voluntary) overseas private investment. That fraction, moreover, has steadily diminished over time. Whereas in the late 1950's direct private investment accounted for almost two-fifths of the net financial flows to the less developed countries, in the last five years for which OECD has published figures, the fraction has dropped to below one-sixth.

One of the original arguments for foreign aid was that development assistance would increase the capacities of poor nations to make productive use of international-investment resources. The record seems to suggest that precisely the opposite has happened. Despite hundreds of billions of dollars of Western development assistance, and a generation of economic growth in the meantime, the less developed countries, taken as a group, obtain a far smaller fraction of their foreign resources from direct private investment today than they did a quarter of a century ago. This must mean either that Third World nations, taken as a group, have grown more hostile to direct private investments, or that they have become less capable of attracting such investment, or both.

The eclipse of direct private investment from the West was made possible in no small part by the ascension of an alternative medium of capital transfer, commercial lending. Unlike direct private investment, bank loans to less developed countries accrue principally to governments and

state-owned public corporations. Such lending effectively severed the connection between the provision of capital and the right to manage it. The
responsibility for determining the use of these funds, and of repaying them,
fell squarely on the state. It was not long before dozens of nations in the
Third World announced that they would be unable to repay their commercial obligations to their Western creditors on schedule.

The attitudes which led to this generalized debt crisis were highlighted
in the subsequent rescheduling negotiations in which many Third World
governments requested debt relief. Such proposals would have converted
a substantial portion of their obligations into a retroactive and unintended
gift from the West. This view of Western capital suggested not only that
it would be appropriate to convert commercial funds into concessional
bequests without warning, but, no less significantly, that there was no reason to expect concessional bequests to earn productive returns.

Within the diverse and disparate amalgam of nations that goes by the
name Third World there has been a dramatic and general improvement in
material living standards during the era of Western transfers. This fact should
be neither ignored nor belittled. Life expectancy for the people of "developing regions," according to the World Health Organization, rose by over 50
percent between the late 1930's and the late 1960's, and has risen still further since then.[3] Although no great confidence can be placed in economic
estimates for the less developed regions, the World Bank says that per-capita
GNP has more than doubled between 1960 and 1980 for the billion people
living in what it terms "middle-income economies."[4] According to the same
source, per-capita GNP rose by over 30 percent in India during this period.
Even that most troubled category of states, the "other low-income economies" of Africa and Asia, are said to have experienced a 20 percent increase
in per-capita GNP during these two decades alone.

But while the peoples of the less developed countries have seen
far-reaching material advances in their societies, their economies have also
typically undergone strange and troublesome transformations. In a great
many countries of the Third World it has proved possible to finance the
ambitious and comprehensive recasting of the national economy in ways
not unlike the mobilizations of societies preparing for protracted and
total war. These exercises in economic conversion have left the structures
of some less developed countries grotesquely distorted, unnecessarily

incapable of meeting either the social needs or the commercial demands of their people. They have left many others in a curious state of economic imbalance: richer than ever before, yet less capable than ever of pursuing self-sustaining growth.

In the Western nations, agricultural development proved to be a key factor in overall economic development. In the era of Western transfer, many governments in Africa, Asia, and Latin America have attempted to bypass agricultural development in their rush to industrialize. They have pursued policies systematically prejudicial to the interests of their rural populations: overtaxing farmers, underpricing their produce, and diverting resources so that the growth of cities and factories may be sustained at a forced pace. Neglect and exploitation have left many poor nations with unnaturally small agricultural sectors in relation to their people's needs or their development potential. Imitating the style of development without capturing its substance, such efforts at development planning have, by and large, succeeded in replicating the structure of the industrialized economies while leaving the populace in poverty.

Some of the resulting distortions may be illustrated by international economic comparisons. (The estimates for poor nations, which come from the World Bank, should not necessarily be treated as reliable or even meaningful, but they are the most commonly used figures in such exercises.) For Peru and Mexico in the early 1980's, the proportion of agriculture in overall GNP was put at roughly 8 percent. This is only half the share that Germany devoted to agriculture in the 1930's, even though Germany then was much more prosperous than Peru or Mexico today by almost any economic measure. By the same token, the share of agriculture in Ecuador's GNP today is apparently smaller than Holland's was in 1950. Bolivia's ratio of agriculture to GNP is lower today than that of Greece, although by any other measure it is Greece which should be considered the more industrialized society. Present-day Nigeria and the Denmark of the early 1950's show roughly equal ratios of agriculture to GNP. Senegal, a nation affected by the Sahelian food crisis, has managed to reduce its current ratio of agriculture to national output down to the level that characterized Japan in the early 1950's. The relation of agriculture to output in Pakistan and India is about the same as in prewar Italy, and is only slightly higher in Bangladesh today than it was in Italy at the turn of the century.[5]

—ᴍ—

The same policies which produce industrialization without prosperity have created an equally paradoxical phenomenon in many less developed countries: investment without growth. By the estimates of the World Bank, in the early 1960's the ratio of gross domestic investment to GNP in Jamaica, Mauritania, Liberia, and what is now the People's Republic of the Congo was equal to or higher than that of Japan in the early 1950's, at the start of its remarkable boom. Yet over the course of the 1960's and 1970's, while Japan was quadrupling its per-capita output, Mauritania and Liberia are said to have raised theirs by less than 40 percent; the People's Republic of the Congo, by the World Bank tally, registered a rise of less than 20 percent; and Jamaica apparently increased its per-capita output by a mere 13 percent. It is worth considering the scale of economic mismanagement necessary to achieve such results. We might also wonder how a poor government could maintain such strikingly high rates of capital accumulation in the face of indisputable and continuing economic mismanagement.

Just as agricultural sectors in the Third World have been artificially restricted and diminished by national policies, so what is termed investment has been artificially swollen. According to the World Bank, the region of the world with the *lowest* overall investment rate today is the West. In the "middle-income economies," overall rates of gross domestic investment are said to be just short of the historically extraordinary levels Japan achieved at the start of its growth spurt in the 1950's. For the "low-income economies," overall rates of gross domestic investment are higher today than they ever were in the United States or the fastest-growing nations of Western Europe.

But these patterns of investment cannot be taken as a sign of economic promise. In many countries, they have already proved to be manifestly unsustainable—the "debt crisis" affecting so many poor nations is only a formal recognition *in extremis* of this fact. To a distressing degree, the capital build-up to which so many Third World governments have committed themselves over the past three decades was guided not by economic logic but by the political imperative of maximizing the resources and power in the hands of the state. The misuse of resources, always costly, is especially hard on the populace of poor societies. It is poor people, after all, who can least easily forgo consumption today, and investment is by definition forgone consumption.

The postwar transfer of resources from Western nations to the less developed countries, as it has been conducted, appears to have accorded with neither of the two original premises for extending "development assistance": it has not improved the climate for productive international investment and it has not contributed generally to self-sustaining economic growth. Ironically, financial transfer from the West may actually have made it possible for many nations to avoid participating more fully in the world economy. Under the best of circumstances, financial aid increases the local money supply, and thus stimulates inflation and reduces international competitiveness unless offsetting measures are enacted. Many regimes have demonstrated that they are not interested in enacting such measures. After all, overvaluing the local currency makes imports cheap, and to the extent that foreign finance is available, exports are unnecessary.

—◊—

The justification for "development assistance" which has been voiced increasingly since the early 1970's is the need to "build human capital." There should be no mistaking the crucial importance of human capital in economic growth. Health, education, knowledge, skills, and other immutably human factors determine the maximum pace at which development may proceed. But returns from human capital, as from any other potentially productive resource, depend upon the environment in which they are put to use. Where physical capital is mismanaged and depleted, it would seem unrealistic to expect human capital to be carefully preserved, augmented, and utilized.

Human capital is much more difficult to measure and evaluate than physical capital—a fact that may not have escaped advocates of new spending programs in this area. Nevertheless, it is possible to make some tentative assessments of the effectiveness of some of the human-capital programs Western aid has helped sponsor. Consider education. As a very rough rule of thumb, the literacy rate in a poor society today should be similar to its primary-school enrollment ratio twenty years earlier. The rule holds in many developing nations, but not in all. According to the World Bank, for example, 47 percent of Bangladesh children were enrolled in primary schools in 1960 but the nation's literacy rate in 1980 was only 26 percent. In Togo, the enrollment ratio was 44 percent in 1960, but literacy is put at 18 percent today. In Zaire, the enrollment ratio was 60 percent in 1960, and the literacy rate today may be as low as 15 percent.[6]

Literacy, of course, is notoriously difficult to measure. Such radical discrepancies, however, appear to speak to something more fundamental than inexact definitions. They suggest that spending in the name of human capital can be wasted, and often has been. The irony is that such wastage seems most likely to occur as governments restrict their societies' contact with the world economy—preventing them from participating in the learning process which has so demonstrably enhanced the productivity of nations at all economic levels in modern times.

In the final analysis, the economic impact of Western financial transfers on the nations of Asia, Africa, and Latin America seems to depend very largely on the attitudes and inclinations of the recipient government. Taiwan and South Korea were both major beneficiaries of foreign aid in the 1950's and early 1960's, and South Korea has been a major borrower of international capital in the 1970's and the early 1980's. Both countries have used these resources in ways that have enhanced their overall economic productivity, improved their international competitiveness, and increased their ability to take advantage of the growing opportunities afforded by world markets. But easy credit and free aid need not be put to economically constructive purposes. They may also be used for quite different goals—even to underwrite practices so injurious that they could not otherwise be afforded.

IV

If opinion surveys are correct, the American people are troubled by our present policies to relieve distress and promote prosperity in the poorer regions of the earth. They are right to be so. As they are currently conducted, American foreign-aid policies cannot be relied upon to encourage economic health or self-sustaining growth in low-income nations; indeed, they may actually subsidize practices that perpetuate or even generate poverty in certain places. Such programs betray the wish of the American people to extend their help to the world's least fortunate groups and dangerously compromise America's moral role in the world.

In the decades since they were initiated, the official development policies of the United States have undergone a progressive divorce from their original purposes and principles. To judge by the results of current foreign-aid programs, the United States government has become comfortable with the idea of conducting a special, separate foreign policy toward the world's poor—a policy whose principles and goals are distinct from, even opposite to, those by which we guide ourselves in the rest of the world. Pursued to their logical conclusion, America's current aid policies would leave poor nations ever less capable of self-sustaining growth, and increasingly dependent on foreign largesse to maintain or improve national standards of living. These same aid policies appear to be indifferent to the politically induced suffering which so many poor peoples must endure at the hands of irresponsible or actively mischievous governments. Would we ever think of guiding our relations with another Western people by such rules?

The terrible irony of this situation is that the United States created a new global order at the end of World War II precisely to eliminate the sorts of suffering we now seem to be inadvertently underwriting in different poor nations. The economic pillars of this new order were an International Monetary Fund, a World Bank, and a generalized arrangement for the promotion of international trade; the political framework for this order was to be the United Nations. The liberal international economic system which was built on those foundations has proved to be the greatest engine of material advance the world has ever known; it has demonstrated its ability to contribute to prosperity in any and all nations willing to avail themselves of its opportunities. The values we impressed upon the original documents of the United Nations not only laid down the guidelines for decent and humane governance, but suggested the approach to policy most likely to relieve suffering and promote general prosperity. These postwar arrangements, which the United States struggled to produce, have created the greatest opportunities for satisfying the wants and needs of mankind that history has yet seen.

A generation of divisive rhetoric and drift has taken its toll on the United States. What is often easy for Americans to forget is that our divisive rhetoric and drift take an even greater toll on other peoples. The fact is that the United States—as a nation, a power, and an idea—is the greatest hope that the world's poor and unprotected peoples have. It is the American people's unmistakable preference that the peoples of the poorer regions of the earth should eventually be liberated—in the true meaning of that word. The United States can do much to help these peoples in their liberation. But we will not be true to our own preferences, or the promise of our system, if we divorce our policies toward the world's poor from the values, institutions, and international economic arrangements which we cherish for ourselves.

Notes

1. Cited in Anders Wijkman and Lloyd Timberlake, Natural Disasters: *Acts of God or Acts of Man?*, London and Washington, Earthscan, 1984.

2. *Geographical Distribution of Financial Flows to Developing Nations*, Paris, OECD, 1984. The calculations here are based on this volume and its predecessor series.

3. World Health Organization, "Mortality Trends and Prospects," in *WHO Chronicle*, 1974, Vol. 28.

4. World Bank, *World Development Report*, 1982, Oxford University Press, 1982.

5. Data for "developing countries" come from various issues of the World Bank's *World Development Report*. Historical figures for Western nations are from Simon S. Kuznets, *Modern Economic Growth* (Yale University Press, 1966) and The Economic Growth of Nations (Harvard University Press, 1971).

6. *World Development Report*, 1982 and 1983. The World Bank did not publish literacy estimates in the 1984 edition of its report.

7

Starved for Ideas

World Food Summit, November 15, 1996

Senator Martino, distinguished guests, and esteemed parliamentarians: Why do we live in a world in which millions upon millions of children and adults suffer from the scourges of extreme hunger and malnutrition? Why does famine, that age-old terror, still stalk the earth today?

These are profound and terrible questions. We gather here at the World Food Summit to confront these questions at the end of a great, but also a terrible, era. Our century has been a time of extraordinary wonder, and of extraordinary horror. It is the paradox of our time that we can marvel at the tempo of technical advance, even as the global gap between what can be done and what is being done grows ever wider, indeed, that in the century when the formula for attaining mass affluence was finally perfected, more people should perish from famine than ever before in human history. This paradox invests your deliberations here in the days ahead with a special and grave responsibility. As we are all too aware from events well within living memory, the power of modern government and the potentialities of collective international action can alter the human prospect for the better, but they can also alter it very much for the worse.

Esteemed parliamentarians. I hope you will indulge me if I speak frankly today, and take my frankness as a sign of my respect. As delegates to the World Food Summit, and as legislators in your own countries, you occupy positions of considerable influence on the global food situation. Through your efforts and activities you can accelerate the pace of progress against global hunger, and bring us closer to the day when famine is permanently conquered. But your official decisions, here and in your home countries, can equally hinder the international struggle for worldwide food security, and exacerbate the risk of mass starvation for vulnerable populations in the years ahead.

Of course we are all gathered here in good will, possessed of noble purpose. It is apparent that we share the same concerns and cherish the same ultimate objective. The success of our venture, however, is not predetermined by the intensity of our intentions. Success will instead depend on just how we choose to pursue our common objective. Effective policies and initiatives must be based on a realistic understanding of the problems we are striving to solve.

Why should I begin with so obvious a point? Because it is often forgotten when people of good will talk about world hunger. For some perhaps primordial reason, it seems that contemplating the problems of starvation and famine can cause the vision of ordinarily brilliant intellectuals, learned academicians and clearheaded statesmen suddenly to blur. This peculiar phenomenon, moreover, is not confined to any particular country or group of countries. All around the world today, specialists and policymakers continue to entertain beliefs and accept premises about the world food situation that are demonstrably invalid, sometimes even glaringly invalid.

To a strange and disturbing degree, modern international man is, quite literally, starved for ideas. Widely accepted misconceptions, stubborn "idees fixes" and crude ideological notions about the nature of hunger and famine in the modern world are impeding the quest to achieve food security for all. Guided, or more exactly, misguided, by fundamentally flawed assessments of the prevalence and causes of global hunger, we cannot hope to attain satisfactory results. At best, our well-meaning efforts will be merely ineffective; at worst, we risk making bad conditions worse, and injuring those we seek to help.

Modern day myths about the world food problem are legion. Today I wish to discuss three that seem to me particularly fashionable, and particularly pernicious. The first concerns the current dimensions of the hunger problem. The second might be described as the "Malthusian specter." The third bears on the relationship between hunger and political morality.

According to what is by now a large body of major studies by reputable and authoritative organizations, the magnitude of the global malnutrition problem in the modern era is vast, so vast, in fact, as to be almost incomprehensible. According to some of these studies, moreover, the problem has, at least in some respects, been worsening over time.

A few citations may be illustrative. In 1950, Lord Boyd-Orr, the first Director General of the UN Food and Agriculture Organization (FAO), warned that "a lifetime of malnutrition and actual hunger is the lot of at least two-thirds of mankind." Thirty years later, a United States Presidential Commission on World Hunger concluded that "(t)his world hunger problem is getting worse rather than better. There are more hungry people than ever before." In 1991, the World Food Council declared that "the number of chronically hungry people in the world continues to grow." And at the World Food Summit today, a principal FAO document puts the undernourished population of the world at well over 800 million, indicating that one out of five persons from developing countries was suffering from chronic undernutrition in the early 1990s.

That most recent FAO estimate seems to suggest both absolute and relative improvement on the world food situation over the long period since Lord Boyd-Orr issued his grim assessment. On the other hand, the FAO's third World Food Survey, back in 1963, concluded that a fifth of the developing world was undernourished at that time. By that benchmark, we would seem to have made no relative progress whatever against Third World hunger over the intervening decades; given the growth of population in the less developed regions (a topic to which I will return) the absolute number of hungry people in the world would have increased tremendously over the past generation.

On the whole, these expert findings paint a disheartening picture. There is just one small thing wrong with this picture: the methodologies of the studies from which it is drawn. Astonishing as it may sound to the non-specialist, the approach underpinning every one of the major international studies over the past two generations that has attempted to quantify global hunger is demonstrably and deeply flawed, although the specific methodological defects vary from one study to the next.

Using the methods employed in any one of these oft-quoted studies, it would be impossible even under ideal circumstances to derive an accurate impression of the global hunger situation, and the conditions under which some of those studies were prepared were far from ideal. For citizens and policymakers committed to charting a course against world hunger, these studies offer a distorted and misleading map.

The troubles with the studies are sometimes technical, but they are never difficult to describe. In every instance, their calculations pivot upon questionable and indeed unsupported assumptions about individual nutritional needs in large populations, and upon equally questionable assumptions about the correspondence between national food supplies and individual food intake. Remember: malnutrition is a condition that affects individuals. Short of clinical or biomedical examination, there is really no reliable means for determining a person's health or nutritional status. Lacking such information, these studies draw necessarily crude inferences about individual well-being from highly aggregated economic and agricultural data. They cannot cope with such exacting, but important, issues as whether individuals with lower caloric intake have lower than average caloric requirements; whether individual metabolic efficiency adjusts in response to changes in the nutritional supply; or whether individuals predicted by their models to be undernourished actually suffer from identifiable nutritional afflictions. To pose these questions is not to presuppose an answer to them; rather it is simply to discharge a basic duty of careful inquiry.

Sometimes the results of these hunger studies could be dismissed after the most casual inspection. In 1980, for example, the World Bank published a paper purporting to show that three-fourths of the population of the less developed regions suffered from "caloric deficits." This ominous conclusion, however, was reached by a chain of dubious suppositions, the final and most spectacular of which was that anyone receiving less than the average "recommended dietary allowance" was underfed. In reality, of course, about half of any population will need less than the average allowance, that is the meaning of the word "average." Consequently, this model could only generate nonsense numbers. Its computations, for example, showed that nearly half the people in prosperous Hong Kong were getting too little food!

To their credit, the World Bank researchers on this particular project recognized that their work failed the "reality test," and went back to the drawing board to improve their product. Unfortunately, others working on the problem have not always met the same standards of intellectual accountability. Lord Boyd-Orr, for example, never explained the method underlying his now famous estimate of the prevalence of world hunger. After reviewing contemporary FAO data, one of the leading agricultural experts of the day, Prof. Merrill K. Bennett, surmised that the estimate might have been an elementary computational mistake, a misreading of the figures in two particular columns of an FAO table. The FAO, however, never replied to Prof. Bennett's inquiry, and has never offered substantiating evidence for Lord Boyd-Orr's original assertion.

Other FAO estimates about world hunger have remained similarly protected against outside inspection: most of the data and calculations in the first three FAO World Food Surveys, for example, are still unavailable to the public. In more recent FAO studies, where somewhat greater intellectual openness is in display, we can see that the FAO's definition of the caloric threshold level for undernutrition has been steadily climbing over time. But why? These upward revisions do not seem to reflect any obvious changes in the scientific consensus concerning nutritional norms, but they do produce higher totals for any given estimate of the number of hungry people in the world.

If we could only for a moment extricate ourselves from this numerical house of mirrors, we would see that there are indeed meaningful data that bear upon the actual nutritional status of humanity, and that they tell a rather different story from the tales you may be hearing here in Rome.

Household spending patterns in less developed regions, for example, can reveal how the poor assess their own nutritional status. If a family treats food as a "superior good," that is to say, if an increase in income raises the overall share of the household budget going to food, it renders a telling judgment that its members have too little to eat. By this criterion, the incidence of serious hunger in the world would be far lower than the FAO currently suggests: about two-thirds lower, for example, in some years for India (a country which happens to have reasonably good household expenditure data).

Mortality rates, for their part, offer a direct and unambiguous measure of the material condition of any population. Despite the limitations of demographic data in some regions today, it is nonetheless clear that the so-called Third World has experienced a revolution in health conditions over the past generation. According to estimates and projections by the Population Division of the UN Secretariat, life expectancy at birth in the less developed regions rose by an average of almost a decade and a half between the early 1950s and the early 1990s; over that same period, infant mortality in the less developed regions is estimated to have dropped nearly by half. Can one really imagine that such dramatic gains were entirely unaccompanied by nutritional progress?

A precise and reliable method for estimating the incidence and severity of worldwide malnutrition has yet to be devised. We can be all too sure that scores of millions in our world suffer from heart-rending, life-impairing hunger. But exaggerating the current scope of the problem, and minimizing the strides we have already made against it, will serve no worthy purpose. Hungry populations certainly do not benefit from such misapprehensions. In an age of "compassion fatigue," these misrepresentations of reality tend instead to discourage action by depicting the problem as almost insurmountably large. To make matters worse, they may misdirect available humanitarian resources away from the places where they might have made the most difference. And by obscuring true patterns of nutritional change, these misrepresentations obstruct our efforts to learn from experience. Denying the existence of progress against global hunger denies us as well the hope of studying, and attempting to replicate elsewhere, local strategies that have actually resulted in progress.

Let us turn now to the Malthusian specter. As you know, the postwar variant of the Malthusian worldview holds that the globe cannot support the enormous increase in human numbers that we are witnessing, and holds further that we will be faced by rising poverty, mass hunger, and perhaps even worldwide catastrophe unless we somehow check this uncontrolled demographic growth. Overpopulation, increasing scarcity of food and natural resources, and famine, Malthusians argue, are clear and present dangers, the existence of which, they say, demonstrably validate their explication of how the world works.

In intellectual and political circles, the influence of Malthusian ideology today ranges wide and often runs deep; not surprisingly, it is especially evident in deliberations about the world food outlook. For its proponents, Malthusianism has some of the trappings of a secular faith. Matters of faith, as we know, do not readily lend themselves to testability, or to disproof. If we try to treat the Malthusian specter as an empirical rather than a theological proposition, though, we will find little evidence that its advent is nigh.

Consider the problem of "overpopulation." So much has been said about this problem over the years that it may surprise you to hear that there is no fixed and consistent demographic definition for the term. I repeat: none exists. How would we define it? In terms of population density? If so, Bermuda would be more "overpopulated" than Bangladesh. In terms of rates of natural increase? In that case, pre-Revolutionary America would have been more "overpopulated" than contemporary Haiti. In terms of the "dependency ratio" of children and the elderly to working-age populations?

That would mean Canada was more "overpopulated" in 1965 than India is today!

We could go on, but I trust you see my point. If "overpopulation" is a problem, it is a problem that has been misidentified and misdefined. The images evoked by the term, hungry children; squalid housing; early death, speak to problems all too real in the modern world. But these are properly described as problems of poverty. The risk of poverty, however, is obviously influenced, indeed, principally determined, by a panoply of nondemographic forces, not the least of these being the impact of a government's policies upon its subjects or citizens. As for the particulars of the relationship between population growth and poverty, these are more complex and far less categorical than one is often led to suppose.

At the very least, we know for a fact that rapid and sustained population growth does not preclude rapid and sustained economic and social advance. If it did, the vast material transformation we have already witnessed in the Twentieth Century could not have occurred.

Since the beginning of this century, according to the best available estimates, the world's population has more than tripled. Nothing like this had ever taken place before, and although the tempo of global population growth appears to have peaked and to be declining, it is still proceeding with extraordinary speed by historical perspective. This unprecedented demographic explosion, however, did not consign humanity to penury and destitution. Just the opposite: it was accompanied by a worldwide explosion of prosperity. According to the eminent economist Angus Maddison, the world's per capita GDP quadrupled between the turn of the century and the early 1990s. In Latin America and the Caribbean, per capita GDP, by his estimates, has more than quadrupled this century; in Asia and the Pacific, it has more than quintupled; and even in troubled Africa it may have more than doubled. While such calculations cannot be exact, there should not be the slightest doubt about the consequence of the trends they represent.

Why has the most rapid period of population growth in the history of our species been the occasion for the most extraordinary economic expansion in human experience? Part of the answer may lie in the "population explosion" itself, or more precisely, in its proximate causes. The modern "population explosion" was sparked not because people suddenly started breeding like rabbits, but rather because they finally stopped dying like flies. That is to say, it wasn't that fertility rates soared; rather, mortality rates plummeted. Since the start of our century, the average life expectancy at birth for a human being has probably doubled, it may have more than doubled. Every corner of the earth has joined in this health revolution, and on the whole, incidentally, health progress in our century has been more dramatic in the less developed regions than the more affluent ones.

Improvements in health are conducive to improvements in productivity. It is not just that healthier populations are able to work harder; improvements in health and reductions in mortality enhance the potentialities of what economists now call "human capital": education, training, skills, and the like. By so doing, they significantly relieve constraints against attaining higher levels of per capita output.

And what about fertility, which so many influential voices today posit as "excessive" in one or another regions of the world? Unlike better health and longer life, which are universally regarded as desirable, there is no "universal" view on optimal family size. The number of children that parents wish to have, like other big decisions in a person's life, is an inescapably subjective choice, while it may surely be shaped by economic, cultural, or religious factors, in the final analysis it is a personal choice. Before we speak of "excess fertility," we should ponder what we imply by questioning other peoples' choices about family size. Let me be blunt. Human beings are not heedless beasts. They do not procreate with utter disregard for their own well-being, much less the welfare of their own children.

With the tremendous growth of human numbers, and of per capita output, the world's GDP has grown phenomenally in our century: Maddison's aforementioned research, for example, suggests a fourteen-fold rise. Despite this awesome surge in demand, however, the prices for foodstuffs and natural resources have not rocketed skywards over the course of the Twentieth Century. In fact, the long-term trend for primary commodity prices has been heading in exactly the opposite direction. According to one careful study, for example, inflation-adjusted prices for primary commodities, including energy products, had dropped by over a third between the turn of the century and the 1980s. And as you may already have heard in the past few days from our friends from UNCTAD and the "Group of 77," the real price of primary commodities has fallen still further since then.

I regale you with these details about price trends because prices are meant to measure scarcity. Other things being equal, scarce items are supposed to cost more; plentiful items, less. Yet by the very information that prices are intended to convey, it would appear that foodstuffs and natural resources have been growing less scarce, not more, despite mankind's steadily increasing demand for them!

For convinced Malthusians, this seeming contradiction constitutes an unsolved mystery, and indeed an unsolvable one, if they are to maintain faith in their doctrine. We may note, however, that there are perfectly good explanations for the divergent directions of these long-term trends, not the least of these involving an appeal to economic reasoning and an attention to the actual workings of the modern economic process.

And what of famine? Malthusians expect famines to strike what they call "overpopulated" regions, what we might call very poor regions. It is surely true that the margin for error for the very poor is perilously thin. But it does not follow that the very poor in the modern world are inexorably consigned to mass starvation, or that they are pushed there by their own fertility trends. If we examine the actual record, we will see that modern famines are a quintessentially political phenomenon. In the modern world, people starve en masse not because famine is unavoidable. They starve instead because their own rulers happen to be indifferent to their plight, or because the state under which they live has actively contrived to bring about their death.

Recall the most fearsome famines that have gripped nations in our century. Over six million people perished in the Ukraine in 1933. That was Stalin's terror-famine: it was provoked by a deliberately punitive collectivization of agriculture, designed to subjugate an unwilling people. As many as three million people died in Bengal, India in 1943. That was when the British Viceregency, with available stocks of grain at hand, refused to enact the empire's stipulated relief procedures, lest those somehow compromise the overall war effort. Between 1959 and 1961, China lost as many as 30 million people through abnormally high death rates. That was Mao's cruel utopian experiment: first his forcible communization of the countryside shattered the nation's agriculture, then his government closed the country to outside view, denied there was a hunger problem, refused foreign help, and made a point of exporting food. Perhaps a million Biafrans perished from famine in the late 1960s. That was the Nigerian civil war, when food blockades were consciously employed literally to starve the rebels into submission.

In the late 1970s, perhaps a million, maybe more, died from abnormal mortality in Cambodia. That was the Khmer Rouge's methodical and barbaric program of auto-genocide. In the 1980s and 1990s, famine has stricken Ethiopia, Sudan, and Somalia. If the details of these more recent tragedies differ in some specifics from the earlier famines I have mentioned, rest assured that the patterns are entirely the same.

Amartya Sen, the distinguished economist and philosopher, and perhaps the pre-eminent student of contemporary famine, has stated it starkly: "Famines are, in fact, extremely easy to prevent. It is amazing that they actually take place, because they require a severe indifference on the part of the government."

Esteemed parliamentarians: in our epoch, famine has been caused not by an ominous excess of people, but instead by a frightening surfeit of callous rulers and killer states. Malthusian delusions would distract us from this central and gruesome fact, just as they divert us from probing too deeply into the reasons that some countries have, anomalously, experienced persistently poor economic performance, or even economic retrogression, in our age of progressive global economic advance.

Finally, let me turn directly to the relationship between hunger and political morality, a topic upon which we have already touched, if indirectly. At international gatherings, it is sometimes regarded as declasse to observe that one form of national political or legal arrangements might be preferable to others manifest elsewhere in the world. To the urbane, the latter view sometimes sounds embarrassingly provincial. In any case, many intellectuals and not a few political figures would contend that such considerations have no bearing on the pragmatic quest to conquer hunger. They would agree with the renowned playwright Bertolt Brecht: "Erst kommt das Fressen, dann kommt die Moral": food first, morality after.

Brecht's famous and seemingly worldly dictum is at once cynical and appallingly naive. How can we reflect upon the history of our century without being struck by the singular role certain political principles have played in abetting mankind's escape from hunger, and the dark role of other political philosophies in perpetuating the threat of hunger and starvation? At the end of the day, this much is crystal clear: economic liberty is the enemy of hunger, and political freedom is the nemesis to famine.

Permit me to quote Amartya Sen once more: "In the gruesome history of famines there is hardly any case in which a famine has occurred in a country that is independent and democratic, regardless of whether it is rich or poor." We can take this point further. There are practically no instances of famine in any setting where local newspapers were free to criticize their own government, or where citizens enjoyed the substantive right to participate in an opposition party. In open and accountable political systems where governments serve at the sufferance of the voter, there is tremendous pressure and incentive for policies that forestall famine. Impoverished as it is often said to be, India has not suffered famine since its independence. Far from being a luxury that only the rich can afford, as some would have it, political freedom is thus actually an indispensable necessity for the very poor.

Marxist-Leninists have sneered at the liberal conception of political freedom; they still dismiss it as a dangerous illusion. But as the nightmare of totalitarianism at last begins to pass, and its legacy of worldwide wreckage is finally laid bare, there can be no more dispute about just who was entranced by perilous political fantasies. For all their proclamations about enshrining "people's rights," Marxist-Leninist regimes never did divide those vaunted rights into individual portions. And while terrible atrocities were committed in our time by regimes of many political hues, only the totalitarians committed atrocities out of cold-blooded principle.

Just as political liberties place a systemic check on the threat of famine, so economic liberties can dynamically reduce the risk of severe malnutrition. This is so, quite simply, because the institutional framework for securing economic liberties happens also to be conducive to material advance, productivity improvement, and, ultimately, the escape from poverty. Rule of law; protection of individual rights, including property rights; enforceability of contracts; sound money; the sanction of mutually beneficial economic exchange: from the standpoint of protecting liberty, all these things are virtues in their own right. But insofar as they decrease the uncertainty, lower the costs of obtaining information, and reduce what are called the "transaction costs" that confront individual economic agents, the underpinnings of economic liberty stimulate economic activity and enhance economic welfare.

One may also make the case, as some of us have elsewhere, that economic liberty is especially important to the poor, the vulnerable and the marginalized, the groups, in other words, least capable of fending for themselves in an economic and political system that is neither regular nor just.

In much of the world, including areas where basic political freedoms are secure, the ordinary workings of domestic and international markets are today regarded with suspicion, even hostility, in many elite circles. Such circles speak gravely of the perils of "market failure," and claim these perils justify far-reaching interventions into economic life. Truth to tell, markets, like all human inventions, are imperfect. Some specific instances of modern "market failure," moreover, have been conspicuous. But before learning all the fascinating exceptions to the rules, it is best to get the rules themselves straight. For it is the opportunities that lie in market development, and under a regimen of economic liberty, that offer the greatest inherent scope for improving the purchasing power of the world's poor, for stabilizing their access to food supplies, and thus for promoting nutritional security for vulnerable populations. What development specialist Deepak Lal termed "the dirigiste dogma" is still deeply entrenched in many of the world's poorest, and hungriest, spots. As many here will recognize, this dogma commands faithful followers within FAO and other multilateral institutions as well. Alas: adherents of the dirigiste dogma have an unsettling tendency to discover "market failures" where none in fact exist, and to misdiagnose the adverse consequences of their own preferred therapies as "market failures" that will only be remedied through further dirigiste treatments. To belabor the obvious once more, such a state of affairs does not relieve the plight of the world's poor, or expedite progress against global hunger.

As we look toward the coming century, we have more than a presentiment of some of the challenges that will face us. With the enormous increases in world population anticipated in the coming generations, we will need to arrange for commensurately enormous increases in agricultural production capabilities, or disproportionately enormous increases, if we hope to improve the world's dietary quality. Moreover, insofar as agricultural production is just one facet of the complex modern economy, we must be prepared to let agriculture make its fullest contribution to overall development; man's needs and desires, after all, extend far beyond a sufficient dinner. And in the world's hungriest regions, establishing effective, responsive, and limited governance is a task barely begun, much as it was when Lord Peter Bauer warned us so over a generation ago.

That will be the hard work. What I have discussed today, the need to redress some obvious misconceptions, is the easy part. But you will not be able to get around to the hard work unless you do the easy work first. Esteemed parliamentarians and distinguished guests: As you begin the work ahead, which will affect millions of lives, I leave you with a reminder, and a plea. Never forget that harm can come from even the best of intentions. And as you consider the tasks before you, set your course by an injunction as old as the desire to go good itself: first, do no harm. First, do no harm. Ladies and gentlemen, please: first, do no harm.

Part III

Demographic Destinies

Demography is the study of human numbers, but it is the human characteristics of those numbers that define world events. What is called a demographic problem may better be described as a moral and intellectual problem that takes demographic form.

— From "Mortality and the Fate of Communist States"

"Demography is destiny" according to the aphorism often attributed to nineteenth century French polymath and socialist Auguste Comte. A less majestic, but arguably more accurate, formulation would be: "Demography gradually but powerfully alters the realm of the possible." Demographic trends unfold over the long run—and this section collects some of my studies that examine the long reach of demographic forces. Demography also affords us a window into the future, a more reliable picture of what a society is likely to look like a decade or two hence than any economic projection can hope to provide. In the following chapters I discuss the implications of the health crisis the Soviet system eventually visited on its own subjects and its subjugated allies in Warsaw Pact Europe; the outlook for aging populations in the major states of Eurasia, all of which are on track to get old before they get rich; and, in a slightly different vein, the necessity to prepare for the reunification of the Korean population as a free, prosperous, and secure nation in the years ahead.

8

Mortality and the Fate of Communist States

Prosperous Paupers and Other Population Problems, 2000

The crisis and collapse of Communist rule in Eastern Europe and the
Soviet Union between 1989 and 1991 was, arguably, one of the defining moments of modern history. It has also proved to be a moment of truth
for the large and established community of Western specialists—within
government, the academy, and private institutes—who have made it their
purpose to study the Soviet bloc countries. For with a sudden flash, the
weaknesses and shortcomings of a generation of extensive studies were
exposed and glaringly illuminated.

One may begin with what did not happen. Students of the Warsaw Pact
region provided virtually no forewarning of the convulsions that were coming to the states they studied. Quite the contrary: the demise of Warsaw
Pact Communism seemed to take the field as a whole by almost complete
surprise. Though a sizeable literature on the Warsaw Pact states was published in the generation before the "revolutions of 1989," one would be
hard pressed to locate more than a handful of items that would seem to
anticipate the fact (much less the timing) of this dramatic political departure from the Eurasian stage.[1]

Prediction of political outcomes, it must be said, remains rather more of
an art than a science. Premonitions about impending political changes may
speak more to intuition than to positive analysis; it may be unreasonable to
fault a specific discipline for failing to announce an advent almost no one
was expecting. More troubling, from a methodological standpoint, than the
unpredicted collapse of Soviet bloc Communism itself has been the light this
collapse has newly thrown on Western studies of the quantitative performance of those economies.

Of course, the closed nature of those societies, and the peculiar nature of
their economic organization, posed obvious and formidable obstacles to any

effort at measuring true patterns of production, consumption, and growth under central planning. But it is equally true that Western researchers devoted formidable resources to developing just such measurements. In fact, by such criteria as expense, duration, or technical manpower absorbed, the U.S. intelligence community's postwar quest to describe and model the Soviet economy was in all likelihood the largest social science research project ever undertaken.

With the crumbling of the Berlin Wall and the "end of the Cold War," it now seems virtually incontestable that this corpus of quantitative studies, for all their apparent rigor, was for the most part off the mark. As late as 1987, for example, the U.S. Central Intelligence Agency (CIA, 1987) was estimating per capita GNP to be somewhat higher in East Germany than in West Germany. As every German taxpayer is today all too aware, the actual level of per capita output in what have become the "New Federal States" was in reality vastly lower than in the rest of Germany on the eve of that nation's reunification.[2] This signal misreading of Communist economic performance was by no means an isolated incident. Comparable overestimates of economic performance by the CIA may be adduced for every other country in the Soviet bloc. And the CIA was hardly alone in overestimating productivity, living standards, and economic growth within the Soviet bloc during the "Cold War." In a defense of his analysts, the Bush Administration's Director of Central Intelligence pointedly (and correctly) observed that many independent scholars and specialists had taken the CIA's old estimates to task for purportedly underestimating the economic performance of Warsaw Pact countries (Gates 1992).

My purpose in reciting these particulars is not to criticize the work of those in the West who strove so diligently to understand the workings of a system, and a way of life, with which they were fundamentally unfamiliar. It is rather to suggest, with all the benefits of hindsight, that our understanding of the Soviet bloc might have been significantly enhanced if students of those countries had paid a little more attention to their demographic trends. More specifically, I wish to suggest that valuable and telling insights into the social, economic, and even political circumstances of these countries could have been gleaned from analysis of their death rates: their schedules of mortality, and their reported patterns of cause of death.

Such an application of demographic technique, one hopes, would have been gratifying to Roger Revelle. It responds, after all, to an invitation he extended a quarter of a century ago. In offering the results of that now-classic project on "Historical Population Studies" to the reader in 1968, Revelle also framed an agenda for future research. "The new science of historical demography," he observed, "has devoted almost all of its efforts to the determinants of population change, and very few to an examination of its consequences." Among the specifics that "we do not understand," in his enumeration, were "the consequences of greater longevity on allocation of resources and the distribution of political power (Revelle 1968)."

What we have witnessed in the Soviet bloc since 1968, however, is an unprecedented demographic phenomenon that could scarcely be imagined at the time: long-term stagnation—even decline—in life expectancy among a group of industrialized societies that were not at war. This was a major and highly visible event, rife with consequence and implication. Some of those consequences and implications will be explored in this paper.

This chapter proceeds through four sections. The first reviews the anomalous history of mortality trends in Eastern Europe and the USSR between the end of the Second World War and the "end of the Cold War." The second draws inferences about economic performance in those countries from their mortality trends. The third examines some characteristic differences in mortality trends between those areas in which Communist rule has recently collapsed and those in which it continues, and speculates about the significance of the distinction. The final section discusses the significance of current mortality trends for post-Communist societies, especially as they pertain to the prospective transition to a stable economic and political order.

I

For the Soviet Union and the Eastern European countries over which it gained mastery during and immediately after World War II, the "Cold War" began with an explosion of health progress. Improvements in mortality, of course, had been underway in these areas before the advent of Marxist-Leninist rule, and had proceeded even during the crisis years for interwar capitalism: between 1929/32 and 1937, for example, Czechoslovakia's life tables recorded an increase in expectation of life at birth of about three years for males and three and a half for females (United Nations 1968). Nevertheless, the pace of mortality decline under Red Army Socialism was noteworthy. Even after recovery to prewar levels had been attained, the tempo continued to be brisk. It was not idle conceit to assert during those years, as the Soviet bloc governments did, that they were outperforming their capitalist rivals in the field of public health.

A few summary figures can lay out the contrast. Between the early 1950s and the early 1960s, according to recent United Nations Population Division estimates, infant mortality dropped by nearly half in Warsaw Pact Europe, and by over half in the USSR (United Nations 1991). This was a much more rapid pace of progress than in Western Europe as a whole, or even in Western Europe's Mediterranean regions (which were arguably more comparable to the Balkans or Ukraine than Switzerland or Sweden would have been). Over that same decade, life expectancy at birth in Warsaw Pact Europe is estimated to have risen by over five years for males, and by nearly six and a half for females; in the USSR the corresponding increments are estimated at five and a half and four and a half years, respectively. Improvements in "imperialist countries" were not nearly so dramatic. In West Germany, for example, the overall increase in life expectancy at birth between 1950/55 and 1960/65 was about two and a half years; in the United States, it was barely one year. Among the OECD countries, Japan could claim to match the average of Warsaw Pact Europe's increments, but her performance was exceptional for a grouping in which she was clearly an atypical member (ibid).

By the mid-1960s, mortality levels in the Warsaw Pact region were very nearly as low as those of the advanced capitalist countries. By the UN's estimate, less than a year separated overall levels of life expectancy at birth in the U.S. and the USSR; the differential between OECD Europe and Eastern Europe was apparently only very slightly greater. If trends were extrapolated only a few years into the future, the Soviet bloc could be seen catching up with, and then surpassing, advanced Western countries by this important, and politically significant, measure.

That general crossover point, of course, was never reached. Instead, the Warsaw Pact countries collectively, and most unexpectedly, entered a new era: one of stagnation, and deterioration, in overall health conditions. The sudden slow-down is highlighted by the official life tables of the countries in question. (Despite the problems with some of these life tables, largely attendant upon underreporting of infant deaths; their results are informative.)

According to its life tables, life expectancy at birth in Poland rose by less than 2 years between the mid-1960s and the late 1980s—and this apparently was the region's star performer. Overall increases of less than one year over this same generation were estimated by Bulgaria, Czechoslovakia, and Romania; Hungary's life expectancy was basically stationary over the period as a whole; and life expectancy at birth is officially reported to have fallen in the USSR. Worse still was the situation for men: according to these life tables, East Germany enjoyed an increase in life expectancy at birth for males of about one year over these decades, and this was the best of the group. Czechoslovakia's male life expectancy in 1988 is placed at the same level as in 1964, while Bulgaria, Hungary, Poland, Romania, and the USSR all report long-term declines. The USSR also reports a slight long-term decline in female life expectancy at birth.[3] Strikingly, the slowdown, and reversal, of health progress within the Soviet bloc coincided with an acceleration in OECD countries. Between the mid-1960s and the late 1980s, according to the latest UN estimates, life expectancy for both sexes rose by an average of about four years in Western Europe, and by about five years in the United States (United Nations 1992).

How is the virtual cessation of overall health progress within the Soviet bloc to be explained? The phenomenon may be better understood by examining component parts. In most of the Warsaw Pact region, infant mortality rates apparently continued their declines through the 1960s, 1970s, and 1980s, although at a slower pace than in the early postwar period. (There are strong indications that Soviet infant mortality actually increased over some portion of the past generation; owing to the poor state of the relevant Soviet data, however, the debate about this possibility has not yet been settled.)[4]

Mortality data tend to be more comprehensive and reliable for those over the age of one than for infants. They are worth examining, not least for this reason. Table 8-1 presents official life table estimates of life expectation at age one for the Soviet bloc countries for the mid-1960s and the late 1980s. A striking pattern emerges from these data. In five of the seven countries, combined male and female life expectancy for the non-infant population registers at least a slight decline. The situation is even starker by age 30: in six of the seven countries, life expectancy for adults fell over these decades, slight increases in female life expectancy being more than offset by the fall in life expectancy for males. In less than a quarter of a century, Bulgarian and Polish life expectancy for men at age 30 dropped by more than 2 years; in Hungary the drop

Table 8-1. Expectation of Life at Age One and Age 30: Warsaw Pact Region, c.1965–c.1989

Country		Life Expectation at One Year of Age (years)		Life Expectation at Age 30 (years)	
		Male	Female	Male	Female
Bulgaria					
	1965/67	70.28	73.81	43.06	45.99
	1987/89	68.42	74.64	40.87	46.53
	– increment	1.86	+0.83	2.19	+0.54
Czechoslovakia					
	1964	68.44	73.96	41.15	45.84
	1988	67.70	75.07	39.73	46.62
	– increment	0.74	+1.11	1.42	+0.78
East Germany					
	1967-68	69.77	74.70	42.46	46.70
	1987-88	69.53	75.46	41.67	47.08
	– increment	0.24	+0.76	0.79	+0.38
Hungary					
	1964	69.08	73.45	41.74	45.45
	1989	65.58	73.86	37.84	45.55
	– increment	3.50	+0.41	3.90	+0.10
Poland					
	1965/66	68.98	74.43	41.68	46.46
	1988	67.37	75.70	39.60	47.29
	– increment	1.61	+1.27	2.08	+0.83
Romania					
	1963	69.36	72.96	42.66	45.65
	1987/89	67.53	73.13	40.55	45.56
	– increment	1.83	+0.17	2.11	0.09
Soviet Union					
	1965/66	— 68.0[1,2] —		— 45.0[1] —	
	1986/87	— 67.2[1,2] —		— 43.5[1] —	
	– increment	negative		at least one year	
	1958/59	65.62	73.07	39.51	46.13
	1989/90	65.29	74.43	38.62	46.78
	– increment	– 0.33	+1.36	– 0.89	+0.65

Notes: [1] = life expectancy for both sexes. [2] = life expectancy at age 5.
Sources: For USSR 1958/59 and 1986/87 = USSR State Statistical Committee, *Tablitsy Smertnosti i Ozhidaemoy Prodalzhitel'nosti Zhizni Naseleniya* (Moscow: Goskomstat, 1989). All others, United Nations, Demo; Yearbook (New York: UN Department of International Economic and Social Affairs), various issues.

Table 8-2. Changes in Age Specific Death Rates for Cohorts Aged 30–69: Warsaw Pact Region, c.1965–c.1989 (percent)

Country and Sex	30/34	35/39	40/44	45/49	50/54	55/59	60/64	65/69
				Cohort Age				
Males								
Bulgaria (1966-89)	+19	+32	+62	+70	+56	+47	16	+14
Czechoslovakia (1965-89)	5	+8	+19	+40	+33	+29	+15	+6
East Germany (1965-88)	5	8	5	+7	+3	+1	15	17
Hungary (1966-89)	+67	+96	+100	+131	+93	+69	+46	+25
Poland (1966-88)	+9	+17	+36	+51	+47	+38	+23	+6
Romania (1966-89)	+32	+36	+43	+61	+44	+32	+35	+15
Soviet Union (1965/66-89)	5	0	+21	+25	+24	+25	+20	+25
Unweighted average	+17	+26	+39	+55	+43	+34	+15	+8
Females								
Bulgaria (1966-89)	11	15	10	+4	4	4	7	6
Czechoslovakia (1965-89)	13	23	14	9	10	0	3	9
East Germany (1965-88)	12	15	14	12	12	10	16	17
Hungary (1966-89)	+33	+26	+26	+33	+23	+22	+7	2
Poland (1965-88)	27	25	9	9	2	1	3	14
Romania (1966-89)	8	+13	+4	3	0	2	3	3
Soviet Union (1965/66-89)	21	17	4	3	+2	+11	+4	+19
Unweighted average	8	8	3	0	1	+2	3	5

Note: All changes rounded to the nearest percentage point. Percentages derived from sources.
Sources: For Soviet Union 1965/66: John Dutton, Jr., "Changes in Soviet Mortality Patterns, 1959-77," Population and Development Review, vol. 5, no. 2 (1979), pp. 276-77. All other data: United Nations, Demographic Yearbook (New York: UN Department of International Economic and Social Affairs), various issues.

was closer to four years. The Soviet Union, for its part, never released any life tables for its population for the mid-1960s. Official tables for the late 1950s and the late 1980s, however, report male life expectancy at age one, and life expectancy at age 30 for the two sexes together, to have been lower in 1989/90 than they were over thirty years earlier!

Age-specific death rates can cast further light on the deterioration of adult health within the Soviet bloc (see Table 8-2). Between the mid-1960s and the late 1980s, all seven countries reported rising death rates for at least some of

their adult male cohorts. Some of these increases were little short of astonishing: in Hungary, for example, death rates for men in their forties doubled
between 1966 and 1989. In most of these countries, women in various adult
cohorts experienced at least some slight declines in age-specific mortality,
although broad increases in female mortality were evident in both Hungary
and the Soviet Union. Although health trends were, by this measure, arguably unfavorable in all these countries for all adult cohorts, they were especially bad for persons in their forties and fifties.

The health situation—call it a health crisis—in the Soviet bloc countries
during their last generation under Communism was without historical precedent or contemporary parallel. Mortality decline in Western countries, it is
true, has been neither smooth nor uninterrupted; various countries—including the Netherlands, Sweden, and the United States—have reported drops
in life expectancy at birth for their male population at some juncture during
the postwar period. These drops, however, have been slight and temporary,
whereas the rise in death rates for broad groups within Warsaw Pact countries has been major, and sustained over the course of decades.

What accounts for these extraordinary trends? A fully satisfactory answer
to this question must await further interdisciplinary study. Some preliminary
indications, however, may be drawn from data on reported cause of death
in these countries. These data must be used with care, for they are shaped
by an unavoidable element of subjectivity under the best of conditions, and
the best of conditions did not obtain in the statistical offices of Warsaw Pact
states. Cause-of-death data, nevertheless, can speak directly to the proximate
reasons for reduced life expectation, and may be broadly suggestive of the
underlying factors driving the decline.

The World Health Organization (WHO) has prepared age-standardized
breakdowns of mortality rates by reported cause of death for all of its corresponding member states for the period extending from the early 1950s to
the present. It offers breakdowns for the 1965/69–1989 period for four of
the seven countries in the Warsaw Pact: Bulgaria, Czechoslovakia, Hungary,
and Poland. Some of the trends highlighted are intriguing. Levels of mortality attributed to accident and injury, for example, are consistently high
among these states; Hungary—the country of the four with perhaps the best
cause-of-death data—reports that age-standardized mortality from cirrhosis
and chronic liver disease was, by 1987, higher for women than it had been for

men only seventeen years earlier. But mortality ascribed to these causes does not trend upward with any consistency in these countries, and in any case cannot account for much of the overall increment in age-standardized death rates. It is, instead, deaths attributed to cardiovascular disease (CVD) that appear to have shaped these countries' age-standardized mortality trends. In all four countries, deaths attributed to CVD accounted for over half of all age-standardized mortality by the late 1980s. Moreover, all four countries are reported to have suffered huge rises in CVD mortality levels between the late 1960s and the late 1980s. Whereas mortality ascribed to CVD has declined substantially in recent decades throughout the Western industrialized world, Bulgaria reported a 52 percent increase in age-standardized CVD mortality for males between 1965/69 and 1989. Over the same period, CVD mortality seems to have risen dramatically for East bloc women as well: by over 16 percent in Bulgaria and 20 percent in Poland, to select two of the more arresting examples. In proximate terms, the explosive rise in CVD-attributed mortality seems to account fully for the rise in age-standardized mortality in these Soviet bloc countries.[5] Diverging levels of CVD mortality, moreover, seem to account for most of the divergence in overall age-standardized mortality rates over the past generation between Western and Eastern European countries.

The underlying factors contributing to this rise, of course, are more difficult to identify than the proximate ones. Deaths from cardiovascular disease are commonly associated with a variety of specific behavioral or lifestyle characteristics, including heavy smoking, heavy drinking, poor diet, lack of exercise, and psychological stress or emotional strain.[6] There is ample evidence to suggest that Warsaw Pact populations may have been increasingly exposed to such "risk factors" as the era of "detente" progressed.

But such behavioral indications, in a sense, beg the question, for they skirt an obvious etiological issue: not only is the phenomenon of secular increases in mortality in industrialized societies at peace a new one, the patterns accounting for this rise are also unprecedented. Higher levels of general mortality are typically associated with higher levels of death from infectious and parasitic disease, whereas the Warsaw Pact group's path back to higher mortality was paved by increases in deaths attributed to chronic, noncommunicable causes. The rise, and its pattern, was unique to populations living under Warsaw Pact Communism, and indeed apparently common to all of them, despite their manifest differences in language, culture, and levels of material attainment. By these forensics, one might surely be drawn to inquire whether the health problems evidenced by the Warsaw Pact countries was not, in some fundamental sense, systemic. Moreover, in an age when health progress is all but taken for granted, and when scientific, technical, and administrative advances have made it possible to attain given levels of mortality at ever lower income levels, an inability of a particular set of governments to prevent severe long-term declines in health conditions for broad segments of its populations is surely suggestive of a systemic crisis.

II

During the Cold War decades, Western efforts to assess the Soviet bloc economies and to measure their performance were hampered not only by secrecy and mutual mistrust, but by features characteristic of Soviet-style command planning.

For one thing, the incentive structure in the Soviet-type planning rewarded overstatement of results at all levels, including the very highest. As Jan Winiecki (1986) once aptly observed, the "law of equal cheating" does not obtain in such a milieu. Even figures for physical output were routinely padded and exaggerated, albeit by varying margins across countries, industries, and time.

Yet even if perfectly accurate time series data had been available for all items of physical output, Western analysts would still have faced a second problem: valuing the goods and services produced in a way that would make them comparable with output from a market-oriented economy. Ingenious attempts to translate a price structure set by the state into one reflecting scarcity costs were devised: most importantly, the "adjusted factor cost" method pioneered by Abram Bergson and his colleagues in the 1950s.[7] But the problem of finding a common valuation process for systems which allocated resources by such fundamentally different principles could neither be finessed, nor ultimately solved.

For all these difficulties, economic estimates for the Warsaw Pact group were produced, and internally consistent time series were developed to trace their performance. The most authoritative of these time series, published by the CIA, did indicate a fairly steady slowdown in the tempo of economic growth for the region as a whole between the mid-1960s and the late 1980s. At the same time, it suggested quite considerable economic progress. For the 24-year span 1966–1989, for example, the CIA estimated per capita output in Warsaw Pact Europe to have risen by over half; per capita growth for the period as a whole was said to average 1.8 percent a year. By this reading, the region's growth rate would have been lower than the European Community's (2.4 percent for those same years), but the ostensible gap was not dramatic. Specific comparisons, moreover, painted a more favorable picture of the Warsaw Pact's performance against its rivals. The CIA's estimates of per capita growth for the U.S. and the USSR for these years, for example, were virtually identical (1.9 percent per annum), and East Germany's per capita growth rate was placed slightly ahead of West Germany's (2.7 vs. 2.6 percent). On the eve of the "revolutions of 1989," furthermore, CIA estimates indicated that the Warsaw Pact economies had attained fairly high levels of productivity. For 1988, per capita output for the USSR was placed at over three-fifths of the West German level. Per capita output in Czechoslovakia was placed at 78 percent of the level for the Netherlands, and per capita output in East Germany was estimated to be virtually the same as for the European Community as a whole (CIA 1988).

Plausible as such numbers may have seemed when juxtaposed solely against one another, they would seem suspicious—indeed anomalous—if held next to mortality data. Mortality statistics, for example, would immediately seem to call into question the proposition that per capita output in Eastern Germany had reached the level of Western Europe's by the late 1980s. After all: in 1989 WHO's age-standardized death rate for males was 26 percent higher for East Germany than for the countries of Western Europe. For females, East Germany's age-standardized death rate was fully 32 percent higher than Western Europe's. Indeed, by this measure of mortality, death rates in Eastern Germany were actually higher than in such places as Argentina, Chile, Uruguay, or Venezuela (WHO 1991)!

Such discrepancies in mortality levels are pertinent to economic performance in a number of respects. General levels of mortality bear more than a passing relation to labor productivity, which in turn establishes constraints on a population's level of per capita output. Mortality levels, moreover, are directly related to a population's living standards, which are in turn related to its level of per capita consumption.[8]

The relationship between mortality and economic performance, of course, is neither tight nor entirely mechanistic. A country's level of per capita output is determined by more than just its supply of "human capital." Human capital, for its part, is a complex fabric of many strands, of which health is but one, and for which mortality rates may not always provide a satisfactory proxy.[9] Finally, the very fact that fairly low levels of mortality can today be purchased in some low-income countries (such as Sri Lanka or China) should qualify generalizations about the relationship between overall levels of per capita consumption and overall levels of mortality. With such caveats in mind, we may nonetheless be able to read an economic significance from the exceptional mortality trends of the Warsaw Pact region.

Consider once more the comparison of fin de regime East Germany with the countries of the European Community on the one hand, and with selected Latin American countries on the other. Is it conceivable that a country with general levels of mortality so much higher than the EC's average could manage to attain the EC's level of per capita output? In theory, yes: but only under three specific, and highly restrictive, conditions.[10] Equivalent levels of output could coincide with such different mortality levels if: 1) the process of resource allocation were markedly more efficient in the high mortality society; 2) the high mortality society enjoyed a markedly superior endowment of such factors of production as capital or technology; and/or 3) the high mortality society mobilized its labor force in a way that allowed it to evince vastly greater hours of work from its typical resident.[11]

Were these conditions satisfied by East Germany in the period leading up to unification? Soviet-type economies may be good at various tasks, but allocative efficiency was never one of these.[12] Thus, Condition 1 does not obtain. The same may be said for Condition 2: even during the "Cold War," it was no secret that East bloc industry lagged considerably behind the EC in most fields of production with respect to deployed technology and capital stocks.[13] What about Condition 3? Soviet-style systems do seem to be effective in achieving high rates of labor force participation: census data, for example, indicated that over 54 percent of East Germany's population was economically active in the 1980s, as against West Germany's 48 percent.[14] But East Germany's extensive employment strategy entailed the induction of more marginal laborers into the workforce; consequently, the average number of hours worked per week was reportedly lower than in West Germany (under 36 vs. over 40 in 1988 in the non-agricultural sectors)(International Labor Office, 1991). Total hours worked per year, on a population-equivalent basis, appears to have been only slightly higher in East Germany than in West Germany (or by extension in other Western European countries). Insofar as none of the conditions adduced appears actually to have obtained, one would conclude from these mortality differentials, in the absence of other evidence to the contrary, that per capita output in East Germany was actually substantially lower than within the EC countries in the years immediately before reunification.

What of the comparison between East Germany and, say, Argentina? Is it plausible that levels of per capita consumption would be higher for the society with the higher general mortality level? Once again, the answer is: in theory, yes, but only under specific conditions. Such a paradox might be explained by peculiarities of the income distributions of the countries in question; by differences in the reach and scope of health care policies; or by differences in the availability and incidence of other "public consumption" goods and services, such as rationed staples, medical care, or education. Yet by any of these criteria one would expect mortality levels to be lower in an Eastern European socialist economy than in a Latin American economy characterized by equivalent levels of per capita consumption. In the absence of other evidence, therefore, mortality levels would appear to indicate that East Germany's level of per capita consumption was rather more like a Latin American country's than that of a Western European country—and that it may actually have been lower than per capita consumption levels in some parts of Latin America. By way of perspective, one may note that the World Bank's "purchasing power parity" adjustments give Argentina a level of per capita output roughly one-third that of West Germany for 1985 (World Bank 1985).

This approach to mortality analysis can be extended to render a more general impression of the performance of Soviet-type economies in the generation before their demise. One instructive comparison comes from matching estimates of change in per capita output with changes in age-standardized mortality (WHO "European Model") for males over roughly the same period. That particular measure of mortality would seem appropriate as an alternate aperture on economic progress for two reasons. First, though it is a summary measure of mortality for all age groups, the model age-structure upon which it rests is heavily weighted toward persons of working ages, and is therefore sensitive to their mortality trends. Second, despite doctrinally stipulated equality of the sexes, labor force participation rates within the Soviet bloc were always higher for men than for women; moreover, Soviet bloc men tended to be disproportionately represented in higher-pay sectors. For these reasons, Soviet bloc output might be expected to be affected more by changes in male mortality than changes in female mortality.

Table 8-3 presents a match-up of CIA and WHO estimates for Soviet bloc countries and selected states from Western Europe. In all of the Soviet bloc countries, rising male mortality levels coincide with what are calculated to be substantial gains in per capita output. The situation in these four countries is contrasted with four of Western Europe's "slow growers": the Netherlands, Sweden, Switzerland, and the United Kingdom. Over the past generation, faster-growing Western European economies have also been characterized by a somewhat faster pace of change in age-standardized mortality; mortality change in the slow growers is less than the Western European average. Even so, these four countries exhibit an entirely different pattern of mortality change from the four Warsaw Pact countries, despite purportedly similar magnitudes of per capita growth. Where the Warsaw Pact group's mortality rates all rise, Western Europe's "slow growers" all register declines. In view of this radical difference, is it really possible that the Eastern and Western European countries in Table 8-3 would actually have experienced similar per capita growth rates over the generation in question? Under certain conditions, possibly so—if, for example, the Soviet bloc had enjoyed a clear and overriding advantage with regard to technological innovation. But as has been noted, no such advantage was in evidence then, or can be seen in retrospect.

As a final comparison, one may match CIA (per GNP capita) and WHO (age-standardized mortality) estimates for the Soviet bloc and for Latin America for the year 1989 (see Table 8-4). According to the CIA's assessment, none of these Soviet bloc countries had a level of per capita output nearly so low as the most affluent of these Latin American nations; as a group, their level of per capita GNP was said to be over three times as high as those Latin American countries listed. Those same Latin American societies, however, reported substantially lower levels of age-standardized mortality. Of the entire Warsaw

Table 8-3. CIA Estimates of Changes in Per Capita GNP vs. WHO Estimates of Changes in Age-Standardized Male Mortality: Selected Warsaw Pact and Western European Countries, c.1965–c.1989

Country	Estimated Changes in Per Capita GNP 1966–89 (percent)	Estimated Changes in Standardized Male Mortality, 1965/69–89 (percent) – Age –
Bulgaria	+ 61.2	+ 13.4
Czechoslovakia	+ 62.7	+ 1.8
Hungary	+ 57.3	+ 12.5
Poland	+ 62.3	+ 7.9
Unweighted average	+ 60.9	+ 8.9
Netherlands	+ 63.4	− 11.5
Sweden[1]	+ 61.1	− 13.3
Switzerland	+ 51.6	− 27.1
United Kingdom	+ 63.0	− 25.1
Unweighted average	+ 59.8	− 19.4

Notes: WHO age standardization is for its "European Model" population. [1] = 1988
Sources: Derived from US Central Intelligence Agency, *Handbook of Economic Statistics*: 1980 edition, p. 29; 1990 edition, p. 44; World Health Organization, *World Health Statistics Annual*: 1988 edition, table 12; 1990 edition, table 10; 1991 edition, table 11.

Pact grouping in 1989, in fact, only East Germany could have passed for an advanced Latin American society on the basis of its age-standardized mortality figures. These mortality data do not offer a precisely calibrated adjustment of official Western estimates of Soviet bloc economic performance, but they appear to provide a strong implicit challenge to such figures, and thereby may be seen as serving something of a corrective function.

Even among market-oriented societies, international economic comparisons remain a complex and exacting business, for reasons both practical and theoretical. It should be no surprise that opportunities for mismeasurement were greater still when surveying the economies of the Soviet bloc. It may have been too much to hope for a single, unambiguous statistical account of the performance of economies so very different from our own.

Table 8-4. CIA Estimates of Per Capita GNP vs. WHO Estimates of Total Age-Standardized Mortality: Warsaw Pact Countries and Selected Latin American Countries, c.1989

Country	GNP ($1989)	Age-Standardized (deaths per 100,000)
Bulgaria	5,690	1,141.0
Czechoslovakia	7,900	1,158.0
East Germany	9,670	1,014.7
Hungary	6,090	1,229.6
Poland	4,560	1,118.7
Romania	3,440	1,240.5[1]
Soviet Union	9,230	1,159.9[1]
Unweighted average	6,654	1,151.8
Argentina	2,250	1,043.7[2]
Chile	1,880	969.0[2]
Mexico	2,340	1,026.3[3]
Venezuela	2,100	1,003.8
Unweighted average	2,143	1,010.7
Ratio of unweighted averages		
(Latin America = 100)	310	114

Notes: WHO age-standardization is for "European Model" population
[1] = 1988; [2] = 1987; [3] = 1986
Sources: Derived from US Central Intelligence Agency, *Handbook of Economic Statistics* 1990 edition, pp. 30-34; *World Health Statistics Annual*, 1990 edition (table 10), 1991 edition (table 11).

Even so, the simple device of inspecting mortality rates might have indicated a great deal about economic performance in these countries. In the absence of countervailing evidence, they would have suggested that long-term per capita growth was negligible, if indeed positive, between the mid-1960s and the late 1980s; that per capita output was closer to the Latin American than the Western European level at the time of Soviet Communism's collapse; and that levels of per capita consumption in the Soviet bloc might approximate those of Latin America as well. With the benefit of hindsight, and a largely unforeseen revolution, it may now be said that such a reading would not look too far off the mark.

III

Though Communist rule has collapsed in the Warsaw Pact region, it continues in other lands: China, Cuba, North Korea, and Vietnam among them. This partial collapse of a once-global political and economic system poses an obvious question: why did some Marxist-Leninist regimes shake and fall in 1989–91, whereas others managed to weather the storm? The question may seem most appropriate for the historian or the student of international affairs, but it can also be framed in demographic terms. For one may wonder: is it entirely a coincidence that the governments which vanished during this crisis of international Communism had all witnessed long-term health reversals among broad segments of the populations under their control, while all the governments that endured had supervised populations characterized by general and continuing mortality improvements?

The contrast in mortality trends of now-defunct and still surviving Communist governments could hardly be more vivid. Comparison of these trends, however, is not a straightforward proposition. Vital registration data, for the most part, are rather less comprehensive in these surviving states than they were within the Warsaw Pact. (Cuba is the exception to this generalization, although even there questions remain as to the quality of its infant mortality data (Hill 1983). For China, North Korea, and Vietnam, demographic trends had to be reconstructed on the basis of census returns and/or incomplete registration system data; such reconstructions do not permit more exacting or specific analyses of mortality conditions (e.g. year-to-year changes in age-specific death rates). They do, however, provide reasonably reliable estimates of long-term changes in general mortality levels. In particular, it is possible to estimate changes in life expectancy at birth over the past generation for these three countries (see Table 8-5).

In all four countries, gains in life expectancy are quite substantial. Whereas life expectancy for males stagnated, or declined, in the Warsaw Pact countries between the 1960s and the 1980s, it is reported to have increased in Cuba by over eight years, and is estimated to have risen by nearly 14 years in North Korea. China and Vietnam appear to have enjoyed gains in life expectancy at birth of nearly a decade for both males and females over the course of that same generation. By any historical measure, progress in reducing mortality in all these countries over the past decades would arguably qualify as rapid.

Table 8-5. Officially Claimed or Independently Reconstructed Changes in Life Expectancy at Birth: Surviving Communist Regimes, c.1965–c.1989

Country and Year	Life Expectancy at Birth for Males (year)	Life Expectancy at Birth for Females (year)
Cuba		
1965	65.4	67.2
1983/84	72.7	76.1
– increment	+ 7.3	+ 8.9
China		
1965	56.6	57.9
1989	66.2	67.0
– increment	+ 9.6	+ 9.1
North Korea		
1965	51.0	57.1
1987	64.7	71.0
– increment	+ 13.7	+ 13.9
Vietnam		
1965	49.7	57.0
1989	62.0	65.9
–increment	+ 12.3	+ 8.9

Notes: Cuban data taken from official life tables. Estimates for China, North Korea, and Vietnam are reconstructions based on census and/or registration data.
Sources: Cuba: United Nations, *Levels and Trends in Mortality Since 1950* (New York: UN Department of International Economic Aid and Social Affairs, 1982), p. 174; *Demographic Yearbook 1990* (New York: UN Department of International Economic and Social Affairs, 1992), p. 490. China and Vietnam: unpublished estimates, U.S. Bureau of the Census, Center for International Research. North Korea: Nicholas Eberstadt and Judith Banister, *The Population of North Korea* (Berkeley, CA: University of California, Institute of East Asian Studies, 1992), pp. 108-9.

This is not to say that health progress in the surviving Communist states has been steady and consistent. China's "Great Leap Forward" (1957–58) brought on a demographic catastrophe, in which tens of millions perished and life expectancy plummeted. More recently, Beijing's anti-natal population policies have been associated with infanticide, and rising mortality, for baby girls; by some estimates these increases were for a while sufficiently conse-quential to reduce life expectancy at birth for females (Bannister 1987). Such reversals, however, were tied to specific political campaigns. With the relaxation or reversal of the afflicting policy, mortality reductions in both cases resumed their downward trend under the same standing government.

Is there a political significance to this broad distinction in mortality trends within the former Communist world? I believe there may well be, and that the distinction may be useful to understanding the very different fates of these two sets of regimes.

Let me be clear. I do not propose to replace the Marxist notion of historical materialism with determinism of a demographic variety, or to deny the significance of individual actions and discrete decisions within the great play of history. The collapse of Soviet bloc Communism can be traced through a progression of specific events that was in no sense "historically inevitable": the accession of Mikhail Gorbachev; Moscow's decision to abide by the results of Poland's 1989 elections; Budapest's announcement later that year that it would permit East German "vacationers" to use Hungary as a transit stop on the way to West Germany; the failed coup in Moscow in August 1991. I wish instead to underscore the fact that, in our era at least, long-term rises in mortality are fraught with an unavoidable political significance. Whatever else they may portend, secular increases in mortality may today be read as an indicator of fragility for a regime, or an entire system.

The systemic political significance of the Warsaw Pact region's long-term health trends may be better appreciated by comparing their circumstances with the experiences of the Latin American and Caribbean region during the 1980s. For that area, after all, the 1980s were a decade of economic crisis and social reversals; of debt default and "structural adjustment." Whatever the inexactitudes of the calculations, the World Bank now estimates per capita output in the region as a whole to have been lower in real terms in 1990 than it had been in 1980; in countries such as Argentina, Panama, Peru, and Venezuela, corresponding estimates suggest that per capita GNP was over 15 percent lower at the end of the decade than at its start (World Bank 1992). Local austerity measures typically targeted public consumption—the "social safety net"—and most countries in the region could point to cutbacks in public expenditures on income support, education, and health. (Even before these cutbacks, Latin America's "social safety nets" were not considered famously sturdy.)

Despite these various shocks and setbacks, there is to date not evidence of pervasive increases in mortality in the Latin American and Caribbean region.

To be sure: the vital registration systems in many of these countries—including some of the ones apparently hardest hit—were poorly developed, and would not have been capable of providing an immediate representation of mortality reversals. Nevertheless, demographers who have examined mortality trends in the region since the advent of "structural adjustment" have concluded—sometimes to their own admitted surprise—that there is as yet no reason to believe that the direction or even the tempo of mortality change has been affected by this great depression.[15]

To judge by their mortality trends, the population of the Warsaw Pact region, in the generation leading up to the fall of their communist regimes, were suffering through a much more drastic crisis than the one that jolted Latin America in the 1980s. We may lack a compass adequate to the task of charting economic change in these communist societies; even so, we know that governments in other parts of the world and in other times have been able to forestall mortality reversal during severe economic downturns and dislocations. Why were these Warsaw Pact regimes not up to the challenge?

The very fact of secular mortality increase is evidence of a serious failure in health policy. But it is suggestive of much more. Mortality conditions are affected by a constellation of social, economic, and environmental factors. Education, housing conditions, and environmental quality are but a few of the areas bearing upon health in which virtually all modern governments routinely intervene. In centrally planned economies, where government arrogates a more far-reaching authority over the social and economic rhythms of life, the correspondence between mortality trends and government performance is presumably all the more comprehensive and direct. For the Warsaw Pact governments, the secular rises in mortality in the populations under their supervision may have been suggestive of an inability to cope—of uncorrectable policy, administrative incapacity, or even of the erosion of the governing power of the state.

In the event, those Marxist-Leninist regimes that outlasted Warsaw Pact Communism may (individually or collectively) be overturned in the near future, or instead may prove able to hold onto power for many more years. If they fall, moreover, their demise (individual or collective) may be preceded by secular mortality decline. After all, most coups and revolutions in our century have been preceded (and followed) by periods of general improvement in local public health conditions. Broad rises in mortality over long periods of time are neither a necessary nor sufficient condition for the collapse of a country's government, or its political system. Such rises, however, do signify the existence of extraordinary social, economic, and even political stresses. As such, they serve as markers denoting risk for the regime in question. Thus, while it was in no sense pre-ordained that the Warsaw Pact states would be the first of the Communist governments to collapse, neither should it be surprising that things happened to turn out this way.

IV

As post-Communist societies in Europe and the former Soviet Union contemplate the course before them, they know they will be traveling in unexplored terrain. What Janos Kornai (1990) has called "the road to economic freedom" is in fact a desired destination, not a route map. Open societies, inviolable civil liberties, established and liberal legal systems, and functioning market economies may be widely desired in the post-Communist region, but in general remain distant objectives. Traversing the no-man's land between Leninist order and a secure market order confronts would-be reformers with a monumental task. Addressing the issue of privatization, Jan Winiecki (1991) has written that the challenge is to "find a way . . . that is both economically efficient and politically acceptable"; the same may be said for the entire process of transition.

Students of politics and economics have been kept busy by the almost daily changes in these areas since the end of Communism. Political and economic plans or recommendations have proliferated; political and economic analyses of local and regional prospects are now something of a cottage industry. But in looking toward this uncertain future, the student of demography may have something to contribute, too. Once again, much of this contribution can draw from the examination of mortality trends.

In transitional economies, mortality trends can be seen as imposing a variety of constraints on the realm of the possible. Mortality levels and trends, for example, will have a direct bearing on the potential productivity of labor, thus on potential economic efficiency and growth. Mortality trends also bear directly upon a household's well being, albeit in a way that does not always show up in conventional income accounts. Dan Usher (1997) and Sherwin Rosen (1988), among others, have made the argument that consumers and individuals are likely to place considerable economic value on the improvement in their own life expectancy (and similar arguments could be extended to cover other aspects of their health status). Conversely, deterioration of health status or life expectancy represents a self-evident reduction in well being and living standards. While mortality decline may not be invested with political significance in the modern era, continued mortality rises, as we have seen, may betoken regime fragility. In transitional situations, one would interpret secular increases in mortality to presage reduced economic potential and administrative incapacity; one might further expect the phenomenon to generate populist pressures that could translate into the political realm.

With these considerations in mind, let us examine the initial indications about mortality trends in post-Communist territories.

Eastern Germany. In a way, Eastern Germany may constitute the best of all possible post-Communist worlds. Before its demise, the GDR was widely viewed as the most efficient and productive of the Communist economies. By virtue of their incorporation into the existing Federal Republic of Germany, moreover, the territories of Eastern Germany almost instantly secured established frameworks for civil and commercial law, and were subsumed into a stable and successful political economy. Eastern Germans, furthermore, have had their transition pains eased by subsidies of a magnitude unimaginable for any other post-Communist population: due to the favorable terms upon which monetary union was concluded, and the guarantees now available through the Federal Republic's welfare state, Eastern Germans have been receiving non-investment transfers amounting (even after PPP adjustments) to about $4,000 per person per year since the end of 1989.16 Finally, Eastern Germany enjoyed the best health conditions of any country in the Warsaw Pact; its infant mortality rate, in fact, compares quite favorably with that of the white American population.

Auspicious as such soundings may be, the contrast between health conditions in Eastern and Western Germany on the eve of unification was stark (see Table 8-6). By the measure of age-standardized mortality, Eastern Germany's male death rate was 22 percent higher than Western Germany's in 1989; for females the gap was 31 percent. By this measure,

Table 8-6. Mortality Differentials in Germany, 1989: Eastern German Death Rates as a Ratio of Western German Death Rates
(Western Germany = 100)

Age Group	Males	Females
0	105	97
1–4	98	112
5–14	131	103
15–24	115	122
25–34	126	126
35–44	135	109
45–54	130	123
55–64	123	132
65–74	122	140
75 +	120	126
Age standardized	122	131

Note: Age standardization refers to WHO "European Model" population.
Source: Derived from World Health Organization, *World Health Statistics Annual 1990* (Geneva: WHO, 1991), pp. 226, 228, 380.

Eastern Germany joined Western Europe with the distinction of being its least healthy member; age-standardized mortality rates in Ireland, heretofore the highest in the EC or EFTA, were 8 percent lower for males and 6 percent lower for females than were the GDR's in 1989 (WHO 1990). The mortality differences between East and West Germany in 1989, one may note, were greatest for the cohorts of working age—not exactly an ideal circumstance for equalizing productivity across this expanse.

Nor do preliminary figures for 1990 provide occasion for satisfaction (see Table 8-7). By these data, age-specific mortality rates would appear to have risen for most cohorts in East Germany between 1989 and 1990. These apparent rises were recorded despite the magnitude, and broad incidence, of hard currency transfers from the Federal Republic to Eastern Germany households, and despite the opportunity to avail of Western German health care. It is possible that some portion of this rise is a statistical artifact, attributable to improved coverage under the Federal Statistical Office, but the GDR's mortality data (if not its cause of death data) had been reasonably good.

Table 8-7. After "Die Wende": Reported Changes in Age-Specific Death Rates
Eastern Germany, 1989–1990 (percent)

	0	1/4	5/9	10/14	15/19	20/24	25/29	30/34	35/39	40/44
Male	− 2	+ 48	+ 11	+ 68	+ 44	+ 37	+ 26	+ 24	+ 24	+ 4
Female	+ 6	+ 23	+ 63	+118	+ 18	+ 12	+ 23	− 3	+ 17	− 2

	45/49	50/54	55/59	60/64	65/69	70/74	75/79	80/84	85/89	90+
Male	+ 36	+ 8	+ 3	0	+ 4	− 15	+ 16	+ 6	+ 2	+ 7
Female	+ 18	0	+ 1	+ 5	+ 2	− 18	+ 10	− 2	− 2	+ 2

Note: Changes rounded to the nearest percentage point.
Sources: Statistches Bundesamt, *Statistiches Jahrbach* 1991 *Fuer Das Vereinte Deutschland* (Wiesbaden: Metzler Poeschel Verlag, 1991), p. 87; unpublished data, Statistiches Bundesamt.

The apparent broad rise in mortality in Eastern Germany, one must note, would actually mark a reversal of trend for the area. Between 1985 and 1989, age-standardized male mortality had declined by about 6 percent for males and about 8 percent for females.

Eastern Europe. 1990 was the first year of the political and economic transition from Communism in Bulgaria, Czechoslovakia, Hungary, and Poland. The details of their reform programs differed, as do the estimates of their respective performance. It is generally agreed that the economies of all these countries contracted dramatically during their first year of post-Communist rule, although the significance of their output declines is an issue of debate among observers.

Less open to debate are their recorded mortality trends (see Table 8-8). According to these figures, age-standardized mortality for males rose in all four of these countries, and overall age-standardized mortality rose in three of them. Age-standardized mortality for females rose in one of them as well: Hungary. However one interprets these numbers, it cannot be reassuring that "adjustment" and "restructuring," in contrast with the Latin American experience, seem here to be coinciding with at least an initial increase in death rates for broad population groups. One may further

Table 8-8. "After the Revolution": Age-Standardized Mortality in Eastern Europe, 1989–1990
Deaths per 100,000 population

Year Country and Sex	1989	1990	% change
Bulgaria			
Males	1396.6	1397.3	+ 0.1
Females	917.8	913.5	− 0.5
Czechoslovakia			
Males	1522.8	1552.1	+ 1.9
Females	888.4	874.1	− 1.6
Hungary			
Males	1624.9	1670.6	+ 2.9
Females	933.4	955.0	+ 2.3
Poland			
Males	1498.0	1670.6	+ 1.2
Females	838.5	833.0	− 0.7

Note: Age-standardization is for WHO "European Model" population.
Sources: World Health Organization, *World Health Statistics Annual* (Geneva: WHO), 1990 edition, table 10; 1991 edition, table 11.

ponder on the coincidence that Hungary, the country of the four with the worst recorded deterioration in mortality conditions between 1989 and 1990, is also widely viewed by international investors as the country in Eastern Europe most receptive to foreign capital, and moving fastest in the transition to a market economy.

These initial upticks, of course, may in the event be followed by sustained and rapid mortality declines. At the very least, however, it is apparent that the "environment" of policy and social or economic conditions that would bring mortality rates down is not yet in place; liberation from Communist rule in and of itself, evidently, is not a sufficient condition. Moreover, even if a rapid and sustained mortality decline could immediately be arranged for these post-Communist regions, they would not reach the levels characteristic of Western Europe today for many years. If one posited a rate of decline of 2 percent a year (an exceptionally rapid rate, equivalent to that which Chile has enjoyed over the past generation), overall age-standardized mortality rates in East Germany would not match today's Western German rates for another twelve years; Hungary would not reach today's Austrian level for twenty-three years; and Ukraine would not reach today's Swiss level for twenty-four years. For obvious reasons, actual convergence might be expected to take much longer.

Reflection upon mortality conditions, in sum, emphasizes the enormity of the challenges, and potential tribulations, that lie in store for post-Communist populations. Marxist-Leninist rule may or may not ultimately be viewed as an enormous historical detour. Those acquainted with mortality statistics for the post-Communist regions, however, will appreciate that repair of the damage experienced under Communism's tenure, and attainment of Western European levels of performance, should probably be viewed as an historical process: one that may take decades, or even generations to complete.

References

Amann, Ronald, and Julian Cooper, eds. *Industrial Innovation in the Soviet Union*. New Haven: Yale University Press, 1982.

Amann, Ronald, Julian Cooper, and R. W. Davies, eds. *The Technological Level of Soviet Industry*. New Haven: Yale University Press, 1982.

Anderson, Barbara A., and Brian D. Silver, "Trends in Mortality in the Soviet Population," *Soviet Economy*, 6 (1990):2, pp. 191–252.

Banister, Judith. *China's Changing Population*. Stanford, CA: Stanford University Press, 1987.

Bergson, Abram. *The Real National Income of Soviet Russia Since 1928*. Cambridge, MA: Harvard University Press, 1928.

idem. "Comparative Productivity: The USSR, Eastern Europe, and the West," *American Economic Review*, 77 (1987):3, pp. 342–57.

Bergson, Abram, and Hans Heymann, Jr. Soviet National Income and Product 1949-48. New York: Columbia University Press, 1954.

Brada, Joseph C. "Allocative Efficiency and the System of Economic Management in Some Socialist Countries," *Kyklos* 27 (1974):2, pp. 270–85.

Collier, Irwin L. "The Estimation of Gross Domestic Product and its Growth

Rate for the German Democratic Republic," World Bank Staff Working Papers, no. 773 (1985).

Davis, Joseph S. "Standards and Content of Living," *American Economic Review* 35 (1945):1, pp. 1–15.

Desai, Padma, and Ricardo Martin. "Efficiency Loss from Resources Allocation in Soviet Industry," *Quarterly Journal of Economics*, 98 (1983):3, pp. 441–56.

Dutton, John, Jr. "Changes in Soviet Mortality Patterns, 1959–77." *Population and Development Review*, 5 (1979):2, pp. 267–291.

Eberstadt, Nicholas. "Health and Mortality in Eastern Europe 1965–85." *Communist Economies*, 2 (1990):3, pp. 347–371.

Eberstadt, Nicholas, and Judith Banister. *The Population of North Korea*. Berkeley, CA: University of California, Institute of East Asian Studies, 1992.

Gates, Robert M. "CIA and the Collapse of the Soviet Union: Hit or Miss?" speech delivered to the Foreign Policy Association, New York, May 20, 1992.

German Federal Statistical Office (Statistiches Bundesamt). Statistiches Jahrbuch. Wiesbaden: Metzler Poeschel Verlag, 1991 and 1992 editions.

idem. Zur wirtschaftlichen und sozialen Lage in der neuen Bundeslaendern. Special edition, April 1993.

Gomolka, Stanislaw. "The Incompatibility of Socialism and Rapid Innovation," *Millenium*, 13 (1984):1, pp. 16–26.

von Hayek, Friedrich, ed. Collectivist Economic Planning. London: George Routledge and Sons, 1936.

Hill, Kenneth. "An Evaluation of Cuban Demographic Statistics, 1938–80." In Paula E. Hollerbach and Sergio Diaz-Briquets, Fertility Determinants in Cuba. Washington, DC: National Academy Press, 1983.

Hill, Kenneth, and Anne R. Pebley. "Child Mortality in the Developing World." *Population and Development Review*, 15 (1989):4, pp. 657–687.

International Labor Office. *Yearbook of Labor Statistics 1989/90*. Geneva: ILO, 1991.

Kornai, Janos. *The Road to Economic Freedom: Shifting from a Socialist System, The Example of Hungary*. New York: W.W. Norton, 1990.

idem. *The Socialist System*. Princeton: Princeton University Press, 1992.

Labedz, Leopold. "Small Change in Big Brother." *Survey* 120 (1984), p. 3.

Lipset, Seymour Martin and Gyorgy Bence. "Anticipation of the Failure of

Communism," Theory and Society (forthcoming).

von Mises, Ludwig. Socialism. London: Jonathan Cape, 1935.

Murray, Christopher J.L. and Lincoln Chen. "Understanding Morbidity Change." Population and Development Review 18 (1992):3, pp. 481–503.

Pohl, Reinhard, ed. Handbook of the Economy of the German Democratic Republic. Guildford, Surrey: Saxon House, 1979.

Powell, Raymond P. "The Soviet Capital Stock from Census to Census," Soviet Studies 31 (1979):1, pp. 56–75.

Revelle, Roger. "Introduction to the Issue 'Historical Population Studies.'" Daedelus, 97(1968):2, pp. 352–362.

Riley, James C. "The Risk of Being Sick: Morbidity Trends in Four Countries." Population and Development Review, 16 (1990):3, pp. 403–432.

Rosen, Sherwin. "The Value of Changes in Life Expectancy." Journal of Risk and Uncertainty 1 (1988):3, pp. 285–304.

Siebert, Horst. Das Wagnis der Einheit Eine Wirtschftspolische Therapie. Stuttgart: Deutsche Verlags-Anstalt, 1992.

Sinn, Gerlinde and Hans Werner Sinn. Kaltstart: Volkswirtschaftliche Aspekte der deutschen Vereinigung. Tuebingen: J.C.B.Mohr, 1991.

Smil, Vaclav. "Coronary Heart Disease, Diet, and Western Mortality." Population and Development Review, 15 (1989):3, pp. 399–424.

United Nations. Demographic Yearbook. New York: UN Department of International Economic and Social Affairs, various issues.

——. Levels and Trends in Mortality Since 1950. New York: UN Department of International Economic and Social Affairs, 1982.

——. World Population Prospects 1990. New York: United Nations Department of International Economic and Social Affairs, 1991.

——. World Population Prospects: The 1992 Revisions. New York: Department of Economic and Social Development, forthcoming.

United States Central Intelligence Agency. Handbook of Economic Statistics. Washington, DC: GPO, 1980, 1988, 1990 editions.

——. World Factbook 1987. Washington, DC: GPO, 1987.

Usher, Dan. "An Imputation to the Measure of Economic Growth for Changes in Life Expectancy." In Milton Moss, ed., The Measurement of Social and Economic Performance (Cambridge, MA: National Bureau of Economic Research, 1977), pp. 192–226.

USSR State Statistical Committee (Goskomstat). Tablitsy Smertnosti i

Ozhidaemoy Prodalzhitel'nosti Zhizni Naseleniya (Moscow: Goskom-stat, 1989).

Winiecki, Jan. "Are Soviet-type Economies Entering into an Era of Long-Term Decline?" *Soviet Studies*, 38 (1986):3, pp. 325-348.

———. "Transition and the Privatization Problem." *Cato Journal*, 11 (1991):2, pp. 299–309.

World Bank. *World Development Report 1992*. New York: Oxford University Press, 1992.

World Health Organization. *World Health Statistics Annual*. Geneva: WHO, 1988, 1990, 1991 editions.

Notes

1. This was not the first time big events had gone unanticipated. Leopold Labedz, longtime editor of the former *Survey of Soviet Studies*, has written that the only Western journal to predict Khrushchev's ouster in 1964 was *Old Moore's Almanac*—an astrological guide. See his "Small Change for Big Brother," Survey, (1984):120, p. 3. For a systematic assessment of the performance of the social sciences in this field, see Seymour Martin Lipset and Gyorgy Bence, "Anticipation of the Failure of Communism," *Theory and Society*, Vol. 23,(1994).

2. The German Federal Statistical Office, for example, estimates per capita GDP in the second half of 1990 in the "new Federal States" to have been at 30.6 percent of the the Western level. *Statistisches Bundesamt, Zur wirtschaftlichen und sozialen Lage in der neuen Bundeslaendern*, Special Edition, April 1993, p. *127.

That precise figure, however, should not necessarily be retrofitted to the Communist period. The collapse of Communism was attended by a massive reallocation of factors of production—and also by a drop in their utilization. But inexactitudes notwithstanding, it is clear now that per capita production was far lower in East than in West Germany in the last days of Ostpolitik.

3. Figures are drawn from various issues of the aforementioned *UN Demographic Yearbook*.

4. For one recent view of this controversy, see Barbara A. Anderson and Brian D. Silver, "Trends in Mortality in the Soviet Population," *Soviet Economy*, 6(1990):2, pp. 191–252.

5. For a more detailed assessment, see Nicholas Eberstadt, "Health and Mortality in Eastern Europe, 1965–85," *Communist Economies*, 2(1990):3, pp. 347–371.

6. For one recent interpretation of the phenomenon and its correlates, see Vaclav Smil, "Coronary Heart Disease, Diet, and Western Mortality," *Population and Development Review*, 15(1989):3, pp. 399–424.

7. See, for example, Abram Bergson and Hans Heymann, Jr., *Soviet National Income and Product 1940–48* (New York: Columbia University Press, 1954). The fullest exposition

of the approach is Bergson's classic study, *The Real National Income of Soviet Russia Since 1928* (Cambridge, MA: Harvard University Press, 1928).

8. For a classic exposition on the distinction between living standards and consumption levels, see Joseph S. Davis, "Standards and Content of Living," *American Economic Review* 35(1945):1, pp. 1–15.

9. The distinction between health trends and mortality trends is not to be minimized. See, for example, James C. Riley, "The Risk of Being Sick: Morbidity Trends in Four Countries," *Population and Development Review*, 16(1990):3, pp. 403–432, and Christopher J.L. Murray and Lincoln Chen, "Understanding Morbidity Change," *Population and Development Review* 18(1992):3, pp. 481–503. For better or worse, however, mortality data are generally more available and more reliable today than are morbidity data.

10. The discussion below is premised on the assumption that the economists under consideration operate with production functions in which output is a function of capital and labour inputs—both adjusted for quality of the stocks included—and of technical and allocative efficiency, where these are exogenous parmeters. Economies of scale do not figure explicitly in the model outlined above. The discussion assumes that mortality levels do not correlate negatively with other components of "human capital stock," and that there is no correlation between mortality levels and economies of scale.

11. Conventionally, of course, one measures hours of total employment against the economically active population, not the total population. The alternate denominator is used here because we are comparing output per capita for the population as a whole, not per worker.

12. The theoretical grounds for expecting socialist economies to have systemic problems with allocative efficiency were laid out in Ludwig von Mises, Socialism (London: Jonathan Cape, 1935), and F. A. von Hayek, ed., *Collectivist Economic Planning* (London: George Routledge and Sons, 1936). Empirical studies of the problem as it actually exists are numerous, but one might point in particular to Josef C. Brada, "Allocative Efficiency and the System of Economic Management in Some Socialist Countries," Kyklos 27(1971):2, pp. 270–85; and Padma Desai and Ricardo Martin, "Efficiency Loss from Resource Misallocation in Soviet Industry," *Quarterly Journal of Economics*, 98(1983):3, pp. 441–56. See also Abram Bergson, "Comparative Productivity: The USSR, Eastern Europe, and the West," *American Economic Review*, 77(1987):3, pp. 342–57, where a measure of the efficiency loss attendant upon Soviet-style socialism is computed (although this loss relates to both technical and allocative efficiency).

13. The literature documenting technological lag in Soviet bloc industry is extensive, but noteworthy studies include Ronald Amann, Julian Cooper and R. W. Davies, eds., *The Technological Level of Soviet Industry* (New Haven: Yale University Press, 1977); Ronald Amann and Julian Cooper, eds. Industrial Innovation in the Soviet Union (New Haven: Yale University Press, 1982), and Stanislaw Gomolka, "The Incompatability of Socialism and Rapid Innovation," *Millenium*, 13(1984):1, pp. 16–26. In the words of Janos Kornai, "To sum up, low efficiency and technological backwardness and conservatism can be attributed to the combined effects of a set of system-specific factors." Janos Kornai, *The Socialist System* (Princeton: Princeton University Press, 1992), p. 301.

As to general issues relating to Soviet capital stock, see Raymond P. Powell, "The Soviet Capital Stock from Census to Census," *Soviet Studies* 31(1979):1, pp. 56–75. For 1975,

Bergson estimated the USSR's per capita Gross Reproducible Capital Stock (GRCS) to be 73 percent of the U.S. level; by his estimates per capita GRCS in a sample of four socialist countries averaged 71 percent of the level in a sample of seven Western mixed-economy countries, and averaged 77 percent of the Western European level in the socialist economies analyzed. See Bergson, "Comparative Productivity," p. 347.

In East Germany as of 1975, the estimated nominal value of the stock of capital assets was roughly 17 percent of West Germany's—with the former measured in Marks and the latter in Deutschemarks. On a per capita basis, East Germany's estimated stock of capital assets, on a nominal basis, would have been roughly 63 percent of the West German level; insofar as the price ratio with respect to investment in 1975 was believed to be about 1.16 DM/M, this would have suggested East Germany's capital stock per capita was roughly 73 percent as great as West Germany's in 1975. See Reinhard Pohl, ed., *Handbook of the Economy of the German Democratic Republic* (Guildford, Surrey: Saxon House, 1979), pp. 31–3, and Irwin L. Collier, "The Estimation of Gross Domestic Product and its Growth Rate for the German Democratic Republic," World Bank Staff Working Papers, no. 773 (1985), p. 27.

14. Note that we are comparing two rather different systems for measuring labor force participation; while the results cannot be presumed totally comparable, they are nonetheless illustrative.

15. For one such assessment, see Kenneth Hill and Anne R. Pebley, "Child Mortality in the Developing World," *Population and Development Review*, 15(1989):4, pp. 657–687.

16. This is not to say that German policies pertaining to the economics of unification did not leave room for improvement. A sustained examination and economic critique of those policies may be found, for example, in Gerlinde and Hans Werner Sinn, Kaltstart: Volkswirtschaftliche Aspekte der deutschen Vereinigung (Tuebingen: J.C.B.Mohr, 1991), and Horst Siebert, Das Wagnis der Einheit: Eine Wirtschaftspolitische Therapie (Stuttgart: Deutsche Verlags-Anstalt, 1992).

9

Growing Old the Hard Way:
China, Russia, India

Policy Review, May 2006

O ver the past decade and a half, the phenomenon of population aging in the "traditional" or already affluent OECD societies has become a topic of sustained policy analysis and concern.[1] The reasons for this growing attention—and apprehension—are clear enough.

By such metrics as median age or proportion of total population above the age of 65, virtually every developed society today is more elderly than practically any human society ever surveyed before the year 1950—and every single currently developed society is slated to experience considerable further population aging in the decades immediately ahead. In all of the affluent OECD societies, the proportion of what is customarily called the "retirement age population" (65 years of age or older) will steadily swell, with the most rapid expansion occurring among those aged 80 or more. Simultaneously, the ratio of people of "working age" (the cohort, by arbitrary though not entirely unreasonable custom, designated at 15–64 years) to those of retirement age will relentlessly shrink—and within the working age grouping, more youthful adults will account for a steadily dwindling share of overall manpower.

Whether these impending revolutionary transformations of national population structure actually constitute a crisis for the economies and societies in the industrialized world is—let us emphasize—still a matter of dispute. To be sure: This literal upending of the familiar population pyramid (characteristic of all humanity until just yesterday) will surely have direct consequences for economic institutions and structures in the world's more affluent societies—and could have major reverberations on their macroeconomic performance. Left unaddressed, the mounting pressures that population aging would pose on pension outlays, health care expenditures, fiscal discipline, savings levels, manpower availability, and workforce attainment could only have adverse domestic implications for productivity and economic growth in today's affluent OECD societies (to say nothing of their impact on the global outlook for innovation, entrepreneurship, and competitiveness).

But a host of possible policy interventions and orderly changes in existing institutional arrangements offer the now-rich countries the possibility (to borrow a phrase from the OECD) of "maintaining prosperity in an aging society"—and in fact of steadily enhancing prosperity for graying populations. Today's rich countries may succeed in meeting the coming challenges (and grasping the potential opportunities) inherent in population aging—or then again, they may fail to do so. The point is that an aging crisis is theirs to avert—and they have considerable scope for so doing.

In contrast to the intense interest currently accorded the issue of population aging in developed countries, the topic of aging in low-income regions has as yet attracted relatively little examination. This neglect is somewhat surprising, for over the coming decades a parallel, dramatic "graying" of much of the Third World also lies in store. The burdens of pronounced population aging, furthermore, are unlikely to be born as easily by countries still poor as by countries already rich. Simply stated, societies and governments have fewer options for dealing with the problems imposed by population aging when income levels are low—and the options available are distinctly less attractive than they would be if income levels were higher.

Over the next generation, it seems entirely likely—indeed, all but inevitable—that a large fraction of humanity, peopling countries within the grouping often termed emerging market economies, will find themselves coping with the phenomenon of population aging on income levels far lower than those yet witnessed in any society with comparable degrees of graying. For such countries, the social and economic consequences of aging could be harsh—and the options for mitigating the adverse effects of population aging may be fairly limited. In some of these countries, population aging could potentially emerge as a factor appreciably constraining long-term growth and development.

As we will detail in the next few pages, rapid and pronounced population aging represents a highly uneven, largely unappreciated, and as yet almost entirely undiscounted long-term risk for the world's emerging markets.

Dynamics and Dimensions

Venturing predictions about the world outlook 20 years hence is a hazardous enterprise. Nevertheless, we can state quite confidently that a tremendous wave of population aging is virtually certain to sweep through the developing regions between now and 2025. How can we talk so boldly—and so categorically—about events that have not yet unfolded? Over the course of two decades, a country's economic or political circumstances can change tremendously. By contrast, given the stubborn realities of population change—demographic evolution tends to be gradual, contingent on previous developments, and tightly bound by existing social tendencies—there is inherently less leeway among plausible alternative demographic scenarios 20 years hence.

Barring a cataclysm of Biblical proportions, about five-sixths of the roughly 5.3 billion people alive in the less developed regions of the world today are likely still to be around in 2025—and something like two-thirds of the approximately 6.7 billion population projected for those areas as of 2025 will comprise people alive now, already inhabiting those regions today.[2]

Between 2005 and 2025, current projections anticipate the population of the less developed regions to increase by about one-fourth. The most rapidly growing cohort within that population, however, will be the 65-plus group: Once again barring only catastrophe, the Third World's senior citizens will roughly double in numbers over those years, to about 570 million person, or about 8.5 percent of the total for 2025.

While the less developed regions in 2025 would meet the United Nations' definition of an "aging population" (i.e., with persons 65 and older accounting for over 7 percent of total population), their overall population profile would nevertheless be roughly as youthful as that of Europe from the late 1950s or Japan in the mid-1970s. But the extent and tempo of population aging will vary tremendously within the less developed regions: Some territories are slated to experience practically no population aging at all over the coming two decades, while others will become positively aged.

The demography of aging explains this differentiation. As a purely arithmetic matter (and perhaps somewhat counterintuitively), the scope and scale of population aging in any regularly convened human society is determined primarily by changes in its fertility levels, not by changes in mortality.[3] It is low birth rates, rather than long life expectancies, that drive population aging—and in much of the Third World, fertility levels are already very low. Today, in fact, the majority of humanity probably already lives in countries with "sub-replacement fertility" regimes (that is to say, childbearing patterns which, if continued, would result in indefinite population decline, absent immigration).[4]

Since the world's more developed regions account for less than a fifth (19 percent) of the current global population, this means that the great majority of the planet's sub-replacement populations today are found in low-income regions. And since fertility levels in low-income areas continue to drop—even in spots where sub-replacement is already the norm—the momentum for rapid population aging continues to build.

Not in sub-Saharan Africa, to be sure: There, median age is likely to remain just barely over 20 years some two decades from now. And certainly not in those parts of the Arab/Islamic expanse where total fertility rate levels still apparently exceed five births per woman per lifetime (for example, Yemen, Oman, Afghanistan). But in much of East Asia, South Asia, the Middle East, Eastern Europe,[5] and Latin America, sub-replacement fertility is now the norm: which is to say that the areas of the developing world presently set on a trajectory for rapid population aging are precisely the areas that encompass today's most promising emerging market economies.

Emerging Markets

To place the low-income regions' population aging phenomenon in international economic perspective, we can begin by comparing the current correspondences between graying and income levels in today's major emerging market economies with the old-age-to-income trajectories charted out by the major Western economies over the course of their postwar development (see Figure 9-1). As may be seen, the picture for the "emerging markets" is highly varied. On the one hand, some developing economies appear to be much more "youthful" today than Western Europe, the United States, or Japan at comparable levels of per capita income: Proportionately, for example, Turkey, Brazil and Mexico presently support barely half as many senior citizens as Western Europe did at those levels of per capita output. (The proximate explanation for this contradistinction is that Brazil, Mexico and Turkey all

Figure 9-1. Percentage of the Population Aged 65+ vs. GDP per Capita: Developing Countries 1950–2000 vs. Emerging Economies 2000

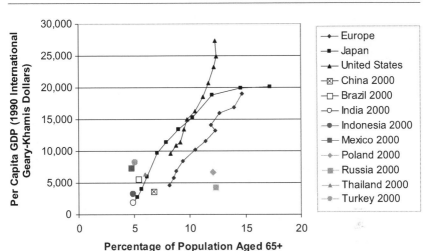

Note: GDP per capita in 1990 Intenational Geary-Kamis Dollars. Europe data for 12 countries: Austria, Belgium, Denmark, Finland, France, Germany, Greece, Italy, Netherlands, Norway, Sweden, Switzerland, U.K.

Sources: Population Division of the Department of Economic and Social Affairs of the United Nations Secretariat, World Population Prospects: The 2004 Revision and World Urbanization Prospects: The 2003 Revision, http://esa.un.org/unpp (April 19, 2005); Angus Maddison, The World Economy: A Millenial Perspective (Development Centre Studies, Organization for Economic Cooperation and Development: Paris 2001), 276, 304, 337, 144, 101, 184, and 194.

had much higher birth rates than the Western countries when approaching the $5,000 GDP per capita threshold.)

Some other emerging market economies appear to be at age–income coordinates almost identical to those traced by Western countries during their economic ascent: India and Thailand, for example, are each separately at points earlier delineated by Japan on its postwar aging/growth path.

But some other emerging market economies already have distinctly higher old age burdens than Western countries bore at similar stages of development. As of the year 2000, China's 65+ cohort accounted for about the same share of population as Japan's in 1970—but per capita output was three times higher for Japan in 1970 than for China in 2000. By the same token, at the point when Western Europe and the United States had the same ratios

Table 9-1. Population Aging in Developed Economies Today vs. Emerging Market Economies Tomorrow

Country/Region	Median Age, yrs (2003)	Percentage of Population 65+ (2003)	GDP per Capita PPP, USD (2003)	GDP per Capita Exchange Rate, USD (2003)
USA	35.8	12.4	37,562	37,648
Japan	42.0	18.5	27,967	33,713
EU-15	39.5	16.9	26,640	26,710*

Country/Region	Median Age, yrs (2025)	Percentage of Population 65+ (2025)	GDP per Capita, PPP 2003	GDP per Capita 2003
Poland	44.2	21.6	11,379	5,280
Russia	43.4	19.8	9,230	2,120
Mexico	32.1	9.8	9,168	6,230
Brazil	36.1	11.0	7,790	2,670
Thailand	39.7	14.6	7,595	2,190
Turkey	36.4	10.8	6,772	2,800
China	39.1	13.7	5,003	1,100
Indonesia	32.8	9.2	3,361	810
India	30.8	7.8	2,892	540

*European Monetary Union only.
Sources: Global Competitiveness Report 2004/2005, Annex Tables 1.01-1.03; World Development Indicators 2004; U.S. Census Bureau International Database.

of elderly to total population as registered by Russia in 2000, their per capita income levels were, respectively, three and six times higher than Russia's.

Turning from the relatively recent past to the immediate future, Table 9-1 indicates the prospective dimensions of the coming wave of population aging for nine of the largest emerging market economies.

By UN criteria, all nine will count as aging societies by 2025—but not surprisingly, the degree of population aging differs greatly from one country to the next. India, Indonesia, and Mexico, for example, will still likely have more youthful age profiles in 2025 than the United States of 2003. By 2025, on the other hand, Turkey and Brazil will be roughly as gray as the United

States today, but not yet so gray as contemporary Japan or today's Western Europe. By 2025, China and Thailand will likely have population profiles almost as elderly as today's EU–15. Russia and Poland, for their parts, will likely have populations more aged in 2025 than Japan's today: That is to say, they will be grayer than any population yet seen in human history.

Although most of these emerging market economies will have age profiles similar to—or in some cases, even more extreme than—today's developed economies, their income levels are far lower than those of the affluent OECD societies today—and in almost every case will almost certainly remain below today's OECD levels two decades from now.

Over a 22-year interim (i.e., 2003 to 2025), Poland could reach today's EU–15 Purchasing Power Parity (PPP)-adjusted per capita output levels if it grew at a steady 4 percent per capita per annum—an ambitious though hardly impossible hope. To hit current Japanese PPP-adjusted income levels, however, per capita Russian growth would have to be maintained at 5 percent a year for nearly a quarter-century. Attaining current EU PPP-adjusted income levels by 2025 would require annualized per capita growth rates of 8 percent for China and over 10 percent for India. One need not be a Russo-pessimist, a Sino-pessimist, or an Indo-pessimist to suggest such tempos may be out of reach.[6]

A closer examination of the Chinese, Russian, and Indian aging problems can lay out the constraints over the coming decades for each of these economies in greater detail.

China: A Tightening "Triple Bind"

China's impending aging wave is illustrated by Figure 9-2, which compares the country's actual population structure in 2000 with its projected profile for 2025. China has evidently experienced subreplacement fertility levels since the early 1990s.[7] Consequently, as may be seen from these projections, every age group under 35 years of age is anticipated to be smaller in China in 2025 than it was in 2000—while all of the older groups are expected to be larger. China's coercive population control program may have succeeded in limiting numbers for the country's rising contingents of young people, but its elderly population will be exploding in the years ahead—waxing at

Figure 9-2. Estimated and Projected Population Structure of China: 2000 vs. 2025

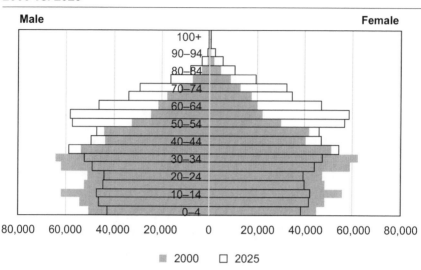

Source: United Nations Population Division, World Population Prospects 2004 Revision. Available online at http://esa.un.org/unpp/index.asp?panel=2.

an annual pace of something like 3.5 percent per year. Between 2005 and 2025, about two-thirds of China's aggregate population growth will occur in the 65+ grouping—and that cohort will likely double in size, to roughly 200 million people. By 2025, under current UN and Census Bureau projections, China would account for less than a fifth of the world's population but almost a fourth of the world's senior citizens.

China, of course, is a vast land with plenty of regional variation: As regards aging and economic development, the country's provinces are characterized both by notable differences in provincial demographic profiles and truly tremendous disparities in levels of per capita output. (In 2001, local per capita GDP was reportedly 13 times as high in bustling Shanghai as in isolated Guizhou.) While there is a broad overall correlation between graying and income levels in China's provinces today, the correspondence is not a tight one—and over the next two decades, some of China's most dramatic aging trends are set to unfold in some of the areas that are poorest today.

We can see this when we compare the U.S. Census Bureau projections of Chinese provincial age structures for 2025 with official Chinese data on per capita levels of GDP by province as of 2001. Currently (2005), Japan reports the world's highest proportion of persons 65 and older, at about 19.5 percent of total population. By 2025, however, the 65-plus cohort is projected to account for 21 percent of total population in one part of China—and that place is not relatively prosperous Beijing or booming Shanghai. Rather, it is Heilongjiang, in China's Manchurian rustbelt—where per capita provincial output (at current exchange rates) was just over $1,100 in 2001.

Currently, Japan also reports the world's highest median age, at about 42.5 years. Yet as of 2025, nine of China's 31 provinces and major municipalities are projected to have higher median ages than contemporary Japan: among them, Liaoning (where the exchange-rate-based GDP per capita was around $1,450 in 2001); Jilin (around $925); and Chongqing (under $690). (Heilongjiang's projected median age in 2025, we might note, would be over 51 years.) No purchasing-power-parity adjustments of these exchange-rate-based figures can alter the basic message they impart: In just 20 years, large parts of China will have to support very aged populations on very low average income levels.

How will China's elderly population be sustained financially two decades hence? All uncertainties about the future notwithstanding, we can fairly confidently surmise that these prospective pensioners will not be supported through the country's existing state pension arrangements. For all the justifiable anxiety about the current actuarial health of national pension systems in various OECD countries, the financial disarray of China's official pension apparatus is in a league of its own. For this patchwork, covering perhaps a sixth of the total Chinese workforce, the net present value of unfunded liabilities is estimated to exceed current GDP—perhaps substantially. China's pension system is clearly unsustainable—but despite the better part of a decade of high-level policy deliberations in Beijing on the national pension problem (the issue has been addressed by directives from the highest levels of government since 1997), no alternative formula has been officially offered.[8] Nor is promulgation of legislation for a new and unified social security system obviously on the policy horizon for China today.[9]

Thus China's national pension system as of 2025 promises today to be more or less the same system that has always provided for the country's elderly and infirm: namely, the family unit. But herein lies a problem: The "success" of the Chinese government's continuing antinatal population drive will necessarily translate in coming decades into a plummeting ratio of working-age children to elderly parents. Whereas the average Chinese woman who celebrated her sixtieth birthday in the early 1990s had borne five children during her lifetime, her counterpart in 2025 will have had fewer than two.

No less important: Over the next 20 years, China's rising cohorts of prospective retirees face a growing "son deficit." In Chinese cultural tradition, it is sons, rather than daughters, upon whom first duty for support of aged parents customarily falls (a daughter is obliged to care for her husband's parents as well as her own). In the early 1990s, about 7 percent of China's 60-year-old women had never borne a son. Today that proportion is about 10 percent. By 2025, the figure will shoot up to roughly 30 percent. Some of the male children in question, furthermore, will not live to adulthood to be able to help support their parents. Taking both fertility and survival trends thus into account, it seems likely that a third or more of Chinese women approaching retirement age two decades from now will have no living sons. For tens of millions of aged Chinese just 20 years from now, seeking financial and material help from one's children will amount to competing for resources with one's son-in-law's parents (given the presumed continuation of China's long-standing cultural norm of near-universal marriage for women). Suffice it to say that such a "niche" is not promising from the perspective of social ecology.

With official government pension guarantees a distinctly more limited and problematic set of options than official policy might wish, and with the traditional social security system known as "the Chinese family" a rather more fragile construct than at any time in the recent past, the grim reality may be that a great many elderly Chinese men and women in the coming decades will have to come to the conclusion that they must sustain themselves by continuing to work. Paradoxically, despite China's tremendous material progress over the half-century beginning in 1975, the nation's elderly will face a continuing need—quite possibly a growing need—to support themselves in old age through their own labor.

But China's elderly population is not ideally placed as competitors in their country's labor markets—either today or tomorrow. And here we enter into the second constraint of China's tightening "triple bind." China's elderly workers occupy a decidedly unfavorable position in the country's labor force today. At the start of the new century, in comparison with China's overall workforce, workers 65 or older are six times as likely to be illiterate or semi-literate, almost 50 percent more likely to have only primary education, and only a tenth as likely to have a high school or college diploma. They are also much more likely to toil in the agricultural sector: In 2000, 87 percent of China's elderly workers were in farming, as opposed to 66 percent for the workforce as a whole.[10] Thus consigned to the low-income sector of the economy, to labor there with low levels of human capital, China's older labor force provides almost a textbook definition for the working poor.

Despite China's educational advances, its older population will still be disadvantaged in 2025. We know this because we have data today on the educational attainment of the people who will make up China's elderly cohorts 20 years from now. As of 2025, something like two-fifths of China's senior citizens will have a primary school education—or less. That circumstance contrasts starkly with prospects for today's developed countries: In both Japan and the United States, for example, nearly five-sixths of the 65-plus population will have at least a high school diploma in 2025.

In 2025, moreover, the fate of China's low-skill older workers will still primarily be to toil in the field. Despite rapid structural transformation in the Chinese economy, agriculture promises to remain a major source of employment two decades from now—and older workers are likely to remain over-represented in China's primary sector.

The point to bear in mind about farming in China is that the occupation entails regular strenuous activity: It is not only low-paying but physically demanding. This point can be drawn more broadly, for even in occupations Western readers do not commonly associate with physical exertion, stamina and muscle-power are routinely required for job performance in China. This is so, quite simply, because China still lacks the capital investment per worker to provide "labor saving" alternatives to human strength in the production process. With mechanization so much more limited in China than in Western economies, the machines powering much of Chinese economic activity today are human bodies—and this circumstance is unlikely to change appreciably over the next 20 years.

Perversely, because China's older workers suffer from lower levels of education and training than the general labor force, they are precisely the cohort most directly obliged to rely upon physical effort to earn a living. This will hold true tomorrow as well as today. And that brings us to the third strand of the "triple bind" that defines China's looming aging problem: In the years ahead, China's senior citizens are not only likely to face real and perhaps mounting pressures to support themselves through paid labor, and not only likely to find that their employment opportunities are principally in low-paying, physically demanding jobs; they are also likely to be less healthy and more fragile than counterparts in other countries where the physical demands of employment are much less forbidding for the elderly and nonelderly alike.

Upon reflection, the proposition that the health of senior citizens in China is more tenuous than that of older populations in Western countries should not surprise: Over their life histories, after all, older people in China have on average been exposed to more in the way of health and nutritional risk, and have less scope for protecting and/or recovering from illness and injury, than older people in affluent societies. In all, China's availability and quality of food, housing, education and health services (and many other factors influencing health status) do not compare favorably with OECD levels. Consequently, China's senior citizens live shorter lives than old people in OECD countries—and their remaining years are more heavily compromised by serious health problems.

Estimates of "disability-free life expectancy" in China and Japan at age 65 make the point.[11] (These particular data come from circa 1990, but the patterns they revealed still obtain.) For men and women alike, overall life expectancy at age 65 was over 50 percent longer in Japan than in China—but whereas Chinese men could reportedly expect to be encumbered by disability for nearly a third of their remaining years, the fraction was just half as high among Japanese men. Chinese women, likewise, could reportedly expect to spend a third of their final years affected by disabilities—whereas the corresponding fraction for Japanese women was one-fifth. These data, incidentally, may considerably understate the extent of health impairment in later life for China's elderly. For one thing, they only refer to disability—not to the broader matter of potentially serious health problems. Secondly, the data on disability come from self-assessments—and as is well known, subjective expectations regarding health tend to be lower for populations with lower income and educational levels.

China's outlook for population aging, in sum, can in some respects be likened to a slow-motion humanitarian tragedy already underway. On the current trajectory, the graying of China threatens many tens of millions of future senior citizens with a penurious and uncertain livelihood in an increasingly successful emerging market. The incidence of individual misfortune implied by current trends looks to be sufficiently broad to suggest that impoverished aging may emerge as a major social problem for China in the years ahead. The impending fault lines for impoverished aging, furthermore, promise to magnify yet further the social inequalities with which China is already struggling.

How the country will deal with the social and political tensions generated by impoverished aging remains to be seen. Since 1997, Beijing's policymakers have recognized the question but have been deferring the response to it. Quite predictably, feasible policy options have narrowed over these years of indecision—and the remaining alternatives are steadily becoming more expensive.

Russia: Graying with "Unhealthy Aging"

In some respects, Russia's outlook for population aging can be regarded as an ordinarily "European" tale. Between 2000 and 2025, total population is expected to decline, while the number of Russians 65 and above is slated to grow substantially. Consequently, Russia's "population support ratio" or PSR—a metric that relates the working age population (15–64 years) to the retirement age population (65+)—falls by Census Bureau projections over this quarter-century from 5.5:1 to 3.3:1.

The implied burden of potential pensioners on the potential Russian workforce of 2025 is high by contemporary standards, to be sure—but such ratios look unexceptional for the Europe that awaits in 2025. By Census Bureau projections, the PSR for all of Europe would be about 3.0:1 in 2025, indicating the Russia would have a slightly higher working age population to retirement age population than the rest of the continent. For 2025, in fact, Russia's proportion of population 65 and older promises to be a bit higher than America's and a bit lower than Western Europe's.

It would be tempting to describe Russia's prospective aging profile as that of a typical developed society—and thus to expect Russia's aging problem to be similar to those of OECD Europe. The weight of the aging

Figure 9-3. Male Survival Schedule, Ages 20–65: Russia vs. Switzerland, 1999

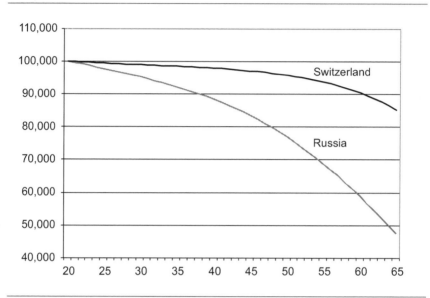

Source: www.mortality.org, accessed July 14, 2005.

burden that Russian society will have to bear in coming years, however, cannot be measured adequately by population pyramids or "population support ratios" alone. Russia's particular vulnerabilities in population aging pivot not so much on the size of the nation's prospective elderly population as on the exceptional fragility of the workforce that will be expected to support it.

Pronounced long-term deterioration of public health for an industrialized society during peacetime is a highly anomalous, indeed counterintuitive proposition for the modern sensibility: Nevertheless, over the four decades between 1961–62 and 2003, life expectancy at birth in Russia fell by nearly five years for males. It also declined for females, although just slightly, making for an overall drop in life expectancy of nearly three years over the past four decades. Between the mid-1960s and the start of the twenty-first century, the country's age-standardized death rates climbed by over 15 percent for women and by a shocking 40 percent for men. This upswing in mortality was especially concentrated among the group of "working age," where the upsurges in death rates were breathtaking. (Between 1970–71 and 2003, for example, every female cohort between the ages of 25 and 59 suffered at least a 40 percent increase in death rates; for men between the ages of 30 and 64, the corresponding figures uniformly exceeded 50 percent, and some cases exceeded 80 percent.)[12]

To get a sense of just how bad health and mortality conditions are for Russian adults nowadays, we can compare survival rates for Swiss men with their Russian counterparts for 1999, thanks to information compiled by the Human Mortality Database[13] (see Figure 9-3). In Switzerland, a 20-year-old man had a five-out-of-six chance of making it to 65 years of age; in Russia, he stood less than even odds. (In 1999, by the way, Russian adult survival schedules were somewhat better than they are today.)

If Russia's adult mortality levels are so "unnaturally" high today, won't more "natural" levels more or less automatically reassert themselves in the coming decades? The dismaying answer is: not necessarily, for in Russia's demography the "abnormal" seems to have become the new norm. Unlike other parts of the industrialized world, Russia's health trends are characterized by a heavy measure of what we might call negative momentum: that is to say, an unfavorable accumulation of immunological insults and health risks in today's adult population by comparison with their parents' generation. To the extent that death rates provide evidence about general health conditions, modern Russia's mortality data strongly suggest that each new cohort is more fragile than its predecessor.

In other industrialized Western societies in the postwar era, younger generations have routinely come to enjoy better survival rates than their predecessors: In contemporary Japan, for example, men born in 1950 have, over their adult life course thus far, experienced age-specific death rates 30 percent to 80 percent lower than those recorded for the cohort born 20 years before them.

By contrast: In Russia today (to invert the popular "boomer" mantra) "30 is the new 40." That is to say, there has been no improvement in survival schedules among the two generations of Russian men born between the late 1920s and 1970. Quite the contrary: Over the life course, each rising cohort of Russian men seems to be charting out a slightly more dismal mortality trajectory than the one traced by its immediate predecessors. (The same sorts of patterns, incidentally, are evident among Russian females.)

This negative momentum makes the objective of major, sustained improvements in public health especially problematic. Partly for this reason, demographers generally have low expectations for health progress in Russia over the years immediately ahead. The U.S. Census Bureau, for example, imagines the male life expectancy in Russia will steadily lag below India's, Pakistan's, and even Bangladesh's through 2025.[14]

Russia's lingering health and mortality crisis promises to be an anchor against rapid economic development, frustrating the effort to move Russia onto a path of swift and sustained material advance. It is difficult to see how Russia can expect, in some imagined future, to achieve an Irish standard of living if its labor force still faces an Indian schedule of survival—or worse. Widespread debilitation and premature mortality among working age cohorts depresses economic potential directly and immediately—but also has adverse and far-reaching effects on longer-term productivity. The expectation of a seriously foreshortened working life alters the cost-benefit calculus for higher education and technical training, lowering investment in human capital. And since Russian working-age adults "present" as far older than Western counterparts of the same calendar birth-year,[15] the scope for "economically active aging"—for enhancing the labor force participation rates and economic contributions of persons in middle age and beyond—will be far more constrained for Russia than for OECD Europe.

Population aging in the context of unhealthy aging poses additional special economic and social challenges to Russia. Given the country's steep and forbidding age-specific health gradient today and the limited prospects for health improvements over the coming two decades, the prospective aging of Russia's working age population—the median age of the population within the 15–64 grouping will be about 42 years in 2025, three-and-a-half years higher than today—means that the health and mortality outlook for Russian manpower could actually be less favorable than today—perhaps even appreciably so. Second, the specter of a swelling population of elderly pensioners[16] dependent for support on an unhealthy and diminishing population of low-income workers suggests some particularly unattractive trade-offs between welfare and growth. Should Russian resources be allocated to capital accumulation or to consumption for the unproductive elderly? Given Russia's population structure, the question cannot be finessed. As of the year 2002, Russia had only 1.7 workers for every pensioner[17]—and that ratio will only fall in the years ahead.

Though the government officially embarked upon pension reform in 2002, that process looks to be a long and complicated one—and what the eventual arrangements will presage on the one hand for the availability of investable funds, and on the other for living conditions of Russia's steadily growing ranks of the elderly and the infirm, is as yet an open question.

India: A Tale of "Two Countries"

India's population profile will age over the coming 20 years, but the country will nevertheless remain relatively youthful. Although projections indicate that India's 65+ cohort is slated to double in size between 2005 and 2025, those elders account for less than 8 percent of overall population 20 years hence; the country's median age then is only just over 30; and the PSR is almost 9:1—a level last witnessed in today's more developed countries before the Second World War.

But in many ways vast India is a sort of arithmetic expression that averages the sum of its many diverse components: so, too, with population aging. Closer examination reveals that with population aging there are in reality two Indias, with very different aging prospects and challenges: one that stays remarkably youthful over the next 20 years; the other already embarked on a very rapid graying.

As already noted, the pace and scale of aging tomorrow is always largely determined by local levels of fertility today. India's total fertility rate has dropped by more than two-fifths over the past three decades—from about 5.4 births per woman per lifetime in the early 1970s to approximately 3.1 today—but the pace of change has varied strikingly from one region and setting to the next.

It will surprise some readers to learn that sub-replacement fertility today prevails in many of India's huge urban centers—New Delhi, Mumbai (Bombay), Kolkata (Calcutta), and Chennai (Madras) among them.[18] But even more surprising, throughout much of rural India—especially rural South India—fertility levels today are also near or already below replacement.

Dr. P.N. Mari Bhat of Delhi University's Institute for Economic Growth has laid out the implications of these discrepant patterns for future aging in the supra-statal regions he labels "north India" and "south India."[19] Currently

(2005), fertility levels for the roughly half-billion population of this "north" are almost twice as high as for the nearly quarter-billion people of this "south." (India's remaining 350 million people live in states and union territories not included in Mari Bhat's "north/south" analysis.)

By 2025, "north" India's population would still be very young. Its projected median age would be just 26—and the 65+ group would account for less than 6 percent of total population. On the other hand, "south" India's population structure in 2025 would bear unmistakable signs of population aging. There, median age would be about 34 (a level comparable to Europe's in the late 1980s), and 9 percent of the population would be 65 or older (about the same share as Japan's in 1980).

Mari Bhat does not break down his 2025 projections to the state level, but Professor Tim Dyson of the London School of Economics has done so for India for 2026.[20] His projections differ from Mari Bhat's in some particulars (most importantly, in positing a slightly faster pace of fertility decline over the next generation), but his calculations similarly depict a growing "aging gap" between north India and south India—with aging by 2026 already having progressed considerably in a number of southern states. In each of India's four southernmost states, median age would be over 35—and over 37 in both Kerala and Tamil Nadu. (For reference, think of Western Europe around 1990.) In these projections, Kerala and Tamil Nadu's proportion of persons 65 and older both exceeded 10 percent by 2025. (Think here of Japan in the mid-1980s.)

A generation before Western Europe's median age reached 35, however, the region's GDP per capita was in the range of $6,000–$8,000 (at 2000 prices and exchange rates); a generation before Japan's share of 65+ to total population hit the 10 percent mark, the country's per capita GDP (at constant 2000 exchange rates and prices) was likewise around $7,000.[21] In 2001— that is to say, 25 years before the two states in question are projected to comport to those same demographic specifics—exchange-rate-based GDP per capita was less than $450 a year in both Kerala and Tamil Nadu. By any international or historical benchmark, indeed, many areas of India are facing the onset of rapid population aging on current levels of per capita output that are astonishingly low.

At the moment, India has nothing like society-wide old-age pension coverage: To the contrary, only about 11 percent of India's workforce participates in any sort of guaranteed retirement income systems. (An "emergency" needs-based monthly stipend is publicly available for persons over 60 in India, but this mechanism offers less than $2 a month to its beneficiaries and is not guaranteed to be available to all who apply for it and meet its hardship qualifications.) Although Indian policymakers and academics have been discussing alternative potential paths to universal old age income protection with a reasonable measure of intellectual seriousness in recent years, no plans for national coverage are even remotely on the national policy agenda.[22] Lacking a tangible comprehensive national retirement pension policy, India's implicit strategy for meeting its coming aging challenge is, at least for now, to "grow its way through it." Like many unspoken and thus unexamined game plans, this one looks highly problematic. Even if India, like the Japan of an earlier day, were poised to grow at a 5.5 percent per capita rate per annum over the coming generation, significant parts of India would be approaching the advent of an "aged society" on income levels almost an order of magnitude lower than those of Japan in the mid-1980s.

A sustained 5.5 percent per capita growth rate for India over the next generation, furthermore, is hardly a matter that can be taken for granted at the moment. In the period since her 1991 economic crisis, India has averaged a highly respectable 4.0 percent annual rate of per capita growth and has become a presence in the global it economy through its enclaves in places like Bangalore. But Bangalore—like the rest of the Indian south—is part of what may soon be known as "old India": While its labor force is relatively skilled, it is also older, and absolute supplies of available manpower will soon peak and begin to shrink. Other parts of India, by contrast, will have abundant and growing supplies of labor—but a disproportionate share of that manpower will be either entirely unschooled or only barely literate.

Figures 9-4 and 9-5 highlight this paradox. They compare projected age/sex/education pyramids in 2026 for the Indian states of Kerala and Bihar (work by Anne Goujon of the Vienna Institute for Demography and Kirsty McNay of Oxford).[23] The extreme contrast is intentional—Kerala is India's most educated state, while Bihar is its least schooled—but the story from the graphics is clear enough. In the Kerala of 2026, almost everyone of working age (15–64) will have some schooling, and the majority of the economically active manpower will have a high school diploma or better—but the largest population cohort would have been people in their 40s, with every successive cohort a little bit smaller. In the Bihar of 2026, on the other hand, each new

Figure 9-4. Age and Education Pyramid for Kerala, India: 2001 and 2026

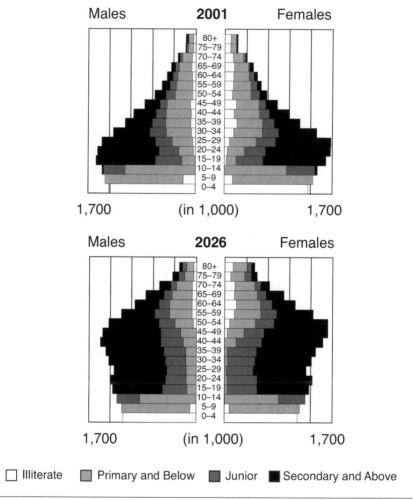

| ☐ Illiterate | ▨ Primary and Below | ▧ Junior | ■ Secondary and Above |

Source: Anne Goujon and Kirsty McNay, "Projecting the educational composition of the population of India: selected state-level perspectives." Applied Population and Policy 2003:1(1) 25–35, Figure 1.

birth cohort entering the labor pool would be larger than the one before—but fewer than one-third of the economically active population (15 to 65 years) would have even completed grade school, and well over two-fifths of the economically active age population would be illiterate, with no schooling whatsoever. (These projections, one may feel compelled to note, posit a

Figure 9-5. Age and Education Pyramid for Bihar, India: 2001 and 2026

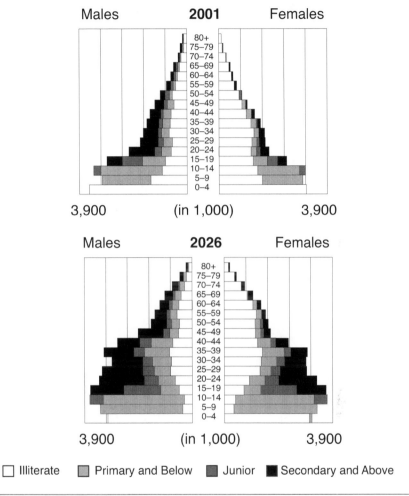

☐ Illiterate	▨ Primary and Below	▨ Junior	■ Secondary and Above

Source: Anne Goujon and Kirsty McNay, "Projecting the educational composition of the population of India: selected state-level perspectives." Applied Population and Policy 2003:1(1) 25–35, Figure 1.

continuation on into the future of the progress achieved over the 1990s in expanding access to education in India.)

To appreciate how very educationally disadvantaged India stands to be a generation hence, we may compare the Goujon-McNay projections with earlier work by Robert J. Barro and Jong-Wha Lee on historical patterns of worldwide educational attainment.[24] By the Goujon–McNay projections, in 2026 nearly one third (32 percent) of Indians 25 years of age or older would be illiterate, with no formal schooling. By contrast, as of 1960—that is to say, nearly three generations earlier—the illiteracy rate for the 25+ group in 23 OECD countries would have been about 6 percent. Even more telling, perhaps, are comparisons with educational levels from other developing regions. To go by the Goujon–McNay projections and the Barro–Lee estimates, India's rate of adult 25+ illiteracy in 2026 would be roughly comparable to the levels in Latin America and the Caribbean or East Asia around 1970 (35 percent and 31 percent, respectively)—that is to say, two generations earlier. Indeed, striking as this may sound, India's future adult illiteracy rates would not be that much lower than the current (2000) levels prevailing in sub-Saharan Africa (43 percent).

Educated and aging, or untutored and fertile—this looks to be the contradiction for India's development in the years immediately ahead. Human resources are the foundation for economic growth in the coming century—but if poor health is the Achilles Heel of Russia's human resources base, seriously inadequate educational opportunity for all too much of the population looks to be the Achilles Heel for India.

What Is to Be Done? Can Anything Be?

In any plausible future, population aging in low-income Eurasia is unlikely to be pretty. Absent only unthinkable catastrophe, the trajectory for a rapid graying is already essentially set for China, Russia, and much of India. Even with rapid and uninterrupted economic growth, by 2025 these aging or aged societies will be far poorer than was the West when Western societies had to face comparable degrees of population aging. There is no "fix" to this basic dilemma—at least, not in the next two decades.

That being said, it is also clear that informed and deliberate public action can still mitigate some of the adverse consequences that rapid graying would otherwise entail.

At first glance, the obvious policy avenue for coping with rapid population aging in Russia, China, and India might appear to be strengthening—and broadening the coverage of—the national pension arrangements in the countries in question. Certainly there is plenty of room for improvement here: Of the three countries, only Russia has a national pension system with anything approaching universal worker coverage (and the soundness of the evolving Russian system still remains to be seen). Moreover, given the enormous economic disparities within all three of these countries, even a relatively small measure of redistribution within the workings of a nationwide pension system could provide an important measure of protection for the most vulnerable of the elderly (a group that will be disproportionately rural, agrarian, and female).

In actuality, however, the potentialities of pension reform may offer less opportunity in each of these countries than would first seem to meet the eye. Post-communist Russia's polity, for example, betrays scant interest (on the part of either policymakers or voters) in protecting the health and well-being of economically productive citizens, much less social dependents. By the same token, the idea of extending pension coverage to the countryside and the slums is not unpopular in India: It simply remains beyond the realm of serious policy discussion. As for China—where political decision making is, shall we say, more "streamlined"—policy interest in extending the nation's pension coverage to poorer rural regions is indeed evident, but action has been precluded by the immense obstacle of the vast existing unfunded pension liabilities for comparatively well-off urban and state employees. However separate those two questions may appear intellectually, in practical terms they are inseparably linked, and the government's inability to deal with the latter means it cannot make progress on the former either.

Perhaps counterintuitively, then, the best hope for controlling the toll of the aging tsunami in low-income Eurasia may lie outside pension policy—more specifically, in embracing politically feasible strategies for poverty-reducing growth. And here it is not hard to identify directions worthy of vigorous pursuit.

In China, for example, the country's banking and financial system fairly begs for overhaul—and a transition to a more transparent, efficient, and sustainable system for financial intermediation will be essential if China is to maintain economic growth in the lower savings rate era that surely lies ahead.

In Russia, public health interventions to reduce premature mortality not only could reduce the country's tragic and unnecessary loss of life, but also could augment the size and the productivity of the working-age population that will be sustaining pensioners (and preparing for self-financed retirement).

As for India, with outward economic orientation and sound macroeconomic policies, high rates of return can be expected from investment in human resources—and the highest returns of all may be expected from extending primary education to those currently excluded from school. (Reaching the young is critical here: A century of efforts around the world has repeatedly demonstrated the limited efficacy of such programs.) India is already committed rhetorically to "Education for all"—but achieving universal primary education will require much more than words from the country's political leadership—and there is no good reason that India should be the sole great modern democracy incapable of meeting this objective.

For China, the case for financial sector reform wins on its own merits—as does the case for public health policy in Russia and universal primary education in India. Yet such policies would have the subsidiary, but hardly trivial, effect of making the scale of the aging problem a little less unmanageable in each of these societies.

Waiting for the "Demographic Dividend"?

Not all emerging markets, of course, are poised to settle their aging populations upon income levels so low as to be without historical precedent. Such middle income economies as Mexico, Brazil, and Turkey—among others—promise to have relatively youthful populations in 2025. Given current productivity levels and reasonable future economic prospects, moreover, a number of these places promise to fall well within the Western age-income experience over their presumed ascent in the coming decades—or perhaps even to remain more youthful than the Western economies were at similar levels of per capita income.

Is there a special economic benefit to be had from relatively youthful development? By some thinking in the economics literature—a hardy strand reaching back nearly half a century—the answer would seem to depend not just upon graying, but upon the ratio of all dependents, young and old, to economically productive workers.

To this way of thinking—oversimplifying the argument, some might say brutally—the lower the "dependency ratio" of children and oldsters to working age people, the higher the rates of capital accumulation and growth. In the argumentation of some economists today, the special moment in the "demographic transition" when birth rates are low and elderly populations are not yet burgeoning provides a sort of "sweet spot" for very rapid economic growth. According to this viewpoint, societies that have recently transited from high to low birthrates—but have yet to experience significant graying—are positioned to reap a "demographic dividend." In this telling, indeed, crucial shifts in demographic structure are integral to the modern era's great development success stories, from East Asia's remarkable economic ascent over the past generation-and-a-half to Ireland's more recent transformation into Europe's "Celtic tiger."[25]

The tale of the demographic dividend is certainly compelling to hear, and it may be heartening for those low-income societies whose dependency ratios are now about to begin a long-term decline—but is the story right? Are dependency ratios critical to a population's prospects for sustained and rapid material advance?

It is surely incontestable that per capita output will be higher, all else being equal, in the society where people of working age account for the greater share of total population. And theoretically, variations in dependency ratios may also plausibly be associated with changes in savings ratios—or more strictly speaking, with changes in a population's disposition to save and the facility with which it can attempt to accumulate savings. But in an era of truly global capital markets, relatively low savings rates in any given locale would not necessarily look like a binding constraint on that area's development. Postwar economic history would seem to indicate that dependency ratios are not a decisive influence on long-run economic performance in our increasingly globalized times. Consider the developmental records of two major global regions—East Asia on the one hand, and Latin America and the Caribbean on the other.

Over the 40 years between 1960 and 2000, dependency ratios for the low-income countries in East Asia and Latin America/Caribbean traced quite similar trajectories (although dependency ratios were always somewhat lower in East Asia). Despite the close correspondence between the indicators for the two regions over the course of the past four decades, economic results in the two areas have been anything but similar: Per capita output septupled for East Asia, whereas it rose by about 85 percent for Latin America and the

Caribbean. In both regions, moreover, the dependency ratio commenced a steady decline around 1975. But while the pace of growth accelerated in East Asia in the quarter-century following this drop, Latin America suffered a growth slowdown. In the high dependency ratio era (1960–75), Latin America's per capita output growth averaged almost 3 percent a year; in the years of steadily falling dependency ratios (1975–2003), annual per capita growth was under 1 percent.[26] Clearly other factors—including government policy—are more important in determining prospects for material progress.

P.N. Mari Bhat's cautious assessment of the possible influence of the demographic dividend on economic growth for India could be extended to other low-income areas as well:

> [D]uring the next 10–20 years demographic conditions would be favorable for growth. . . . However, as Bloom and Williamson note, their effect is by no means inevitable. To realize the effect, it is necessary to support it with appropriate economic, social and political institutions and policies. Otherwise it would only lead to higher levels of unemployment.[27]

Countries with declining dependency ratios, in short, may enjoy some potential for economic advantage—under the right cultural, institutional, and policy conditions. But demographic dividends are nothing to bank on.

Global Implications?

All other things being equal (which is to say, without proactive policy and institutional adjustments), the pronounced population aging that awaits the affluent OECD countries over the generation ahead would be expected to have a depressing effect on both local savings rates and local rates of economic growth. Much the same may also be said of the aging trends that are due to affect some of the major "emerging markets" in the next few decades. The conjunction of population aging in the world's developed economies and important parts of the developing world naturally raises the question of potential global impact. Global capital markets may be efficient in allocating investment to promising countries, corporations, and projects—but the availability of capital will affect the cost of capital and thus the profitability or attractiveness of undertakings worldwide. By the same token economic slowdowns in one major region would be expected to have spillover impacts on growth in other regions in an environment of liberalized global trade. Will the aging of the Third World have unanticipated spillover effects for the world economy? The answer is not yet clear—but it is none too early to begin asking the question.

Notes

1. A select representation might include: Alan J. Auerbach, Laurence J. Kotlikoff and Robert Hageman, "The Dynamics of an Aging Population: The Case of Four OECD Countries," *NBER Working Papers* 2797 (1989); David Cutler et al., "An Aging Society: Opportunity or Challenge?" *Brookings Papers on Economic Activity 1* (1990), 1–56; Richard Disney, *Can We Afford To Grow Older? A Perspective on the Economics of Aging* (MIT Press, 1996); OECD, *Maintaining Prosperity in an Ageing Society* (Paris: OECD, 1998); United Nations Population Division, *Replacement Migration: Is It a Solution to Declining and Ageing Populations?* (UN Department of Economic and Social Affairs, March 2000); Peter S. Heller, *Who Will Pay?: Coping with Aging Societies, Climate Change and Other Long-Term Fiscal Challenges*, (IMF, 2003); Landis MacKellar et al., *The Economic Impacts of Population Ageing in Japan*, (Elgar, 2004); James Proterba, "The Impact of Population Aging on Financial Markets," *NBER Working Papers* 10851 (2004); *International Monetary Fund, World Economic Outlook: The Global Demographic Transition* (IMF, September 2004). More popularized presentations include Peter G. Peterson, *Gray Dawn: How the Coming Age Wave Will Transform America—and the World* (Times Books, 1999); Robert Stowe England, *Global Aging and Financial Markets: Hard Landings Ahead?* (CSIS Press, 2002); Philip Longman, *The Empty Cradle: How Falling Birth Rates Threaten World Prosperity and What To Do About It*, (Basic Books, 2004); and Laurence J. Kotlikoff and Scott Burns, *The Coming Generational Storm: What You Need To Know About America's Economic Future* (MIT Press, 2004).

2. Demographers today generally use global population projections by the United Nations Population Division and the United States Census Bureau as their reference standards: UNPD's "World Population Prospects" are available electronically at http://www.unpopulation.org; USCB's "International Data Base" can be accessed at http://www.census.gov/ipc/www. Either set of projections (UNPD "medium variant" or USCB sole-variant) can be used to support the calculations above.

3. An illustrative example will emphasize the point. In a high-mortality society where female life expectancy stayed at 50 years and births per lifetime forever averaged six per woman, median age would eventually stabilize at about 16 years. On the other hand, if female life expectancy were 50 but births per lifetime averaged two instead of six, median age would stabilize close to 40! With an average of two children and a female life expectancy of only 50, in fact, the 65-plus group would ultimately account for over

15 percent of total population—a higher fraction than that estimated for the "more developed regions" at the dawn of the twenty-first century. (Estimates derived for "stable population" structures with female life expectancy of 50 under either West, North, East, or South "model" life tables—cf. Ansley J. Coale and Paul Demeny with Barbara Vaughan, *Regional Model Life Tables and Stable Populations* (Academic Press, 1983) and USCB International Data Base.)

4. Chris Wilson and Gilles Pison, "La majorité de l'humanité vit dans un pays où la fécondité est basse," *Population & Sociétés* 405 (October 2004).

5. Technically, Eastern Europe is defined as "more developed" rather than "less developed" in the UN's global taxonomy. Because these "more developed" countries are nonetheless relatively low-income societies, we will include them for consideration here.

6. The task of reaching today's OECD per capita income levels, incidentally, may be even more daunting than those numbers suggest, for China, Russia and India all enjoy extremely generous PPP adjustments in this table, each of which scales up the country's actual exchange-rate-based per capita output level by a factor of four or more. By actual exchange-rate-based per capita GDP estimates, Russia's is one-fifteenth of Western Europe's, and China's is less than a twentieth of Japan's.

7. The UNPD currently suggests that China's total fertility rate was about 1.92 in 1990–95, a level roughly 16 percent below that required for long-term population replacement, and that China's TFR has subsequently declined to a bit over 1.7 today. The U.S. Census Bureau's reading is quite similar: For 2005, it projects a TFR of 1.72 for China. These estimates, of course, are prepared under uncertainties, the most important of these being the lack of complete annual vital registration data for China, and the unknown degree of under-reporting of infants and children in the country's censuses and demographic surveys. For background, see Daniel Goodkind, "China's missing children: The 2000 census underreporting surprise," *Population Studies* 58:3 (2004), 281–295, and Guangyu Zhang and Zhonwei Zhao, "China's Fertility Puzzle: Data Collection and Data Use in the Last Two Decades," paper presented at Population Association of America 2005 Annual Meeting, Philadelphia, Pennsylvania (April 1, 2005).

8. For background, see *World Bank, Old Age Security: Pension Reform in China* (World Bank, 1997); Song Xiaowu, ed., *Perfect the Pension System* (Enterprise Management Publishing House, 2001) [in Chinese]; Jinxing Huang, "Economic Restructuring, Social Safety-Net and Old-Age Pension Reform in China," *American Asian Review* 21:2 (2003), and Xin Wang, "China's Pension Reform and Capital Market Development," *China & World Economy* 12:3 (2004).

9. Professor Mark W. Frazier of Lawrence University may have pinpointed a critical factor in this continuing delay: "Until the fundamental question of what the state owes its citizens in terms of guaranteed basic pension benefits is resolved, the debate over the necessity of pension legislation to supplant the current patchwork of national and local regulatory controls is largely academic." "What's in a Law?: China's Pension Reform and its Discontents," in Neil J. Diamant, Stanley J. Lubman, and Kevin J. O'Brien, *Engaging the Law in China: State, Society and Possibilities for Justice* (Stanford University Press, 2005), 108–130, cite at 125.

10. Data drawn from China Ministry of Labor and Social Security, China Labour Statistical Yearbook 2003, Tables 1–43, 1–51, and China National Bureau of Statistics,

Tabulation on the 2000 Population Census of the People's Republic of China, Volume 2, Tables 4–4, 4–4c.

11. Yasuhiko Saito, Xiaochun Qiao and Sutthichai Jitapunkul, "Health Expectancy in Asian Countries," in J.M. Robine et al., *Determining Health Expectancies* (Chichester, England: John Wiley & Sons, 2003), 289–317.

12. How are we to explain modern Russia's awful health tragedy? The fact is, demographers and public health specialists do not fully understand the reasons for these gruesome results. Diet, smoking, sedentary lifestyles, and health care (or the lack of it) all play their part. Russia's romance with the vodka bottle is also deeply implicated here. Part of the mystery of the ongoing Russian health disaster, however, is that the problem looks to be worse than the sum of its parts: that is to say, death rates are significantly higher than one would predict on the basis of observed risk factors alone.

13. Available at http://www.mortality.org.

14. Those Census Bureau projections, furthermore, do not formally take into account the possibility that additional and perhaps severe new health setbacks may lie in store for the Russian Federation. Yet precisely such problems are, quite plainly, on the horizon today: Think of the country's still-gathering HIV/AIDS and drug-resistant tuberculosis epidemics.

15. A single example: In 1999—by no means the worst year for health in post-Communist Russia—the same death rates experienced by 40-year-old Russians were matched in Italy by women at age 55 and by men at age 60, respectively. (Estimates from the Human Mortality Database, www.mortality.org.)

16. Given Russia's grim health problems, it may seem paradoxical that the population should be aging so rapidly. Remember, however, our earlier discussion: Population aging is driven much more by fertility patterns than mortality—and Russia's fertility levels today are far below replacement.

17. For a penetrating overview and analysis of the Russian pension situation, see Leon Aron, "Privatizing Pensions," AEI Russian Outlook (Summer 2004).

18. See, for example, Christophe Z. Guilmoto and S. Irudaya Rajan, "District Level Estimates of Fertility from India's 2001 Census," Economic and Political Weekly (February 16, 2002), data from Table a–1. For a more comprehensive treatment, see Christophe Z. Guilmoto and S. Irudaya Rajan, eds., Fertility Transition in South India (Sage Publications, 2005).

19. P.N. Mari Bhat, "Demographic Scenario, 2025," Study #S-15, Research Projects on India—2025 conducted by Centre for Policy Research (New Delhi, July, 2003).

20. Tim Dyson, "India's Population—The Future," in Tim Dyson, Robert Cassen and Leela Visaria, eds., *Twenty-First Century India: Population, Economy, Human Development, and the Environment* (Oxford University Press, 2004), 74–107. Professor Dyson also generously shared with me some of the additional unpublished details from this same series of projections.

21. Derived from World Bank, World Development Indicators 2004 CD-ROM. Estimates for Western Europe are for the 12 current countries of the European Monetary Union for 1960–65; estimates for Japan are for 1960.

22. For background, see *First Report of Project Oasis* (Old Age Social and Income Security), India Ministry of Social Justice and Empowerment (February 1, 1999); World Bank,

India: "The Challenge of Old Age Insurance Security," Report 22034-IN (April 5, 2001); B.C. Purohil, "Policymaking for diversity among the aged in India," *Journal of Aging and Social Policy* 15:4 (2003); and Robert Palacios, "The Challenge of Pension Reform in India," in Edgaro M. Favaro and Ashok K. Lahiri, *Fiscal Policies and Sustainable Growth In India* (Oxford University Press, 2004), 282–300.

23. Anne Goujon and Kirsty McNay, "Projecting the educational composition of the population of India: selected state-level perspectives," Applied Population and Policy 1:1 (2003). The discussion below benefits from additional unpublished projections from that effort, kindly transmitted to me by Dr. Goujon. The discussion refers to the Goujon-McNay "Scenario One" projections.

24. Robert J. Barro and Jong-Wha Lee, *International Data on Educational Attainment: Updates and Implications*, Harvard University Center for International Development Working Papers 42 (April 2000).

25. For example: Ansley J. Coale and E.M. Hoover, *Population Growth and Economic Development in Low-Income Countries* (Princeton University Press, 1958); Stephen Enke, "The economic aspects of slowing population growth," *Economic Journal* 76 (1966); David Bloom and Jeffrey Williamson, "Demographic Transitions and Economic Miracles in Emerging Asia," *World Bank Economic Review* 12 (1998), 419–456; David Bloom, David Canning, and Jose Sevilla, *The Demographic Dividend: A New Perspective on the Economic Consequences of Population Change* (Rand, 2003).

26. Comparisons derived from World Bank, World Development Indicators (2004) CD-ROM.

27. Mari Bhat, "Demographic Scenario, 2025," 9.

10

Hastening Korean Reunification

Foreign Affairs, March/April 1997

Whatever their differences, the five governments that must contend most directly with Pyongyang—Seoul, Washington, Beijing, Tokyo, and Moscow—all assume that a rapid reunification of Korea is not only unlikely, but would run contrary to their national interests if it occurred. In fact, a rapid implosion of the North is more likely than a gradual reunification, and with the opposite range of consequences.

The cherished vision of a gradual and orderly drawing together of the two Koreas is today nothing more than a fantasy. As time goes on, North Korea will only grow poorer and more dangerous. For all parties affected, the faster reunification takes place, the better. Many details of reunification remain uncertain, but Western powers must begin to consider what a sudden reintegration might mean. The Korean question is no longer a problem that can be postponed and then muddled through.

A Widening Gulf

The vision of a gradual reintegration of the two Korean economies that many South Koreans so fondly entertain assumes that North Korea's government will someday embrace a program of economic liberalization and somehow survive to complete the decades of transformation the program would entail. Yet Pyongyang to date has vigorously opposed any liberalization of economic policies worthy of the name. There is nothing to suggest that North Korea is contemplating any such reorientation. The weight of the evidence, furthermore, indicates that the leadership believes economic liberalization would be lethal for the regime. If the North cleaves to its traditional policy, the most likely outlook is continued economic decline. For the South, on the other hand, the most reasonable prognosis for the decades ahead is steady and perhaps substantial economic growth. Under such circumstances, both the relative and the absolute gap between the North's and the South's per capita income will continue to widen. Meanwhile, the cost of unification—the investment needs of North Korea in relation to South Korean output—will likely grow steadily and perhaps swiftly every year reunification is delayed. The further apart the two economies get, the greater the cost of bringing the North to parity with the Republic of Korea (ROK).

If, however, the specter of German-style unification expenses is terrifying to some South Korean policymakers, they tremble before a chimera. Any number of careful studies have pointed out that the bulk of western German transfers to the new federal states since 1990 have been for social welfare payments, not investment. There is no reason for these particular expenses to be replicated elsewhere—especially not in the ROK, which for better or worse still lacks most of the adornments of a full-fledged welfare state. Moreover, Korean reunification will yield benefits as well as costs.

In the short run, reunification with a poorer partner could help relieve South Korea's incipient labor shortage, reduce pressures on wages and other production costs, and enhance Korea's international competitiveness. A fusion of the two Korean work forces could increase purchasing power and living standards for the great majority in both the North and the South. Over the long run, as northern Korea's infrastructure and industrial capacity are renovated, all of Korea could experience dynamic supply-side effects. The flip side of North Korea's current infrastructural obsolescence is the coming opportunity to replace decrepit plants with state-of-the-art equipment embodying the latest technology.

The Weapons Ledger

If the economic prospects of a more immediate and deliberate Korean unification are decidedly less menacing than so often depicted, what of its possible political and strategic ramifications? Unfortunately, as difficult or contentious issues are deferred, the costs of maintaining the unstable balance in the Korean peninsula stand only to rise. From a financial perspective, in addition to underwriting military deterrence in South Korea, Western governments now envision substantial outlays to Pyongyang for economic and humanitarian aid. The "Agreed Framework" Washington reached with Pyongyang in 1994 is but one of several mechanisms for such transfers. To the extent that the great Pacific powers think about Korean security in a two-state framework, they will be ineluctably drawn to subsidizing the Northern system as its internal crises mount.

On a separate ledger, given the North's constantly improving arsenal, the extended survival of the Democratic People's Republic of Korea (DPRK) will raise both the probability and the expected intensity of out-of-theater security threats facilitated by DPRK sales or transfers of arms to extremist governments or terrorist groups in other parts of the world. While none of the policy alternatives facing the North Korean leadership today can look terribly attractive, a strategy of continuing to augment the North's potential to inflict devastation on both neighboring and more distant countries may appear more promising—and indeed, more logical—than any other option. After all, what sort of consideration could Pyongyang expect from the world community if "the North Korean question" were merely a humanitarian problem? To extend the life of the state, by this reasoning, it is imperative to upgrade the threat posed by weapons of mass destruction. Indeed, as best can be told, this is exactly what North Korean policymakers are attempting to do. For while the effectiveness of a conventional army will eventually be compromised by the decay of the national economy, the killing force of these particular instruments is much better insulated against such adverse trends.

Although North Korea's program for developing nuclear weapons is widely thought to be suspended, the DPRK has reportedly established a nuclear warfare command and may have one or more atomic bombs in its possession. The nuclear option, in any case, is only one component of the DPRK's overall program. North Korea has extensive capabilities for manufacturing chemical weapons, including nerve gas; according to some reports, it may have the world's third-largest inventory of these compounds. And North Korea has been working feverishly for decades on long-range missiles.

Although such threats would likely prove most burdensome to the United States, the only one of the four Pacific powers with truly global interests and obligations, all of the others would be affected by the destabilization that weapons of mass destruction can cause in distant venues, such as the Middle East.

North Korea Is the Nuclear Problem

Every government in northeast Asia can help improve the chances for rapid reunification. But two constraints loom large. The first is that neither China nor Russia can be counted on to cooperate in multilateral deliberations about what follows the end of North Korea. The second is that the allies most likely to cooperate in those preparations—the South, Japan, and the United States—have already restricted their freedom of maneuver through the Agreed Framework.

For obvious historical reasons, Washington's security relationships with Beijing and Moscow are vastly different from its relationships with Seoul and Tokyo. For similar reasons, China and Russia can be expected to regard an American design for a new Korea with considerable suspicion. China in particular has reason to appreciate the Korean status quo. Given its close economic and political ties with both Korean governments, the Chinese state now enjoys a more favorable position in Korea than at any point in the past century and a half.

Weighing against the impediments to cooperation, though, is the compelling fact that the current order in Korea cannot last. It is in both China's and Russia's interests to help shape the order that will follow. Moreover, Chinese and Russian interests coincide with the joint interests of South Korea, Japan, and the United States in fundamental respects.

If Middle Eastern oil exports were disrupted tomorrow by a crisis involving North Korean-made weapons of mass destruction, for example, China would suffer directly. Conversely, both Russia and China would reap commercial and security benefits from a successful Korean reunification. Therefore, they have strong incentives for approaching reunification together with the United States and its allies. The task for U.S., Japanese, and South Korean diplomacy, then, is not to convince Russian and Chinese leaders to submit to a Western strategy for Korea, but rather to encourage them to think clearly and realistically about where their own interests lie.

The Agreed Framework poses a rather different set of problems. This complex document outlines an extended schedule of financial, material, and diplomatic benefits that Pyongyang may obtain from a U.S.-led international consortium if and when the North passes a variety of milestones, mainly concerning compliance with the nuclear Nonproliferation Treaty but also involving such things as detente with South Korea and arms control. As negotiators on both sides have pointed out, the document is not a formal agreement, but a road map. Some, however, have observed that the agreement's ambiguities expose the United States and its allies to the worst of two diplomatic worlds, possibly obliging Washington to behave as if it were bound by treaty while permitting Pyongyang to decide when and whether it will honor its corresponding obligations. The range of envisioned Western-DPRK engagements restricts the range and scope of Western reunification strategies.

If Western governments are not to be ensnared, they must honestly recognize the Agreed Framework for what it is. The document does not solve the North Korean nuclear problem, but simply permits both sides to settle the matter later on. The North Korean nuclear "problem," for its part, does not derive from the technical specifications of the North's Soviet-style reactors, but rather from the inherent character and intentions of the North Korean state. The North Korean regime is the North Korean nuclear problem, and unless its intentions change, which is unlikely, that problem will continue as long as the regime is in place. If Western governments believe they can influence the nature of that state, they should assess their progress—or lack thereof—carefully and unflinchingly. But to allow this document to compromise preparations for Korean unification would be a grave mistake.

Southern Hospitality

The Western countries with the greatest prospective influence on Korea's reunification are South Korea, the United States, and Japan. What sorts of things could each of them do, bilaterally or multilaterally, to improve the odds of a free, peaceful, and successful reunification? As a first but vital step, Seoul should make preparation an immediate national priority and begin to design long-range policies. Political leadership in the South must increase the South Korean public's awareness of the tests that lie ahead and make the case that these tests can only be successfully surmounted by sensible strategy and concerted collective effort.

If a free and peaceful reunification is indeed consummated, the subsequent success of the project will also depend greatly on the dynamism of the South's economy, the resilience of its society, and the stability of its polity. Despite the South's great strides in these areas over the past generation, there is unfinished business in each of them.

Preventing war and forging a successful reunification will require close cooperation with all the South's allies, including Japan. Although Seoul's ties to Tokyo have been deepening and warming for decades, there is ample room for improvement here, as well.

With regard to North Korea, the South must begin to think not only about deterrence but about reconciliation. Healing the wounds of divided Korea promises to be a monumental task—one that may take generations to complete. But the process can begin now. Committing the South to a "malice toward none" policy after Korean unification, and to guaranteeing ordinary northerners the same civil and political rights as southerners, would send an important and stabilizing message. Working to open lines of communication and expand people-to-people contacts could increase familiarity and reduce misunderstandings on both sides. South Korean society today is strong enough to withstand any attempts Pyongyang might make to manipulate such overtures; Seoul would be wise to capitalize on that strength.

The United States can shape the prospects for Korea's reunification through diverse instruments, but its unique and indispensable contribution is in the realm of security. Just as the U.S. military commitment to the South has been the sine qua non of deterrence on the peninsula, a vibrant U.S.–South Korean security relationship in a united Korea will be critical to the success of reunification.

For Washington, however, preparing for Korean reunification will mean more than thinking about bases and planes. As the world's predominant economy, and as the presumptive leader of any strategic Western initiative in northeast Asia or other regions of the globe, responsibilities for coordinating an international approach to Korean unification will almost naturally devolve on the United States. Managing such an effort wisely and effectively will be a tremendous task—no less taxing or delicate than the historic endeavor that united Germany in 1990.

To consider Japan's prospective influence on Korean unification is to beg the question of Japan's role in the world. In this century, Japan has never had a "normal" foreign policy: before World War II, it was an insatiable and revisionist power; after its terrible defeat, it has been a meek, one-legged giant. To this day, it is difficult for the Japanese to discuss their national interests—even in the Korean peninsula, where those interests are so directly and dramatically affected.

For better or worse, until Japan can play a role on the international stage in the same manner as other industrial democracies, its contributions to a successful Korean reunification are most likely to be made through the two diplomatic channels that Tokyo is most comfortable with: international finance and multilateral institutions. Japan's government and the Japanese business community can begin now to focus on the potential of mutually beneficial economic cooperation in a united Korea and on the problems that must be avoided or solved if such cooperation is to bear fruit. In multinational forums, Japan could be a persuasive lobbyist for an effective nuclear nonproliferation regime. In the years ahead, Japan could use its growing influence at the World Bank and other multilateral development banks to encourage those institutions to devote their technical expertise and financial resources to meeting the challenges that Korea's reunification would entail.

The list of possible initiatives and policies could be extended and elaborated. The point, however, is short and simple. Northeast Asia can live with a united Korea—in fact, it could be considerably more comfortable with a single free Korea than with the present arrangement. It is time for statesmen in the Pacific and beyond to think about how to make Korean reunification a success—because success or no, reunification is coming.

PART IV

Human Imperatives

Security comes first. First in the hierarchy of human needs. First in the prerequisites for economic progress. Nothing so elevated as "law and order.". . . Just physical safety and security. Without security, efforts to better the national plight will be doomed to frustration, or worse. Foreign economic assistance will be mainly wasted, or worse. Humanitarian assistance efforts will find themselves on an endless treadmill. Economic and humanitarian assistance are no substitute for security and safety—cannot substitute for it, cannot themselves create it.

— From "Haiti in Extremis"

One of the most enduring—and troubling—aspects of the human condition is that the most vulnerable and desperate among us are also those who lack a voice. It is therefore incumbent upon those who sleep comfortably and safely at night to go out of our way to try to listen for their voices—so that we might better understand their plight and if possible help relieve their affliction. The chapters in this section are all efforts at listening—or in today's jargon, studies in human security. The first of these examines the reasons that a distinct fraction of humanity—proportionately small, perhaps, but nonetheless encompassing hundreds of millions of souls—should find themselves in countries that have so conspicuously failed to join in the global escape from extreme poverty over the past generation. The following study, on Haiti, attempts to draw attention to the critical but often overlooked distinction between poverty and misery—and makes the case that physical safety and security of person

195

must be the very first "developmental priority" for any society. We then focus on the global spread of the phenomenon of sex-selective abortion—a barbaric practice that ironically is only possible thanks to technological advance, and one which cannot not be extirpated without profound changes in social conscience. Last but not least is an address I delivered in Seoul on the parlous condition of North Korean refugees in China, where I urged my South Korean friends to open their doors—and their hearts—to those brothers in need and "bring them home."

11

The Global Poverty Paradox

Commentary, October 2010

For a brief, glorious, and unforgettable moment 20 years ago, it seemed as if a great and terrible question that had been perennially stalking humanity had finally been answered. That profound question was as old as human hope itself: could ordinary men and women, regardless of their location on this earth or their station in this life, hope that deliberate social arrangements could provide them—and their descendants thereafter—with permanent and universal protection against the grinding poverty and material misery that had been the human lot ever since memory began? For those exhilarating few years back in the 1990s, it seemed to many of us that the 20th century had indeed answered this age-old question: decisively, successfully, and conclusively.

Brute facts, after all, had demonstrated beyond controversy that human beings the world over could now indeed create sustained explosions of mass prosperity—rather than temporary and transient windfalls—that would utterly transform the human material condition, relegating the traditional conception of desperate want from a daily personal concern to an almost abstract textbook curiosity.

According to estimates by the late economic historian Angus Maddison, the world's average per capita output quadrupled between 1900 and 1989/91, with even greater income surges registered in the collectivity of Western societies where the process of modern economic growth had commenced.[1] Membership in this "Western" club, though, manifestly did not require European background or heritage, for the Asian nations of Japan, South Korea, and Taiwan had come to embrace political and economic arrangements similar to those pioneered in Western Europe and its overseas offshoots, and had in fact enjoyed some of the century's fastest rates of long-term income growth.

The formula for generating steady improvements in living standards for a diversity of human populations, in short, had been solidly established. The matter at hand was now to extend that formula to the reaches of the earth where it could not yet be exercised—most obviously at that time for political reasons, given the fact that nearly a third of the world's peoples were still living under Communist regimes in the late 1980s.

By the early 1990s, with the final failure of the Soviet project and the widely heralded idea of the "End of History," it suddenly seemed as if the liberal political ideals that promoted the spread of the Western growth formula would no longer encounter much organized global resistance. It now seemed only a matter of time until every part of the world could join in a newly possible economic race to the top. Prosperity for all—everywhere—no longer sounded like merely a prayer. Quite the contrary: the end of global poverty was increasingly taken to be something much more like a feasible long-term-action agenda.

Alas, in the years since, new brute facts have asserted themselves, while other awkward facts of somewhat older vintage have reasserted themselves, demanding renewed attention. All too many contemporary locales have managed to "achieve" records of long-term economic failure in our modern era. The plain and unavoidable truth is that countries with hundreds of millions of inhabitants today are not simply falling behind in a global march toward ever-greater prosperity: they are positively heading in the wrong direction, spiraling down on their own distinct, but commonly dismal, paths of severe, prolonged, and tragic retrogression.

Haiti is a particularly awful case in point.

The Case of Haiti

Conditions of life in Haiti, wretched for most Haitians even in the best of times, took a sharp turn for the worse earlier this year, when an earthquake measuring 7.0 on the Richter scale struck not far from the capital of Port-au-Prince. The resultant carnage was heartrending; the chaos, stomach-churning. At this writing, the official estimate of the death toll from the disaster has risen above 200,000—although it is a telling sign of Haiti's sheer underdevelopment that an exact death count from the earthquake and its aftermath is regarded by foreign relief workers on the scene as an utterly unrealistic proposition.

Yet there was absolutely nothing "natural" about the human cost of this natural disaster. Massive earthquakes do not always unfold as calamities of biblical proportions, even when they are visited on major urban population centers. In October 1989, a massive earthquake suddenly struck the Bay Area of California. In sheer magnitude, that earthquake was almost as violent as Haiti's (6.9 vs. 7.0); its epicenter was roughly as far from downtown San Jose as Haiti's was from central Port-au-Prince. The final death toll in the Bay Area tragedy: 63 lives.

At first glance, such wildly disparate death counts in the face of arguably comparable natural calamities may seem to serve as a grim metaphor for the seemingly perennial yawning gap that separates life chances in rich and poor regions today. In reality, however, the backstory is still sadder than these raw numbers might of themselves suggest: for the awful fact of the matter is that the United States and Haiti are societies whose capabilities for meeting human needs (and protecting human beings) have been moving in fundamentally different directions for decades.

A society's material capabilities for meeting human needs are very broadly indicated by its levels and trends in per capita output (GDP). America is not one of the modern world's most rapidly growing economies—over the past century, in fact, per capita growth has averaged a little under 2 percent a year—but thanks to the power of compound interest, such a tempo of growth brings dramatic and salutary transformations over time, if it can be sustained. In the roughly six decades between 1950 and 2008, indeed, America's per capita output more than tripled. But over that same half century or so, by Maddison's reckoning, per capita output in Haiti actually declined—by more than a third.

Thanks to its prolonged economic retrogression, Haiti today is not simply immiserated; it is in fact substantially poorer than it was half a century ago. By the hardly insignificant yardstick of income levels, the country appears to be less developed now than it was two generations before. (Appalling death tolls in the face of earthquakes, tropical storms, and other forces of nature are merely one manifestation of the more general deterioration in material capabilities for meeting human needs that are implied by such trends.)

Haiti, moreover, is only one of many countries in the modern world to have been heading down—not up—in economic terms for decades on end.

Summary statistics from the World Bank and the World Trade Organization (WTO) outline the dimensions of this global problem.

By the World Bank's calculations, nearly two dozen countries suffered negative per capita economic growth over the course of the quarter century from 1980 to 2005. And the World Bank does not even attempt to estimate economic trends for a number of national problem cases—Kim Jong-il's North Korea and Robert Mugabe's Zimbabwe among them—where pronounced and prolonged economic decline have almost certainly taken place. When one tallies up the global totals, it would appear that close to half a billion people today live in such countries—societies beset not merely by long-term stagnation but also by a quarter century or more of absolute deterioration in income levels.

At the same time, WTO numbers point to a jarring drop in the long-term export performance of many contemporary societies. Adjusting for inflation, these WTO data suggest that more than 30 countries were actually earning in real terms less from merchandise exports in 2006 than they did in 1980, over a quarter century earlier. The picture is still worse when we take intervening population growth into account. Real per capita export revenue, measured in U.S. dollars, looks to have been lower in more than 50 countries in 2007 (the last year before the current worldwide economic crisis) than in 1980. In all, such places today account for roughly three quarters of a billion of the world's 6.8 billion current inhabitants—about a ninth of the globe's total population.

Thus, it is not just that an appreciable swath of humanity today lives in countries that have not yet managed to customize, and apply, the global formula for sustained growth that has been propelling the rest of the world out of poverty and into material security, or even affluence. No—hundreds of millions of people in the modern world live in places where the development process is manifestly stuck in reverse.

For these hapless societies, pronounced and relentless economic failure is not an awful aberration but rather the seemingly "natural" way of things: the only way things have ever been in living memory for most locals, and most international observers. After all, the median age of the world's present population is less than 30 years; this means that most people today can recall only long-term economic failure for these dozens of countries.

National examples of prolonged economic failure dot the modern global map: in the Caribbean (Cuba, Haiti); in Latin America (Paraguay, Venezuela);

even in dynamic East Asia (North Korea). But the epicenter of prolonged economic failure is sub-Saharan Africa.

The Case of Sub-Saharan Africa

Sub-Saharan Africa comprises an extraordinary diversity of peoples, and the economic records of each of the region's 50-plus countries is separate and distinct. Yet taken together, their overall development record in the post-colonial period has been utterly dismal.

Some improvement in the region's economic performance has been registered since the mid-1990s. Even so, according to estimates by both Angus Maddison and the World Bank, per capita income for the region as a whole was slightly lower in 2006 than it was in 1974. Much the same holds true for real per capita export earnings. According to the WTO's numbers, Africa's overall per capita merchandise export revenues, adjusted for inflation, showed absolutely no improvement between 1974 and 2006—and after the global economic crisis, they appear to have been around 10 percent lower in 2009 than they were in 1974.

This is very bad news for a very large number of people: as of last year, according to U.S. Census Bureau projections, sub-Saharan Africa's population was well over 800 million people, roughly one-eighth of all human beings on earth today.

The sub-Sahara is not simply an epicenter of economic failure; it is also the epicenter of a pervasive failure in what might be called human development. Poorer countries, of course, tend to suffer from poor health and education as well, and sub-Saharan Africa is by far the poorest region of the planet today. But it is not just that Africa's health and educational profiles are much worse than for any other major region of the world; they are also markedly worse than would be predicted on the basis of the region's woeful economic performance alone.

Consider life expectancy at birth—the single best summary measure of a population's overall health conditions. Sub-Saharan life spans today are on average roughly 10 years lower than in other countries with comparable starting points in health four decades ago and comparable income levels today. This awful result has much to do with the HIV/AIDS tragedy, which to date has been concentrated in Africa and has sent life expectancy in some sub-Saharan societies plummeting.

But analogous patterns are evident for educational attainment in the sub-Sahara—trends that cannot be traced so easily to the unpredictable outbreak of communicable pandemics. Through painstaking effort, Robert J. Barro of Harvard and Jong-Wha Lee of Korea University have compiled a database detailing changes in adult educational levels in more than 100 countries for the years 1960 to 2000.[2] For the world as a whole, average years of schooling for a country's adult population as of the year 2000 can be pretty accurately predicted by the country's level of adult education 40 years earlier and its income level at the end of the intervening period.

Here again, sub-Saharan educational profiles in 2000 were even more modest than the region's very low income levels would have of themselves predicted: to go by World Bank data, this "sub-Sahara effect" amounted to an average of 1.2 years of schooling forgone for each and every person 15 years of age and older. In a region where adult men and women had an average of just 3.5 years of schooling as of 2000, this would have been a far from trivial loss; on the contrary, it suggests that sub-Saharan Africans would have enjoyed fully one third more years of adult education, its low income levels notwithstanding, if only they had been living in a place more like other regions of the Third World.

A Poor-Friendly Era

The problem of sustained socioeconomic retrogression is all the more dismaying, and puzzling, when one bears in mind the phenomenal explosion of prosperity that has transformed the world as a whole in the modern era— and the potentialities for material advance that are afforded even the poorest societies.

In the half century between 1955 and 2005, by Maddison's reckoning, the planet's per capita income levels nearly tripled, growing at an average tempo of more than 2 percent per year, despite the unprecedented pace of population increase in the Third World over those same years. The expansion of international trade—and thus by definition, of markets for export produce— was even more dramatic: on a worldwide basis, real per capita demand for international merchandise and commodities jumped almost tenfold during those same years.

Scientific and technical advances have immensely improved life prospects in the planet's poorest and least scientifically proficient reaches. Thanks largely to progress in life sciences and public-health know-how and the concomitant spread of basic education, longer lives are now possible worldwide at ever lower national-income levels. No country on earth registered a female life expectancy at birth of 65 years before the end of World War I; the first society to breach that threshold was apparently New Zealand, somewhere around 1920. Today average female life expectancy at birth for poor countries as a whole is well above 65 years. Even places like Nepal are thought to have reached this once-impossible level of life expectancy—and Nepal does this today on less than a fifth of New Zealand's income level circa 1920.

There should be no doubt whatsoever that the health revolution facilitated by the postwar era's knowledge explosion, and all that has accompanied it, has been fundamentally "poor-friendly." In the early 1950s, by the estimates of the UN Population Division, life expectancy at birth was 25 years higher in the more developed regions than in the less developed regions; 50 years later—despite the AIDS catastrophe—that differential had been cut in half. By this most basic measure of all, inequality between rich and poor has by no means increased; rather, during our era of modern global economic development, it has been shrinking, progressively and dramatically.

The worldwide surge in prosperity over the past two generations has been nothing like the winner-take-all race that some insinuate it to be. The plain fact is that countries at every income level have benefited tremendously from the global economic updrafts of our modern age. World Bank estimates underscore this point. If we take high-income economies completely out of the picture, average real per capita output for the rest of the world more than tripled between 1960 and 2006. (By Maddison's calculations, incidentally, per capita incomes in Brazil, Mexico, and Turkey are higher than they were in Scandinavia and the Netherlands in the early 1950s.)

For the "low middle income economies" (countries including China, Egypt, India, and the Philippines), estimated per capita incomes rose more than fivefold. And even for the "low income economies" as a whole—the 1.3 billion people in the world's poorest contemporary societies—per capita output is thought to have risen by almost 150 percent over those same years.

Salutary political changes—including what the late Samuel Huntington termed "waves of democratization"—have swept through the less developed regions over the past two generations. But First World levels of institutional and administrative acumen are by no means necessary for sustained economic growth in poor countries today. In fact, the political and policy prerequisites for eliciting enormous improvements in local incomes may be less exacting in our modern era than ever before.

A few examples will suffice to make this point. Take Bangladesh, a country widely written off as a hopeless basket case at its independence in 1971. Political stability has not exactly been Bangladesh's métier: over the past four decades, the country has experienced dozens of attempted political coups, three of which overturned the seated government. Bangladesh still does not qualify as an open society or a full-fledged democracy; Freedom House, for example, rated the country as only "partly free" earlier this year. Yet despite all this, per capita output in Bangladesh has roughly doubled since the early 1970s, according to both Maddison and the World Bank's World Development Indicators (WDI).

The case of the Dominican Republic may be even more instructive. In 1961, the country's longtime dictator, Rafael Trujillo, was assassinated. A period of political instability ensued; in 1965, U.S. troops had to occupy that country for a year to restore order. In the decades that followed, the country's "economic climate" might at best be described as mediocre: the country ranked 99th on the 2009 Corruption Perceptions Index, and 100th on the Fraser Institute's 2009 Index of Economic Freedom. Yet over the four decades between 1965 and 2005, per capita income in the Dominican Republic more than tripled, increasing over these years at an average pace of almost 3 percent per annum. Between the early 1960s and the early 2000s, moreover, overall life expectancy in the Dominican Republic jumped by nearly two decades: today, according to the U.S. Census Bureau, it stands at 74 years—just four years behind that found in the United States.

The Dominican Republic's progress in economic development is noteworthy in its own right—but it is all the more striking when juxtaposed against the gruesome and prolonged developmental failure still underway in Haiti. The two countries, of course, share the Caribbean island of Hispaniola.

So, given the pervasive scope and scale of worldwide economic advance in our age—and the apparently increasing ease of achieving sustained economic progress, even for populations at the lowest levels of material attainment—how are we to explain, and deal with, the phenomenon of persisting socio-economic failure in Haiti and dozens of other contemporary societies? How have these places managed to avoid self-enrichment, given the apparently increasing worldwide odds against such an outcome? And what can be done to end the syndrome of developmental decline on the lands that have been subject to it?

One diagnosis, insistently tendered in some parts of the academy and the international community, pegs the problem as a sheer insufficiency of foreign aid; the correlative prescription from these quarters—a lot more of it. Currently, the most vocal and articulate advocates of this point of view are Jeffrey Sachs of Columbia University and the United Nation's Millennium Development Goals (MDG) project. The MDG project avers that the primary impediment to more rapid progress against poverty in low-income countries nowadays is the lack of funding for practical, tested programs, and policy measures that would reliably and predictably raise living standards in the world where they are lowest today. Sachs and the UN's MDG apparatus consequently urge an immediate doubling of official Western-aid transfers to low-income areas and offer a detailed array of plans for absorbing these proposed additional flows (which are envisioned at almost $190 billion a year above "baseline" levels by the year 2015).[3]

The trouble with this narrative is that foreign aid is not exactly an untested remedy for global poverty in our day and age. To go by figures from the Organisation for Economic Cooperation and Development, total flows of development assistance to recipient countries since 1960, after adjusting for inflation, by now add up to something like $3 trillion.

Now, in some places and times, international aid appears not only to have enhanced material advance but also to have promoted the transition to self-sustaining growth (i.e., growth without aid). Aid transfers seem to have been most productive in the hands of governments that supported economically productive policies and practices. But foreign aid quite clearly is neither necessary nor sufficient to elicit growth and development in our modern era—nor is it even capable of preventing long-term economic retrogression in recipient states. In today's dollars, Haiti has received more than $10 billion since 1960 in official development assistance alone (and vastly more if private aid, humanitarian assistance, and security assistance are taken into account). On a per capita basis, this works out to more than four times as much assistance per capita as Western European populations received during the Marshall Plan era. Yet Haiti's per capita income, according to Maddison, was less than two-thirds as high in 2008 as it had been in 1960.

Similarly, since 1970, sub-Saharan African states have taken in the current equivalent of more than $600 billion of official development assistance—over three times as much aid on a per capita basis as Marshall Plan states received. As we know all too well, these subventions neither forestalled long-term economic decline for the region as a whole nor prevented the rise of poverty in many "beneficiary" states in the sub-Sahara.

How does one account for these inconvenient facts? Evidently, by ignoring them. To make their case for aid as the necessary remedy for contemporary global poverty, proponents of the Sachs-MDG plan are willing to undertake breathtaking, even patently absurd, intellectual contortions. Thus the plan's overview document asserts, without any hint of irony, that "many well-governed countries [today] are too poor to help themselves."[4] Social-science and policy-research literature, to be sure, has committed a fair share of howlers during the past century, but this may be the single most empirically challenged sentence of the new millennium.

The too-little-aid theory in essence attempts to explain—or blame—the prolonged economic failure of large portions of the modern world on external factors (in this case, the stinginess of affluent Western populations). A much more plausible explanation, however, relates to domestic factors within the countries and societies in question. Perhaps most important, these concern the deep, complex, historically rooted, and interconnected issues of "culture" on the one hand and what is now called "governance" on the other.

Culture and Governance

The proposition that a local population's viewpoints, values, and dispositions might have some bearing on local economic performance would hardly seem to be controversial. Decades ago, the great development economist Peter Bauer wrote that "economic achievement depends upon a people's attributes, attitudes, mores and political arrangements." The observation was offered as a simple and irrefutable statement of fact, and it would still be unobjectionable today to most readers who have not been tutored in contemporary "development theory." But for development specialists, discussion of "culture"—much less its relationship to such things as work, thrift, savings, entrepreneurship, innovation, educational attainment, and other qualities that influence prospects for material advance—is increasingly off-limits.

In the erudite reaches of development policy, indeed, discussion of such matters at all is often regarded as poor form at best—and at worst is taken to smack of condescension, paternalism, or even latent prejudice. Paul Collier's bestselling 2007 exposition, *The Bottom Billion*, is a case in point.[5] Remarkably, Collier manages to complete his opus without ever referring to cultural impediments to economic progress in the world's poorest and most economically stagnant societies. In fact, he utters the world culture only once—and that once as a reference to the contending worldviews and approaches of various parties involved in international-aid negotiations.

To be sure, the record of historical efforts to predict and explain economic performance on the basis of cultural attributes is, let us say, checkered. Up through the 1950s and even into the early 1960s, for example, researchers and self-styled experts were offering confident and detailed explanations of why "Confucian values" constituted a serious obstacle to economic development in East Asia. A decade or so later—after the huge boom all around the East Asian rim was well underway—the profession was still united in the consensus that the Confucian ethos mattered greatly in economic performance, but they had quietly shifted their estimate of that impact from negative to positive.

This gets us to the crucial issue of governance—which is shaped by, and in turn independently shapes, local attitudes, expectations, and motivations. Throughout the reaches of the world characterized by long-term economic failure, governance has generally been abysmal. Violent political instability and predatory, arbitrary, or plainly destructive state practices have shaken, or sometimes altogether destroyed, the institutions and legal rules upon which purposeful individual and collective efforts for economic betterment depend. In a few spots on the map—such as North Korea— pronounced economic failure is due to "strong states": monster regimes that starve their subjects as a matter of principle or ideology, given their own twisted official logic. For many more of today's failed economies, the trouble instead is that governance has been the charge of "weak" states or even "failed states": polities with extremely fragile capabilities, sometimes lacking the ability to maintain order or guarantee their subjects' physical security at all (think Liberia, Sierra Leone, Somalia).

In these wretched locales, economic failure and continuing developmental decline are unlikely to be arrested absent some serious successes in state-building. But how, exactly, does one proceed with that task? As Francis Fukuyama, who was studied the history of state-building, has cautioned, even under the best of circumstances, the quest to forge sturdy, competent, and trusted state apparatuses promises to be difficult, risky, and time-consuming ventures in these places—and expensive to boot.[6] Yet state-building is still hardly even on the agenda of the international-aid community, where moving Western "development" money to stricken regions assumes a much higher administrative priority. Scarcely less important, the challenges of state-building today are compounded by the burdens of history. In South Korea, state-building, from today's perspective, looks to have been a relatively undemanding mission, difficult as it was: Korea was a nation with a tradition of self-rule under a fairly sophisticated indigenous administrative system for a people with a long civilization and their own written language. In sub-Saharan Africa today, apart from South Africa, the only country that can be similarly characterized is perhaps Ethiopia. But even self-rule is no guarantee that state-building will be easy. Haiti, for example, has enjoyed more than two centuries of formal political independence.

If state-building is the precondition for any real hope of ending the prolonged economic failure and enduring poverty of the hundreds of millions of people currently condemned to this fate in the modern world, the precondition to state-building looks, quite unavoidably, to be foreign intervention—and quite possibly, sustained foreign intervention.

Unfortunately, in the wake of America's unpopular and in many ways bungled intervention in Iraq, such a prospect is if anything even less palatable for the Western governments that might undertake it than it would have been before the Iraq war. Given sensitivities about their own past colonial activities, postwar voters in Japan and most of Europe have always been reluctant to send troops abroad on indefinite latter-day "civilizing missions." For example, public support in those countries for the existing, arguably modest, state-building mission currently underway in Afghanistan is tenuous, and any broader commitment to such an international objective simply is not in the cards, now or in the foreseeable future. A number of development economists who recognize the imperative of state-building (not that they would call it by that name) have proposed intriguing schemes for promoting security in poor regions through outside interventions. Collier, much to his credit, flatly states that "external military intervention has an important place in helping the societies of the bottom billion" and argues that "these countries' military forces are more often part of the problem than a substitute for external forces." In fact, he devotes the better part of a chapter of his tome to hypothesizing just how the European Union could be encouraged to provide "credible guarantees of external military intervention" to prevent coups in democratically elected Third World governments.[7] Paul Romer, the father of modern economics' "new growth theory," floats the idea of "charter cities" protected by international security arrangements to which impoverished inhabitants in violent and lawless environments could migrate to enjoy the protections of person, property, and pragmatic rule. Such ideas, unfortunately, are only thought experiments—with little chance of moving off the shelf of theory and into practice, barring a tremendous change in the norms by which international relations are today conducted.

So where does this leave us?

On the one hand, the formula for achieving sustained long-term economic growth on a national basis has pretty clearly been developed, if not perfected—and applying this formula looks to be easier than ever before in human history. Most people, moreover, live in countries that have accepted the arrangements to undergird this growth formula—some by deliberately and enthusiastically embracing them, others by more inadvertently stumbling upon them. Barring global catastrophe—some unforeseen worldwide conflagration or environmental debacle—these populations in general can expect their descendants to enjoy higher incomes and greater affluence than they themselves have ever known. Moreover, thanks to what the economic historian Alexander Gerschenkron described as "the advantages of backwardness," untapped technological and economic potentialities provide the poorer populations in this group with the possibilities of even more rapid growth than those facing the richer world.

On the other hand, many hundreds of millions of people—a fraction of humanity that may rise, not fall, in the years immediately ahead—cannot avail themselves of the basic political arrangements that set the global growth formula into action. For now, and for the foreseeable future, these miserables can look forward only to relative economic decline—or even further absolute decline, difficult as that may be to imagine.

Nearly half a century ago, Peter Bauer warned presciently that "if attitudes, mores and institutions uncongenial to material progress have prevailed for long historical periods, with corresponding effects on material advance, it may be difficult to reverse their effects except after long periods." We are living in the world Bauer prophesied. Global prosperity for all is not yet at hand—and, painful and indeed shocking as this may be to recognize, the day in which all humanity can expect to be included in the march toward ever greater affluence cannot be foreseen with any confidence.

Notes

1. Angus Maddison, "Statistics on World Population, GDP and per Capita GDP, 1-2008 AD" (March 2010), available electronically at http://www.ggdc.net/maddison.

2. Robert J. Barro and Jong-Wha Lee, "International Data on Educational Attainment: Updates and Implications" (Harvard Center for International Development Working Paper No. 42, April 2000)—Appendix Data Tables, available electronically at http://www.cid.harvard.edu/ciddata/ciddata.html.

3. Investing in development: a practical plan to achieve the Millennium Development Goals/UN Millennium Project, Jeffrey D. Sachs, Director (New York: United Nations Development Programme, 2005).

4. Sachs, p. 17.

5. Paul Collier, The Bottom Billion: Why the Poorest Countries Are Failing and What Can Be Done About It (New York: Oxford, 2007), p. 124.

6. Francis Fukuyama, State-Building: Governance and World Order in the 21st Century (Ithaca: Cornell, 2004).

7. See, for example, Paul Romer, "For Richer, for Poorer," Prospect (London), no. 167, February 2010, available electronically at http://www.prospectmagazine.co.uk/2010/01/for-richer-for-poorer/.

12

Haiti in Extremis

The Weekly Standard, October 4, 2006

A brief summer visit to Haiti—the beautiful, perpetually tormented trop-ical purgatory that occupies the western third of the Caribbean island of Hispaniola—cannot help but focus the comfortable and well-fed foreign visitor's attention on two profound issues of the modern era: the reasons for the persistence of so much misery in an ever more affluent world, and the practical measures that might permit our world's poorest countries to escape from the heart-rending deprivation that they continue to suffer.

With an area comparable to the state of Maryland and a population (at about eight and a half million) roughly the size of New York City's, Haiti is closer to Florida—just an hour and a half from Miami by jet—than is Washington, D.C. But in a very real sense, the distance between the United States and Haiti is almost unimaginable.

By the yardstick of income, Haiti is by far the poorest spot in the Western Hemisphere, and in fact one of the very poorest places on the planet. State Department and CIA guesses put the country's per capita income at about $550 a year, or about a dollar and a half per day—but these formal, exchange-rate based estimates are highly misleading, if not meaningless. (Could anyone in the United States today survive for a year consuming no more than $1.50 worth of goods and services a day?) A better sense of Haiti's plight comes from comparisons of purchasing power. Perhaps the most authoritative global esti-mates of this sort have been done by Angus Maddison, the eminent economic historian. At the start of this decade, according to Maddison, Haiti's per capita output was thirty-five times lower than that of the United States. To get a sense of what this means: Think how things would go for your family if you had to get by for the entire year on just ten days of your current earnings.

Haiti looks impoverished even next to other impoverished countries. By Maddison's reckoning, per capita purchasing power in Haiti is one third that of Bolivia, the poorest country in South America. There is no country in the Middle East or Asia with an income level as low as Haiti's, not even Bangladesh. And although sub-Saharan Africa is the epicenter of desperate poverty in the modern world, a majority of sub-Saharan countries enjoy per capita income levels that are higher than Haiti's.

Income numbers alone, however, cannot convey an accurate impression of the terrible deprivation that is the inescapable lot of the ordinary Haitian. For this, one must take a stroll through La Saline, or Bel Air, or any of the other wretched slums that account for most of the living quarters in Haiti's capital, the sprawling city of Port-au-Prince.

From high up in the hills that ring this city by the bay, the place looks sublime: On the horizon a perfect blue sky meets a shimmering sea to frame the vast metropolis below. The illusion is maintained only so long as one is sufficiently removed to view actual human beings. As one makes the descent into town, the picture quickly changes: The eye of Bierstadt is replaced by the eye of Bruegel, and then by the eye of Bosch. Once in the city proper, one realizes that the urban sky is so clear because Haiti is too poor to have air pollution. Gasoline and diesel vehicles are out of almost everyone's reach, and garbage is too precious to be burned on the street. But Port-au-Prince is not too poor to have sewage: That humid choking stench is everywhere. Unending makeshift shacks stretch from clogged "canals," through which water the color of petroleum slowly trickles: This is at once the communal latrine and the water supply for washing the evening's cookware.

Tiny storefronts, stocked with a few handfuls of merchandise, advertise their wares with homemade signs in French or Creole (the Africanized French fusion most Haitians actually speak), but many—perhaps most—of the thronging passersby cannot understand these because they have never learned to read. Children are everywhere, many of them painfully thin—some are clothed, some partially clothed, others not clothed at all; not a few bear the marks of illness, infections, or growths that have never been diagnosed or treated. The graying decayed remnants of a few kites entangled on telephone lines provide the only hint that any of these children has ever possessed or enjoyed a toy. As for the grown-ups on the street, some seem agitated, some enervated, but almost all are shrunken and weathered, aged far beyond their years: Young women here look middle-aged, middle-aged men positively ancient. And these are the adults strong enough and healthy enough to be out on the streets: The victims of Haiti's chronic life-threatening epidemic afflictions—malaria, tuberculosis, and (now) HIV/AIDS—are more likely to be out of sight, in the hovels of the back alleyways, resting and trying to cling to life.

Yet things are even worse—much worse—for most Haitians than this bleak street picture might suggest. For there is an important qualitative difference between grinding poverty and utter misery, and Haiti today lies on the wrong side of that divide. These impoverished Haitians lack more than money, food, medicine, schooling, decent housing, shoes, clean water, and regular electricity: They also lack personal safety and physical security. Haiti is a territory trapped between a state of siege and a state of nature—a Hobbesian nightmare in which violent and well-armed crime gangs operate essentially at will, effectively controlling much of the area in which ordinary people have to live.

The personnel of most foreign embassies simply will not visit many inhabited regions of the country without armed escort—and are specifically enjoined from visiting other places (such as the Cité Soleil slum, home to perhaps half a million people) under any circumstances at all. The third day of my Haiti visit, word went around that a man had been not just murdered but deliberately beheaded on the same street as the U.S. ambassador's residence—an effective message to the island that absolutely no spot in Haiti is beyond the reach of the crimelords.

The more well-to-do Haitians I met spoke of the daily terror of crime and violence that they face—robbery, kidnappings, murder just for the fun of it—and these are the Haitians who can afford safer neighborhoods, protective walls adorned with barbed wire and broken glass, or perhaps armed guards. The greatest burden of crime, violence, and lawlessness falls on the poor. "We can't even hand things out to people in the slums—it would endanger them," explained a foreign social worker with nearly two decades' experience in Haiti's worst neighborhoods. "You know what would happen if we gave little radios? The bad guys would know about it right away—and they'd come into those homes to take the radios, and more."

Lest there be a thought that Haiti's poor have nothing to lose from gangs and crime but their radios, Dr. Jean William Pape, the latter-day Haitian-born Albert Schweitzer who directs GHESKIO, the country's leading HIV-research institute/clinic, told me that the connection in Haiti between violent chaos and forcible rape was so immediate and direct that his staff compiles a "rape index" that serviceably mirrors changes in Haiti's security environment just by tabulating the number of victims streaming into his clinics after sexual assaults. In a country where the government does not even bother to compile crime statistics, this may be the closest thing to a proxy for local crime rates that exists.

Why is there no physical security in Haiti today? The problem speaks to an abject failure of both the government of Haiti and the U.N.'s latest Haitian intervention force (MINUSTAH—the Francophone acronym for "United Nations Stabilization Mission in Haiti") in their most fundamental of charges.

The Haitian government maintains no standing army—merely a police force of perhaps 7,000. Only some of those police show up for work, and a troubling proportion of those who do show up are compromised, on the take from the very predators against whom they are supposed to protect the public. To put the problem in perspective, consider this: New York City—with a population roughly comparable to Haiti's, and an environment incomparably more stable and secure—employs about 35,000 sworn police officers, a force perhaps ten times larger than the number of reliable Haitian police (the latter scattered over a country about two orders of magnitude larger in area than the five boroughs).

Apart from the occasions when they are identified as abetting kidnappings or gang rampages, Haiti's police force is largely invisible. In my first two days of ranging through Port-au-Prince, I spotted police officers exactly twice— one of these instances being a spin near the presidential palace, the Haitian "White House." In the slums of La Saline I passed a police station—but no one seemed to be there. Where were the officers—hiding inside? Possibly so: The téléjiol—Haiti's national word-of-mouth grapevine and main communications medium in this densely-packed, illiterate nation—was saying that a band of police had just found themselves outgunned in Port-au-Prince in a shoot-out with local gangsters, and had retreated to their headquarters. The police situation, however, is said to be improving. U.S. embassy personnel informed me that Haiti was training new police recruits in classes of 250—at which pace, by rough calculation, Haiti could muster a New York City-sized police force somewhere around the middle of this century, assuming zero attrition or mortality.

As for MINUSTAH and their 8,800 soldiers and police, some Haitians have taken to calling them TOURISTAH. As one explained to me, "We see them in our best restaurants, dating our women, and on our nicest beaches. The only place we don't see them is where the crime and violence are taking place, where they are needed." Constrained by extraordinarily restrictive "rules of engagement," these U.N. forces remain far from their goal of "stabilizing" Haiti. Indeed, when U.N. secretary general Kofi Annan briefly visited Haiti in August to praise progress and call for more international aid, his advance team—even with the MINUSTAH force at hand—judged the security situation too perilous to risk scheduling a visit to Dr. Pape's model GHESKIO clinic, located in downtown Port-au-Prince.

In a purely arithmetic sense, Hkaiti's poverty today is a consequence of prolonged and severe economic retrogression—we might even say economic implosion. According to Angus Maddison's estimates, per capita GDP in Haiti is roughly 25 percent lower now, at the beginning of the new century, than it was in 1945. Per capita GDP was nearly twice as high in Haiti as in Bangladesh back in 1950—but by 2001, per capita output was higher in Bangladesh than in Haiti (by about 15 percent). And Haiti has been overtaken by Bangladesh not only in raw economic performance, but also in basic social performance: By World Bank estimates, life expectancy today is fully a decade higher in Bangladesh than in Haiti; according to the U.N., in fact, Haiti's life expectancy is no higher today than it was 20 years ago.

Indications of protracted decline abound. According to the World Bank, Haiti's level of total cereal production is 20 percent lower today than it was in 1961: this, for a still predominantly rural society whose population more than doubled in the interim. Likewise, aggregate electricity generation is lower than it was a decade and a half ago—a modern record for futility surpassed perhaps only by Kim Jong Il's North Korea. Haiti once had a national railway line—but it is missing now, engulfed and absorbed in the brush. (Haiti has practically no forests—all the free firewood has already been taken.) Old State Department "Area Handbooks" speak of Haitian coffee as the country's main export; modern-day U.S. agricultural officials talk of "Haitian blue" in tones akin to the North American bison—i.e., a magnificent species, sadly no longer much seen.

For any small island economy, international trade is vital—yet Haiti barely engages in it. According to the World Trade Organization, total merchandise exports for Haiti in 2005 amounted to $473 million, or about $55 per person. And as with so much else in Haiti, trends are heading in the wrong direction.

In the capital's tiny Port Authority, where cargo from vessels docked in the harbor is still unloaded mainly by hand, officials tell me that freight volume is down 50 percent over the past two years. Rough calculations suggest that Haiti—a country self-sufficient in nothing—is bringing in through its port system rather less than a pound per person per day of merchandise: food, gasoline, cement, trucks, clothing, paper, machinery—everything.

Haiti's other aperture to the world economy is an inland road through the highlands linking it to the Dominican Republic, its larger and markedly more successful neighbor on Hispaniola—but for the month before my arrival, that access point had been closed to all international commerce. It seems that Haiti had a newly appointed head of customs who entertained the peculiar idea of actually attempting to collect the statutory import duties listed on the books for incoming goods. Affronted and incensed, Haiti's major smugglers organized a trucking roadblock of the border, and then enforced it through menace. The government to date has proved incapable of lifting this self-embargo. There is quite a bit of talk about the lonely honest Haitian official at the center of this trade crisis. It is said, for example, that Transparency International is thinking of honoring him with an award—if he lives long enough.

It is no more than stating the obvious to say that Haiti's historical and political saga is intimately entwined with the dismal results we see today. We need not revisit every sorry stage and tragic step in the country's anguished 200-plus years of independence to understand the awful humanitarian spectacle. Yet the milestones of this historical legacy must be at least mentioned in passing. The African roots: over 100 tribes or peoples involuntarily transplanted to the New World to form the workforce of the French slave plantation system. The colonial interlude: the briefest, as a matter fact, for any country in the New World (French rule in Haiti lasted only just over a century). The slave revolt: following the American Revolution chronologically, but informed by the merciless logic of the French Revolution, killing or driving out virtually all of the country's "white" former masters. And then, with independence on New Year's Day in 1804, the troubled triumph of this Black Spartacus nation.

In 202 years of sovereignty, Haiti has celebrated over 20 constitutions; nine presidents-for-life; a handful of self-proclaimed kings and emperors—and, if one is counting generously, three peaceful and legal transfers of presidential authority from one legitimately elected government to the next, one of which involves the current occupant of the National Palace, President René Préval, who assumed office under MINUSTAH's aegis earlier this year.

Recurring military interventions from abroad are also part of the Haitian legacy, usually though not always by American forces. Most memorable were the 19-year Marine Corps occupation of the country that commenced during World War I; and, more recently, the U.N.-sanctioned American mission in the 1990s that temporarily restored to power Jean-Bertrand Aristide—the exiled, vengeful, radicalized, and corrupt, but popularly elected, president. (In 2004, when Aristide—reelected but by then disgraced—reluctantly relinquished the presidency of a Haiti in turmoil and disarray, U.S. Marines returned once again, before handing off international responsibility for the policing of Haiti to others under the United Nations flag.)

Haiti's heritage is so very African (only a tiny fraction of its people claim to be mixed-blood or "mulatto") that the West African traditions of the 17th and 18th centuries—the culture of modern Haiti's original enslaved ancestors—have not only survived, but taken on a life of their own in the New World. Voodoo is a touchstone here (a word, by no coincidence, that came from a language spoken in the West African country now called Benin). A local aphorism has it that "Haiti is 90 percent Catholic and 100 percent voodoo." Voodoo is, indeed, one of the country's two state-recognized religions. In its forbidding supernatural world, ordinary helpless mortals are at the mercy of a pantheon of loa and lesser undead beings—zombies, loups-garous (werewolves), and the like—who must be feared, and may occasionally be traduced, but cannot always be propitiated.

The correspondence between voodoo and modern Haitian politics is more than incidental. Indeed, Haiti's most powerful and arguably most successful political figure from the past century—François "Papa Doc" Duvalier—was, literally, a voodoo doctor. "Papa Doc" had an M.D. in modern medicine, and trained at the University of Michigan—but he also carefully garbed himself in the dark black suit and the dour, unforgiving demeanor of Baron Samedi, the voodoo god of the graveyard. His control over Haiti was so total that his proposal to confer the next presidency-for-life upon his 19-year-old son "Baby Doc" carried a plebiscite by a vote of 2.5 million to one—so total that his decree to recast the Lord's Prayer as an appeal to the Almighty Papa Doc did not evoke laughter from the Haitians obliged to recite it. Papa Doc ruled through fear, and his agents of terror were his personal gangs of armed, unsmiling, sunglass-wearing thugs. These were the tontons macoutes: creole for "bogeymen," another homage to voodoo. They were not Haiti's first criminal marauders in de facto authority, inflicting misfortune or tragedy by whim on the uncharmed and unlucky—nor, as we sadly see today, were they the last.

Modern Haiti has experienced a "withering away of the state," to borrow a phrase from Karl Marx, but not at all in the way Marx anticipated for his Communist utopia. The government has ceased to provide security and physical safety in any regular or credible fashion. It no longer provides regular and reliable postal service. Its provision of electricity and water is limited and irregular. Health services rely mainly on the charity of strangers (also known as foreign aid).

Hardly less important, the government has excused itself from the task of educating the nation's young. It is only a slight exaggeration to say there is no public system, or even structure, for primary and secondary education in Haiti. The Haitian government, as best I can tell, does not collect and disseminate educational statistics any more—and has basically no idea how many of the country's children are in school, or out of it. There is no question, however, that the educational profile is dismal: According to the country's 2003 census, for example, less than a quarter of all Haitians live in families where the main provider has gone further than sixth grade, and half of Haiti's families rely on breadwinners who have no formal schooling at all.

Knowledgeable Haitians and foreigners with whom I talked guessed that maybe half or three-fifths of Haiti's children enter primary school these days, with maybe one third of that fraction completing their primary education. They also guessed that the Haitian government provides no more than a tenth of the spaces for primary school these days—the rest coming from private-sector "écoles" and "colleges," most of which are tiny, store-front for-pay operations whose modest tuitions nevertheless pose a grim food-or-schooling question to families who wish to see their sons and daughters get an education.

In today's Haiti, even a rudimentary education looks to be beyond the reach of the majority of children; mass illiteracy is the likely prospect for the rising generation. If the failure to provide security deprives Haitians of the environment in which material advance is possible, the failure to educate deprives the population of the tools by which to achieve such advance.

Where does foreign aid and foreign assistance fit into this gruesome tab-leau? In the United States and elsewhere, there are voices quick to attribute Haiti's dire circumstances to inadequate foreign generosity. According to the USAID "Green Book," however, Haiti received a cumulative total of about $3.5 billion (in 2004 dollars) in American aid (economic and security assis-tance) between 1946 and 2004—that is to say, over the roughly six decades in which its per capita output achieved a decline of 25 percent. U.S. aid, moreover, was just one of many sources of concessional official transfers to Haiti. According to the World Bank, since 1969, Haiti has enjoyed a cumu-lative total of $8.3 billion in official development assistance (measured in 2004 dollars).

To put these sums in perspective: The U.S. government places Haiti's official, exchange rate-based GDP for the year 2005 at $4.3 billion. While there are reasons to remain skeptical about that precise figure, as already noted, we can be more confident about another measure of the country's economic performance: merchandise export earnings. In 2004, according to the World Trade Organization, Haiti generated a little less than $400 million through international sales of its own goods. Against that benchmark, foreign aid transfers would amount to over two decades' worth of Haitian exports. Whatever Haiti's many problems may be, an inadequate volume of foreign aid is not one of them.

Although Haiti's prospects are severely clouded, the picture is not totally without hope. Haiti now relies upon a million-plus community of émigrés in the United States, Canada, and elsewhere for remittances that may be the country's most effective economic lifeline at the moment; those same émi-grés could be pivotal in reconstructing and developing Haiti if the business climate warranted the effort, investment, and risk. Haitians are resourceful and hard-working, as their very survival under current conditions should attest. The nation of Haiti has capable, dedicated, and loyal allies, both for-eign and domestic.

Some of the good works now underway are truly inspiring (among them, the Mother Teresa Missionaries of Charity home for abandoned children and the aforementioned GHESKIO HIV clinic/institute, both of which I had the privilege to visit). Other projects underway are incontestably beneficial and worthwhile, such as the microfinance initiative at SOGEBANK, providing loans of a few hundred dollars at a time to striving market-women who can put these to good use. And against all odds, some initiatives are bearing fruit: The nation's HIV prevalence, for example, has been dropping in recent years, and may have been cut by as much as half over the past decade. But all of these individual pockets of promise are as exposed and vulnerable as sand castles at low tide—every speck of progress could be swept away, given the wild, unpredictable, and still-uncontrolled savagery into which this unhappy country has descended.

Haiti will be in a much better place than it is today when we can complain about corruption there. Haiti will be in a much better place than it is today when we can focus our policy criticisms on bureaucratic inefficiency, or wrongheaded economic and financial policies. What Haiti needs, more than any other single thing, is physical safety and security—for the sake of the poor as well as the rich. By itself, physical safety would constitute an immense improvement in the local standard of living (measured in any real human sense). An environment of safety and security would make it possible—at least theoretically—to achieve social and economic development and material advance.

For now, those desiderata are not even remotely realistic objectives. A cautious political survivor, President Préval now talks of "social appeasement" (a term that sounds no better in French or Creole than in English) and of opening a "dialogue" with the gangs that are murdering and terrorizing his countrymen. Safer streets are hardly the most likely outcome from such entreaties.

Under current conditions, foreign economic assistance—from the United States or elsewhere—can serve little more than a palliative function, akin to changing bandages on an open wound. While some will argue there is merit and even nobility in such service, we should have no illusions about what such service can—and cannot—do.

What do we—the fortunate souls holding U.S. passports, with warm beds and hot meals awaiting us—come home learning from a brief fact-finding sojourn to Haiti? In a sentence: Security comes first. First in the hierarchy of human needs. First in the prerequisites for economic progress. Nothing so elevated as "law and order"—apart from its unfondly remembered interlude under U.S. Marine Corps occupation in the early 20th century, it is not clear that Haiti has ever had that, and maybe not even then. Just physical safety and security.

Without security, efforts to better the national plight will be doomed to frustration, or worse. Foreign economic assistance will be mainly wasted, or worse. Humanitarian assistance efforts will find themselves on an endless treadmill. Economic and humanitarian assistance are no substitute for security and safety—cannot substitute for it, cannot themselves create it. And what holds for Haiti holds just as true for other tortured regions of the world where governments receive foreign aid, but local populations do not receive safety.

13

The Global War Against Baby Girls

The New Atlantis, January 12, 2012

Over the past three decades the world has come to witness an ominous and entirely new form of gender discrimination: sex-selective feticide, implemented through the practice of surgical abortion with the assistance of information gained through prenatal gender determination technology. All around the world, the victims of this new practice are overwhelmingly female—in fact, almost universally female. The practice has become so ruthlessly routine in many contemporary societies that it has impacted their very population structures, warping the balance between male and female births and consequently skewing the sex ratios for the rising generation toward a biologically unnatural excess of males. This still-growing international predilection for sex-selective abortion is by now evident in the demographic contours of dozens of countries around the globe—and it is sufficiently severe that it has come to alter the overall sex ratio at birth of the entire planet, resulting in millions upon millions of new "missing baby girls" each year. In terms of its sheer toll in human numbers, sex-selective abortion has assumed a scale tantamount to a global war against baby girls.

Initial Signal in China

A regular and quite predictable relationship between total numbers of male and female births is a fixed biological characteristic for human populations, as it is for other species of mammals. The discovery of the consistency, across time and space, of the sex ratio at birth (SRB) for human beings was one of the very earliest findings of the modern discipline of demography. (One of the founders of the field, the German priest and statistician Johann Peter

Süssmilch, posited in 1741 that "the Creator's reasons for ensuring four to five percent more boys than girls are born lie in the fact that it compensates for the higher male losses due to the recklessness of boys, to exhaustion, to dangerous occupations, to war, to seafaring and immigration, thus maintaining the balance between the two sexes so that everyone can find a spouse at the appropriate time for marriage.")

Medical and demographic research subsequently identified some differences in SRB that correspond with ethnicity, birth order, parental age, urbanization, environmental conditions, and other factors. But such differences were always quite small; until the 1980s, the SRB for large human populations tended to fall within a narrow range, usually around 103 to 106 newborn boys for every 100 newborn girls and typically centering no higher than 105. Until the 1980s, exceptions to this generality were mainly registered in small populations, and attributable to chance.

The modern phenomenon of biologically unnatural increase in the sex ratio at birth was first noticed in the 1980s for China, the world's most populous country. In 1979, China promulgated its "One Child Policy," a compulsory and at times coercive population-control program that continues to be enforced to this day (albeit with regional and temporal variations in severity). In 1982, China's national population census—the first to be conducted in nearly two decades—reported an SRB of 108.5, a striking and disturbing demographic anomaly. Initially, researchers surmised that this abnormal imbalance might be in large part a statistical artifact, under the hypothesis that Chinese parents might be disposed to conceal the birth of a daughter so as to have another chance for a son, given the strict birth quotas so often decreed by the One Child Policy. But successive Chinese population censuses registered ever-higher SRBs. By the 2005 "mini-census"—a survey of 1 percent of the country's population, conducted between the full censuses—China's SRB approached 120, and the reported nationwide sex ratio for children under 5 was even higher (see Table 13-1). Although, as recently noted in a study by Daniel M. Goodkind in the journal *Demography*, there remain some discrepancies and inconsistencies among data sources (census numbers, vital registration reports, hospital delivery records, school enrollment figures, and so on) concerning China's SRBs and child sex ratios over the past two decades, there is absolutely no doubt that shockingly distorted sex ratios for newborns and

Table 13-1. The Rise of Gender Imbalance in China

Reported Sex Ratios at Birth and Sex Ratios of the Population Age 0-4: China, 1953-2005 (boys per 100 girls)

Year	Sex Ration at Birth	Sex Ratio, Age 0–4
1953	—	107.0
1964	—	105.7
1982	108.5	107.1
1990	111.4	110.2
1995	115.6	118.4
1999	117.0	119.5
2005	118.9	122.7

Sources: William Lavely, "First Impressions of the 2000 Census of China" (http://csde.washington. edu/pubs/wps/01-13.pdf), as well as unpublished data from the Chinese Academy of Social Sciences, Institute for Population and Labor Economies, 2008.

Figure 13-1. Reported Sex Ratio in China by Province, 2005

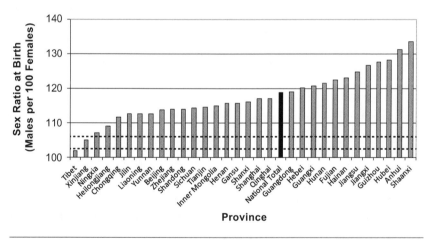

Source: China's 2005 "mini-census."

children prevail in China today—and that these gender imbalances have increased dramatically during the decades of the One Child Policy.

Chinese census data outline the basic geo-demography of China's imbalanced sex ratios at birth. For the country as a whole, SRBs since

Figure 13-2. Reported Child (0–4) Sex Ratio in China by Country, 2000

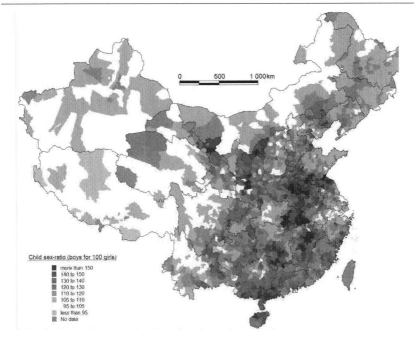

Source: Christophe Z. Guilmoto and Sébastien Oliveau, "Sex ratio imbalances among children at micro-level: China and India compared," paper presented at Population Association of America 2007 annual meeting. Based on data from the National Bureau of Statistics of China (2003).

1982 have consistently been lowest for China's cities, and highest for rural areas; in the 2005 mini-census, reported SRBs were roughly 123 for rural areas, 120 for towns, and 115 for cities. But there are major SRB variations within China at the regional level; as of 2005, only three provinces reported essentially "normal" SRBs, while many more reported SRBs of 125 or more, with two provinces reporting levels in excess of 130 (see Figure 13-1). The geography of China's gender imbalance is further highlighted by a county-level breakout of sex ratios for young children in the year 2000 (see Figure 13-2). As may be seen, sex ratios are essentially "normal" (105 or lower) in much of Western China and along parts of the country's northern border—areas where non-Han ethnic minorities predominate—while unnatural gender imbalances characterize virtually the entirety of the Han-majority areas in China's east and south. There are tremendous variations in the extremity of the condition within this Han expanse: a number of inland and coastal areas stand out as epicenters of the problem, and are marked by concentrations of counties, each encompassing millions or tens of millions of people, wherein child sex ratios of 150 or greater prevail. Demographers Christophe Z. Guilmoto and Sébastien Oliveau describe these radical-imbalance areas as "hot spots"—and since the phenomenon has spread across China's population over the past three decades, Figure 13-2 may be regarded as the map of mounting national casualties.

Parity-Specific Imbalance

Further light is cast on the cause of Chinese SRB imbalances by patterns of parity-specific SRBs—that is to say, sex ratios at birth by birth order—since 1982 (see Figure 13-3). Significantly, SRBs for firstborn Chinese children have remained relatively low and were actually in the biologically "normal" range around 105 until the early 1990s. By contrast, SRBs for higher-parity births (children born after the first child) from the late 1980s onward have been stratospheric and continued to rise until the year 2000, at which time the SRB for higher-parity births exceeded 150. (Higher-parity SRBs reportedly declined somewhat between 2000 and 2005—but as of 2005 nonetheless amounted to 143 for second births and to 156 for third births.) An influential 2006 Harvard dissertation by Emily Oster hypothesized that the emerging gender imbalances in China and elsewhere were primarily a consequence of the spread of the hepatitis B virus, which is known to skew SRBs in favor of male babies in maternal carriers—but clearly that theory cannot account for the extraordinary and continuing disparities between first births and higher-order births in China. Instead, it is by now widely recognized that these gender disparities are the consequence of parental intervention—namely, mass feticide, through the agency of medically induced abortion and prenatal gender determination technology. Chinese parents appear to have been generally willing to rely upon biological chance for the sex outcome of their first baby—but with increasing frequency they have been relying upon health care technology and services to ensure that any second- or higher-order

**Figure 13-3. China: Reported Sex Ratios at Birth by Birth Order
(parity), 1982–2005**

Sources: Full Chinese population censuses in 1982, 1990, and 2000 and "mini-censuses" (1 percent population surveys) in 1987 and 2005. Adapted from Li Shuzhou, "Imbalanced sex ratio at
birth and comprehensive intervention in China," 4th Asia Pacific Conference on Reproductive and
Sexual Health and Rights, United Nations Population Fund, October 2007.

baby would be a boy. (Although China's population program is known as
the "One Child Policy," in practice it permits the birth of some second,
third, and even higher-order babies. For the country as a whole, the total
fertility rate, or number of births per woman per lifetime, is estimated by
the U.N. Population Division as 1.64 for the 2005-2010 period, and by
the U.S. Census Bureau International Data Base at 1.54 for the year 2010.)

The critical health service elements in this tableau are China's universal and
unconditional availability of abortion conjoined with access to reliable and
inexpensive obstetric ultrasonography. According to Chinese researchers, in
1982 diagnostic ultrasound scanning devices were available in health clinics
in about one-sixth of Chinese counties; by 1985, over half of Chinese counties had them, and by 1990 virtually all did. By 2000, sex-selective abortion
had become astonishingly commonplace in China: rough calculations for that
year suggest that no less than half of the nation's higher-parity female fetuses
were being aborted, and that well over half of all abortions were female fetuses

terminated as a consequence of prenatal gender determination. In effect, most of contemporary China's abortions are thus intentional female feticides.

Drivers of Imbalance

Though Western sensibilities may be inclined to attribute the national embrace of mass female feticide to "backward" thinking in China, important basic facts are uncomfortably inconsistent with that proposition. For one thing, abnormal sex ratios appear to be almost entirely a Han phenomenon within China—and China's Han are, generally speaking, better educated and more affluent than the country's non-Han minorities. Second, although SRBs are lower in urban than in rural China, these differences may have less to do with education and income than with fertility levels. After all, fertility levels are decidedly lower in urban than in rural China, meaning that a smaller proportion of babies born in China's cities are higher-parity births, which tend in China to be overwhelmingly male. Third, China has enjoyed a historically extraordinary surge of development and prosperity over the very years that SRBs and child sex ratios have been rising. Between the 1982 census and the 2005 mini-census, China's reported adult (15 and older) female illiteracy rate dropped from 25 percent to 4 percent, and mean years of schooling for Chinese women rose by nearly 50 percent over roughly that same period, from 5.4 to 8.0. Moreover, China's estimated per capita income jumped nearly fivefold between 1982 and 2005, while the fraction of the population living in extreme poverty (as defined by the World Bank) plummeted from roughly 75 percent in 1981 to roughly 15 percent in 2004. Despite continuing political restrictions and state-administered censorship, China is also vastly more open to the outside world today than it was in the early 1980s (as attested by statistics on everything from international trade, investment, and finance to travel and communications). China's increasingly unnatural sex ratios for babies and children and its growing army of "missing girls" must therefore be regarded as a feature—indeed, a defining feature—of so-called "globalization with Chinese characteristics." (Note, incidentally, that Beijing outlawed prenatal sex determination in 1989, and criminalized sex-selective abortion in 2004—yet these legal strictures have obviously been ineffective despite the Chinese state's considerable police powers.)

Figure 13-4. Sex Ratios at Birth Reported in East Asia: 1980–2005

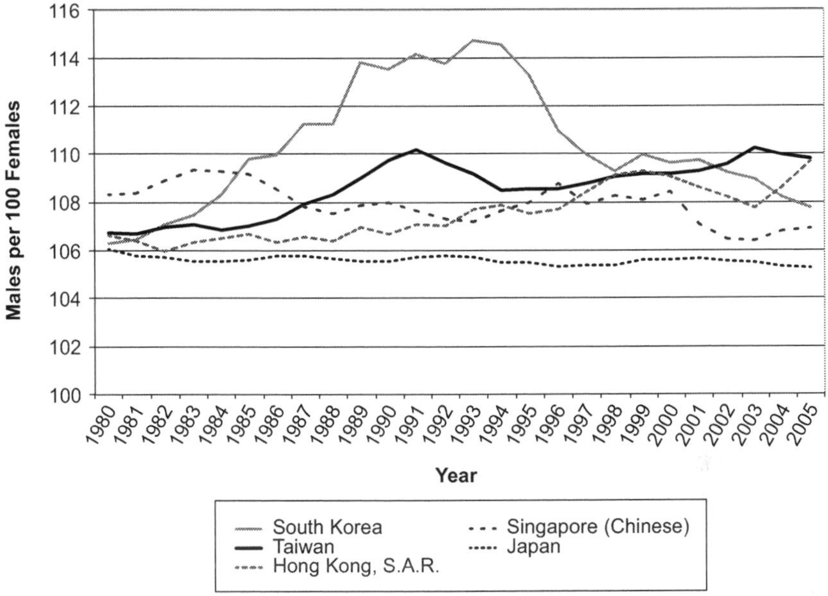

Source: Daniel Goodkind, "Child underreporting, fertility, and sex ratio imbalance in China," *Demography* (2011) 48:291-316.

Imbalances in the "Little Dragons" and Vietnam

China's unnatural long-term rise in SRBs emerged under a draconian state-run population-control program. But coercive family-planning programs are neither a necessary nor a sufficient condition for widespread female feticide. This much is evident from SRB trends in East Asia's four "Little Dragons": Hong Kong, Singapore (more specifically, Singapore's ethnic Chinese), South Korea, and Taiwan. All of those societies maintain voluntary family-planning programs—nevertheless, each of them has registered eerie increases in SRBs in the era of unconditional abortion and widespread access to inexpensive obstetric ultrasonography (see Figure 13-4). Approaching the dawn of the twenty-first century, SRBs in all four of these affluent and highly educated populations were a naturally impossible 108 or higher; and just as in China, SRBs were typically lowest (often "normal") for the first-born babies and suspiciously elevated for all higher-parity births, as

Figure 13-5: Reported Child (0–6) Sex Ratio, India, Re-aggregated Sub-Districts, 2001

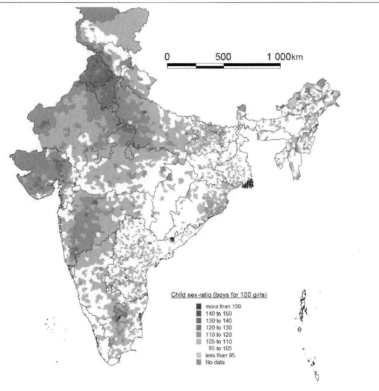

Source: Christophe Z. Guilmoto and Sébastien Oliveau, "Sex ratio imbalances among children at micro-level: China and India compared," paper presented at Population Association of America 2007 annual meeting. Based on data from the 2006 Indian census.

reported by Chai Bin Park and Nam-Hoon Cho in 1995—a telltale sign of parental intervention through sex-selective abortion. Like China, these Little Dragons all had laws on their books proscribing prenatal gender determination and sex-selective abortion that did not forestall subsequent rises in their SRBs. Of all the Little Dragons, South Korea reached the most demographically disfiguring heights: an SRB of well over 114 in the early 1990s, not too different from China's at that time. But South Korea's SRB declined steadily thereafter, and by 2009 was, according to official state statistics, a practically "normal" 106—a matter to which we shall return.

The Imbalance Elsewhere

In West Asia, the Caucasus region has emerged since the end of the Cold War as another front in the global war against baby girls. Between the final collapse of the Soviet Union in 1991 and the year 2000, SRBs in Armenia, Azerbaijan, and Georgia all rose from about 105 to about 120. Ultrasound diagnostics were generally unavailable in these countries in the Soviet era. Inferential evidence—including increased general access to diagnostic ultrasound and newly increasing SRBs for higher-parity births, especially third and higher-order births—strongly suggests that these countries are subject to the same syndrome observed in so much of East and South Asia. Recent data indicate that SRBs in the Caucasus have declined, but only slightly: to 116 in Armenia and Azerbaijan (as of 2008) and to 112 in Georgia (as of 2004).

The ten societies with biologically unnatural SRBs examined thus far represent most of the world's major religious and cultural traditions: Confucianism, Buddhism, Hinduism, Islam, and Christianity. But these are by no means the only contemporary settings in which evidence of the phenomenon is emerging at a population-wide level (see Tables 13-2 and 13-3). Recent vital statistics for places with complete or near-complete registration, and census returns for other places, point to almost twenty additional countries or territories with populations of one million or greater with suspiciously high SRBs. Other places in Asia with high recent SRBs and/or child sex ratios include the Philippines, Brunei Darussalam, Papua New Guinea, Bangladesh, Kyrgyzstan, and Turkey. In North Africa and the Middle East, both Lebanon and Libya betray the same disturbing demographic characteristics. In Latin America and the Caribbean, elevated SRBs or child sex ratios are seen in Cuba, Puerto Rico, and El Salvador. But it is important to recognize that the phenomenon is also now evident in over half a dozen European countries as well. Albania's officially reported 2004 SRB was 113. In Serbia and Montenegro—portions of the former Yugoslavia—2008 SRBs were 109 and 108, respectively. And in the nominally Catholic-majority populations of Austria, Italy, Portugal, and Spain, officially reported 2008 SRBs were all 107.

Naturally impossible SRBs are also now seen in the United States and the United Kingdom—within particular ethnic groups. In America, as Douglas Almond and Lena Edlund have reported in the Proceedings of the National Academy of Sciences (PNAS), SRBs of 108 were characteristic of the

Table 13-2. Selected Countries with Populations over 1 Million Reporting Sex Ratios at Birth over 107 in a Recent Year (and Near-Complete Vital Registration)

Country (year)	Sex ratio at birth	Midyear pop. (2010), UNPD
Albania (2004)	113	3,204,000
El Salvador (2007)	110	6,193,000
Philippines (2007)	109	93,261,000
Libya (2002)	108	6,355,000
Serbia (2008)	108	9,856,000
Austria (2008)	107	8,394,000
Cuba (2008)	107	11,258,000
Italy (2005)	107	60,551,000
Kyrgyzstan (2008)	107	5,334,000
Portugal (2008)	107	10,676,000
Spain (2008)	107	46,077,000

Note: All data derived from civil registration, estimated at over 90 percent complete.
Sources: Table 10 ("Live births by age of mother and sex of child, general and age-specific fertility rates: latest available year, 1990-2008"), Demographic Yearbook 2008, Statistics Division, Department of Economic and Social Affairs, U.N. Secretariat; and World Population Prospects: The 2010 Revision (http://esa.un.org/unpd/wpp/index.htm).

Table 13-3. Selected Countries with Populations over 1 Million Reporting Child (0-4) Sex Ratios Above 107 in a Recent Population Census

Country (year)	Sex ratio at birth	Midyear pop. (2010), UNPD
Lebanon (2007)	110	4,228,000
Bangladesh (2001)	108	148,692,000
Papua New Guinea (2000)	108	6,858,000
Albania (2001)	107	3,204,000
Turkey (2000)	107	72,752,000

Note: Lebanon data from sample survey, de facto, all others from census, de facto, complete tabulation.
Sources: Table 7 ("Population by age, sex and urban/rural residence: latest available year, 1999–2008") Demographic Yearbook 2008, Statistics Division, Department of Economic and Social Affairs, U.N. Secretariat; and World Population Prospects: The 2010 Revision (http://esa.un.org/unpd/wpp/index.htm).

"Asian-Pacific" population (Chinese-Americans, Korean-Americans, Filipino-Americans, etc.) in the 2000 census, and in vital statistics thereafter. These are all populations whose SRBs were within the natural biological range a generation ago. In England and Wales, sex ratios at birth for Indian-born mothers have also risen markedly, from 104 in the 1980s to 108 in the late 1990s, as noted by Sylvie Dubuc and David Coleman in *Population and Development Review*. In both the United States and the United Kingdom, these gender disparities were due largely to sharp increases in higher-parity SRBs, strongly suggesting that sex-selective abortions were the driver. The American and British cases also point to the possibility that sex-selective abortion may be common to other subpopulations in developed or less developed societies, even if these do not affect the overall SRB for each country as a whole.

The Demographic Effect

Sex-selective abortion is by now so widespread and so frequent that it has come to distort the population composition of the entire human species: this new and medicalized war against baby girls is indeed truly global in scale and scope. Estimates by the United Nations Population Division (UNPD) and the U.S. Census Bureau's International Programs Center (IPC)—the two major organizations charged with tracking and projecting global population trends—make the point. According to estimates based on IPC data, a total of 21 countries or territories (including a number of European and Pacific Island areas) had SRBs of 107 or higher in the year 2010; the total population of the regions beset by unnaturally high SRBs amounted to 2.7 billion, or about 40 percent of the world's total population. For its part, UNPD estimates that 24 countries and territories (a slightly different roster from IPC's, including some additional European, South American, Middle Eastern, Asian, and Pacific settings) had SRBs of 107 or higher for the 2005-2010 period, for a total population similar to the IPC figure. Additionally, UNPD and IPC list several countries with child (age 0-4) sex ratios of 107 or higher; those lists partially overlap with the SRB lists. If we tally all the places that IPC and UNPD flag as having unnaturally high SRBs or child sex ratios, along with the places listed in Tables 2 and 3 whose official demographic statistics report unnaturally high SRBs or child sex ratios, we would have a total of over 50 countries and territories accounting for over 3.2 billion people, or nearly half of the world's total population.

By the reckoning of UNPD, the overall global sex ratio at birth has already assumed naturally impossible heights in the era of sex-selective abortion, rising from 105 in 1975-80 to 107 for 2005-10. By the same token, IPC puts the worldwide under-5 child sex ratio at 107 for 2010.

To go by both UNPD and IPC reconstructions of local age-sex structures, today's societies with unnaturally high SRBs and/or child sex ratios had an aggregate "boy surplus" of over 55 million males under the age of 20 by the year 2010; and if we assume that the SRBs and child/youth sex ratios in these societies should be around 105, the unnatural "girl deficit" for females 0-19 years of age as of 2010 would have totaled roughly 32-33 million by both UNPD and IPC figures. In both the UNPD and the IPC reckonings, the world's two most populous countries, China and India, would account for the overwhelming majority (31-32 million) of the world's "missing girls" under 20 years of age in our era of sex-selective abortion (although the implied UNPD and IPC totals for China and India themselves differ substantially, in accordance with their assumptions concerning such things as the extent of undercounting of girls). Note, in any case, that irrespective of differences in IPC- and UNPD-based estimates for given countries, these global estimates for missing girls under 20 are arguably conservative figures. The IPC and UNPD estimates exclude numerous countries—some of them quite populous— where, as Therese Hesketh and Zhu Wei Xing have reported in PNAS, evidence of unnaturally high SRBs has been emerging from vital registration or national census data. Also, the figures could be considered conservative because they only consider countries with SRBs or child sex ratios of 107 or higher, even though anything over 105 could be considered unnatural, and other research sometimes uses thresholds of 104, 103, or even lower.

Social Implications

The consequences of medically abetted mass feticide are far-reaching and manifestly adverse. In populations with unnaturally skewed SRBs, the very fact that many thousands—or in some cases, millions—of prospective girls and young women have been deliberately eliminated simply because they would have been female establishes a new social reality that inescapably colors the whole realm of human relationships, redefining the role of women as the disfavored sex in nakedly utilitarian terms, and indeed signaling that their very existence is now conditional and contingent.

Moreover, enduring and extreme SRB imbalances set the demographic stage for an incipient "marriage squeeze" in affected populations, with notably reduced pools of potential future brides. China's persistently elevated SRBs, for example, stand to transform it from a country where as of 2000 nearly all males (about 96 percent) had been married by their early 40s to one in which nearly a quarter (23 percent) are projected to be never married as of 2040, less than 30 years from now, according to a 2008 analysis by the demographer Zeng Yi and colleagues in the journal *Genus*. Such a transformation augurs ill in a number of respects. For one thing, unmarried men appear to suffer greater health risks than their married counterparts, even after controlling for exogenous social and environmental factors; a sharp increase in the proportion of essentially unmarriageable males in a society with a universal marriage norm may only accentuate those health risks. In a low-income society lacking sturdy and reliable national pension guarantees for the elderly, a steep rise in the proportion of unmarried and involuntarily childless men begs the question of old-age support for that rising cohort. Economists such as Gary Becker and Judge Richard Posner have hypothesized that mass feticide, in making women scarce, will only increase their "value"—but in settings where the legal and personal rights of the individual are not secure and inviolable, the "rising value of women" can have perverse and unexpected consequences, including increased demand for prostitution and an upsurge in the kidnapping and trafficking of women (as is now being witnessed in some women-scarce areas in Asia, as reported by Mara Hvistendahl in her new book *Unnatural Selection*).

Finally, there is the speculative question of the social impact of a sudden addition of a large cohort of young "excess males" to populations with sustained extreme SRBs: depending on a given country's cultural and institutional capabilities for coping with this challenge, such trends could quite conceivably lead to increased crime, violence, and social tensions—or possibly even a greater proclivity for social instability. (For a decidedly pessimistic but studied assessment of these prospects, see Valerie M. Hudson and

Andrea M. den Boer's 2004 book *Bare Branches: The Security Implications of Asia's Surplus Male Population.*)

All in all, mass sex selection can be regarded as a "tragedy of the commons" dynamic, in which the aggregation of individual (parental) choices has the inadvertent result of degrading the quality of life for all—and some much more than others.

What are the prospects for mass sex-selective feticide in the years immediately ahead? Unfortunately, there is ample room for cautious pessimism. Although biologically unnatural SRBs now characterize an expanse accounting for something approaching half of humanity, it is by no means clear that this march has yet ceased.

As we have seen, sudden steep increases in SRBs are by no means inconsistent with continuing improvements in levels of per capita income and female education—or, for that matter, with legal strictures against sex-selective abortion. Two of the key factors associated with unnatural upsurges in nationwide SRBs—low or sub-replacement fertility levels and easy access to inexpensive prenatal gender-determination technology—will likely be present in an increasing number of low-income societies in the years and decades immediately ahead. The third factor critical to mass female feticide—ruthless son preference—is perhaps surprisingly difficult to identify in advance. In theory, overbearing son preference should be available from demographic and health surveys—such as India's National Family and Health Survey, which demonstrated that prospective mothers in the state of Punjab desired their next child to be male rather than female by a ratio of 10 to 1. Yet ironically, despite the many tens of millions of dollars that international aid and development agencies have spent on the hundreds of demographic and health surveys they have supported in low-income countries over recent decades, information on sex preference is almost never collected. (Evidently, Western funders of Third World population programs are concerned about the number of babies local parents desire, not their genders.)

Differential infant and child mortality rates arguably also offer clues about son preference: societies where female rates exceed male rates (patterns arising from systemic discriminatory mistreatment of little girls) may be correspondingly disposed to prenatal gender discrimination as well. According to the World Health Organization's 2009 Life Tables, over 60 countries currently experience higher infant or age 1-4 mortality rates for girls than for boys: a roster including much of South-Central Asia, North Africa and the Middle East, parts of Latin America and the Caribbean, and over a dozen countries in sub-Saharan Africa. If such gender bias in mortality turns out to be a predictor of sex-selection bias, this global problem may get considerably worse before it gets better.

Considerations for the Future

There is, however, one country thus far that has managed to return from grotesquely imbalanced SRBs to normal human ratios: South Korea. As explained by Woojin Chung and Monica Das Gupta in 2007 in Population and Development Review, there is still considerable dispute about the factors involved in this turnaround, with many institutions and actors ready to take credit (as the old saying goes: success has many fathers). Available evidence, however, seems to suggest that South Korea's SRB reversal was influenced less by government policy than by civil society: more specifically, by the spontaneous and largely uncoordinated congealing of a mass movement for honoring, protecting, and prizing daughters. In effect, this movement—drawing largely but by no means exclusively on the faith-based community—sparked a national conversation of conscience about the practice of female feticide. This conversation was instrumental in stigmatizing the practice, not altogether unlike the way in which nationwide conversations of conscience helped to stigmatize international slave-trading in other countries in earlier times. The best hope today in the global war against baby girls may be to carry this conversation of conscience to other lands. Medical and health care professionals—without whose assistance mass female feticide could not occur—have a special obligation to be front and center in this dialogue.

14

Bring Them Home

The Weekly Standard, June 6, 2005

In recent decades, more than one constitutional democracy has been faced with the prospect of a humanitarian crisis afflicting compatriots living beyond its borders. And on more than one occasion, such states have come to the rescue of their countrymen—by welcoming them into the homeland, embracing them as fellow citizens, and permitting them to enjoy the opportunities and benefits of life under secure, constitutional and democratic rule.

The Federal Republic of Germany faced such a crisis in the very earliest days of its existence, when the ethnic Germans who came to be called Vertriebene—most of them women and children—were fleeing from the harsh and vindictive Soviet expansion. West Germany welcomed these unfortunates, even though it was not clear that the still-devastated German economic terrain could provide for all these new mouths. Accommodating this influx of needy refugees—a population of over 11 million, disproportionately made up of the elderly, the infirm, and casualties of war—was more than an incidental inconvenience for a then-fragile West German society, where semi-starvation rations were the norm. Informed opinion, both in West Germany and abroad, held that the prospects for the Vertriebene were bleak—and that the burden of supporting them could only compromise the future of a free Germany. Yet in the event, the miserable unfortunates who flooded into the Federal Republic were soon to prove integral to what became known as the Wirtschaftswunder—the German postwar economic "miracle."

As West Germany flourished, the Federal Republic not only continued to welcome in its kinsmen, but sought them out, financing their transit and even purchasing their freedom from the odious dictatorships that held them in bondage. In addition to the Vertriebene, the Federal Republic of Germany was to absorb another 8 million ethnic German Aussiedler (from the former

Soviet Union, Poland, and elsewhere) in the four decades between the early 1950s and the German nation's ultimate reunification.

The state of Israel also has faced recurrent humanitarian refugee crises. Hapless, impoverished, and persecuted Jewish populations figured all too prominently within the worldwide Jewish diaspora. From the very founding of the Israeli state in 1948, the government of Israel made a point not only to welcome these Jews into their country with open arms, but also actively to seek them out, and to aid in their passage to their promised land.

Particularly dramatic mass rescue efforts were organized for the endangered Jews of Yemen, and then, decades later, for the starving Beta Israel (Jews sometimes called Falasha) from Ethiopia. These bold and successful air missions are recorded by history as "Operation Flying Carpet," "Operation Moses," "Operation Solomon," and "Operation Sheba." In an inconstant and often heartless world, their inspiring example has demonstrated the potential of humanitarian rescue if a free society is genuinely committed to serving as "its brother's keeper."

Those stirring Israeli rescue missions, it is worth noting, raised their own concerns and questions among the populace receiving the desperate pilgrims. The impoverished and benighted Jews from Yemen and Ethiopia were utter strangers to modernity. Most of them could not read; many of them had never owned a pair of shoes; some had never seen an airplane until the moment of their deliverance. How could such people stand a chance of meeting the challenges of life in a sophisticated industrial society?

Today we know the answer. The story of Yemeni and Ethiopian assimilation into modern Israeli society was not perfect—tales involving human beings never are. With the passage of time, nevertheless, integration has worked remarkably well—far better than many would have dared to hope. The Yemeni and Ethiopian refugees and their descendants are loyal and productive citizens in their newfound homeland—proud supporters of Israeli democracy and participants in the Israeli economy. Moreover, by this loving gesture to "the least of her people," Israel's democracy was itself further affirmed and further strengthened.

Today, it is the Republic of Korea that faces a humanitarian crisis among exiled compatriots. This is a terrible saga, an ongoing tragedy. It is not "breaking news," nor has it exactly escaped international notice. Quite the contrary: Over the past decade, this piteous situation has been chronicled in practically every tongue (all the languages of the United Nations, at the very least). But let me recount it anyway.

Not far from Seoul—maybe a half hour's journey north, by jet plane—an untold number of terrified Koreans are hiding in a foreign land, engaged in a grave and uncertain struggle for survival. (There may be tens of thousands in the ranks of these misérables, or there may be hundreds of thousands—it is a chilling indication of their plight that we should have no reliable information about such a basic fact.) These wretched vagabonds—most of them women and children—are escapees from North Korea. They have crossed the Yalu and the Tumen into China in tiny groups, driven into the unknown by Kim Jong Il's man-made famine. That catastrophe—the only peacetime famine to befall an urbanized, literate society in all of human history—claimed hundreds upon hundreds of thousands of victims in the 1990s; though the death toll from the ongoing North Korean food crisis seems for the moment to have subsided, hunger remains a dire problem there—especially for that society's officially disfavored strata.

For the North Korean border-crossers in China, existence is stripped of the most modest vestiges of ordinary human dignity. Local rules of survival oblige these people to live like animals—if they hope to live at all. Many of the border-crossers stay in the woods, sleeping by day and foraging by night, alone and in constant fear of discovery by fellow humans. The women can be sold, like cattle; the men are regularly hunted down and rounded up, almost like dogs.

These escapees are at the mercy of the least scrupulous element of the populace north of the Yalu River. They can be robbed without recourse—or raped, or beaten and killed just for the fun of it. And that is the peril when their hunters are simply ordinary villagers or townsmen. When they are captured by local security agents or members of the secret police, their fate is possibly even more frightening—for then they are deported back to North Korea, a receiving state that regards any voluntary departure from Kim Jong Il's "paradise" as a crime, an act of betrayal verging on treason. The deportees forced back into North Korea face unspeakable punishments in political prisons, reeducation camps, and special detention camps for children. In addition to the tortures returnees can expect to face themselves, there is the added pain of knowing that their family line is subject to retribution—for in the North Korean control system, horrible penalties can fall on family members as many as three generations removed from the perpetrator of a so-called political crime.

The conditions facing today's North Korean border-crossers are no less grim than those of the Vertriebene or Falasha/Beta Israel before them, and likely are more dire. The case for a Republic of Korea rescue of these escapees—that is to say, for aiding in their relocation to the South, for welcoming them into South Korean life, and for positively determining to abet their integration as citizens and members of South Korean society—is compelling, in fact, overwhelming.

Indeed, it is imperative that the Republic of Korea—for legal, and for moral, but also for entirely practical reasons—accept the challenge posed by the distress of these very vulnerable fellow Koreans and rise to meet it.

Here are just a few of those reasons. Welcoming and embracing North Korean escapees who wish to come to the Republic of Korea (ROK) and enjoy the guarantees of constitutional democracy is not simply a sentimental impulse. Rather it is a position consistent with the ROK's most basic laws. The rights and jurisdiction of people living in the northern part of the Korean peninsula are spelled out in the ROK constitution. Though the constitution went through nine revisions between 1948 and 1987, the basic promise of citizenship held out to brethren in the North never waivered. Nor does it today—from the standpoint of the written law.

After stipulating that the government of the ROK has the right to define nationality for the country, the constitution goes on to define the legal conception of the Korean nation in Article 3: "The territory of the Republic of Korea shall consist of the Korean peninsula and its adjacent islands." And it goes further, stipulating that "the State shall protect its citizens abroad as provided by Act." Are ordinary North Koreans who wish to claim South Korean citizenship eligible for it under ROK law? The answer is unambiguously yes. The question in fact has been reviewed and settled by the ROK Supreme Court.

On November 12, 1996, the Court ruled on a pending deportation case that one Ms. Lee Young Soon, a North Korean who had been living in China, but had made her way to the South, was in fact automatically qualified for ROK citizenship. The relevant portion of the ruling reads as follows: "Under Clause 3 of the [ROK] Constitution, North Koreans should be acknowledged as citizens of the Republic of Korea."

Reaffirming the Republic of Korea's constitutional obligations to North Korean escapees would have intangible but far-reaching and salutary effects for South Korea, both domestically and internationally. Such a declaration would strengthen the rule of law in South Korea, reinforcing the political foundations upon which the ROK's own freedom, prosperity, and security ultimately rest. And it would provide a magnificent demonstration to the world that South Korea's commitment to its basic legal principles is not merely rhetorical or opportunistic.

South Korea, it bears remembering, is still a state under siege—like Israel, the Republic of Korea remains locked in conflict with neighboring forces that entirely deny its authority or even its right to exist at all. No gesture would better remind the international community of the reasons that the Republic of Korea is the legitimate state in the intra-peninsular contest than welcoming the refugees home.

Rescuing the North Korean escapees is unquestionably the right thing to do from a humanitarian standpoint, as well. The circumstances that have forced North Koreans to risk their lives crossing the Chinese border to forage and beg are so awful as to defy understanding by the comfortable, the well-fed, and the well-protected. North Korea's subjects have long suffered under a police state once described by Robert Scalapino, the eminent Asia scholar, as "the closest approximation of totalitarianism that could be achieved by a society operated by human beings." As many as a million—or more—were killed in the Great North Korean Famine of the 1990s.

Because of the extreme secrecy of the North Korean state, we do not know just how serious the privation facing ordinary North Koreans actually is. Even the international humanitarian organizations that have supplied Pyongyang with hundreds upon hundreds of millions of dollars worth of supplies over the past decade have not been given honest information about the distress that they are paying to relieve. But we know that ordinary North Korean children and young people these days are stunted and wasted—so small and slight on average that, by comparison to their South Korean brethren, they look as if they were drawn from a different race. (That is why the North Korean military has steadily relaxed its height and weight prerequisites to the point where the height requirement could reportedly be met by a typical 8-year-old South Korean schoolboy.)

News reports suggest that North Korea's food situation is taking a turn for the worse—reports seemingly confirmed by announcements that rations are again being cut. Under such circumstances, the argument for humanitarian rescue would appear self-evidently arresting.

Welcoming these escapees from North Korea will also create direct and acute pressure upon Pyongyang to attend to the needs and aspirations of its subjects. Sending the signal throughout the North that escapees have a real alternative to the hell of Kim Jong Il's "workers' paradise" and the purgatory of a no-man's land just across the Chinese border will compel the Kim Jong Il regime to re-examine the destructive policies and practices that are driving North Koreans to flee.

Addressing the reality of a beckoning safe haven for escapees would require the North Korean regime to adopt a more pragmatic and humane food policy, to tolerate a wider scope for self-betterment through individual initiatives, and to build sturdier links to the world economy. In short, the possibility of a real alternative to life in the North will push that regime, much against its wishes, to open the door a bit to a less illiberal order—not to a liberal order, to be sure, but perhaps to a system with less malevolence than any they have yet known.

We do not know and cannot know the status of the discourse within the inner circles of Kim Jong Il's hierarchy about the question of "reform." And it is probably fruitless to speculate about just who among that country's top mass-murderers may secretly be a "closet reformer," or what "reform" would actually mean to them: For North Korea today, after all, ordinary Stalinism might count as a liberal advance.

We do know, however, that the North Korean state can be moved in the direction of more pragmatic policies and practices: The small economic steps of recent years—changes termed "the July 2002 North Korean reforms" in some circles—show that the system can bend in the direction of rationality. Perhaps all that is needed for the North Korean system to bend still further in that direction is a heavier weight of exigency.

There is no question, incidentally, that North Korea's leadership regards the exodus of escapees as a weight that may force them to bend. If they did not, why was it that after the July 2004 repatriation to Seoul of 468 North Koreans, the media in the North published a long and hysterical fulmination denouncing the "enticement" of its citizens to the South, and declaring that such migration was a "plot to topple our system"? Rescuing North

Korean escapees will not only unequivocally improve the quality of life for the escapees themselves—it will help to improve the quality of life for those who cannot yet escape the North.

Welcoming and embracing North Korean escapees will constitute a concrete and tangible step in the reconciliation between North and South. These escapees, indeed, will constitute a living bond across the divided peninsula—and because they will be well treated in the South, it will be a bond of healing. Indeed, rescuing and embracing the escapees will send a multiplicity of signals to the North, all of them propitious: that Northerners are truly regarded in the South as long-lost brothers; that South Korea is not the "Hell on Earth" they have been taught to fear this past half century and more; that a humanistic liberal democracy awaits on the other side of the DMZ. And word will assuredly get back to the North. As the people of North Korea learn the fate of escapees to the South, this will generate further pressure for more humane rule in the North.

Finally, accepting North Korean escapees into the South will provide invaluable experience and guidance as South Koreans consider all the practical preparations that will be needed for the eventual reconciliation of the entire populations of the North and South. We know already about the challenges and difficulties North Korean immigrants face in the South as they struggle to assimilate from the frozen monochrome of their former existence into the splendid, dizzying Technicolor of modern life. Now is the time to learn more about the steps and measures in education, training, support, and acceptance that will be needed to help these ordinary people stream into the vibrant flow of South Korean life. Now is the time to learn how small businesses, NGOs, religious groups, and all the other wonderful panoply of civic associations in a "civil society" can best aid these former outcasts in their transformation into citizens of a free and democratic Korea.

Needless to say, learning how to make this integration work brings us one step closer to the day when the entire Korean people will be able to live as one—reconciled, united, secure, prosperous, and free.

If the arguments for a rescue campaign to bring North Korean escapees to South Korea are so compelling, why have they not been translated into political action? Why are the escapees not already being rescued en masse? The answer is quite clear. The self-styled "human rights" champions who came to power in the ROK in 1998, and who have subsequently governed uninterrupted through two successive presidencies, have to the very best of their abilities ignored the tears, the prayers, and the heart-rending distress of endangered compatriots with lives flickering as precariously as candle-flames just across the Yalu and the Tumen.

Perverse and improbable as it may seem, these one-time dissidents—activists who sought office by promising the South Korean public to speak up for the vulnerable, to stand up for the disempowered, and to embody solidarity with the victimized—have done almost everything within their power to avert their gaze from a human rights disaster second to none in the contemporary world: a disaster befalling their own Korean minjok.

This part of the saga of North Korea's escapees is painful to recount. But it must be recognized, if only out of respect for the suffering of victims alive and dead, and in our capacity as witnesses for future generations.

Christians distinguish between "sins of omission" and "sins of commission"—a useful taxonomy for believers and nonbelievers alike in examining the South Korean government's response to the plight of the North Korean escapees. That the escapees still huddle in hiding nearly 10 years into this crisis speaks clearly enough to the "sins of omission." Let us focus then on what might be described as Seoul's "sins of commission."

We can note the milestones without rehearsing every detail. We may, for example, go back to the year 2002, when handfuls of North Korean escapees were breaching the boundaries of Western embassies in Beijing, seeking asylum. Chinese security operatives stormed some of those diplomatic compounds, in a number of cases beating the asylum-seekers and physically dragging them away. After Beijing came under a storm of international criticism for its shocking, violent, probably illegal abuse of these asylum-seekers, the Chinese foreign ministry spokesperson retorted that the South Korean government had been secretly asking China's help in keeping North Korean escapees out of the ROK diplomatic compound. The government in Seoul never refuted this assertion. That episode occurred on the watch of a Nobel Peace laureate and human rights role model, President Kim Dae Jung.

With the transition from the Kim Dae Jung presidency to the Roh Moo Hyun administration, it is true that more North Korean refugees were repatriated than ever before: over 3,000 since President Roh's inauguration, more than half of the total since the 1953 Korean War cease-fire. But such numbers still constitute a mere trickle—and it is a flow that has hardly been encouraged by official policy.

Quite the contrary: In December 2004, the Republic of Korea's unification ministry announced that it was slashing the government's per capita resettlement stipend for North Korean newcomers by almost two-thirds (from approximately $28,000 to approximately $10,000)—and that it would be stepping up its screening and interrogations of would-be resettlers.

One rationale indicated for the increased scrutiny of escapees was the possibility that spies were posing as defectors. If so, that would mark an unusual—one is tempted to say unique—expression of concern about the risks of domestic subversion by the current administration, since the Roh government has otherwise reined in longstanding police and intelligence counterespionage activities, and cut back the government's prosecution of suspected spies and agents to less than a handful of cases a year.

As the Roh government was changing its rules to let escapees know they could expect a chillier welcome in the South, it was also embracing what might be called a "see no evil" policy regarding the escapees, diligently neglecting reports that might morally obligate increased concern for their well-being, and responding with ruthlessly optimistic spin to ominous accounts of the fate of North Korean border-crossers.

For a full month last year, for example, the ROK foreign ministry officially denied that China was rounding up hundreds of escapees and sending them back to North Korea—only to be forced eventually to admit that those stories were true. Subsequent news accounts by the ROK's own semi-official Yonhap newswire have reported the execution of dozens of North Korean returnees "to discourage North Koreans from seeking political asylum in South Korea." Then there was the stunning video smuggled out of North Korea that documents horrifying daytime public executions; if you live in South Korea, you will not have seen it on TV. The video has been broadcast all over the rest of the free world, but the Roh administration has made sure that South Korean television will not carry it.

Could Seoul's posture toward the plight of the North Korean escapees possibly get any more callous? As we learned earlier this year, apparently so. In January, the minister of unification repeated what had earlier been described in the local press as "virtually an official statement of regret to the North" about the aforementioned repatriation of 468 North Korean refugees from a third country in July 2004. This time he went further, declaring, "We disapprove of the mass defections," and promising that "there will not be another large-scale movement of North Korean refugees" into the South. "North Korea takes the refugee issue as a threat to its regime," he said, and "undermining the North is not our policy." The minister was not misspeaking: To the contrary, he was providing an absolutely faithful description of his government's broader approach to North Korea.

It is an approach that has prompted the ROK ministry of national defense to deny that North Korea is the "main enemy" for South Korea's armed forces, striking all such references from this year's ministry "White Paper." It is an approach that recently led the South Korean government to abstain—for the third year in a row—from voting on the United Nations Human Rights Commission resolution condemning human rights abuses in North Korea. "There is no need to provoke the North by voting on the resolution," unnamed South Korean officials explained.

Nor, apparently, to provoke the North with any expressed disapproval of the condition of Pyongyang's subjects. *The Wall Street Journal* has quoted a previous Roh administration unification minister as dismissing talk of political rights in North Korea with the memorable phrase "political freedom is a luxury, like pearls for a pig."

There is an awful coherence to this approach to relations with the North. Plainly put: It is an approach that regards the jailers who run North Korea as "partners for peace," while it treats the captives and escapees from this huge open-air prison as troublesome claimants who only get in the way of Seoul's grand designs for peninsular peace. It should go without saying that the obstacle to peace, reconciliation, and unification is not the North Korean population—it is the wicked regime that enslaves them.

While enslaving them, that same regime strives to destroy the South. The ministry of defense may pretend otherwise, but South Koreans are the true intended targets of the North's chemical weapons, biological weapons, its short-range missiles, and now perhaps, its atomic weapons. There is no contradiction whatever between the North's treatment of its subjects and its program of perfecting WMD threats against the South: Both are animated and guided by a single worldview and strategy.

At this point let me dispel any intimations of partisanship in the above indictment. It is true that South Korea's current opposition party has raised a few voices in honorable exception to the current "see no evil" policy for North Korean escapees. But it is a fact that the opposition party controlled the National Assembly for a number of years during both the Kim Dae Jung and the Roh Moo Hyun administrations. Over that tenure I am unaware of any legislation passed, or even hearings convened, to assuage the distress of North Korea's escapees.

There are, to be sure, many practical problems and objections to be considered in any effort of humanitarian rescue for the North Korean escapees. Let me mention two of them. The first concerns China, the escapees' most unwelcoming host. Despite its international treaty obligations— Beijing is signatory to the U.N. Convention and Protocol on Refugees, the U.N. Convention Against Torture, and the Vienna Conventions on Diplomatic and Consular Relations—the Chinese government routinely hunts downs, rounds up, and deports North Korean escapees to a certainty of savage punishment back in the North. As we have already noted, some of these hunts have taken Chinese agents into the embassies and consulates of foreign governments against the express wishes of foreign diplomatic representatives.

China asserts that it is not bound in this instance by the Refugee Convention and Protocol because the North Korean escapees are "economic migrants" rather than "refugees." Legal analyst Benjamin Neaderland also raises the possibility that China may face conflicting international legal obligations with respect to the escapees: If China, as may be the case, has a secret bilateral pact with Kim Jong Il—a sort of Fugitive Slave Act requiring the repatriation of illegal emigrants—a "Chinese argument that they are bound to return North Koreans found to be traveling illegally [would] not [be] without merit in international law."

Still and all, China's current intransigence is not necessarily an insuperable obstacle. The wordplay China uses to evade its Refugee Convention responsibilities is of course grotesque, and transparent. China is, however, a dictatorship—a government that takes liberties with the law through sheer force of habit. And China is emboldened to take liberties with these particular laws precisely because the Republic of Korea—a constitutional democracy under rule of law—is today so very conspicuously avoiding its own legal responsibilities toward those same escapees. China's leeway for legal obfuscation would be tremendously reduced if South Korea made it clear that Seoul intended to resettle any and all escapees who wished to head South—and was willing to make an international issue of this.

The possible contradiction between presumed bilateral obligations to Pyongyang and international treaty obligations, moreover, seemingly evaporates if Seoul remembers its constitutional obligation to make citizens of ordinary North Korean escapees desirous of that status. Here again Neaderland:

If the South Korean government were to assert that the North Koreans in China possess South Korean nationality, it could plausibly claim that China is treaty-bound by the Vienna Convention to allow access to any North Korean seeking to enter a South Korean consulate in China. While there may be policy reasons . . . that stand in the way of South Korea asserting such a claim, it is a claim potentially supported by international law and one that China would have to take seriously if offered by South Korea.

If Seoul adopts an activist stance and insists upon observance of the law—starting with its own laws—many of the problems encountered with China today may solve themselves.

The second issue concerns the United States. With the passage of the North Korean Human Rights Act of 2004, Washington is now committed to taking in an as-yet-undetermined number of North Korean asylum-seekers. Shouldn't a big country like the United States—a country peopled through immigration—shoulder a major share of the burden of resettling North Korean escapees? One could certainly hope that the active Korean-American community and Korean-American religious organizations would take the lead in helping them adjust to their newfound freedom.

That being said, we must also recognize that there is an international division of labor in the struggle for freedom. In this division of labor, the United States' indispensable contribution in its bilateral relationship with South Korea has been—and remains—the guarantee, underwritten by the lives of U.S. soldiers and the treasure of U.S. taxpayers, that South Korea could be the home for freedom in the Korean peninsula. South Korea's indispensable contribution in this arrangement is to act on that guarantee.

There is constant talk of "burden sharing" in the Washington-Seoul relationship, but discussions of "burden sharing" in this humanitarian rescue challenge must not become an excuse for delay or avoidance of Seoul's own special duties in this particular emergency.

Korea is a nation with a long and venerable history—the myth of Tangun takes us back almost 5,000 years. Nevertheless, Korea's greatest and most glorious days still lie ahead: The reunification of the Korean people under free and democratic governance, which will be an epochal event not just in Korean history, but in world history.

Against great odds, South Korea has become the home of freedom in the peninsula. Now the task is to extend that freedom to the North, if need be, one escapee at a time. The duty for the South could not be clearer: Bring them home.

PART V

O My America

For the most part, the concept of "American exceptionalism" has been applied to the political differences that separate America's experience and behavior from that of states in the "Old World": the USA's striking absence of any socialist movement worthy of a name; the spirit of 'manifest destiny' long informing US foreign policy, and so on. But America's "exceptionalism" extends well beyond the realm of the explicitly political, and into the realms of the nation's very rhythms of life.

> – From "Demographic Exceptionalism
> in the United States"

The United States of America is a most unusual country. "American exceptionalism" is more than a slogan: for deep, historical reasons, our nation happens to be distinctively different. This may help to explain why, for example, American politics and political decision making are so often and so surprisingly misunderstood by overseas observers (including foreign adversaries), despite the extraordinarily open nature of our society. But Americans also seem to misunderstand much about their own society, including some of our most important social and economic problems. In the following chapters I attempt to use empirical evidence to dispel misperceptions and to illuminate neglected realities. America's persistently high infant mortality rate, for instance, cannot be explained by a lack of health care, though it does appear to be shaped by a number of other important but less examined factors, including parental behavior. The prevalence of poverty in postwar America, for its part, appears to be systematically mismeasured by the government's official poverty rate, a badly flawed statistical indicator in urgent need of repair or replacement. America's population patterns today are appreciably different from those of other affluent countries—sufficiently so, I argue, that we may fairly speak nowadays of "American demographic exceptionalism." And America's seemingly special discomfort with government entitlement programs, I suggest, also may have to do with "American exceptionalism," for the modern welfare state was designed in Europe to deal with European problems and realities, which differed substantially from America's own.

15

America's Infant Mortality Puzzle

The Public Interest, Fall 1991

During the 1980s, America's infant-mortality rate (the number of children per thousand born who die in their first year of life) became a focus of increased attention, commentary, and public concern. Though the U.S. infant-mortality rate has declined steadily over the past several decades, dropping most recently from 12.6 in 1980 to 9.1 in 1990, America still has an unusually high rate in comparison with other countries.

The U.S. Department of Health and Human Services' Health United States 1990 provides an official assessment of the problem. In 1987, the U.S. infant-mortality rate was reportedly higher than in twenty-three other countries or territories, including most of Western Europe, Hong Kong, Singapore, and the then-communist state of East Germany. Between 1981 and 1987, despite the continuing decline in its reported infant-mortality rate, America's international ranking fell by five places. By 1987, the U.S. infant-mortality rate was almost 20 percent higher than in Norway, nearly 50 percent higher than in the Netherlands, and fully twice as high as in Japan.

America's persistently high infant-mortality rate is conventionally attributed to two underlying factors: the prevalence of poverty and a corresponding lack of adequate health care. This view is accepted not only by many specialists in public health but also by a number of Washington policymakers. In March 1990, for instance, the chairman of the House Select Committee on Children, Youth, and Families opened a day of hearings on "Child Health: Lessons from Developed Nations" with this observation:

> [C]hildhood poverty, the greatest predictor of poor health among children, is worse in the United States than in most other industrialized countries. Financial barriers are the most common and

significant reason that women and children do not receive the health care they need. By contrast, in Europe or Canada, no pregnant woman has to ask how, or where, she will receive prenatal care, or who will pay for it. . . .

He suggested, moreover, that "the time ha[d] come to thoughtfully consider the practices of other comparable countries, which in many important areas are achieving better health and economic outcomes for their children and families, despite their smaller gross national product." As compelling as this may sound, however, there is reason to question whether it adequately describes the nature of the current infant-mortality problem in the United States.

Historical Perspectives

In the late 1980s, America's infant-mortality rate did seem unusually high in relation to its level of per capita output (a broad but useful measure of the nation's prosperity). That circumstance, however, was by no means new. In the late 1920s, United States had also registered an unusually high rate of infant mortality in relation to its per capita productivity. While the United States had the highest per capita output of any Western country during this time—one-third higher than Switzerland, the country with the second-highest level—its infant-mortality rate ranked near the middle. Sweden and Norway, with less than half of America's estimated level of per capita output, each reported lower rates of infant mortality than the United States between 1925 and 1929.

America's relatively high infant-mortality rate also predates the development of the modern welfare state, a fact that challenges the widespread perception that our poor performance can be traced directly to shortcomings in social services. In 1925, the welfare state was still in its infancy throughout the Western world. Sweden, the first modern state to establish such a system of social guarantees, was barely through its first decade of experimentation by the mid-1920s. Social-welfare provisions were correspondingly more modest in other Western nations, yet several had distinctly lower reported infant-mortality rates than that of the United States. In the

Netherlands, for example, the reported infant-mortality rate in the late 1920s was only about five-sixths the level registered in the United States, despite per capita government expenditures that were only three-fourths the contemporary American level.

It should be noted that the well-known disparity between black and white infant-mortality rates does not explain America's unfavorable standing among other Western countries throughout the century. The black infant-mortality rate in America is about twice the rate for whites. Yet the infant-mortality rate of U.S. whites alone, when compared to those of other members of the Organization for Economic Cooperation and Development (OECD), dropped from sixth to fifteenth place between 1955 and 1985.

Reliability of Data

How is America's comparatively high level of infant mortality to be explained? In some measure, the differential between the United States and other Western societies may be a statistical artifact.

World Health Organization (WHO) guidelines stipulate that all births showing any signs of life be included for the purposes of defining infant mortality, regardless of the duration of pregnancy or the size of the newborn. American procedures conform to these guidelines fairly rigorously. In 1988, for example, U.S. vital statistics registered almost 24,000 infants weighing less than one kilogram (about 2.2 pounds). Survival rates for this high-risk cohort are extremely low. Though the group accounted for just over one-half of one percent of that year's registered births, it accounted for over a third of registered infant deaths in 1986. In Switzerland, by contrast, an infant must be at least thirty centimeters long at birth to be counted as "living"; the restriction effectively excludes most infants weighing less than a kilogram. The country's relatively low reported rate of infant mortality reflects in part the categorical exclusion of these high-risk births.

Switzerland, moreover, is not the only Western country to enforce its own particular definition of infant deaths. In Italy, for example, there are at least three different definitions in use in different regions of the nation. A recent twenty-three-country study on European vital statistics concluded that "there are many indications of differences in recording and reporting live birth, fetal death, and infant death within the European region of the WHO. Even where [WHO] recommendations are adopted as the legal definition, some countries have incomplete registration or reporting. . . ."

Further evidence of underreporting also seems apparent in the proportion of infant deaths different countries report for the first twenty-four hours after birth. In Australia, Canada, and the United States, over one-third of all infant deaths are reported to take place in the first day; in Sweden and Japan, where infant-mortality rates are currently lowest, such deaths account for about a quarter of the total. In other places, corresponding fractions are suspiciously low. Less than one-sixth of France's infant deaths are reported to occur in the first day of life. In Hong Kong, such deaths account for only one-twenty-fifth of all infant deaths.

Increased standardization of infant-mortality data would undoubtedly alter America's ranking within the OECD grouping. The potential impact of such revisions, however, should not be exaggerated. Better reporting might move the United States from the bottom third towards the middle, but no higher. Australia and Canada, whose distributions of infant death by age most closely match those of the United States, report rates markedly lower than those of America—lower, indeed, than for the U.S. white population. The comparatively poor health and survival prospects for American babies—white and black alike—still requires explanation.

Poverty and Medical Care

The conventional explanation for the high U.S. infant-mortality rate focuses upon poverty. According to this theory, high levels of infant mortality are a predictable consequence of the high proportion of children in poverty. Though plausible on its face, it appears to be less convincing when examined in detail.

Poverty in the United States is regularly measured by the "poverty rate," an official government index devised in the mid-1960s. (To this date, no other Western government calculates such an index for its population.) But the "poverty rate" is a poor measure of material deprivation. Deprivation is characterized, and indeed defined, by inadequate consumption. The "poverty rate," by contrast, is defined in relation to income—and then only to income in a given year. Consumer Expenditure Surveys (CES) conducted by the U.S. Bureau of Labor Statistics consistently indicate the actual consumption of households below the "poverty line" to be well above the average annual stated earnings and benefits—for the lowest income brackets, typically two, three, or even four times greater. This result should not be surprising: purchasing power in any given year depends not only on annual income, but upon savings, assets, loans, and a variety of other financial arrangements.

The actual spending patterns of the poor in America also raise questions about the extent to which the poor assess themselves to be materially needy. In 1988, less than one-fifth of the expenditures in households reporting annual incomes of $5,000 or less were allocated to food and beverages, even though all persons in this group were defined as "poor." A century of research on consumer spending patterns has shown that poor people tend to devote a higher percentage of their budget to food than do more affluent households. Yet the proportion of consumption allocated to food and non-alcoholic beverages was actually lower for this American "poverty" group than for the national populations of such places as Finland, France, Ireland, Italy, and Norway in 1985. All of those countries, however, had infant-mortality rates significantly lower than that reported for the United States in the mid- and late-1980s, despite spending patterns that suggest greater material need.

Whatever the limitations of the American "poverty line" as an index of deprivation, researchers have attempted to apply it to other Western societies. The results are intriguing. According to one such effort, child-poverty rates in 1980 were virtually identical in Australia and the United States, yet America's infant-mortality rate at the time was almost one-fifth higher. For white Americans, the child-poverty rate was lower than for Australians (13.6 percent versus 16.9 percent), yet the infant-mortality rate was higher (11 per 1,000 versus 10 per 1,000). Conversely, while white Americans in 1980 reported a much higher rate of child poverty than West Germans, their infant-mortality rate was actually slightly lower. In view of the purportedly strong correlation between child poverty and infant mortality, such inexact correspondences are surprising.

By the same token, the case against the availability and adequacy of American health care looks less compelling when examined in its particulars. An international comparison of perinatal mortality rates and their components attests to this.

Perinatal mortality refers to fetal deaths that occur after twenty-eight weeks or more gestation and to infant deaths that take place within seven days of birth. Data comparing birth-weight distribution and perinatal mortality in Japan, Norway, and the U.S. for the early 1980s are available from the International Collaborative Effort on Perinatal and Infant Mortality (ICE). These figures reveal a surprising finding: at any given birth weight, perinatal mortality rates in Norway and Japan were significantly higher than for American babies, whether white or black. If Japanese babies had enjoyed U.S. birth-weight-specific survival odds, their perinatal-mortality rate would have been cut by over a third. This fact is all the more striking because Japan already reports virtually the lowest perinatal-mortality rates in the world.

While biological, social, and economic factors undoubtedly afflict the perinatal-mortality rate, the quality of medical care is commonly the decisive factor—especially for high-risk infants at low-birth weights. Compared with other Western societies enjoying especially low rates of infant mortality, American babies at any given birth weight appear to have unusually good chances of surviving the perinatal period, regardless of race. All other things being equal, this would seem to suggest that medical care for infants in the United States is actually better than in some other advanced industrial societies.

Biological and Behavioral Factors

As is widely known, the proportion of low-birth-weight babies in the U.S. black population is extremely high compared to virtually every other Western population. What may be less known is the extent to which white babies in the United States suffer from low birth weight. Even though the median birth weight is currently lower in Japan than in the United States, white American babies have nearly twice as high an incidence of low birth weight. To understand the nature of the American mortality problem, then, one must account for the high incidence of high-risk, low-weight births for black and white Americans alike.

Although controversial, the theory that the extremely high incidence of low birth weight in the American black population may be due in part to biological factors cannot yet be dismissed. Even after controlling for

Table 15-1. Estimated Proportion of Low-Birth-Weight Babies: Single Live Births, 1982, by Selected Maternal Characteristics

	All Races	White	Black
All births	6.6	5.6	12.2
Family Income			
– 149 percent of poverty line or less	7.7	5.6	12.9
– 150 percent or more of poverty line	6.2	5.6	11.4
Mother did not smoke during pregnancy	4.2	3.3	9.0
Fifteen or more cigarettes per day	12.9	12.6	18.6
Child wanted at time of conception	5.8	5.3	10.2
Mistimed or unwanted	7.9	6.2	13.6

Note: Low birth weight defined as 2500 grams or less.
Source: E.R. Pamuk and W.D. Mosher, Health Aspects of Pregnancy and Childbirth, United States, 1982 (Hyattsville, MD: National Center for Health Statistics, Series 23, No. 16, 1988), pp. 52-53.

mother's age, education, and income, the proportion of low-birth-weight babies is roughly twice as high for blacks as for whites. Recent research suggests the same may be true when one controls for the number of visits for prenatal medical care.

Whatever the proportion of low-birth-weight differentials that proves to be attributable to biological factors, it is apparent that parental attitudes and behavior have an influence on a child's chances of being born at a low birth weight (see Table 15-1). In 1982, the National Center for Health Statistics (NCHS) conducted an extensive survey on pregnancy and child health in the United States. Among its objectives was to collect data on the correlates of low birth weight. According to its findings, there was no measurable difference in the incidence of low birth weight for white infants born into families above or below an income line set at 150 percent of the poverty rate (though poverty was associated with higher low-birth-weight rates for blacks).

While no measurable differences in the incidence of low birth weight by income were reported for white infants, they were about one-sixth more likely to be born into this high-risk group if their parents described them as "mistimed or unwanted at conception" rather than "wanted at conception." Black babies who were described as "mistimed or unwanted" were one-third more likely to be born at low birth weight than those described as "wanted at conception."

Even greater differences were associated with cigarette smoking. Among women who reported smoking fifteen or more cigarettes per day during pregnancy, the incidence of low birth weight was two times greater for blacks and nearly four times greater for whites than among self-described non-smokers. At a time when American doctors routinely and forcefully recommend against smoking during pregnancy, the decision to smoke heavily during pregnancy may be taken as a proxy for a set of parental attitudes and practices that do not bode well for the infant's general well-being.

Illegitimacy

Another proxy for behavior and attitudes that affect the health of an infant may be the decision to bear a child out of wedlock. The incidence of low birth weight is consistently, and often considerably, higher for illegitimate babies, irrespective of the age or race of the mother. In fact, so substantial are the differentials associated with illegitimacy that an American baby born to a teenage mother is less likely to be born at low birth weight if the mother is married and black than if she is unmarried and white.

Among American public-health specialists, it is commonly held that the association between illegitimacy and higher rates of infant mortality is spurious. A 1990 "editorial note" in the Centers for Disease Control's Morbidity and Mortality Weekly Report (MMWR), stated that "the marital status of the mother confers neither risk nor protection to the infant; rather, the principal benefits of marriage to infant survival are economic and social support." In the recent past, when few data were available on the social correlates of illegitimacy in America, such a viewpoint was perhaps intuitively plausible. In light of newly gathered data, however, it no longer looks so tenable.

Since the early 1980s, the NCHS has been conducting a project linking births and infant deaths for the entire country, and tabulating data on infant deaths against various maternal characteristics. An eight-state pilot survey in 1982 cross-tabulated infant-mortality rates not only against the race and age of the mother, but also against her marital status and level of education (see

Table 15-2. Infant-Mortality Rates by Race, Education, and Marital Status for Women Age Twenty Years or Older: Eight Pilot States, United States, 1982 Birth Cohort (per 1,000 Live Births)

Years of Education	All Races	White	Black
All Women	10.5	9.0	21.9
– 0 to 8 years	13.0	12.0	27.5
– 9 to 11 years	16.7	12.9	29.1
– 12 years	10.1	8.8	20.0
– 13 to 15 years	9.5	8.1	18.6
– 16+ years	8.6	7.9	20.6
Married Women	9.1	8.4	18.2
– 0 to 8 years	11.1	10.6	24.5
– 9 to 11 years	12.4	11.1	24.9
– 12 years	8.9	8.4	16.4
– 13 to 15 years	8.5	7.8	16.8
– 16+ years	8.3	7.9	19.2
Unmarried Women	20.7	16.2	25.2
– 0 to 8 years	20.7	18.1	29.8
– 9 to 11 years	24.9	19.2	30.7
– 12 years	18.6	14.6	23.1
– 13 to 15 years	18.9	15.1	20.9
– 16+ years	18.4	11.6	26.8

Note: The eight pilot states include Illinois, Indiana, Massachusetts, Michigan, Missouri, New Hampshire, Vermont, and Wisconsin. "All races" includes races other than white and black.
Source: National Center for Health Statistics, Pilot Linked Birth and Infant Death File, unpublished data.

Table 15-2). According to these data, infant-mortality rates for white mothers over age twenty were higher for unmarried but college educated women than for married high school—or even grade school—dropouts. The same pattern held true among black mothers.

In the past, Census Bureau reports on poverty have not disaggregated poverty rates for various types of families by the educational level of the household head. For the first time, however, the 1988 report on poverty in America did. According to its findings, the 1988 poverty rate for households with children headed by a white woman with a year or more of college education was 18.1 percent. By contrast, the corresponding poverty rate for two-parent families headed by a person with less than a high school education was estimated to be 19.0 percent. For black Americans, the findings were similar: corresponding family-poverty rates were reported to be 24.3 percent and 28.0 percent, respectively. These categories do not correspond precisely with the categories outlined in Table 15-2 nor, of course, to the year in question. Even so, they would seem to challenge the presumption that poverty, as officially defined, would explain the high rates of infant mortality for educated but unmarried mothers.

Parental Practices and Infant Health

Such findings are broadly consistent with other recent data that have been compiled on the health of American children. In analyzing the results of the NCHS's 1988 National Health Interview Survey on Child Health, for example, NCHS researcher Deborah Dawson found that "health vulnerability . . . scores were elevated" for children in single-parent homes, even after controlling for race, income, and maternal education.

Why should the health of infants and children in single-parent homes be worse than what race, age, education, or income would seem to predict? Such differentials may be partly explained by the attitude of single parents toward the care and treatment of offspring. For all mothers, the number of maternal visits for prenatal care during the course of pregnancy may be used as a serviceable, if imperfect, indicator of such attitudes. Unpublished data from the NCHS's "Linked Birth and Infant Death Files" show a strong correlation between infant-mortality rates and the numbers of prenatal medical visits by the pregnant mother (see Table 15-3).

In 1986, infant mortality among blacks who reported no visits for prenatal medical care was over three times the U.S. black national average. Among whites, the infant-mortality rate for such mothers was three-and-a-half times the corresponding national average. For both black and white infants, infant-mortality rates were over seven times higher among mothers who sought or received no prenatal care than for those reporting thirteen to sixteen prenatal visits. Although overall infant-mortality rates were over twice as high for blacks as whites in 1986, infant-mortality rates for black mothers

Table 15-3. Infant-Mortality Rates by Race of Mother and Number of Prenatal Visits: United States, 1986 Birth Cohort (Deaths per 1,000 Live Births)

Number of Prenatal Visits	White	Black
Total	8.6	18.1
No Visits	31.2	56.5
1–4 Visits	39.2	49.8
5–8 Visits	15.8	20.2
9–12 Visits	5.2	8.8
13–16 Visits	4.1	7.4
17 Visits or More	6.3	8.2

Source: National Center for Health Statistics, Linked Birth and Infant Death File, unpublished data.

who reported thirteen to sixteen prenatal medical visits were actually lower than the white national average.

Of course, education and income levels probably correlate positively with the number of prenatal medical visits a mother makes. Maternal age may also be a factor. And some high-risk premature births may be associated with fewer prenatal visits simply by virtue of their shorter gestation period. Nevertheless, the relationship between infant mortality and the frequency of prenatal medical visits is so robust that a strong correspondence may be expected to remain even after controlling for such exogenous influences. A parent's interest in prenatal care suggests a broader set of outlooks and practices. Unmarried mothers are decidedly less likely to seek medical care for the infants they are bearing during the course of their pregnancy. In 1987 illegitimate black babies were nearly four times as likely to have received no prenatal care as black babies born in wedlock. Illegitimate white infants were about five times as likely to have received no prenatal care as white babies born in wedlock. Although further research will be required to answer the question conclusively, it seems unlikely that social and economic factors alone could account for such disparities.

Indeed, illegitimacy has played a role in retarding improved prenatal care. According to a recent supplement to the NCHS's Monthly Vital Statistics

Report (MVSR), "much of the lack of improvement in early receipt of prenatal care (between 1979 and 1988) is associated with the increasing proportion of births to unmarried mothers who are less likely than married mothers to begin care early."

Since 1960, childbearing in the United States has been profoundly affected by a sweeping change in patterns of illegitimacy. Although fewer children were born in 1988 than in 1960, the number of births reported for unmarried mothers rose at an average pace of over 5 percent a year over this period. By 1988, over one-quarter of all births in America were to unmarried women. As the MVSR noted, the profile of the unmarried mother has changed with the increase in illegitimate births:

[In 1988] increases were greater for white women, continuing a pattern that has been observed in recent years. . . . Rates of nonmarital childbearing and proportions of nonmarital births among black women continue to be substantially higher than among white women. In recent years, however, because the increases have been much more rapid for white than black women, the differentials by race have diminished. . . . In recent years . . . the largest increases in nonmarital childbearing have occurred among relatively older women. One third of unmarried mothers were 25 years and older in 1988 as compared with 24 percent in 1980. . . . The pattern of more rapid increases in rates for older than for younger unmarried mothers is generally replicated in rates for white and black women, but the pace of increase has been greater for white women.

By 1988, black teenage mothers accounted for less than one-seventh of the illegitimate births in the United States. Nearly one-quarter of the children born to white women in their early twenties were out of wedlock. And although illegitimacy ratios varied considerably by state, in every state unmarried mothers accounted for at least 10 percent of the total white births.

Compared with some other Western societies, of course, illegitimacy ratios in the United States today are not exceptional. Illegitimacy has been reported on the rise in virtually all Western countries over the past generation. While the reported ratios in the United States in the late 1980s were over twice as high as in West Germany, and over four times as high as in Italy, they were roughly the same as in France and the United Kingdom and less than half that of Sweden—the society with the lowest reported infant-mortality rate in Europe.

Different patterns of parental behavior, however, appear to be associated with illegitimacy in Sweden and in the United States. In Sweden, despite a reported illegitimacy ratio of almost 50 percent, only 17 percent of family households in 1988 were single-parent households; consensual unions or cohabitation appear to be common. The United States, with 23 percent of all families with children in single-parent households in 1988, appears to have the highest proportion of such families of any major Western country—a pattern that has characterized the United States since the 1960s.

Local-Level Data

The contribution of parental behavior or life styles to higher levels of infant mortality is further emphasized by an examination of local-level data. Considerable variations both in socioeconomic characteristics and patterns of family formation are reported among the fifty states and the District of Columbia. These variations tend to highlight underlying nationwide patterns.

In the mid-1980s, the unweighted average rate of infant mortality for the five areas reporting the highest levels was over 60 percent higher than for the five lowest. Per capita personal income, however, was officially estimated to be greater in the areas with the higher reported rates of infant mortality than in the states with the lowest reported rates. Indeed, per capita personal income in the lowest infant-mortality states was officially estimated to be below the national average, and above the national average in the highest infant-mortality areas. On the other hand, differences in illegitimacy ratios correspond directly with state-level differences in infant mortality: the unweighted average illegitimacy rate for the five highest infant-mortality areas in the mid-1980s was over twice as high as for the five lowest infant-mortality states.

Data from the 1980 U.S. Census were somewhat more comprehensive. Characteristics conventionally thought to explain the health differential seem to offer little insight into the gap between high and low infant-mortality states. For 1979-1981, the estimated family-poverty rate for the five highest infant-mortality states was higher for the high infant-mortality group, but it was also above the national average for the states with the lowest infant-mortality rates. Similarly, although unemployment rates were on average slightly lower for the low infant-mortality states, they were no higher than the national average for the group with the highest rates of infant mortality. On the other hand, the proportion of children receiving government benefits through the Aid to Families with Dependent Children (AFDC) program corresponds directly with infant-mortality differences. The AFDC program is itself significant, insofar as it has become a vehicle for financing illegitimacy and maintaining the families of unmarried mothers. By 1987, over half the children receiving AFDC benefits qualified for the program because their parents were unmarried; their total numbers would account for over nine-tenths of all children for American never-married mothers.

It is quite possible that race plays a confounding role in these state-level comparisons, given that black Americans—whose high infant-mortality rates might skew overall data considerably—constitute a widely varying proportion of the total population of the different states. 1980 Census data allow us to compare high and low infant-mortality areas within the American black population by itself (see Table 15-4). For the five states reporting the lowest rates of black infant mortality, the unweighted average was less than three-fifths the level of the high-mortality group. Median family income was virtually identical for the high and low infant-mortality groups, and above the black national average for both.

While the family-poverty rate was notably lower for the low infant-mortality group, it was also distinctly below the black national average in the high infant-mortality group. Median years of education of the household head was above the black national average for both groups. A distinct difference between the two groups, however, was in illegitimacy ratios: in 1980, the proportion of children born out of wedlock in the highest infant-mortality areas was 150 percent higher than in the lowest infant-mortality states. The illegitimacy ratio in the highest infant-mortality areas, moreover, was significantly higher than the black national average.

The Limits of Policy Interventions

If parental life styles and family-formation patterns play a direct and important role in determining infant survival chances, the prospects for reducing American infant-mortality rates through government income support and health-care policies may be less substantial than is sometimes supposed.

Table 15-4. Characteristics of Children, Families, and Persons in States with Highest and Lowest Reported Black Infant-Mortality Rates c. 1980

	Infant Mortality (per 1,000)	Median Income (1980 dollars)	Family Poverty Rate (percent)	Median Education (years)	Illegitimacy Rate (percent)
Lowest					
Hawaii	11.4	12,764	11.5	12.9	11.4
Washington	14.9	15,833	17.3	12.7	40.7
Colorado	15.4	15,732	18.7	12.7	40.3
Mass.	16.4	13,249	23.8	12.4	52.9
California	17.1	14,887	26.7	12.6	52.8
Unweighted average	15.0	14.493	16.4	12.7	39.6
Highest					
Delaware	27.4	13,127	25.1	12.0	66.1
District of Columbia	26.3	16,362	18.6	12.2	64.3
Illinois	25.9	14,478	27.0	12.2	66.0
Michigan	24.0	15,817	23.5	12.2	52.7
W. Virginia	23.2	12,318	21.4	12.1	52.0
Unweighted average	25.4	14,420	23.1	12.1	60.2
U.S. average	21.0	12,598	26.5	12.0	55.3

Sources: U.S. Department of Health and Human Services, Social Security Administration, 1979 Recipient Characteristics Study: Part1: Demographic and Program Statistics (March 1982), p. 37; U.S. Bureau of the Census, State and Metropolitan Area Data Book 1986, p. 509; U.S. Department of Health and Human Services, Health United States 1984 (Hyattsville, MD: National Center for Health Statistics, 1989), p. 55: U.S. Department of Commerce, 1980 Census of Population (Washington, DC: Bureau of the Census, 1981), various volumes.

Given the complex interactions between illegitimacy and infant mortality, for example, estimating the extent to which expanding AFDC eligibility might reduce infant-mortality rates would be an intricate calculation.

Parallel questions arise about the expansion of public health-care programs. It is widely argued today that poorer Americans have inadequate access to health care. In much of this discussion, however, a critical distinction has been obscured: the difference between availability and utilization. As long as health-care treatment is a voluntary option for the potential patient—or the potential patient's parents—utilization will depend not only upon availability, but also upon the attitudes, inclinations, and preferences of individual decisionmakers.

Table 15-5. Average Number of Physician Contacts for American Children Under Eighteen Years of Age by Selected Characteristics: 1985–1987

	White	Black
All Children	4.5	2.8
Family Income		
– under $10,000	4.4	3.2
– $10,000 to $19,999	4.1	2.5
– $20,000 to $34,999	4.7	2.8
– $35,000 or more	5.0	3.3
Poverty Status		
– in poverty	3.9	3.1
– not in poverty	4.7	2.8
Children Assessed in Fair or Poor Health	15.5	6.5
Family Income		
– under $10,000	13.6	6.2
– $10,000 to $19,999	12.8	6.8
– $20,000 to $34,999	19.6	11.3
– $35,000 or more	21.0	7.1
Poverty Status		
– in poverty	13.0	7.0
– not in poverty	17.5	7.0

Source: P. Ries, Health of Black and White Americans, 1985-87 (Hyattsville, MD: National Center for Health Statistics. Series 10, No. 171, 1990), pp. 58, 62.

These attitudes and preferences bring an interesting perspective to the current debate about "affordability" of health care in contemporary America. In 1985-1987, according to a recently released NCHS study, white children averaged 4.5 physician contacts a year—over three-fifths more than black children (see Table 15-5). The difference is not totally explained by "poverty" or income level. Black families were on average poorer than white families, and more affluent families tended to have more physician contact for their children. But the average number of physician contacts was higher for whites at every income level. For families with incomes of $35,000 or more, for example, white children averaged 5.0 contacts a year—50 percent more than black children in the same income grouping. Distinctions were even more dramatic for children whose health parents described as fair or poor. In this group, white children averaged two-and-a-half times more physician contacts than black children; in families with incomes above $35,000, white children averaged nearly three times as many contacts with physicians as their black counterparts. It is true that black families tend to have much lower net financial worth than white ones, and health-care decisions may be affected to some degree by a family's wealth. For whatever reason, though, it would appear that white parents found health care to be more "affordable" for their children than relatively well-off black parents.

The Bureau of Labor Statistics Consumer Expenditure Survey (CES) reveals still more about popular perceptions of the "affordability" of current health-care services. Table 15-6 details reported expenditures in 1988 on health care, entertainment, alcohol, and tobacco for households reporting incomes of less than $20,000 by age of household head. Generally speaking, households in this lower half of the income scale indicated that they could "afford" to spend several times as much on entertainment, alcohol, and tobacco as on health care. It is hard to know exactly how much confidence to place in such reported expenditures; for one thing, many respondents have received free health care under the Medicaid program. But it would appear that among these households the income elasticity of expenditure was substantially higher for health care than for entertainment, alcohol, and tobacco. To judge by the preferences revealed in this survey, lower-income consumers seemed to treat health care as an optional but dispensable luxury good, whereas they appeared to regard entertainment, alcohol, and tobacco as necessities "affordable" at any level of household income.

As long as health-care treatment is the prerogative of the patient—or the patient's parents—some fraction of the population will always deem treatment to be "unaffordable," regardless of its actual nominal cost. In such circumstances, the only way to ensure adequate coverage would be to deny the patient his or her option over treatment—for example, by making routine assessments mandatory, independent of the preference of the patient, and proscribing nonnegotiable therapies on their basis. One may doubt that such a proposal would be favorably received by the American public at large.

Table 15-6. Patterns of Consumer Expenditure by Reported Household Income and Age of Head of Household (1988 U.S. Dollars)

	Less than $5,000	$5,000–$9,999	$10,000–$14,999	$15,000–$19,000
Under 25 Years				
Health Expenditures	177	207	484	625
Entertainment	450	649	896	1,053
Alcohol and Tobacco	282	465	529	614
25 to 34 Years				
Health Expenditures	247	349	471	613
Entertainment	510	496	796	1,007
Alcohol and Tobacco	359	461	472	574
35 to 44 Years				
Health Expenditures	749	448	808	957
Entertainment	595	564	786	1002
Alcohol and Tobacco	419	454	403	512
Ratio of Expenditures on Entertainment, Alcohol and Tobacco to Health Care (Health Care = 100)				
Under 25 Years	414	538	294	267
25 to 34 Years	352	274	269	258
35 to 44 Years	135	227	147	158

Source: U.S. Department of Labor, Bureau of Labor Statistics, unpublished tables.

More than in many other societies, Americans pay close attention to their individual freedoms and rights. For better or worse, one of those rights—within very broad limits—is the right to be a negligent parent. One may feel that too many parents and parents-to-be misuse this particular freedom. Yet simple governmental remedies to the injuries possible under these liberties are not immediately evident. Even when American parents are demonstrably abusive to their children, the state's options are limited and hardly ideal; can the state proceed more confidently against parents who merely expose their fetuses or infants to potential risks without malice aforethought? It is far from obvious what role public policy should play in this problem if it aims to avoid creating new injuries in the course of redressing existing ones.

16

The Mismeasure of Poverty

Policy Review, August/September 2006

For well over a century, with ever-expanding scale and scope, the United States government has been generating statistics that might illuminate the plight of society's poorest and most vulnerable elements. From the beginning, the express objective of such efforts has always been to abet purposeful action to protect the weak, better the condition of the needy, and progressively enhance the general weal. America's official quest to describe the circumstances of the disadvantaged in quantitative terms began in the 1870s and the 1880s, with the Massachusetts Bureau of Statistics of Labor and the U.S. Bureau of Labor Statistics, and the initial efforts to compile systematic information on cost-of-living, wages, and employment conditions for urban working households in the United States.[1] U.S. statistical capabilities for describing the material well-being of the nation's population through numbers have developed greatly since then.

Today the United States government regularly compiles hundreds upon hundreds of social and economic indicators that bear on poverty or progress on the domestic scene. Within that now-vast compendium, however, one number on deprivation and need in modern America is unquestionably more important than any of the others—and has been so regarded for the past four decades. This is what is commonly known as the "poverty rate" (the informal locution for the much more technical mouthful "the incidence of poverty as estimated against the federal poverty measure.")

First unveiled in early 1965, shortly after the launch of the Johnson administration's "War on Poverty," the poverty rate is a measure identifying households with incomes falling below an official "poverty threshold" (levels based on that household's size and composition, devised to be fixed and unchanging over time). Almost immediately, this calculated federal poverty measure was accorded a special significance in the national conversation on the U.S.

271

poverty situation and in policymakers' responses to the problem. Just months after its debut—in May 1965—the War on Poverty's new Office of Economic Opportunity (OEO) designated the measure as its unofficial "working definition" of poverty. By August 1969, the Bureau of the Budget had stipulated that the poverty thresholds used in calculating American poverty rates would constitute the federal government's official statistical definition for poverty. It has remained so ever since.[2]

The authority and credibility that the official poverty rate (OPR) enjoys as a specially telling indicator of American domestic want is revealed in its unique official treatment. The OPR is regularly calculated not only for the country as a whole, but for every locality down to the county level and beyond—on to the level of the school district. (It is even available at the level of the census tract: enumerative designations that demarcate the nation into subdivisions of as few as one thousand residents.)

Furthermore, U.S. government antipoverty spending has come to be calibrated against, and made contingent upon, this particular measure. Everywhere in America today, eligibility for means-tested public benefits depends on the relationship between a household's income and the apposite poverty threshold. In Fiscal Year 2002 (the latest period for which such figures are readily available), perhaps $300 billion in public funds were allocated directly against the criterion of the "poverty guideline" (the Department of Health and Human Services' version of poverty thresholds).[3] The poverty rate currently also conditions many billions of dollars of additional public spending not directly earmarked for anti-poverty programs: for example, as a component in the complex formulae through which community grants (what used to be called "revenue sharing") dispense funds to local communities.

Given its unparalleled importance—both as a touchstone for informed public discussion and as a direct instrument for public policy—the reliability of the official poverty rate as an indicator of material deprivation is a critical question. How accurately—and consistently—does the OPR reflect changing patterns of material hardship in modern America or changes in the living standards of the U.S. "poverty population?" How faithfully, in other words, does our nation's poverty rate describe trends and patterns in the condition that most Americans would think of as poverty?

Although our official poverty rate is now by and large taken for granted, having become widely regarded with the passage of time as a "natural" method for calibrating the prevalence of material deprivation in American society, the measure itself was originally an ad hoc improvisation—and arguably a fairly idiosyncratic one—and in practical terms appears to be a problematic descriptor of poverty trends and levels in modern America. For one thing, its reported results do not track well with other indicators that would ordinarily be expected to bear directly on living conditions across the nation. In fact, over the past three decades, the relationship between the OPR and these other indicators has been perversely discordant.

While the official poverty rate suggests that the proportion of the American population living below a fixed "poverty line" has stagnated—or increased—over the past three decades, data on U.S. expenditure patterns document a substantial and continuing increase in consumption levels for the entire country—including the strata with the lowest reported income levels. And while the poverty threshold was devised to be measuring a fixed and unchanging degree of material deprivation (i.e., an "absolute" level of poverty) over time, an abundance of data on the actual living conditions of low-income families and "poverty households" contradicts that key presumption—demonstrating instead that the material circumstances of persons officially defined as poor have improved broadly and appreciably over the past four decades.

In short, America's most relied-upon metric for charting a course in our national effort to reduce and eliminate poverty appears to offer unreliable, and indeed increasingly misleading, soundings on where we are today, where we have come, and where we seem to be headed.

History of a Calculation

The current conception of the U.S. federal poverty measure was first introduced to the American public in January 1965 in a landmark study by Mollie Orshansky, an economist at the Social Security Administration.[4] Drawing upon her own earlier work, in which she had experimented with household income thresholds for distinguishing American children living in poverty conditions, Orshansky proposed a countrywide annual income criterion for identifying households in poverty, based on money income requirements set "essentially on the amount of income remaining after allowance for an adequate diet at minimum cost."

As devised, Orshanksy's "poverty thresholds" were established as scalar multiples of the annual cost of a nutritionally adequate—but humble—household diet. For the base food budget in calculating poverty thresholds, Orshansky chose the U.S. Department of Agriculture (USDA) "economy food plan" (known today as the "thrifty food plan")—the lower of the two such budgets USDA prepared for nonfarm families of modest means (one specifically proposed by USDA "for temporary or emergency use when funds are low").

The selection of a particular poverty-level food budget then immediately raised the question of the appropriate multiplier for an overall "poverty line" for demarcating total annual income for the officially poor. The answer to that question was by no means obvious. While the cost of the economy food plan could be justified in terms of sheer empirical exigency—people must eat to survive; food costs money—the choice of a food budget multiplier was a much more subjective affair.

From the pioneering work of the Prussian economist Ernst Engel in the 1850s onward, a century of household budget studies around the world had demonstrated that food did not account for a fixed percentage of household expenditures—but rather that the share of food in total spending steadily and predictably declined as household income levels increased. In impoverished low-income countries, 60 percent or more of the household budget was allocated for food—while on the other hand, a much smaller fraction of total income went to food in the richest countries in the postwar era. What was the correct proportion to use in constructing a U.S. poverty threshold?

In the event, Orshansky suggested a multiplier of roughly three times the minimum food budget for poverty-level incomes. While readily noting that her proposed multiplier was "normative," Orshansky also argued that her coefficient had a solid grounding, and indeed reflected the norms in U.S. contemporary living standards.

A USDA national food consumption survey, conducted in the U.S. in the spring of 1955 (the most recent such survey available at the time of Orshansky's study), indicated that American nonfarm families of two or more were devoting an average of roughly one-third of their after-tax money incomes to food. Orshansky seized this three-to-one relationship for the general guideline for the poverty line she computed, and accordingly established her poverty threshold as a sort of multiplicative product of a nutritionally adequate (but stringent) food budget otherwise suggestive of poverty conditions on the one hand and, on the other, the then-conventional ratio of food to nonfood expenditures for "Main Street" Americans.

But not all households were accorded a poverty threshold of exactly three times their corresponding "economy food plan" budget. Orshansky tailored those thresholds further, to account for variations in household size and composition and the presumed impact of these demographic factors on what is known as the Engel coefficient. (Larger poor households, for example, were posited to allocate a higher share of their income to food than smaller ones, and senior citizens living alone were presumed to require a larger share of their budgets for nonfood necessities than younger one-person households.) In her calculations, Orshansky drew upon USDA economy food plan budgets, Bureau of Labor Statistics (BLS) expenditure surveys, and 1960 census returns from the U.S. Census Bureau, crafting detailed weightings for estimated food needs in diverse household structures, and then adjusting the Engel coefficients actually observed for such households in BLS expenditure surveys in accordance with judgments about the role that economies of scale—or sheer deprivation—had played in influencing those outcomes.

The USDA economy food plan offered separate budgets for 19 types of household configurations. For her part, Orshansky created poverty thresholds for 62 separate types of nonfarm households—58 varieties of different sorts of families, and an additional four for persons living alone (differentiated by age and gender). She also estimated the 62 corresponding poverty thresholds for the U.S. farm population, for a nationwide total of 124 U.S. poverty thresholds.

Using these poverty thresholds (all initially benchmarked against the 1964 USDA economy food plan), Orshansky calculated the total population below the poverty line for the United States as a whole—and for regional and demographic subgroups within the country—for calendar year 1963, relying upon Census Bureau data on pretax money income for that same year. (The statistical distinction between pretax income—the figures used for determining whether a family fell below the poverty threshold—and after-tax money income—the criterion against which those same poverty thresholds had been originally constructed—was finessed through a presumption that the poor would not be paying out much, or anything, in taxes.)

Although Orshansky's study did not actually use the term poverty rate—it talked instead about the incidence of poverty—the poverty rate quickly came to mean the proportion of persons or families below the poverty line in the apposite reference group, and has been so understood ever since.

The schema and framework for estimating official poverty rates in the United States today are basically the same as in 1965. Annual OPRs are still determined on the basis of poverty thresholds maintained and updated by the U.S. Census Bureau (currently calculated for "only" 48 family subtypes); official poverty status is still contingent upon whether a household's measured annual pretax money income exceeds or falls below that stipulated threshold. While a number of minor revisions have been introduced (such as the elimination of Orshansky's farm/nonfarm differentials, and also of her differentials between male- and female-headed households), the original Orshansky approach of computing poverty rates on the basis of poverty thresholds and annual household income levels remains entirely intact.

The most significant change in the original poverty thresholds is their annual upward adjustment to compensate for changes in general price levels. In 1969, the Bureau of the Budget directed that the poverty line would thenceforth be pegged against the Consumer Price Index (CPI) and ruled that the CPI deflator would also be used to establish official "poverty thresholds" back to 1963, the base year for Orshansky's original study. (CPI-scaled adjustments were subsequently utilized to calculate poverty thresholds, and thus official poverty rates, back as far as 1959—i.e., the year against which the household money incomes in the 1960 census were reported.)

To this writing, official U.S. poverty thresholds continue to be updated annually in accordance with changes in the CPI—and with CPI changes alone. Implicit in this decision is the important presumption that America's official poverty rate should be a measure of absolute poverty rather than relative poverty. Whereas a relative measure might take some account of general improvements of living standards in assessing material deprivation, the determination to hold poverty thresholds constant over time, adjusting only for inflation, is to insist upon an absolute conception of poverty: a standard of deprivation held as constant over time as the index problem will permit.

In her seminal 1965 study, Orshansky acknowledged more than once that her measure of poverty was "admittedly arbitrary"—although she also vigorously defended it as "not unreasonable." Though she did not dwell on the point, a considerable degree of the apparent arbitrariness in this poverty measure was conditioned by the imperative of fashioning a serviceable and regularly updateable index from the limited data sources then readily at hand.

Whatever the intellectual merits of representing material deprivation in terms of a nationwide annual reported pretax money incomes standard—a variety of objections to which practice could be drawn from basic tenets in microeconomics—the singular virtue of such a poverty indicator was that the Census Bureau was already producing detailed and continuous data of just this sort through its P–60 (i.e., Consumer Income) Series of "Current Population Reports."

By the same token, Orshansky's poverty thresholds were open to criticism on a number of conceptual and empirical grounds, as she herself recognized. But those constructs also happened to represent concoctions—arguably quite insightful and ingenious ones—based on the somewhat haphazard ingredients then at hand in the statistical larders of USDA, the Census Bureau, and the BLS.

As of 2005, the U.S. official poverty rate is the single longest-standing official index for assessing deprivation and material need in any contemporary country. That fact alone makes it unique. But America's OPR is unique in another sense, as well. For although a multitude of governments and international institutions have pursued quantitative efforts in poverty research over the past two decades, and have even fashioned particular national and international poverty indices, none has elected to replicate the Orshansky approach to counting the poor. This curious fact is not often remarked upon by U.S. statistical authorities—but it is not only worth bearing in mind, it is also worth pondering as one evaluates the U.S. poverty rate and its long-term performance.

Stark Numbers

Estimates of the official poverty rate for the United States are available from the year 1959 onward. For the total population of the U.S., the OPR declined by nearly half over this period, from 22.4 percent in 1959 to 12.7 percent in 2004, and dropped by roughly similar proportions for America's families, from 20.8 percent to 11.0 percent. Measured progress against poverty was more pronounced for older Americans (the OPR for persons 65 and older fell from 35.2 percent to 9.8 percent) but more limited for children under 18 (27.3 percent vs. 17.8 percent). For African Americans, the official poverty rate declined by almost three-fifths—by over 30 percentage points—between 1959 and 2004, but in 2004 remained over twice as high for whites.

One may note that most of the reported reduction in overall U.S. poverty, according to this federal poverty measure, occurred at the very beginning of the series—that is to say, during the first decade for which numbers are available. Between 1959 and 1968, the OPR for the total population of the United States fell from 22.4 percent to 12.8 percent, or by more than a point per year. In 2004, by contrast, the U.S. poverty rate was only imperceptibly lower than it had been in 1968—and actually slightly higher than it had been back in 1969.

Indeed, to judge by the official poverty rate, the United States has suffered a generation and more of stagnation—or even retrogression—in its quest to reduce poverty. Figure 16-1 illustrates the situation. For the entire U.S. population, the lowest OPR yet recorded was for the year 1973, when the index bottomed at 11.1 percent. Over the subsequent three decades, the OPR nationwide has remained steadily above 11.1 percent, often substantially; in 2004, the rate reported was 12.7 percent.

This long-term rise in the official poverty rate for the U.S. as a whole was not a statistical artifact—an arithmetic consequence of averaging in some particularly grim trends for some smaller subpopulation within the nation. To the contrary, long-term increases in OPRs were characteristic for the overwhelming majority of the U.S. public during the period in question. Between 1973 and 2004, the official poverty rate did decline for older Americans as a whole (16.3 percent vs. 9.8 percent) and for persons living alone (25.6 percent vs. 20.5 percent); it also declined for African Americans overall (31.4 percent vs. 24.7 percent). But for the rest of the country, the official poverty rate was in general higher at the start of the new century than it had been in the early 1970s. Measured poverty rates, for example, were higher in 2004 than they had been in 1973 for children under 18 (14.4 percent in 1973 vs. 17.8 percent in 2004) and for people of working ages, i.e. 18 to 64 (8.3 percent vs. 11.3 percent). The nationwide OPR for U.S. families likewise rose over those years (from 9.7 percent to 11.0 percent). Outside of the South, where the OPR registered a slight decline (from 15.3 percent to 14.1 percent), poverty

Figure 16-1. No Progress for Three Decades? U.S. Poverty Rate, 1973–2004

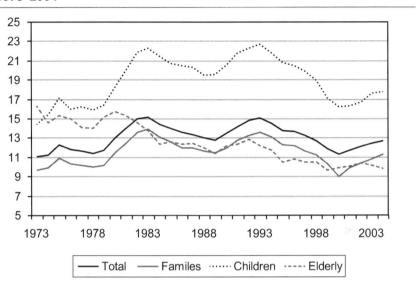

Source: U.S. Census Bureau Historical Poverty Tables, available online at http://www.census.gov/hhes/poverty/histpov/hstpov2.html. Accessed 10/18/05.

rates were higher in every region of America in 2004 than in 1973. Overall poverty rates for non-Hispanic whites—so-called Anglos—were also higher than they had been in 1973 (7.5 percent vs. 8.6 percent). No less striking, the overall poverty rate for Hispanic Americans was exactly the same in 2004 as in 1973—21.9 percent—implying that the circumstances of this diverse but often socially disadvantaged ethnic minority had not improved at all over the course of three full decades.

Taken on their face, these stark numbers would seem to be a cause for dismay, if not outright alarm. To go by the official poverty rate, modern America has failed stunningly to lift the more vulnerable elements of society out of deprivation—out from below the income line, according to the author of the federal poverty measure, where "everyday living implied choosing between an adequate diet of the most economical sort and some other necessity because there was not money enough to have both." This statistical portrait of an apparent long-term rise in absolute poverty in the contemporary United States evokes the specter of profound economic, social, and political dysfunction in a highly affluent capitalist democracy. (It is a picture that conforms disturbingly well with some of the Marxian and neo-Marxist critiques of industrial and global capitalism, which accused such systems of inherently generating "immiserating growth.") All the more troubling is the near-total failure of social policy implied by such numbers, for despite the War on Poverty and all subsequent governmental antipoverty initiatives, official poverty rates for the nation have mainly moved in the wrong direction over the past three decades.

Other Measures

Although the official poverty rate is accorded a special official status as an index of poverty conditions in modern America, it is by no means the only available indicator that might provide insight on poverty conditions and material deprivation in the country. Many other indices bearing upon poverty are readily available, and their trends can be compared with the reported OPR. Curiously, the official poverty rate does not seem to exhibit the normal and customary relationship with any of these other poverty proxies.

Table 16-1 illustrates the problem. It contrasts results for the years 1973 and 2001 for the official poverty rate and several other indicators widely recognized as bearing directly upon the risk of poverty in any modern urbanized society. (The choice of these two specific end-years is admittedly and deliberately selective—but it is a selection that highlights the underlying contradictions discussed below.)

In the period between 1973 and 2001, for example, per capita income in the United States rose very significantly in real (inflation-adjusted) terms: by roughly 60 percent, according to estimates from the Census Bureau's cps series. Other official U.S. data, incidentally, suggest the gains over those years may have been even more substantial: The National Income and Product Accounts from the Bureau of Economic Analysis (BEA), for example, estimate an increase in per capita output of about 67 percent for 1973–2001.[5]

By the same token, the measured rate of unemployment for persons 16 and older was somewhat lower in 2001 (4.7 percent) than it had been in 1973 (4.9 percent). Alternative measures of the availability of remunerative employment also indicated that a higher fraction of the American

Table 16-1. Poverty Rate and Other Possible Indicators of Progress Against Poverty: 1973 vs. 2001

	Poverty rate	Unemployment rate (%)	Per capita income (2002 $)	Percent of people with a high school degree	Total medical means-tested govt. spending (mil 2002 $)
1973	11.1	4.9	14,291	59.8	109,008
2001	11.7	4.7	22,970	84.1	230,595

Sources: U.S. Census Bureau Historical Poverty Tables, Table 2. Available online at http://www.census.gov/hhes/poverty/histpov/hstpov2.html. Accessed 2/25/05; U.S. Census Bureau Historical Income Tables, Table P-1. Available online at http://www.census.gov/hhes/income/histinc/incperdet.html. Accessed 2/15/05; House Ways and Means Committee Prints: 108-6, 2004 Green Book, Appendix F and K. Available online at http://www.gpoaccess.gov/wmprints/green/2004.html. Accessed 2/15/05; and U.S. Census Bureau, Statistical Abstract of the United States: 2003, Mini Historical Statistics Table HS-22. Available online at http://www.census.gov/statab/hist/HS-22.pdf. Accessed 2/15/05.

population was gainfully occupied in 2001 than in 1973: Labor force participation rates for those 16 and older, for instance, were over six points higher in 2001 (66.9 percent) than they had been in 1973 (60.5 percent), and the employment-to-population ratio for the 16-plus group was almost seven points higher in 2001 (63.7 percent) than in 1973 (56.9 percent).

As for educational attainment, America's working-age adults clearly had completed more years of schooling in 2001 than in 1973. In 1973, nearly 40 percent of U.S. adults 25 or older had no high school degree; by 2001, the corresponding fraction was under 16 percent. Among youths and young adults, the profile for access to schooling also improved between 1973 and 2001, if less dramatically: Whereas the ratio of net enrollment in high school for children 14–17 years of age had been 91.0 percent in 1973, it was a projected 94.8 percent for 2001.

Then there are the trends in spending by government at the federal, state, and local levels on means-tested benefit programs: that is to say, public anti-poverty outlays. Between Fiscal Year 1973 and Fiscal Year 2001, real spending on such programs more than tripled, leaping from $153 billion to $484 billion (in constant 2002 dollars), or by over 150 percent on a per capita inflation-adjusted basis. One can make arguments for excluding the health and medical care component from the measure of antipoverty program spending; doing the sums, nonhealth antipoverty spending would still rise in constant 2002 terms from $109 billion in 1973 to $231 billion in 2001, or by 57 percent per capita.[6] These data, one must emphasize, account for just the government's share of anti-poverty programs: Private charitable donations provide additional resources for meeting the needs of America's poor, and those resources are considerable. In the year 2001, total private philanthropic giving was estimated at $239 billion—in real terms, 156 percent more than in 1973; and in real per capita terms, an increase of over 90 percent. Although we cannot know the exact proportion of these private funds earmarked for poverty alleviation, it seems safe to say that antipoverty spending by both the public and the private sectors increased very significantly on a real per capita basis between 1973 and 2001.

As it was constructed, the official poverty rate was meant to measure only pretax money incomes; in-kind benefits, such as food or housing, would be excluded from this calculus automatically, and by design. Given the prevailing perceptions that cash aid accounts for only a small fraction of U.S. antipoverty spending—and the common belief that means-tested cash aid has been substantially reduced in the United States since "welfare reform" laws of 1996—one might assume that antipoverty spending ought not to have too much of an influence on long-term trends in the official poverty rate. Yet cash transfers through official antipoverty policies are by no means trivial today, nor has the rise over the past three decades in such spending been insignificant. In 2001, government-provided cash aid programs for the poor dispensed over $100 billion—81 percent more in real terms than in 1973, and nearly 35 percent more on real per capita basis. If we were to factor in private-sector cash aid, total anti-poverty transfers for 2001 would be that much higher.

Per capita income, unemployment, educational attainment, and antipoverty spending are factors that would each be expected to exert independent and important influence on the prevalence of poverty in a modern industrialized society—any modern industrialized society. When trends for all four of these measures move conjointly in the direction favoring poverty reduction, there would ordinarily be a strong expectation that the prevalence of measured poverty would decline as well (so long, of course, as poverty was being measured against an absolute rather than a relative benchmark). Yet curiously, the official poverty rate for the United States population was higher for 2001 (11.7 percent) than for 1973 (11.1 percent).

Needless to say, this is a discordant and counterintuitive result that demands explanation. Further examination, unfortunately, reveals that the paradoxical relationship between the poverty rate and these other indicators of material deprivation in Table 16-1, while perverse, is not at all anomalous. To the contrary: For the period since 1973, the U.S. poverty rate has ceased to correspond with these other broad measures of poverty and progress in any common-sense fashion. Instead, the poverty rate seems to have become possessed of a strange but deeply structural capriciousness: For while it continues to maintain a predictable relationship with these other indicators, the relationship is by and large precisely the opposite of what one would normally expect for a poverty indicator.

The curious behavior of the official poverty rate in relation to these four other important measures bearing on material deprivation is underscored by simple econometrics, through regression equations in which these other measures are utilized in an attempt to "predict" the poverty rate for a 30-year period (1972–2002). Under ordinary circumstances, we would expect unemployment and poverty to be positively associated (the higher the unemployment level, the higher the poverty level), while per capita income, educational attainment, and anti-poverty spending should all correlate negatively with any absolute measure of poverty.

Between 1972 and 2002, however, the official poverty rate happens to correlate positively with increases in per capita income—and the statistical association is a strong one. Indeed, controlling for changes in unemployment levels, a rise in real U.S. per capita income of $1,000 (in 2002 dollars) would be predicted to push up the official poverty rate for the entire population by over half a percentage point.

If we exclude per capita income from the tableau, the other three measures—unemployment, education, and anti-poverty spending—can in tandem do a very good job of predicting changes in the poverty rate, together explaining over 90 percent of the variation in the poverty rate during the period in question. But the relationships between the poverty rates and these other variables are perverse: The poverty rate falls when unemployment rises; and when education or anti-poverty spending rise, the poverty rate rises too.

And if we use all four measures to try to predict the poverty rate, the common-sense (i.e. negative) correlation between per capita income and poverty at last emerges, and that relationship is statistically strong—yet strong relations between the poverty rate and the other three measures also emerge, and all of those are perverse. Those relationships, in fact, imply that an eight-point jump in the unemployment rate would reduce the official poverty rate by a point, while a ten point drop in the percentage of adults without high school degrees would raise it by a point! No less striking: A nationwide increase in means-tested public spending of $1,000 per capita (in 2002 dollars) would be predicted to make the official poverty rate rise— by over three percentage points.

Clearly, something is badly amiss here. And unless someone can offer a plausible hypothesis for why U.S. data series on per capita incomes, unemployment rates, adult educational attainment, and anti-poverty spending should be collectively flawed and deeply biased for the post–1973 period, the simplest explanation for these jarring results would be that the officially measured poverty rate happens to offer a highly misleading, or even dysfunctional, measure of material deprivation and has, moreover, been doing so for some considerable period of time.

A Major Discrepancy

Over the years a number of criticisms have been lodged against the official poverty rate, among them:

- The OPR takes no account of regional differences in U.S. price levels.

- It embraces an inappropriate deflator for its inter-temporal adjustments in price levels.

- It takes no account in "money income" of either personal taxes paid or capital gains reaped—quantities that have been on the rise over the past generation.

- It is biased because it makes no imputation for the implicit rental "income" homeowners enjoy through occupying their own properties.

- It is biased because it takes no account of the noncash benefits that households consume (including means-tested public benefits and such private services as employer-provided health insurance).

The Census Bureau has attempted to deal with most of these objections. A series of Census Bureau studies, in fact, have calculated "alternative poverty estimates" for the United States using both a different price index (CPI-U-RS, whose calculated tempo of increase has been somewhat slower than CPI-U), and a variety of more inclusive measures of "income"—and all the associated permutations for the two.[7] (The Census Bureau has not been able to calculate regional poverty thresholds for different regions within the United States, due mainly to a lack of necessary detailed data on local price levels.)

There is, however, an additional problem with the official poverty rate— one possibly more significant than any of the criticisms just mentioned. This is its implicit assumption that a poverty-level household's annually reported money income will equate to the level of its annual expenditures.

The original Orshansky methodology estimated "poverty thresholds" to designate consumption levels consonant with poverty status, and matched these against annually reported household incomes—but it made no effort to determine the actual consumption levels of those low-income households. Instead, it posited an identity between reported money income and expenditures for these families. To this date, the method by which the official poverty rate is calculated continues to presume an identity between measured annual money incomes and annual expenditure levels for low-income households. Yet this presumption is dubious in theory, and it is confuted empirically by virtually all available data on spending patterns for America's poorer strata.

From the standpoint of economic theory, a corpus of literature extending back to the early postwar period, and including the contributions of at least two Nobel laureates in economics (Milton Friedman and Franco Modigliani) has outlined the entirely logical reasons for expecting expenditures to exceed income for consumers who end up in the lowest income strata in any given year. Both the "permanent income hypothesis" and the "life cycle income hypothesis" tell us that families and individuals base their household budgets not just on the fortunes (and uncertainties) of a single year, but instead against a longer life-course horizon—stabilizing their long-term living standards (and smoothing their consumption trajectory) against the vagaries of short-term income fluctuations. Such behavior naturally suggests that the marginal propensity to consume will tend to be disproportionately high for lower-income households—and for the perhaps considerable number of households where expected "permanent income" exceeds current income (i.e. "transitory income"), current consumption will likewise exceed current income if financial arrangements permit.[8]

From the standpoint of empirics, U.S. survey data document a by now major discrepancy between reported annual expenditure levels and reported annual income levels for poorer households in the United States—a disproportion that seems to have been widening steadily over the decades since the official poverty rate was first devised. These trends are evident from the Consumer Expenditure (CE) Survey, produced by the Bureau of Labor Statistics. Unlike the Census Bureau's P–60 series on money incomes of U.S. households, which has been prepared continuously since the late 1940s, the BLS CE surveys have until recently been episodic, taking place about once a decade between the end of World War II and the start of the 1980s. From 1984 onwards, the CE survey has been published annually. Like the P–60 series, this one in principle measures pretax money income of households, but it also cross-references reported annual income against a detailed breakdown of reported out-of-pocket expenditures (net of reimbursement).

In the four decades between 1960–61 and 2002, according to CE surveys, real per household expenditures in the United States rose overall by roughly 65 percent—but since average household size declined over those years from 3.2 persons to 2.5 persons, unweighted real per capita expenditures rose by about 111 percent.[9] Over that same period, real expenditures rose substantially for lower-income Americans as well: In 2002, constant expenditures for the poorest fifth (lowest income quintile) of U.S. households were 77 percent higher than they had been for the poorest fourth (lowest quartile) in 1960–61; between 1972–73 and 2002, real expenditures for the lowest quintile of households increased by 57 percent. Given changes in household size, unweighted per capita expenditure levels were 130 percent higher in real terms for the poorest fifth of U.S. households in 2002 than they had been for the poorest fourth in 1960–61—and for the lowest income quintile were about 43 percent higher in 2002 than for 1972–73.

It is striking that real levels of household expenditures for the poorest fifth of U.S. households have risen by over half during a period in which the official

Table 16-2. Consumer Expenditure Patterns for Low-Income Americans: 1960/61–2002

	1960/61 (Families, lowest quartile)	1972/73 (Families, lowest quartile)	2002 (Consumer units, lowest quintile)
Persons per unit	2.2	1.6	1.7
Reported annual current consumption expenditures (constant 2002 $)	10,756	12,166	19,061
Reported annual pretax income (constant 2002 $)	9,613	8,719	8,316
Reported consumption as a percent of reported income	112	139	229

Note: Earlier surveys deflated by CPI-U-RS index, mean value of reported years used for 1960/61 and 1972/73.
Source: Handbook of Labor Statistics 1975—Reference Edition, BLS Bulletin 1856 (1975), Table 137; Consumer Expenditures Survey 1972–73, BLS Bulletin 1997 (1978), Volume 1, Table 10; "Consumer Expenditures in 2002," BLS Reports 974, February 2002, available electronically at http://www.bls.gov/cex/csxann02.pdf.

poverty rate should also have risen (from 11.5 percent of the population in 1972–73 to 12.1 percent in 2002)—and during which, according to the same CE survey data, real incomes for the poorest fifth of U.S. households reportedly fell. The contradiction is explained, in proximate terms, by a dramatic increase in the ratio of expenditures to income for poorer U.S. households. Whereas the ratio of expenditures to pretax income remained fairly stable for U.S. households overall between 1960–61 and 2002 (rising from 81 percent to 86 percent), that same reported ratio has skyrocketed for poorer Americans since the advent of the official poverty rate. In 1960–61, the lowest income quartile of U.S. households reportedly spent about 12 percent more than their annual pretax income. By 1972–73, however, the poorest fifth of households were spending nearly 40 percent more than their annual income—and by 2002 were spending well over double their reported annual income. (See Table 16-2.)

Statisticians and economists at the BLS caution that theirs is an expenditure survey, rather than an income-and-expenditure survey, and explicitly recommend that "for users interested only in income information, data published by the Census Bureau of the U.S. Department of Commerce may be a better source of information." Substituting Census Bureau estimates for pretax money income for the poorest quintile, however, does not vitiate the apparently widening gap between incomes and expenditures for poorer American households. Comparing CE survey data on expenditures and Census Bureau data on money incomes, we find reported expenditures for the lowest fifth of households 24 percent higher than pretax income in 1972–73, but over 90 percent higher in 2002. Furthermore, the gap between money incomes for the poorest fifth (as reported by the Census Bureau) and expenditure levels for the poorest fifth (as reported by the BLS) appears to have widened gradually over the 1980s and 1990s.

It is worth noting that virtually all of the 13.6 percent of the U.S. population in the lowest income quintile of the CE surveys in 2002 would have counted as officially poor under contemporary poverty thresholds and BLS soundings on their annual income. Yet paradoxically, as of 2002 the average expenditure level for this poorest fifth of U.S. households was 50 percent above the official poverty threshold for a two-person family—even though the average household size of for those in the lowest quintile was less than two persons (1.7). Furthermore, since the CE surveys report only out-of-pocket expenditures (excluding unreimbursed employer and government noncash benefits), actual levels of consumption of goods and services for low-income households may be higher still than these nominal results suggest.

In the early 1960s—the period whose data Orshansky relied upon in devising her original poverty rate—a surfeit of reported expenditures over reported pretax income among low-income households was already evident in national consumer expenditure surveys, but that discrepancy was relatively modest: about 12 percent for the lowest income quartile. By the turn of the century, that reported discrepancy was truly enormous: It had risen to almost 130 percent for the lowest income quintile of U.S. households. The arguably unexpected but in any case continuing and now-extreme divergence between reported income and reported expenditure levels for low-income households represents a critical blind spot for the official American poverty indices. With reported pretax income levels an ever poorer predictor of true household consumption levels, the official poverty rate— contingent as it is on income rather than consumption numbers—would correspondingly appear to be an increasingly biased estimator of the actual prevalence of deprivation among United States households.

Temporary Poverty

The stark and increasing mismatch between reported annual incomes and reported annual expenditures for low-income households in contemporary America may go far in helping to explain why the official poverty rate—predicated as it is on reported annual money income—seems so very out of keeping with other data series bearing on the incidence of material deprivation in modern America. But how is this widening gap to be explained? How did the reported surfeit of expenditures over pretax income for low-income households in America in CE surveys vault from about 12 percent in the early 1960s to almost 130 percent in 2002?

One hypothesis for the growing discrepancy between income levels and expenditure levels for poorer Americans might be that low-income Americans are "overspending"—i.e., going ever deeper into debt. By the reasoning of this surmise, the apparently widening gap between income and expenditures reported for poorer Americans, far from being an artifact, would represent an all-too-genuine phenomenon: an unsustainable binge that must eventually end, with ominous consequences for future living standards of the vulnerable and the disadvantaged.

On its face, this hypothesis might seem plausible. In the event, however, it appears to be confuted by data on the net worth of poorer American households. If expenditures for lower-income households were being financed through a steady draw-down of assets or accumulation of debt, we would expect the net worth of poor Americans to decline steadily over time in absolute terms. No such trend is evident from the two government data sources that attempt to estimate the net worth of poorer Americans: the Census Bureau's Survey of Income and Program Participation (SIPP) and the Federal Reserve Board's Survey of Consumer Finance (SCF).[10] To be sure, poorer American households do appear to have very modest means by comparison with the rest of contemporary America. At the turn of the century, according to both SIPP and SCF, the median net worth for U.S. households in the bottom income quintile was less than $8,000 (in 2001 dollars). But available data do not suggest that median net worth of poorer households is declining steadily over time. The SIPP data report that median net worth of poorer U.S. households dipped between the mid-1980s and the early 1990s, but then rose back to close to their earlier levels by the turn of the century; SCF data corroborate a steady rise in median net worth for poorer households over the 1990s.

A slightly more sophisticated version of the same spend-down thesis might propose that net worth was holding for low-income households only because fixed-value liabilities were being accumulated against nominal (and potentially transient) increases in assets values. (We might term this a "second-order overspending" hypothesis.) Available data argue against this conjecture as well. The SCF provides estimates not only of mean net worth, but also of mean assets and liabilities for the poorest fifth of U.S. households. Between 1989 and 2001, the estimated mean value of those assets appreciated much more substantially than mean liabilities ($24,000 versus $8,000, in constant 2001 dollars). Consequently, the mean net worth of the poorest fifth of U.S. households was estimated to rise in real terms by roughly half over those same years, from about $34,000 to over $52,000 (in constant 2001 dollars). Poorer U.S. households, taken as a whole, may have been "spending down" a portion of their appreciating asset values—but only a portion of those gains.

If the growing statistical discrepancy between incomes and expenditures for poorer Americans cannot be explained by a growing indebtedness of lower-income households, how, then, can we account for it? Three partial explanations come immediately to mind.

- *Changes in CE survey methods and practices.* The growing mismatch between reported income and reported expenditures for lower-income households could in part be an artifact of changes in the CE survey itself. The University of Texas's Daniel Slesnick, a trenchant student of U.S. poverty data, has noted that the correlation between reported income and reported expenditures on the CE surveys as a whole dropped substantially between the early 1960s and the 1980s,[11] but Harvard's Christopher Jencks has counseled against imputing too much significance to the apparent change. Jencks observes that the CE survey currently entails fewer built-in checks and safeguards than in the past: Whereas inconsistent or curious responses would be likely to invite re-interviews—and emendations—in the 1960–61 survey, similarly suspicious data might simply be entered into the official data-base in more recent surveys.[12] Neither Slesnick nor Jencks, however, offers us an indication of the actual quantitative impact of these alterations in the conduct of the CE survey.

- *Income underreporting.* A second potential problem, related to the first, might be a tendency over time toward increased misreporting of income. As already mentioned, the BLS staff responsible for the CE surveys carefully note that users should place more confidence in their expenditure estimates than their income estimates, especially for the lowest reported income deciles. (The CE staff seems especially concerned by the relatively large number of respondents who report extremely low or even negative incomes but healthy spending patterns.) As a possible corrective for the survey's income underreporting, CE researchers have proposed the ranking of households by outlays rather than income. Ranking households by current outlays rather than income radically changes the ratio of outlays to income for the bottom quintile: In the 1992 CE survey, for instance, that ratio drops from 2.05 (income-ranked) to a mere 0.67 (outlay-ranked).[13]

This innovative exercise casts an interesting additional light on U.S. expenditure patterns—but as a corrective for income underreporting, it has some problems of its own. For one thing, an outlays-based ranking of household incomes and expenditures produces the entirely anomalous result that America's greatest "savers" are the quintile of households with the very lowest incomes (with a pretax income-to-outlays ratio of 1.50), while the greatest dis-savers are the very top quintile (with a ratio of only 0.88).

Accounting for the growing discrepancy between reported income and reported expenditures in the CE survey, moreover, would require some evidence of increased misreporting of incomes for the lowest quintile of households. In actuality, the discrepancies between CE and Census Bureau estimates for pretax money incomes have been diminishing over the past two decades. CE estimates for the lowest quintile's money incomes were 44 percent below Census Bureau estimates in 1984—whereas the difference was 17 percent in 2002. The gradual reconciliation of CE and Census Bureau estimates would not argue for increasing misreporting unless the Census Bureau were itself the main source of the problem.

- *Increased year-to-year income variability.* One possible explanation for a secular rise in the expenditure-to-income ratio for households in the lowest annual income quintile would be a long-term increase in year-to-year variations in household income. If U.S. consumer behavior comports with the "permanent income" hypothesis, and if the stochastic year-to-year variability (i.e., transitory variance) in American income patterns were to increase, then we would expect, all other things being equal, that the ratio of reported annual expenditures to reported annual incomes would increase.

This ratio would be expected to rise because intensified transitory variance would mean that, at any given time, a higher proportion of effectively nonpoor households would be experiencing a "low income year"—and since their consumption levels would be conditioned by their "permanent income" expectations, they would still be spending like nonpoor households, even if they were temporarily classified as poor households by the criterion of current income. The greater the proportion of "temporary poor" in the total poverty population, the greater the discrepancy between observed income levels and observed expenditures levels should be within the poverty population.

If poverty is defined in terms of a particular income threshold, it should be readily apparent that poverty status is not a fixed, long-term condition for the overwhelming majority of Americans who are ever designated as poor. Quite the contrary: Since American society and the U.S. economy are characterized by tremendous and incessant mobility, long-term poverty status appears to be the lot of only a tiny minority of the people counted as poor by the official U.S. poverty metric.

The Census Bureau's longitudinal Survey on Income and Program Participation documents this central fact. For the calendar year 1999, nearly 20 percent of the noninstitutionalized American population was estimated to have experienced two or more months in which their household income fell below the poverty threshold. And at some point during the four years 1996–1999, fully 34 percent of the surveyed population spent two months or more below the poverty line. On the other hand, just 2 percent of the population spent all 48 months of 1996–99 below the poverty line. The long-term poor (or "permanent poor"), in other words, accounted for barely one-tenth of those who passed through officially designated poverty at some point in 1999, and

Figure 16-2. Long-Term Probability of Staying in Poverty, by Age 1996–99

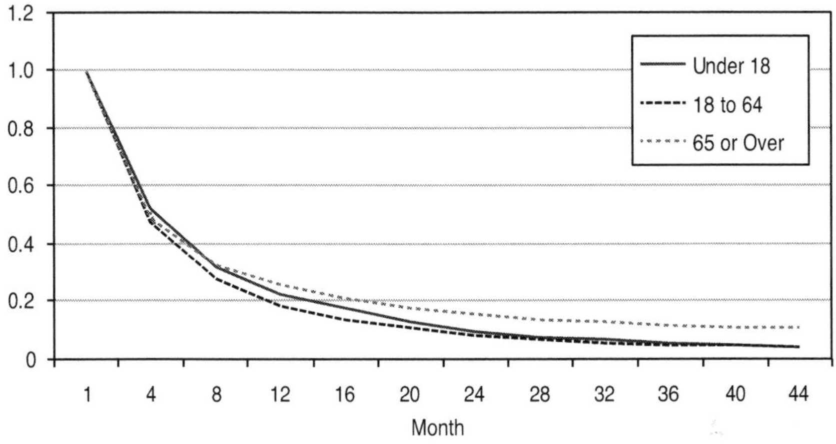

Source: U.S. Census Bureau: "Poverty—Poverty Dynamics 1996-1999 Table 4". Available online at http://www.census.gov/hhes/www/poverty/sipp96/table04.html, accessed 2/27/05.

less than 6 percent of those who were counted as poor at any point between the start of 1996 and the end of 1999. (See Figure 16-2.)

As might be expected, the incidence of chronic or long-term poverty varies according to ethnicity, age, household composition, and location. Whereas just 1 percent of the non-Hispanic white population is estimated to have spent all of 1996–99 below the poverty line, the rate was over 5 percent for both African-Americans and Hispanic-Americans; long-term poverty rates of over 5 percent also typified female-headed households and persons living alone. Yet even for the groups with the highest measured rates of long-term poverty, these permanent poor accounted for a very small fraction of the "ever poor": Fewer than a sixth of the Hispanics counted as poor at any time during 1999, for example, had been below the poverty line throughout 1996–99.

Given the high proportion of the temporarily poor within the overall population of those counted as poor, it should not be surprising that reported expenditures would exceed reported income among America's lower-income strata, as they apparently do today. But while the dynamics illustrated by the SIPP data speak to high, steady, and rapid rates of transition into and out of poverty status for American households in the late 1990s, those data do not indicate whether or not the longer-term trend in year-to-year household income variability has been increasing.

More extended longitudinal data series would be required for such calculations—and fortunately, such data bases are currently available. One of these is the Panel Series on Income Dynamics (PSID), an ongoing in-depth socioeconomic survey that commenced in 1968 and currently follows 7000 sample families. Several researchers have attempted to estimate longer-term trends for transitory variance in U.S. household income based on these data. Their findings all point to a single general pattern: one of secular, and quite significant, increases in such variability between the early 1970s and the beginning of the twenty-first century.

Although the concept of transitory income—and thus variance in transitory income—is clear enough in theory, the task of computing transitory variance is not straightforward in practice, owing to the nature of the observational problem; consequently, a variety of techniques has been advanced for decomposing "permanent variance" and "transitory variance" within the spectrum of overall income differences within a given population.

One recent approach to decomposing the two was developed by Johns Hopkins University's Robert A. Moffitt and Boston College's Peter Gottschalk, applying their method to PSID household earnings data. Relying on this same technique, Yale University's Jacob S. Hacker calculated that the year-to-year variability of pretax income for U.S. families rose dramatically over the last quarter of the twentieth century, more than doubling between 1973 and 1998. By those calculations, transitory variance (or what Hacker labels "income instability") rose quite steadily over the course of the 1970s and 1980s, then spiked upward in the early 1990s—dropping off in the mid-to-late 1990s, but nevertheless remaining in 1998 well above the average level of the 1973–90 period.

Further work by Hacker updated those calculations to cover the 1973–2000 period, and changed the metric from pretax family income to post-tax, post-transfer family income (arguably a more representative measure for permanent income). Those computations also indicated a substantial long-term rise in transitory variance for U.S. household income. Like his initial findings, these updated calculations report a curious and unexplained spike in transitory variance for the year 1993—but even excluding that observation, there is an unmistakable secular increase in measured year-to-year variability over this period.

Further analysis of the PSID survey corroborated Hacker's findings and expanded on them. For a special series of articles on economic insecurity in the United States today for the *Los Angeles Times*,[14] Moffitt was commissioned to supervise an additional breakdown of trends in transitory variance in U.S. family income over the 1970–2000 period. Utilizing Moffitt-Gottschalk techniques, he and two graduate students calculated, among other things, the changes in transitory income variance for families at different rungs on the income ladder, and the absolute change in transitory variance for median-income households in the United States.

According to those calculations, inflation-adjusted variations in annual U.S. family income registered a steady and consequential climb over the 1970–2000 period. For a median-income American household—a family in the very middle of overall income distribution—the maximum expected random volatility in year-to-year income more than doubled over these years, rising from about $6,00 in 1970 to nearly $13,500 in 2000 (in constant 2003 dollars).[15] (See Figure 16-3.) Since inflation-adjusted median family income (in the PSID data series) rose by just 28 percent over those same years, maximum random annual volatility in relation to annual income rose significantly—from about 16 percent in 1970 to about 27 percent in 2000.

The correspondence between income shocks and family income levels, moreover, was not uniform across the income spectrum. Moffitt calculated what statisticians call the "coefficient of variation" (variance as a proportion of the sample's mean) for families at three separate positions in the income scale: the twentieth percentile (designated as the working poor), the fiftieth percentile (labeled the middle class), and the ninetieth percentile (upper income). In 1970, the coefficient of variation was lowest for the highest of these income groupings, and highest for the lowest income grouping; proportional income variability was about twice as high for families at the 20 percent mark in the overall income distribution as for those at the 90 percent threshold.

Between 1970 and 2000, the coefficient of variation rose for families at all three spots in the overall U.S. income distribution—but it was measured as rising especially sharply for those bordering the bottom income quintile. Whereas proportional income variability increased by about three-fifths for the upper-income grouping, and by about three-fourths for the middle-class

Figure 16-3. Absolute Annual Income Variability, 1970–2000: Median-Income Families (constant 2003 Dollars)

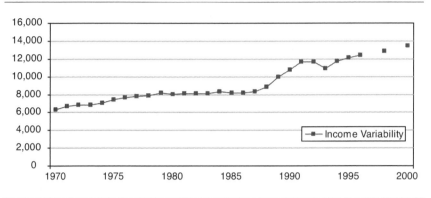

Note: Variability defined statistically as one standard deviation of variance.
Source: "The Source of the Statistics and How They Were Analyzed" Latimes.com (December 29, 2004). Calculations by Robert A. Moffitt of Johns Hopkins University. Available at http://www.latimes.com/business/la-fi-riskshift3oct10-method,1,2775842.story. Accessed 11/2/2005.

grouping, it fully doubled for the working poor families at the boundary between the bottom income quintile and the second income quintile in the overall income distribution.

The long-term increase in proportional income variability for American households evident within the PSID data series—and the disproportionate increase in such variability for Americans at the lower rungs of the income ladder—are highly suggestive. If corroborated through other longitudinal data series (such as the Census Bureau's SIPP), these would qualify as truly major socioeconomic trends for contemporary America. Yet the finding is so robust within the PSID data that it merits immediate discussion, even before exploring other longitudinal series.

Certainly the measured long-term increases in transitory income variance reflected in the PSID would be consistent with the by now generally accepted finding that secular differences in overall household earnings and overall household income both increased during the last quarter of the twentieth century in the United States.[16] The causes of, and relative contributions of different socioeconomic factors to, the phenomenon of increased U.S. earnings and income dispersion in contemporary America are matters of extensive ongoing research and active debate among informed specialists.

The social consequences of increased income equality, and the policy implications of those trends, are likewise matters of widespread interest and continuing, intense dispute. For our limited purposes here, it may suffice to underscore a single statistical consequence of the measured rise in U.S. income inequality. If (as PSID data strongly suggest) the proportional variation in American annual household income has been on the rise over the past generation—and if, moreover, such increases have been especially pronounced at the lower quintiles of the overall income distribution (as PSID also strongly suggest)—then we would correspondingly expect a rise, possibly even a sharp rise, in the discrepancy between reported annual income and reported annual expenditures for households in the bottom quintile of the income distribution.

Clearly more research is warranted here. For now, however, we may note that the curious divergence between reported income and expenditure patterns that has been recorded in consumer expenditure surveys for the period since the early 1970s appears to be matched by a simultaneous reported rise in transitory income variance for U.S. families in the PSID survey—and with a particularly marked increase in proportionate year-to-year variations for families on the borderline of the bottom income quintile.

Incontestably Better Off

By indexing annual changes in nominal poverty thresholds against the Consumer Price Index, the official poverty rate for the U.S. is, in principle, devised to track over time a set of fixed and constant household income standards for distinguishing the poor from the nonpoor. While there are conceptual justifications for both absolute and relative measures of poverty, the incontestable fact is that the OPR was intended to be an absolute measure—one that would identify people living in conditions determined by a specific and unchanging budget constraint.

Thus constructed and thus interpreted because contemporary specialists on poverty in the United States widely understand the poverty line to demarcate the population within the United States whose absolute material circumstances have not improved since the advent of the War on Poverty. This understanding is implicit in the comments of economist Sheldon Danziger, a leading authority on America's poverty problem, upon the release of official poverty numbers for the country in 2004 that were higher than the ones reported in the mid-to-late 1970s: "We have had a generation with basically no progress against poverty. . . . The economic growth is not trickling down to the poor."[17]

The notion that the official poverty rate tracks a fixed and unchanging material condition, however, is contradicted by a wide array of physical and biometric indicators. These data demonstrate steady and basically uninterrupted improvements in the material conditions and consumption levels of Americans in the lowest income strata over the past four decades.

Mollie Orshansky intended her original standard for counting the poor to designate an income level below which "everyday living implied choosing between an adequate diet of the most economical sort and some other necessity because there was not money enough to have both." In purely material terms, today's American poverty population is incontestably better off than were Orshansky's original poor back in 1965.

To track the changing material circumstances of America's low-income population, we will follow trends in four areas: 1) food and nutrition; 2) housing; 3) transportation; and 4) health and medical care. From the early 1960s through the beginning of the twenty-first century, American consumers, poor and nonpoor alike, devoted the great majority of their personal expenditures to these four categories of goods and expenditures. Between 1960–61 and 2002, food, housing, transport, and health/medical care together accounted for about 70 percent of mean U.S. household expenditures, and for about 80 percent of the expenditures of households in the lowest income quintile. And while the composition of these allocations by category shifted over these decades, their total claim within overall expenditures remained remarkably stable. Let us then examine in turn trends in food and nutrition, housing, transportation, and health/medical care.

Food and Nutrition. In the early 1960s—the years for which the poverty rate was first devised—undernourishment and hunger were unmistakably in evidence in the United States. Indeed, self-assessed food shortage was clear from the expenditure patterns of American consumers: In the 1960–61 consumer expenditure survey, for example, the marginal propensity of consumers to spend income on food rose between the lowest and the next lowest income groupings. With an income elasticity for food of more than 1.0, this poorest grouping of Americans—accounting for about 1 percent of the households surveyed—defined a grouping for which foodstuffs were "luxury goods." In no subsequent consumer expenditure surveys for the United States, however, is it possible to identify sub-categories of the U.S. population with income elasticities of expenditure for foodstuffs in excess of 1.0.

Biometric assessments of nutritional status amplify and extend the evidence from consumer expenditures surveys. Health survey data collected by the National Center for Health Statistics (NCHS) of the U.S. Centers for Disease Control and Prevention (CDC) make the point. Between the early 1960s and the end of the century, for example, the proportion of the adult population 20 to 74 years of age assessed "probabilistically" as underweight from weight-for-height readings (i.e., with a measured body mass index of under 18.5) dropped by half, from 4.0 percent to 1.9 percent.[18] The main nutritional problem to emerge over those years in the anthropometric data was obesity, the prevalence of which (as predicted by weight-for-height data) soared from 13 percent in 1960–62 to 31 percent in 1999–2002.

For purely biological reasons, a society's most nutritionally vulnerable groups are typically infants and children. Anthropometric and biometric data suggest that nutritional risks to American children have declined almost continuously over the past three decades. Even for low-income children—i.e., those who qualified for means-tested public health benefits—those nutritional risks look to have been declining progressively. According to the National Pediatric Surveillance System of the CDC, for example, the percentage of low-income children under five years of age who were categorized as underweight (in terms of BMI for age) dropped from 8 in 1973 to 5 in 2003; since the cutoff for "underweight" was defined probabilistically as the fifth percentile on normed pediatric growth charts, the 2003 finding would be consistent with observations for a normalized population with an underweight prevalence of zero. Similarly, the proportion of medically examined low-income children who presented height-for-age below the expected fifth percentile level on pediatric growth charts declined from 9 percent in 1975 to 6 percent in 2003. Blood work for these same children suggested a gradually declining risk of anemia, to judge by the drop in the proportion identified as having a low hemoglobin count.

Housing and Home Appliances. Statistical information on U.S. housing conditions and home appurtenances are available today from three main sources: 1) the decennial census of population and housing; 2) the Census Bureau's American Housing Survey (AHS), conducted in 1984 and every few years thereafter; and 3) the Department of Energy's Residential Energy Consumption Survey (RECS), initially conducted in 1978 and currently re-collected every four years. Since 1970, the decennial census has cross-classified household housing conditions by official poverty status; AHS and RECS also track poverty status and its correlates in their surveys.

Basic trends in housing conditions for poverty households and officially nonpoor households are highlighted in Table 16-3. In terms of simple floorspace, the homes of the officially poor were more spacious at the dawn of the new century than they had been three decades earlier. In 1970, almost 27 percent of poverty-level households were officially considered overcrowded (the criterion being an average of over one person per room).[19] By 2001, according to the AHS, just 6 percent of poor households were "overcrowded"—a lower proportion than for nonpoor households as recently as 1970. Between 1980 and 2001, moreover, per capita heated floor-space in the homes of the officially poor appears to have increased substantially—to go by official data, by as much as 27 percent or perhaps even more. By 2001, the fraction of poverty-level households lacking some plumbing facilities was reportedly down to 2.6 percent—a lower share than for nonpoor households in 1970.

Trends in furnishings and appurtenances for American households similarly record the steady spread of desirable consumer appliances to poor and nonpoor households alike. From 1970 to the present, poorer households' access to or possession of modern conveniences has been unmistakably increasing. For many of these items—including telephones, television sets, central air conditioning, and microwave ovens—prevalence in poverty-level households as of 2001 exceed availability in the typical U.S. household as of 1980, or in nonpoor households as of 1970. By the same token, the proportion of households lacking air-conditioning was lower among the officially poor in 2001 than among the general public in 1980. By 2001, over half of all poverty-level households had cable television and two or more television sets. Moreover, by 2001 one in four officially poor households had a personal computer, one in six had internet access, and three out of

Table 16-3. Selected Housing Characteristics, Poor and Other Households, USA: 1970–2001

	Non-poor HHS 1970	Poor HHS 1970	All HHS 1980	Poor HHS 1980	Poor HHS 1990	Poor HHS 2001
Households with 1.00+ persons per room (%)	9.8	26.9	4.5	n/a	n/a	6.0
Lacking some plumbing facilities (%)	3.4	17.4	2.2	n/a	n/a	2/6
Home not heated (%)	0.6	0.9	0.6	1.1	n/a	2.2
Mean heated square feet of home	n/a	n/a	1,499	1,095	1,105	1,227
Average square feet heated per household member	n/a	n/a	534	371	385	472

Note: n/a = not available, "poor" = below official poverty threshold.
Sources: Derived from *Census of Population* 1970: *Subject Reports, Low-Income Population Final Report* PC (2)-91: *Low-Income Population* (Bureau of the Census, 1973), Table 36; *1980 Census of Housing: Volume 1: Characteristics of Housing Units* HC 80-1A (Bureau of the Census, 1983), Table 1; *Residential Energy Consumption Survey: Housing Characteristics* 1980 Edition (Department of Energy, Energy Information Administration, 1982), Tables 9, 26, 1990 Edition (DOE, 1992), Table 15; 2001 edition (DOE, 2003) Tables CEI-5.1A, CEI 5.2A, CEI-5.1U, CE 2.3C, available electronically at http://www.eia.gov/emeu/recs/contents.html; American Housing Survey of the United States (Bureau of the Census), 2001 edition (2003), Tables 2-3, 2-4.

four had at least one VCR or DVD—devices unavailable even to the affluent a generation earlier.

These data cannot tell us much about the quality of either the housing spaces that poverty level households inhabit or the appurtenances furnished therein. They say nothing, furthermore, about nonphysical factors that bear directly on the quality of life in such housing units—most obvious among these being crime. These data, however, strongly support the proposition that physical housing conditions are gradually improving not only for the rest of America, but for the officially poor as well. In any given year, a gap in physical housing conditions separates the officially poor from the nonpoor—but the data for today's poor appear similar to those for the nonpoor a few decades earlier.

Transportation. At the time of the 1972–73 consumer expenditure survey, almost three-fifths of the households in the lowest income quintile had no car. Since the official poverty rate for families in those years was only about 10 percent, we may suppose that the proportion of poverty-level households without motor vehicles at that time was somewhat higher. By 2003, however, over three-fifths of U.S. poverty-level households had one car or more—and nearly three of four had some sort of motor vehicle. (The distinction is pertinent, owing to the popularity and proliferation of suvs, light trucks, and other motor vehicles classified other than as cars from the late 1970s onward.)

By 2003, quite a few poverty-level households had multiple motor vehicles: Fourteen percent had two or more cars, and 7 percent had two or more trucks. In 2003, to be sure, vehicle ownership was more limited among the officially poor than among the general public; for the country as a whole, fewer than 9 percent of households reported being without any motor transport whatever. The increase in motor vehicle ownership among officially poor households has followed the general rise for the American public—albeit with a very considerable lag. As of 2003, auto ownership rates for poverty-level households mirrored ownership rates for U.S. families in general in the early 1950s; for all forms of motor transport, U.S. poverty households' ownership levels in 2003 matched overall U.S. families' auto ownership levels from the early 1960s; and poverty households' ownership levels for two or more motor vehicles paralleled that of the general U.S. public in the late 1950s or early 1960s.

Health and Medical Care. NCHS data can be used to illuminate two separate aspects of health status and medical care in modern America: outcomes and service utilization. The most critical datum for health status is arguably mortality: All other health indicators are subsidiary to survival. The single most intuitively clear mortality indicator may be expectation of life. Unfortunately, however, available data do not permit the construction of "life tables" and attendant survival schedules by official poverty status. But mortality data are available for adults by their educational attainment—and this proxy affords us a glimpse at some of the socioeconomic differences in death rates in contemporary America.

Perhaps not surprisingly, adults without a high school diploma had significantly higher age-standardized death rates than the general population: In 2002, the differential was over 50 percent among both men and women. Despite the relative magnitude of this disparity, however, in absolute terms

Figure 16-4. Poverty Rates vs. Infant Mortality Rates: USA, White Children 1959–2001

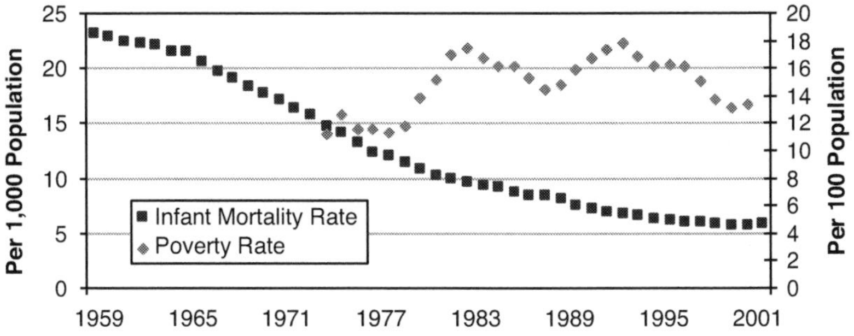

Sources: "Supplemental Analysis of Recent Trends in Infant Mortality," by Kenneth D. Kochanek, M.A., and Joyce A. Martin, M.P.H. Available online at http://www.cdc.gov/nchs/products/pubs/pubd/hestats/infantmort/infantmort.htm. Accessed 2/14/05. U.S. Census Bureau Historical Poverty Tables, available online at http://www.census.gov/hhes/poverty/histpov/perindex.html. Accessed 2/14/05. "Health USA 2004," National Center for Health Statistics. Available online at http://www.cdc.gov/nchs/data/hus/hus04trend.pdf. Accessed 2/23/05. National Center for Health Statistics, "Deaths: Final Data for 1997," available online at http://www.cdc.gov/nchs/data/nvsr/nvsr47/nvsr47_19.pdf. Accessed 2/14/05. Statistical Abstract of the United States, US Census Bureau, 1979 edition, Table 87; 1982 edition, Tables 90, 111.

death rates in 2002 for this educationally disadvantaged group were lower than they had been among the general public some years earlier. The overall age-standardized death rate for women 25 to 64 years of age in 1970, for example, was slightly higher than the 2002 rate for their counterparts who had not completed high school. Among adult men, death rates for the general public in 1970 were about 10 percent higher than among high-school dropouts in 2002.

For babies and infants, the single most important measure of health status is surely the infant mortality rate. Between 1970 and 2002, the infant mortality rate in the United States fell by nearly two-thirds, from 20 per 1,000 live births to 7 per thousand. The infant mortality rate continued its almost uninterrupted annual declines after 1973, when officially measured poverty rates for U.S. children began to rise. The contradistinction is particularly striking for white babies. Between 1974 and 2001, their infant mortality rates fell by three-fifths, from 14.8 per 1,000 to 5.8 per 1,000; yet over those same years, the official poverty rate for white children rose from 11.2 percent to 13.4 percent. (See Figure 16-4.)

These survival gains were achieved not only in the face of purportedly worsening poverty status, but also despite unfavorable trends in biological risk. In 2001, the proportion of white babies born at high-risk "low birth weight" (below 2,500 grams) was actually somewhat higher than in 1974. Yet despite these troubling trends in low-birth-weight disposition, infant mortality rates improved dramatically. Since the inherent biological disparities in mortality risk between low-birth-weight and non-low-birth-weight newborns did not diminish over this period, the reasonable inference might be that medical and health care interventions—changes in the quality and availability of services—accounted for most of the difference. And since low-birth-weight infants are disproportionately born to mothers from disadvantaged socioeconomic backgrounds, a further reasonable inference is that these improvements in quality and availability of medical care extended to America's poorer strata, not just the well-to-do.

One particularly revealing indicator of health status and health care availability is dental health. From at least the nineteenth century, with its path-breaking reform-movement studies of the English working classes, the condition of a population's teeth has been recognized as a telling reflection of social well-being. Dental health is also an informative proxy for health care access because dentistry is still widely regarded as an optional medical service. Between the early 1970s and the late 1990s, the share of the U.S. adult population with untreated dental cavities is estimated to have dropped by nearly half, from 48 percent to 26 percent. Of officially poor adults, fully two-fifths still had untreated cavities in the 1999–2000 NCHS survey—but since nearly two-thirds of poverty-level adults had untreated cavities in the 1971–74 surveys, this represented a considerable advance over circumstances a generation earlier. For older Americans, the loss of all natural teeth was always a likely outcome in later life—but a majority of Americans 65 and older can now expect to avoid that fate. According to NCHS health examination surveys, the fraction of edentulous senior citizens declined from about 50 percent in 1960–62 to about 30 percent in 2000. (No data are available here for trends for poverty-level seniors.)

Such improvements in dental conditions are suggestive of improved dental care. Time series data on dental visits are not immediately available, but data for recent years could be consistent with increased use of dentistry by the official poverty population. By 2002, nearly half of poverty-level

Figure 16-5. Percent of Children Under 18 Years Without a Reported Health Care Visit in the Past Year, by Percent of Poverty Threshold

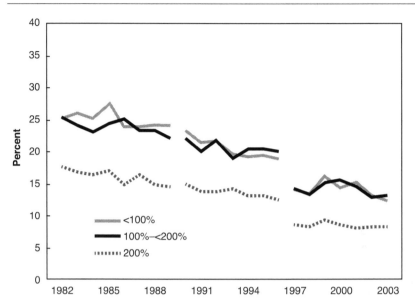

Source: *National Health Interview Survey.*

adults aged 18 to 64 and nearly two-thirds of poverty-level children 6 to 17 years of age were reportedly making at least one dental visit a year. Such rates would look comparable to the ones reported for the general population in the early 1960s.

Trends in utilization of health care for the poor are further illustrated by the circumstances of children under 18—more particularly by the proportion reporting no medical visits over the year preceding their health interview survey. (See Figure 16-5.) While the percentage of children without an annual medical visit is always higher among the poor than among the nonpoor, steady declines are reported for both groups—and the declines were substantial. The proportion of children without a reported annual medical visit, in fact, was significantly lower for the poverty population in 2002 (12.1 percent) than it had been for the nonpoverty population 20 years earlier (17.6 percent). Figure 16-5 cannot address the question of preexisting health needs—it could be that pediatric medical problems were on the rise during this period. These data thus do not conclusively demonstrate that "access" or "availability" of health and medical care have been improving. But they are strongly suggestive of this possibility—all the more so in conjunction with the salutary trends in health status outcomes.

To summarize the evidence from physical and biometric indicators: Low-income and poverty-level households today are better-fed and less threatened by undernourishment than they were a generation ago. Their homes are larger, better equipped with plumbing and kitchen facilities, and more capaciously furnished with modern conveniences. They are much more likely to own a car (or a light truck, or another type of motor vehicle) now than 30 years earlier. By most every indicator apart from obesity, their health care status is considerably more favorable today than at the start of the War on Poverty. Their utilization of health and medical services has steadily increased over recent decades.

All of this is in one sense reassuring. These data underscore the basic fact that low-income Americans have been participating in what Orshansky termed "America's parade of progress." Orshansky had worried that the poor in modern America might be watching that parade and "wait[ing] for their turn—a turn that does not come"; fortunately, her apprehension has proved to be unfounded.

To state this much is not to assert that material progress for America's poverty population has been satisfactory, much less optimal. Nor is it to deny the importance of relative as opposed to absolute deprivation in the phenomenon of poverty as the poor themselves experience it. Those are serious questions that merit serious discussion, but they are questions distinct and separate from the focus of this study—i.e. the reliability of the official poverty rate per se as an indicator of material deprivation.

As we have seen, the U.S. federal poverty measure is premised on the assumption that official poverty thresholds provide an absolute poverty standard—a fixed inter-temporal resource constraint. Such a standard should mean that general material conditions for the poverty population should remain more or less invariant over time. Yet quite clearly, the material condition of the poverty population in modern America has not been invariant over time—it has been steadily improving. The OPR thus fails—one is tempted to say that it fails spectacularly—to measure what it purports to be tracking over time. As an indicator of a condition originally defined in 1965, the official poverty rate seems to have become an ever less faithful and reliable measure with each passing year.

Biases and Flaws

In some quarters, criticism of the various shortcomings of America's official poverty rate will be taken as evidence of indifference to the plight of America's disadvantaged and poor. Such an inference is illogical at best. Proponents of more effective antipoverty policies should be in the very front ranks of those advocating more accurate information on America's poverty problem. Without such information, effective policy action will be impeded; under the influence of misleading information, policies will be needlessly costly—and ineffective.

The official poverty rate is incapable of representing what it was devised to portray: namely, a constant level of absolute need in American society. The biases and flaws in the poverty rate are so severe that it has depicted a great period of general improvements in living standards—three decades from 1973 onward—as a time of increasing prevalence of absolute poverty. We would discard a statistical measure that claimed life expectancy was falling during a time of ever-increasing longevity, or one that asserted our national finances were balanced in a period of rising budget deficits.

Central as the "poverty rate" has become to antipoverty policy—or, more precisely, especially because of its central role in such policies—the official poverty rate should likewise be discarded in favor of a more accurate index, or set of indices, for describing material deprivation in modern America.

The task of devising a better statistical lodestar for our nation's antipoverty efforts is by now far overdue. Properly pursued, it is an initiative that would rightly tax both our formidable government statistical apparatus and our finest specialists in the relevant disciplines. But such exertions would also stand to benefit the common weal in as yet incalculable ways.

Notes

1. Joseph P. Goldberg and William T. Moye, *The First Hundred Years of the Bureau of Labor Statistics*, Bureau of Labor Statistics Bulletin 2235 (September 1985).

2. For informative background on the origin and evolution of the poverty rate, see Gordon M. Fisher, "The Development of the Orshansky Poverty Thresholds and Their Subsequent History as the Official U.S. Poverty Measure," U.S. Census Bureau Poverty Measurement Working Papers (May 1992, partially revised September 1997).

3. Douglas J. Besharov and Peter Germanis, "Reconsidering the Federal Poverty Measure: Project Description," http://www.welfareacademy.org (June 14, 2004), 5. Poverty guidelines are based on poverty thresholds but differ from them in that they are more currently updated to reflect intervening changes in price levels and have a slightly more simplified schema for determining household eligibility levels, with fewer categories for family size and composition than are found in the Census Bureau's poverty threshold tables.

4. Mollie Orshansky, "Counting the Poor: Another Look at the Poverty Profile," *Social Security Bulletin* 28:1 (January 1965).

5. Real per capita GDP estimates derived from NIPA BEA Tables and mid-year population for 1973 and 2001 as reported in *Statistical Abstract of the United States 2004–2005*, Table No. 2.

6. Derived from Vee Burke, *Cash and Noncash Benefits for Persons with Limited Income: Eligibility Rules*, Recipient and Expenditure Data, FY2000–FY2002, Congressional Research Service Report rl32233 (November 25, 2003), Table 5, and *Statistical Abstract of the United States 2004–2005*, Table 2.

7. See Joe Dalaker, *Alternative Poverty Estimates in the United States: 2003*, U.S. Census Bureau Series P–60:227 (June 2005).

8. The concept of transitory income can be traced back at least as far as Milton Friedman and Simon S. Kuznets, *Income from Independent Professional Practice* (National Bureau of Economic Research, 1945), Chapter 7, where the term itself was perhaps coined. Consumer behavior theory would suggest that annual incomes would equate to annual expenditures in the lowest income strata only where those low income levels were in fact consonant with a household's expectations of its long-term financial outlook—or where institutional barriers prevented the household from financing additional near-term consumption.

9. We use unweighted per capita consumption here rather than a weighted adjustment because the former measure is more straightforward. There are good arguments for the latter, insofar as we might expect consumption needs of children and the elderly to be lower than those of working-age adults—but since there are no generally accepted differentials for such weightings, we opt here for transparency over sophistication.

10. SCF appears to offer more a comprehensive inventory than SIPP of the various components of household wealth. For a detailed comparison and evaluation, see John L. Czajka, Jonathan E. Jacobson, and Scott Cody, *Survey Estimates of Wealth: A Comparative Analysis and Review of the Survey of Income and Program Participation* (Mathematica Policy Research Inc., August 22, 2003).

11. Daniel T. Slesnick, *Consumption and Social Welfare: Living Standards and Their*

Distribution in the United States (Cambridge University Press, 2001).

12. Christopher Jencks, comments at Second Seminar on Reconsidering the Federal Poverty Measure, (September 14, 2004), as reported in Summary Report by Douglas J. Besharov and Gordon Green, http://www.welfareacademy.org (October 18, 2004), 10.

13. John M. Rogers and Maureen B. Gray, "CE Data: Quintiles of Income Versus Quintiles of Outlays," *Monthly Labor Review* (December 1994), 32–37. As defined by BLS, "current outlays" is a slightly more comprehensive measure of spending than "total expenditures."

14. Peter G. Gosselin, "The New Deal: If America Is Richer, Why Are Its Families So Much Less Secure?" (Three Part Series in the *Los Angeles Times*, October 12–December 30, 2004).

15. Technically speaking, Moffitt's measure in Figure 16-3 uses the statistical benchmark of a single standard deviation of variance to establish what the *Los Angeles Times* series refers to as the "maximum fluctuation in annual household income for 68 percent of U.S. families." That is to say, assuming the year-to-year variations in family income conform to the bell-shaped normal distribution, this calculation delineates the mark within which just over two-thirds of observed stochastic variations in income for median-income families would be expected to fall.

16. For the official U.S. data on these trends, see Arthur F. Jones Jr. and Daniel H. Weinberg *The Changing Shape of the Nation's Income Distribution*, 1947–1998, U.S. Census Bureau, Series P–60:204 (June 2000) and, for some updated data for 1967–2001, the U.S. Census Bureau's "Historical Income Inequality Tables."

17. David Leonhardt, "More Americans Were Uninsured and Poor in 2003, Census Finds," *New York Times* (August 27, 2004).

18. Weight-for-height designations of obesity should be regarded as probabilistic because they do not actually measure or estimate a given individual's actual proportion of body fat (as is done clinically through skin-fold tests, etc.)

19. RECS 2001 (upon whose figures the calculation above was based) places the mean heated floor space per poverty household at 472 per person; the AHS 2001, for its part, indicates a median value of 739 square feet per person for poverty households, although this total appears to include both heated and unheated floor space and pertains only to the 55 percent of poverty-level households in single, detached and/or mobile/manufactured homes. (American Housing Survey 2001, Table 2–3.)

17

Demographic Exceptionalism in the United States: Tendencies and Implications

Agir, 2007

The idea that the American political experiment bears profound signifi-cance for all humanity is one rooted deep and long in American soil—it far predates the actual establishment of the United States of America (witness Governor John Winthrop's famous "city on a hill" sermon in Massachusetts in 1630, nearly a century and a half before the American Revolution). By the same token, the notion that America was characteristically different from all of the societies from which its emigrant populations had been drawn (the "American difference") was an early and continuing theme of discussion about United States, not only among the revolutionaries who created this independent federalist state in the late Eighteenth Century, but also among discerning observers and well-wishers from the Continent. The concept of "American exceptionalism" was in fact formalized by Alexis de Tocqueville in his opus Democracy in America, after his travels through the USA in the early 1830s.

For the most part, the concept of "American exceptionalism" has been applied to the political differences that separate America's experience and behavior from that of states in the "Old World": the USA's striking absence of any socialist movement worthy of a name; the spirit of 'manifest destiny' long informing US foreign policy, and so on.[1] But America's "exceptionalism" extends well beyond the realm of the explicitly political, and into the realms of the nation's very rhythms of life. These surprising but very palpable ten-dencies may be described as "American demographic exceptionalism".

Paradoxically, although the United States may well count as the "first new nation" (to borrow a phrase from Seymour Martin Lipset) to embark upon the project of democratic modernity, US demographic patterns have not homogenized with those of the world's other industrial democracies. To the contrary: after several decades of seeming convergence in population patterns in the early postwar era, we have witnessed more than a generation of strong and stubborn "demographic divergence" in population profiles between the United States on the one hand and virtually all other OECD members on the other—with potentially even more dramatic divergences seemingly in store.

Two demographic tendencies separate the United States from virtually all developed counterparts in Europe and Asia. The first is childbearing patterns: at a time in which it is the norm for rich countries to report markedly, often astonishingly, low birth rates, fertility levels in the United States are very close to the level needed for long-term population replacement—which makes the USA peculiarly and insistently fecund for a contemporary affluent democracy. The second is immigration patterns: the USA's absorption of foreigners continues apace, with high and continuing inflows of immigrants from the "Third World", but without (as yet) the symptoms of "cultural indigestion" that have troubled Western Europe of late.

US "demographic exceptionalism" would be a fascinating academic side-note if America were today a tiny and distant state, as was the case in 1790. As it happens, however, the USA is now the world's dominant power— and it is also the most populous of the developed societies: over twice as large as Japan, over three times as large as Germany, and over five times the size of France, Italy, or Britain. America's exceptional demographic trends are of interest not only to demographers and sociologists, but to economists, strategists and policymakers looking at the international environment that beckons over the coming generation.

Exceptional American Fertility

From its earliest Colonial origins, childbearing was believed to be markedly higher in this frontier society than in the settled regions of Europe from whence most Americans traced their roots. This American fertility premium was noted and discussed by leading thinkers on both sides of the Atlantic—Malthus in Britain; Crevecoeur in France; Benjamin Franklin in America (who offered the vision of Americans "swarming across the countryside like locusts").

Those perceptions were grounded in demographic reality. The U.S. Bureau of the Census now estimates a "total fertility rate" (TFR) in 1800 for America's "whites" of over 7 births per woman per lifetime, compared with contemporaneous rates around 5.7 in England and 4.5 in France.[2] Fertility levels were even higher for the USA's African-American slaves: according again to the Census Bureau, the US black TFR for the 1850s was nearly 8—a level over 40 percent higher than for contemporary US whites.[3]

From this exceptionally high starting point, the United States moved more or less steadily over the course of the 19th Century through a "demographic transition" toward lower death rates and lower birth rates. By 1900 the United States was the world's most modernized and affluent large country (excepting then only Britain),[4] and with its "white" TFR by then down to 3.6, her "fertility transition" had progressed rather further than in most of her European counterparts (excepting again England, and of course, and also France, whose historical fertility transition, as French readers will know, was distinctive among the now-developed countries in its own way).

After World War II, in the era of the developed regions' "baby boom", US fertility levels once again jumped above Europe's. According to the UN Population Division, America's TFR in the 1950s was over 3.5, whereas Europe's was under 2.7—just three-fourths the US level.[5] But in the pervasive "baby bust" that was to follow, US fertility declined even more sharply than Europe's, dropping to levels that, if continued, would have presaged steady population decline in the absence of immigration. By 1976, America's "period" TFR was 1.74[6]— lower than the fertility level of the EU-15 that same year, less than half of America's own level from the late 1950s, and 18% lower than the requirements for long-term population stability.

At that juncture, "modernization theory" seemed triumphant: socio-economic development appeared to have brought about a basic convergence in fertility trends (at sub-replacement levels) for the world's more developed regions. But a funny thing happened on the road to depopulation: America's reported fertility levels turned upward, since then persistently skirting the replacement level. In 1989, America's "period" TFR rose slightly above 2.0—and has remained in that neighborhood ever since. In the sixteen years from 1989 to 2004, America's TFR averaged 2.02 births per woman, suggesting a "net replacement rate" (NRR) of 98% from one birth cohort to the next.

America's limited but unmistakable upsurge in fertility over the past generation marks a striking and indeed dramatic departure from the march toward seemingly ever-lower levels of sub-replacement childbearing in almost every other developed society. In the first half of the current decade, according to UN Population Division estimates and projections, America's TFRs and NRRs were fully 50% higher than Japan's, and about 45% higher than the averages for Europe as a whole.

Europe's overall fertility levels, to be sure, may currently be depressed by the post-Communist "demographic shocks" that some former Soviet bloc countries (most notably, Russia) continue to experience—but even compared with the amalgam of Western European societies, the US-European fertility gap now looks like a yawning divide. By the calculations and projections of the US Census Bureau, America's TFR is currently over 35% than in "Western Europe" (the EU-15 plus Norway, Switzerland and the region's tiny republics, principalities and islands); and although current fertility levels within Western Europe differ from one society to the next, in some cases quite substantially, the region's overall fertility levels have clearly tended down over the past three decades, while America's have trended up. Such indeed is the distinctiveness of America's recent fertility trends that a wide divide has now opened between the USA and Canada—countries that, in many respects, were long regard as something like "demographic twins". [See Figure 17-1] In the year 2004—the latest year for which data are available—the TFR in the USA was 35% higher than in Canada (with a still greater fertility differential separating the USA and the French-speaking province of Canada).

How can we explain the fertility gap now separating the United States from practically the rest of the developed world? Possible factors might include two distinctive current American social phenomena already widely discussed in the USA and internationally: 1) America's increasingly multiethnic composition (due in large measure to high rates of net immigration, about which more shortly) and 2) the partly-related phenomenon of American teenage fertility levels, which are famously high in the USA in relation to other contemporary affluent democracies.[7] Yet however plausible such factors may sound, they do not actually explain away most of the current fertility gap between the United States and Western Europe.

Consider teenage childbearing patterns: although America's high rates may be notorious within today's OECD societies, the fact of the matter is that

Figure 17-1. US "Demographic Exceptionalism": TFRs, Canada vs. USA, 1975–2004

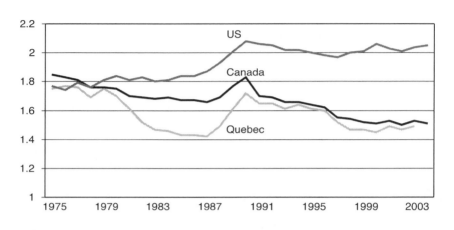

Source: Updated from Barbara Boyle Torrey and Nicholas Eberstadt, "The North America Fertility Divide", Policy Review, no. 132 (August/September 2005), http://policyreview.org/aug05/torrey.html.

US teenage birthrates fell by about one third between 1990 and 2004, even though the overall US TFR remained relatively high and steady. By the year 2004, moreover, teen births comprised just one tenth of all American births and about a tenth of America's overall TFR: meaning, in practical terms, that a total cessation of childbearing by women under 20 years of age would still leave US fertility levels over 20% higher than Western Europe's.

As for fertility differences by ethnicity in the United States, these are real enough—but it is also easy to exaggerate their moment. With the single, albeit highly significant, exception of Hispanic-Americans, fertility levels for US minorities have by and large been converging with those of the non-Hispanic "White" majority. [See Table 17-1] Indeed: average fertility levels for Asian-Americans are almost identical to those for "Anglo" Americans, and Native Americans levels are now lower. While birth rates remain higher for African-Americans than for Anglos, the current black-white differential (of just 9%) is in fact the lowest in at least 150 years (i.e., since the era of slavery in the South). The Hispanic-Anglo fertility gap, for its part, is mainly a matter of the high reported birth levels for Mexican-Americans (whose calculated TFRs currently touch 3.0). Some other Hispanic Americans register

Table 17-1. TFR by Ethnicity: USA, 2004

Total Population	2.05
Non-Hispanic White	1.85
Non-Hispanic Black	2.02
American Indian	1.73
Asian/Pacific Islander	1.90
Hispanic:	2.82
– Puerto Rican	(2.06)
– Cuban	(1.73)
– Mexican	(3.02)
– Other Hispanic	(2.65)

Source: US Centers for Disease Control and Prevention (CDC), "Births: Final Data for 2004", *National Vital Statistics Reports*, vol. 55, (September 29, 2006), available online at http://www.cdc.gov/nchs/data/nvsr/nvsr55/nvsr55_01.pdf.

fertility levels fairly close to Anglo levels (e.g., Puerto Ricans), or actually below them (Cuban-Americans).

In proximate terms, the single most important factor in explaining America's "high" fertility level these days is the birth rate of the country's "Anglo" majority—who still, it is worth noting, account for roughly 55% of the country's births. Over the past decade and a half, the TFR for non-Hispanic White Americans averaged 1.82 births per woman per lifetime—sub-replacement, to be sure, but well over 20% higher than corresponding national fertility levels for Western Europe today—and even higher if one were to compare "Anglo" TFRs with the TFRs of Western Europe's native born populations.

One may of course object that treating Western Europe as a single unit obscures the diversity of fertility patterns within this collectivity, and fair enough—but fertility levels for America's Anglo population also happens to vary by state, and the contrast between the two at the regional level is instructive. [See Figure 17-2] In the year 2000, France reported the highest fertility of any EU member—yet matched against the TFRs of "Anglos", France's TFR would have ranked it in the bottom half of US states. Conversely, America's New England region consistently reports America's lowest levels of Anglo fertility—yet if White New England were a European country, its fertility

Figure 17-2. TFRs, Europe vs. "Anglo" USA: 2000

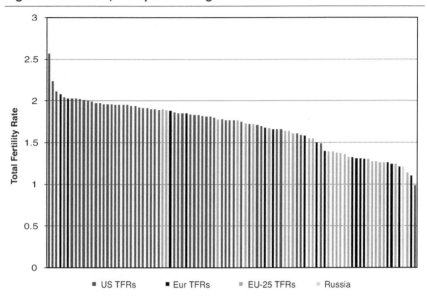

Note: "Anglo" = non-Hispanic White. "Period" total fertility rates in 2000 presented for European countries and for the 50 American federal states. "EU" is pre-accession.

Sources: Eurostat, Population Data, http://epp.eurostat.ec.europa.eu/portal/page?_pageid= 1996,45323734&_dad=portal&_schema=PORTAL&screen=welcomeref&open=/popula/ pop/demo/demo_fer&language=en&product=EU_MASTER_population&root=EU_MASTER_ population&scrollto=171 (accessed June 14, 2007); National Vital Statistics Report: Vol 52, No. 19 May 10, 2004.

level would be distinctly above the EU-15 average. Present-day Turkey may seem fearsomely prolific to some Europeans contemplating the prospect of a Turkish accession to the EU, but Turkey's current TFR of somewhere around 2.0 would be utterly unexceptional in White America today: in much of the American West, in fact, Turkey's current childbearing profile could scarcely be distinguished from that of native-born Anglo locals.

What then accounts for Anglo America's unexpectedly high and stable propensity to reproduce? Carefully tailored pro-natalist government policies certainly cannot explain it: the USA has none! Washington, to the contrary, is known within the OECD for the stinginess of its taxpayer-supported pro- grams for mothers and children. By the same token, US labor patterns do not seem especially "family-friendly"; indeed Americans work longer hours and enjoy less vacation time than any of their European friends across the Atlantic. And a run-through of the checklist of other possible economic and/ or policy explanations for the growing fertility gap between US Anglos and Western European is similarly unsatisfying.

It may be that the main explanation for the US-Europe fertility gap lies not in material factors, but rather in the seemingly ephemeral realm of values, ideals, attitudes, and outlook. It is fairly well established through public opinion surveys, for example, that Americans tend to be more optimistic about the future than their European counterparts: a disposition, one might easily surmise, that could weigh on the decision to bring children into this world. Similarly, the proportion of Americans reporting that they are "proud" to be Americans invariably registers at higher levels than the corresponding soundings in Europe: all other things being equal, such patriotism or nationalism may also plausibly be imagined to conduce to additional births. Perhaps most portentously, survey data indicate that the USA is still in the main a believing Christian country, with high percentage of households actively worshipping on a monthly or even weekly basis. In striking contrast to Western Europe, which might provocatively (but not unfairly) be described as a post-Christian, post-secular territory these days, religion is alive and well in the USA—the most modern, developed and affluent of the modern world's developed affluent societies still seems to be stirred, animated and moved by the basic Judeo-Christian religious texts.

It is not hard to imagine how the religiosity gap between America and Europe would translate into a fertility gap. Unfortunately, the proposition is devilishly difficult to test. Although the USA is (in the taxonomy of the great sociologist Pitirim Sorokin) a "quantophrenic" society, hungry for all manner of facts and figures, an Executive Order of over three decades standing has all but forbidden the federal government's gathering of statistics on the religious affiliation of US citizens. (French readers will appreciate that they are in a similar situation, albeit for different reasons.) Consequently, there are virtually no official national data for the United States that would permit a rigorous testing of the hypothesis that America's unusual disposition to religiosity is directly related to her also unusual disposition to childbearing. Although America is clearly an outlier among developed countries with respect to both religiosity and fertility, assertions that attempt to connect those two factors on the basis of broad, aggregate observations and trends run the risks of committing what statisticians call "ecological fallacy" (i.e., mistakenly associating two actually unrelated phenomena for want of examining the relationships revealed at the level of the individual). Consequently, the proposition that Americans are more fertile because they are more devout must be treated as just an intriguing speculative surmise—at least for now.

Exceptional American Immigration Patterns

The United States is historically a nation populated overwhelmingly by immigrants and their descendants. Immigration—both officially authorized and extra-legal—remains a central feature of the country's demographic life. The scale of undocumented or illegal immigration into the United States in recent years was suggested by the US 2000 census count, which tabulated six million more inhabitants than the "intra-census projection" had prepared US officials to expect!

Western Europe, to be sure, has experienced its own influx of newcomers over the past generation—but in both relative and absolute terms, the influx of migrants to the United States continues at a distinctly higher tempo. By the estimates and projection of the US Census Bureau, net migration into Western Europe over the past decade (1996–2005) averaged roughly 740,000 persons a year—making for a rate of about 1.9 per thousand in comparison to the existing settled population. For the United States, by contrast, the corresponding figures are an average of about 980,000 a year and a rate of 3.5 per year. There are some developed societies whose net immigration rates today are higher than America's—Australia, Canada and New Zealand, for example—but no large country today has a rate even close to the USA's. Indeed: while the USA accounts for one fourth of the population of the so-called "developed regions" (including Eastern Europe and Russia), it accounts for nearly half of the area's annual net migration.

In purely arithmetic terms, America's high flows of net immigration explain much of the country's steady and continuing population growth. Currently, about a third of the US annual demographic increase can be attributed to the net immigration of that given calendar year. But of course immigrants and their descendants account for an even greater share of that annual change:

and depending upon how far back we set the benchmark, we could end up ascribing virtually all US population growth to immigrants and their progeny. One particularly apposite benchmark might be the year 1965, when US immigration laws were decisively liberalized, and much higher, more geographically diverse quotas were established to supersede the restrictive immigration legislation enacted in 1924.

Estimating the precise proportion of population growth in the USA since 1965 due to immigrants and their descendants is a little more tricky than one might first assume; to my knowledge, no published work has offered such calculations. Fortunately, however, Dr. Jeffrey Passel of the Urban Institute in Washington, DC, a specialist on US immigration patterns, has examined this question: his unpublished estimates suggest that over half (about 53%) of the USA's population growth in the period since 1965 can be ascribed to immigration, broadly viewed.[8] Since America's population has grown by over 100 million persons over that interim—from about 194 million in midyear 1965 to just under 300 million at this writing—this would mean that post-1965 immigrants and their descendants account for well over 50 million of the inhabitants of contemporary America—more than one sixth of its residents.

According to official estimates, as of 2003 the foreign-born population of the United States totaled over 33 million, close to 12% of the country's total population—and in many of America's leading urban centers, the proportion of immigrants is now considerably higher. According to the 2000 census, for example, 22% of the population of Chicago was foreign-born; corresponding proportions exceeded 30% for Boston, 35% for both New York and San Francisco; and 40% for Los Angeles. Since less than a fifth of these migrants originated from Europe, Canada, or Australia, America's new wave of immigration is overwhelmingly "Third World". Over one fourth of America's foreign born, for example, now come from Asia. An overall majority (an estimated 52%) of the newcomers are Latin American, with Mexican-born immigrants accounting in turn for the majority of these Latinos. The Census Bureau estimates that over 9 million Mexican-born men, women and children live in the USA today—and that over half of them are unauthorized to be in the United States.[9]

America's latest wave of immigration has certainly exacerbated, and possibly enflamed, some domestic tensions—and has stimulated an undeniable measure of "nativist" political backlash. (Witness the current proposals in Washington for erecting what would be the world's largest fence, a gigantic thousand-plus mile barrier to seal off the US-Mexico border!) In the post-9/11 America, furthermore, the idea that 7 million or more people have entered the country without official authorization (as current Census estimates suggest) is now inescapably regarded by the public through the prism of national security.

Yet when all is said and done, America's new wave of immigrants can be seen as assimilating tolerably well—in the pattern of earlier historical migrations to the USA. Despite the high concentration of relatively poor, and poorly educated, immigrants in big cities, America's urban areas have not as yet become tinderboxes for violent unrest by the foreign-born—a conspicuous contrast with modern-day Europe.[10] Furthermore, despite alarms and warnings that "some" immigrants (i.e., Mexicans) are failing to assimilate or are positively resisting assimilation, the weight of evidence seems to point in just the opposite direction. (A recent study in Southern California, for instance, suggests that Spanish-speaking at home among Mexican Americans declines steadily from one generation to the next—and at a pace similar to that witnessed for the decline of foreign "kitchen talk" in America's highly successful Korean and Chinese immigrant communities.[11])

The United Sates, to be sure, has experienced anti-immigrant paroxysms in the past (such as the one resulting in America's 1924 Immigration Act). Economic historian Jeffrey G. Williamson has argued that the last great US clamp-down on immigration was decades in the making, bringing to a flashpoint tendencies that had been building from the 1890s. This was an era, Williamson recalls, characterized by rising economic differences, high volumes of migration, significant pressure on wages for low-skilled native-born Americans, and gradually increasing political calls for immigration restrictions.[12] In this earlier era, Williamson argues, America's radical cut-back in immigration was finally catalyzed by a "triggering event": namely, World War I. Williamson's analysis is compelling precisely because so many of those same social, economic, and political tendencies can be seen gathering in the United States today. It also begs the question: can one now imagine a new "triggering event" of a similar anti-immigration policy?

The Future of American "Demographic Exceptionalism"

American fertility and immigration trends cannot be forecast with any great accuracy over the coming generation (no more so than for any other developed country). If American "demographic exceptionalism" should continue for another decade or so, however, its consequences could be truly profound.

Just what such "exceptionalism" would portend may be seen in Figure 3, which compares US Census Bureau projections for the USA and Western Europe for 2025. [See Figure 17-3] These Census Bureau projections assume a gradual improvement in life expectancies in both regions. More critically, they posit an increase in both Western European and American TFRs (to 1.62 and 2.18 in 2025, respectively) and a slight absolute decline in average annual net migration inflows for both regions (to about 700,000 and 900,000, respectively). One may of course quibble with these assumptions, and some reputable demographers do (the United Nations Population Division's "medium variant", for example, envisions a drop of US TFRs to under 1.9 by 2025). In any case, the projections highlighted in Figure 17-3 vividly illustrate the longer-term implications of US "demographic exceptionalism", if that phenomenon should indeed continue.

In demographic terms, Western Europe and the USA would be strikingly different places two decades hence. Western Europe's total population would be shrinking, despite continuing immigration, while America's would still be growing by about 2.8 million a year. Western Europe would be much "grayer" than the US, with a median age of 46 years (as against the USA's 39 years) and nearly 23% of all people 65 or older (versus 18% in America). In this future world, children under 15 would make up just one seventh of Western Europe's population, whereas they would account for nearly a fifth of the US populace, and whereas senior citizens (65+) would outnumber children (<15) in Western Europe by a ratio of roughly 160 to 100, the US would still have more children than seniors.

In absolute terms, although Western Europe's total population would still exceed America's by around 50 million (400 million versus 350 million), all of that differential would accrue from older age groups (50-plus), with the disproportion especially notable for among septuagenarians and octogenarians. For the under-25 population, on the other hand, Americans would outnumber Western Europeans.

Figure 17-3. Population Structure, 2025: Western Europe vs. USA (US Census Bureau Projections)

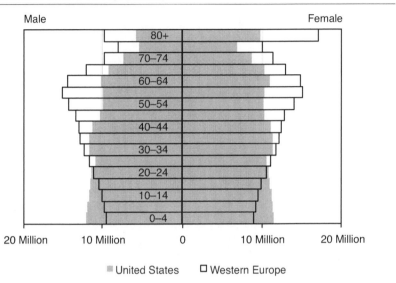

Note: "Western Europe" is defined by the US Census Bureau to include the EU-15, Sweden, Switzerland, and adjoining or nearby smaller islands, kingdoms, and republics
Source: U.S. Census Bureau, International Data Base, available at http://www.census.gov/cgi-bin/ipc/idbagg [accessed August 3, 2006].

(This projected tableau, it is worth emphasizing, relies less on surmise and conjecture than might first be assumed, even though the world it describes is nearly twenty years distant. The overwhelming majority of Americans and European who will inhabit their respective regions are already alive, living there today. The 20-to-25-year-olds of 2025, we may note, are already here on earth, having been born in the years 2000 through 2005; by the US Census Bureau's estimates and projections, births in the US exceeded those in Western Europe for the first time in the year 2004.)

America's prospective demographic divergence, however, impends not just against Western Europe, but rather against the entire developed world. By these same Census Bureau projections for 2025, America's population growth rate would be the very highest in the more developed regions—and America's median age would be (apart from fascinating exceptions like Albania) virtually the lowest. In these projections, moreover, the USA would be the only developed country with over 5 million citizens to be home to more children than senior citizens—and the only developed country at all whose working-age population (15–64) would still be growing!

To the extent that population structure in and of itself can be said to influence economic performance, America's "exceptional" demographic profile could be seen as conferring some modest developmental advantages upon US society. All other things being equal, America's relatively youthful population should experience less pressing burdens from pension and health costs in the years ahead than the rest of the world's (more elderly) developed democracies. A growing labor force, for its part, offers opportunities for innovation, start-up, and re-allocation of productive resources that are plainly harder to seize in the context of a declining workforce. The best-educated elements of any developed country's workforce tend to be its youngest entrants—but while that group stands to shrink relatively and absolutely throughout the developed regions as a whole over the next two decades, America's pool of young manpower will almost certainly continue to grow.

Beyond population composition, absolute numbers also matter in international affairs. America's aggregate population size has some incalculable, but nonetheless genuine, bearing on the country's global predominance today. The US is the world's third largest country today (after only China and India), and projections suggest it will remain Number Three in the decades immediately ahead. But with its exceptional and robust projected population growth, America is poised to account for an increasing share of the now-developed countries' population. Whereas the ratio of Americans to Russians today is just over 2-to-1, by 2025 that same ratio may be almost 3-to-1. In Census Bureau projections, there are 3.6 Americans for every German today but there would be 4.4 in 2025. There are five Americans for every Italian today, but there would be six in less than two decades. And so on. All other things being equal, such trends might seem to some extent to reinforce US international predominance (even though the divergence in demographic profiles between the US and the rest may also portend an era of diminishing affinities between the US and her historical Western allies.)

Assessing the implications of trends that have yet to unfold is, to be sure, only speculation. But as these projections should indicate, US "demographic exceptionalism" is not only here today, but it may be here to stay for a long time. It is by no means beyond the realm of the possible that America's demographic profile will look even more "exceptional" a generation hence than it does today.

Notes

1. Seymour Martin Lipset, *American Exceptionalism: A Double-Edged Sword*, (New York: W. W. Norton, 1996).

2. Jean-Claude Chesnais, *The Demographic Transition: Stages, Patterns And Economic Implications*, (New York: Oxford University Press, 1992).

3. Susan B. Carter, *Historical Statistics of the United States: Earliest Times to the Present*, (New York: Cambridge University Press, 2006), Table Ab1-10.

4. Angus Maddison, *The World Economy: Historical Statistics*, (Paris: OECD, 2003).

5. United Nations Population Division, "World Population Prospects, the 2004 Revision", available online at http://www.unpopulation.org.

6. "Period" fertility rates are synthetic "snapshot" of childbearing patterns displayed by women of all ages in a given year—which is to say, they represent the fertility levels that would result from an indefinite continuation of the childbearing trends of a given and particular year.

7. Another possible, somewhat technical, factor is what demographers call the "tempo effect". Since "period" TFRs are a sort of social snapshot, they may misrepresent long-term fertility trends if mores about the timing of childbearing are undergoing significant change. In the United States in the 1970s, we now know, "period" rates dropped sharply in part because American woman were deciding to delay childbearing—they ended up having their average of two children, but at later ages than their parents. There is a head debate among demographers today about just how much of a "tempo effect" Europe may experience in the years ahead. If European countries do enjoy a substantial "tempo effect", this would of course narrow the transatlantic fertility gap. For obvious reasons, however, this is for now a question that cannot as yet be answered.

8. Dr. Jeffrey Passel, Urban Institute, personal communication August 2006.

9. US Census Bureau, *Statistical Abstract of the United States: 2006*, (Washington DC: Government Printing Office, 2006), Tables 7, 42, 44, 45; idem, "Table FBP-1: Profile of Selected Demographic and Social Characteristics, 2000—People Born in Mexico", available electronically at http://www.census.gov/population/cen2000/stp-159/STP-159-Mexico.pdf.

10. One may note, of course, that the United States has a much smaller foreign-born population of Arabs and Muslims than does Western Europe—true enough. Even so, the assimilation of first-generation immigrants of Islamic heritage seems to be progressing more successfully in the United States than in Western Europe on the whole. Cf. "Look out, Europe, they say: why Muslims find America easier than Europe to blend into", *The Economist*, June 24, 2006.

11. Rubén G. Rumbaut, Douglas S. Massey, and Frank D. Bean, "linguistic life expectancies: Immigrant language retention in Southern California", *Population and Development Review*, September 2006, pp. 447-460.

12. Jeffrey G. Williamson, *The Political Economy of World Mass Migration: Comparing Two Global Centuries*, (Washington, DC: American Enterprise Institute Press, 2005).

18

American Exceptionalism
and the Entitlement State

National Affairs, January 5, 2015

I f social policy were medicine, and countries were the patients, the United States today would be a post-surgical charge under observation after an ambitious and previously untested transplant operation. Surgeons have grafted a foreign organ—the European welfare state—into the American body. The transplanted organ has thrived—in fact, it has grown immensely. The condition of the patient, however, is another question altogether. The patient's vital signs have not responded entirely positively to this social surgery; in fact, by some important metrics, the patient's post-operative behavior appears to be impaired. And, like many other transplant patients, this one seems to have effected a disturbing change in mood, even personality, as a consequence of the operation.

The modern welfare state has a distinctly European pedigree. Naturally enough, the architecture of the welfare state was designed and developed with European realities in mind, the most important of which were European beliefs about poverty. Thanks to their history of Old World feudalism, with its centuries of rigid class barriers and attendant lack of opportunity for mobility based on merit, Europeans held a powerful, continentally pervasive belief that ordinary people who found themselves in poverty or need were effectively stuck in it—and, no less important, that they were stuck through no fault of their own, but rather by an accident of birth. (Whether this belief was entirely accurate is another story, though beside the point: This was what people perceived and believed, and at the end of the day those perceptions shaped the formation and development of Europe's welfare states.) The state provision of old-age pensions, unemployment benefits, and health services—along with official family support and other household income guarantees—served a multiplicity of purposes for European political economies, not the least of which was to assuage voters' discontent with the perceived shortcomings of their countries' social structures through a highly visible and explicitly political mechanism for broadly based and compensatory income redistribution.

But America's historical experience has been rather different from Europe's, and from the earliest days of the great American experiment, people in the United States exhibited strikingly different views from their trans-Atlantic cousins on the questions of poverty and social welfare. These differences were noted both by Americans themselves and by foreign visitors, not least among them Alexis de Tocqueville, whose conception of American exceptionalism was heavily influenced by the distinctive American worldview on such matters. Because America had no feudal past and no lingering aristocracy, poverty was not viewed as the result of an unalterable accident of birth but instead as a temporary challenge that could be overcome with determination and character—with enterprise, hard work, and grit. Rightly or wrongly, Americans viewed themselves as masters of their own fate, intensely proud because they were self-reliant.

To the American mind, poverty could never be regarded as a permanent condition for anyone in any stratum of society because of the country's boundless possibilities for individual self-advancement. Self-reliance and personal initiative were, in this way of thinking, the critical factors in staying out of need. Generosity, too, was very much a part of that American ethos; the American impulse to lend a hand (sometimes a very generous hand) to neighbors in need of help was ingrained in the immigrant and settler traditions. But thanks to a strong underlying streak of Puritanism, Americans reflexively parsed the needy into two categories: what came to be called the deserving and the undeserving poor. To assist the former, the American prescription was community-based charity from its famously vibrant "voluntary associations." The latter—men and women judged responsible for their own dire circumstances due to laziness, or drinking problems, or other behavior associated with flawed character—were seen as mainly needing assistance in "changing their ways." In either case, charitable aid was typically envisioned as a temporary intervention to help good people get through a bad spell and back on their feet. Long-term dependence upon handouts was "pauperism," an odious condition no self-respecting American would readily accept.

The American mythos, in short, offered less than fertile soil for cultivating a modern welfare state. This is not to say that the American myth of unlimited opportunity for the rugged individualist always conformed to the facts on the ground. That myth rang hollow for many Americans—most especially for African-Americans, who first suffered for generations under slavery and thereafter endured a full century of officially enforced discrimination, as well as other barriers to self-advancement. Though the facts certainly did not always fit the ideal, the American myth was so generally accepted that the nation displayed an enduring aversion to all the trappings of the welfare state, and put up prolonged resistance to their establishment on our shores.

Over the past several decades, however, something fundamental has changed. The American welfare state today transfers over 14% of the nation's GDP to the recipients of its many programs, and over a third of the population now accepts "need-based" benefits from the government. This is not the America that Tocqueville encountered. To begin to appreciate the differences, we need to understand how Americans' relationship to the welfare state has changed, and with it, the American character itself.

An American Revolution

The road to our modern welfare state traces its way through northern Europe, most notably through Bismarck's social-insurance legislation in late 19th-century Germany, Sweden's pioneering "social democracy" policies during the interwar period, and Britain's 1942 "Beveridge Report," which offered the embattled nation a vision of far-reaching and generous social-welfare guarantees after victory.

Over the first three decades of the 20th century, while welfare programs were blossoming in Europe, in the United States the share of the national output devoted to public-welfare spending (pensions, unemployment, health, and all the rest) not only failed to rise but apparently declined. The ratio of government social outlays to GDP looks actually to have been lower in 1930 than it was in 1890, due in part to the death of Civil War veterans (of the Union army) and their dependents who had been receiving pensions. Thirty-six European and Latin American countries—many of which lagged far behind the U.S. in terms of educational attainment and socioeconomic development—already had put in place nationwide "social insurance" systems for old-age pensions by the time the United States passed the Social Security Act in 1935, establishing our first federal legislation committing Washington to providing public benefits for the general population.

Suffice it to say, the United States arrived late to the 20th century's entitlement party, and the hesitance to embrace the welfare state lingered on well after the Depression. As recently as the early 1960s, the "footprint" left on America's GDP by the welfare state was not dramatically larger than it had been under Franklin Roosevelt—or Herbert Hoover, for that matter. In 1961, at the start of the Kennedy Administration, total government entitlement transfers to individual recipients accounted for a little less than 5% of GDP, as opposed to 2.5% of GDP in 1931 just before the New Deal. In 1963—the year of Kennedy's assassination—these entitlement transfers accounted for about 6% of total personal income in America, as against a bit less than 4% in 1936.

During the 1960s, however, America's traditional aversion to the welfare state and all its works largely collapsed. President Johnson's "War on Poverty" (declared in 1964) and his "Great Society" pledge of the same year ushered in a new era for America, in which Washington finally commenced in earnest the construction of a massive welfare state. In the decades that followed, America not only markedly expanded provision for current or past workers who qualified for benefits under existing "social insurance" arrangements (retirement, unemployment, and disability), it also inaugurated a panoply of nationwide programs for "income maintenance" (food stamps, housing subsidies, Supplemental Social Security Insurance, and the like) where eligibility turned not on work history but on officially designated "poverty" status. The government also added health-care guarantees for retirees and the officially poor, with Medicare, Medicaid, and their accompaniments. In other words, Americans could claim, and obtain, an increasing trove of economic benefits from the government simply by dint of being a citizen; they were now incontestably entitled under law to some measure of transferred public bounty, thanks to our new "entitlement state."

The expansion of the American welfare state remains very much a work in progress; the latest addition to that edifice is, of course, the Affordable Care Act. Despite its recent decades of rapid growth, the American welfare state may still look modest in scope and scale compared to some of its European counterparts. Nonetheless, over the past two generations, the remarkable growth of the entitlement state has radically transformed both the American government and the American way of life itself. It is not too much to call those changes revolutionary.

The impact on the federal government has been revolutionary in the literal meaning of the term, in that the structure of state spending has been completely overturned within living memory. Over the past half-century, social-welfare-program payments and subventions have mutated from a familiar but nonetheless decidedly limited item on the federal ledger into its dominant and indeed most distinguishing feature. The metamorphosis is underscored by estimates from the Bureau of Economic Analysis, the unit in the federal government that calculates GDP and other elements of our national accounts. According to BEA figures, official transfers of money, goods, and services to individual recipients through social-welfare programs accounted for less than one federal dollar in four (24%) in 1963. (And, to go by BEA data, that share was not much higher than what it had been in 1929.) But by 2013, roughly three out of every five federal dollars (59%) were going to social-entitlement transfers. The still-shrinking residual—barely two budgetary dollars in five, at this writing—is now left to apply to all the remaining purposes of the federal government, including the considerable bureaucratic costs of overseeing the various transfer programs under consideration themselves.

Thus did the great experiment begun in the Constitution devolve into an entitlements machine—at least, so far as daily operations, budgetary priorities, and administrative emphases are concerned. Federal politics, correspondingly, are now in the main the politics of entitlement programs— activities never mentioned in the Constitution or its amendments.

The Road to Welfare

Scarcely less revolutionary has been the remolding of daily life for ordinary Americans under the shadow of the entitlement state. Over the half-century between 1963 and 2013, entitlement transfers were the fastest growing source of personal income in America—expanding at twice the rate for real per capita personal income from all other sources, in fact. Relentless, exponential

Table 18-1. Entitlement Dependence in America, 1983 v. 2012

Recipiency Status & Program	3rd Quarter 1983 Number in Millions (Percent)	3rd Quarter 2012 Number in Millions (Percent)	Difference Number in Millions (Percent)
All People	224.3 (100.0)	308.9 (100.0)	84.6 (—)
Received Benefits from ≥1 Programs	66.5 (29.6)	152.9 (49.5)	86.4 (19.9)
Social Security	31.7 (14.1)	51.5 (16.7)	19.8 (2.6)
Medicare	26.7 (11.9)	48.2 (15.6)	21.5 (3.7)
≥ 1 Means-Tested Programs	42.1 (18.8)	109.3 (35.4)	67.2 (16.6)
– Federal SSI	3.2 (1.4)	20.4 (6.6)	17.2 (5.2)
– Food Stamps	18.7 (8.3)	50.8 (16.5)	32.1 (8.2)
– AFDC	9.3 (4.2)	5.4 (1.8)	−3.9 (−2.4)
– Women, Infants, & Children	2.4 (1.1)	22.7 (7.3)	20.3 (6.2)
– Medicaid	17.5 (7.8)	83.1 (26.9)	65.6 (19.1)

Source: U.S. Census Bureau.

growth of entitlement payments recast the American family budget over the course of just two generations. In 1963, these transfers accounted for less than one out of every 15 dollars of overall personal income; by 2013, they accounted for more than one dollar out of every six.

The explosive growth of entitlement outlays, of course, was accompanied by a corresponding surge in the number of Americans who would routinely apply for, and accept, such government benefits. Despite episodic attempts to limit the growth of the welfare state or occasional assurances from Washington that "the era of big government is over," the pool of entitlement beneficiaries has apparently grown almost ceaselessly. The qualifier "apparently" is necessary because, curiously enough, the government did not actually begin systematically tracking the demographics of America's "program participation" until a generation ago. Such data as are available, however, depict a sea change over the past 30 years.

By 2012, the most recent year for such figures at this writing, Census Bureau estimates indicated that more than 150 million Americans, or a little more than 49% of the population, lived in households that received at least one entitlement benefit. Since under-reporting of government transfers is characteristic for survey respondents, and since administrative records suggest the Census Bureau's own adjustments and corrections do not completely compensate for the under-reporting problem, this likely means that America has already passed the symbolic threshold where a majority of the population is asking for, and accepting, welfare-state transfers.

Between 1983 and 2012, by Census Bureau estimates, the percentage of Americans "participating" in entitlement programs jumped by nearly 20 percentage points. One might at first assume that the upsurge was largely due to the graying of the population and the consequent increase in the number of beneficiaries of Social Security and Medicare, entitlement programs designed to help the elderly. But that is not the case. Over the period in question, the share of Americans receiving Social Security payments increased by less than three percentage points—and by less than four points for those availing themselves of Medicare. Less than one-fifth of that 20-percentage-point jump can be attributed to increased reliance on these two "old age" programs.

Overwhelmingly, the growth in claimants of entitlement benefits has stemmed from an extraordinary rise in "means-tested" entitlements. (These entitlements are often called "anti-poverty programs," since the criterion for eligibility is an income below some designated multiple of the officially calculated poverty threshold.) By late 2012, more than 109 million Americans lived in households that obtained one or more such benefits—over twice as many as received Social Security or Medicare. The population of what we might call "means-tested America" was more than two-and-a-half times as large in 2012 as it had been in 1983. Over those intervening years, there was population growth to be sure, but not enough to explain the huge increase in the share of the population receiving anti-poverty benefits. The total U.S. population grew by almost 83 million, while the number of people accepting means-tested benefits rose by 67 million—an astonishing trajectory, implying a growth of the means-tested population of 80 persons for each 100-person increase in national population over that interval.

In the mid-1990s, during the Clinton era, Congress famously passed legislation to rein in one notorious entitlement program: Aid for Families with Dependent Children. Established under a different name as part of the 1935 Social Security Act, AFDC was a Social Security program portal originally intended to support the orphaned children of deceased workers; it was subsequently diverted to supporting children from broken homes and eventually the children of unwed mothers. By the 1980s, the great majority of children born to never-married mothers were AFDC recipients, and almost half of AFDC recipients were the children of never-married mothers. The program's design seemed to create incentives against marriage and against work, and it was ultimately determined by bipartisan political consensus that such an arrangement must not continue. So with the welfare reforms of the 1990s, AFDC was changed to TANF—Temporary Aid to Needy Families— and eligibility for benefits was indeed restricted. By 2012, the fraction of Americans in homes obtaining AFDC/TANF aid was less than half of what it had been in 1983.

The story of AFDC/TANF, however, is a one-off, a major exception to the general trend. Over the same three decades, the rolls of claimants receiving food stamps (a program that was officially rebranded the Supplemental Nutrition Assistance Program, or SNAP, in 2008 because of the stigma the phrase had acquired) jumped from 19 million to 51 million. By 2012 almost one American in six lived in a home enrolled in the SNAP program. The ranks of Medicaid, the means-tested national health-care program, increased by over 65 million between 1983 and 2012, and now include over one in four Americans. And while the door to means-tested cash benefits from the Social Security program through AFDC/TANF had been partly (though not entirely) closed, a much larger window for such benefits was simultaneously thrown open in the form of Supplemental Security Income, a program intended to provide income for the disabled poor. Between 1983 and 2012, the number of Americans in households receiving Federal SSI more than sextupled; by 2012, over 20 million people were counted as dependents of the program.

All told, more than 35% of Americans were taking home at least some benefits from means-tested programs by 2012—nearly twice the share in 1983. Some may be tempted to blame such an increase on increasingly widespread material hardship. It is true that the American economy in 2012 was still recovering from the huge global crash of 2008, and unemployment levels were still painfully high: 8.1% for the year as a whole. But 1983 was a recovery year for the U.S. economy, too; the recession of 1981 and 1982 was the most severe in postwar American history up to that point, and the unemployment rate in 1983 was 9.6%, even higher than in 2012.

By the same token, although the official poverty rate was almost identical for the two years—the total population estimated to be below the official poverty line was 15.2% in 1983 and 15.0% in 2012—the proportion of Americans drawing means-tested benefits was dramatically higher in 2012. By 2012, there was no longer any readily observable correspondence between the officially designated condition of poverty and the recipience of "anti-poverty" entitlements. In that year, the number of people taking home means-tested benefits was more than twice the number of those living below the poverty line—meaning a decisive majority of recipients of such aid were the non-poor. In fact, by 2012 roughly one in four Americans above the poverty line was receiving at least one means-tested benefit.

How could this be? America today is almost certainly the richest society in history, anywhere at any time. And it is certainly more prosperous and productive now (and in 2012) than it was three decades ago. Yet paradoxically, our entitlement state behaves as if Americans have never been more "needy." The paradox is easily explained: Means-tested entitlement transfers are no longer an instrument strictly for addressing absolute poverty, but instead a device for a more general redistribution of resources. And the fact that so many are willing to accept need-based aid signals a fundamental change in the American character.

The Moral Fabric

Asking for, and accepting, purportedly need-based government welfare benefits has become a fact of life for a significant and still growing minority of our population: Every decade, a higher proportion of Americans appear to be habituated to the practice. If the trajectory continues, the coming generation could see the emergence in the United States of means-tested beneficiaries becoming the majority of the population. This notion may seem absurd, but it is not as fanciful as it sounds. In recent years, after all, nearly half of all children under 18 years of age received means-tested benefits (or lived in homes that did). For this rising cohort of young Americans, reliance on public, need-based entitlement programs is already the norm—here and now.

It risks belaboring the obvious to observe that today's real existing American entitlement state, and the habits—including habits of mind—that it engenders, do not coexist easily with the values and principles, or with the traditions, culture, and styles of life, subsumed under the shorthand of "American exceptionalism." Especially subversive of that ethos, we might argue, are essentially unconditional and indefinite guarantees of means-tested public largesse.

Some components of the welfare state look distinctly less objectionable to that traditional sensibility than others. Given proper design, for example, an old-age benefit programs such as Social Security could more or less function as the social-insurance program it claims to be. With the right structure and internal incentives, it is possible to imagine a publicly administered retirement program entirely self-financed by the eventual recipients of these benefits over the course of their working lives. The United States is very far from achieving a self-funded Social Security program, of course, but if such a schema could be put in place, it would not in itself do violence to the conceptions of self-reliance, personal responsibility, and self-advancement that sit at the heart of the traditional American mythos. (Much the same could likewise be said of publicly funded education.) Moral hazard is inherent, and inescapable, in all public social-welfare projects—but it is easiest to minimize or contain in efforts like these. By contrast, the moral hazard in ostensibly need-based programs is epidemic, contagious, and essentially uncontrollable. Mass public provision of means-tested entitlements perforce invites long-term consumption of those entitlements.

The corrosive nature of mass dependence on entitlements is evident from the nature of the pathologies so closely associated with its spread. Two of the most pernicious of them are so tightly intertwined as to be inseparable: the breakdown of the pre-existing American family structure and the dramatic decrease in participation in work among working-age men.

When the "War on Poverty" was launched in 1964, 7% of children were born outside of marriage; by 2012, that number had grown to an astounding 41%, and nearly a quarter of all American children under the age of 18 were living with a single mother. (In the interest of brevity, let us merely say much, much more data could be adduced on this score, almost all of it depressing.)

As for men of parenting age, a steadily rising share has been opting out of the labor force altogether. Between 1964 and early 2014, the fraction of civilian men between the ages of 25 and 34 who were neither working nor looking for work roughly quadrupled, from less than 3% to more than 11%. In 1965, fewer than 5% of American men between 45 and 54 years of age were totally out of the work force; by early 2014, the fraction was almost 15%. To judge by mortality statistics, American men in the prime of life have never been healthier than they are today—yet they are less committed to working, or to attempting to find work, than at any previous point in our nation's history.

No one can prove (or disprove) that the entitlement state is responsible for this rending of the national fabric. But it is clear that the rise of the entitlement state has coincided with these disheartening developments; that it has abetted these developments; and that, at the end of the day, its interventions have served to finance and underwrite these developments. For a great many women and children in America, and a perhaps surprisingly large number of working-age men as well, the entitlement state is now the breadwinner of the household.

Entitlements and Exceptionalism

Changes in popular mores and norms are less easily and precisely tracked than changes in behavior, but here as well modern America has witnessed immense shifts under the shadow of the entitlement state. Difficult as these shifts may be to quantify, we may nevertheless dare to identify, and at least impressionistically describe, some of the ways the entitlements revolution may be shaping the contemporary American mind and fundamentally changing the American character.

To begin, the rise of long-term entitlement dependence—with the concomitant "mainstreaming" of inter-generational welfare dependence—self-evidently delivers a heavy blow against general belief in the notion that everyone can succeed in America, no matter their station at birth. Perhaps less obvious is what increasing acceptance of entitlements means for American exceptionalism. The burning personal ambition and hunger for success that both domestic and foreign observers have long taken to be distinctively American traits are being undermined and supplanted by the character challenges posed by the entitlement state. The incentive structure of our means-based welfare state invites citizens to accept benefits by showing need, making the criterion for receiving grants demonstrated personal or familial financial failure, which used to be a source of shame.

Unlike all American governance before it, our new means-tested arrangements enforce a poverty policy that must function as blind to any broad differentiation between the "deserving" and "undeserving" poor. That basic Puritan conception is dying today in America, except perhaps in the circles and reaches where it was already dead. More broadly, the politics surrounding the entitlement system tends to undermine—by and large deliberately—the legitimacy of utilizing stigma and opprobrium to condition the behavior of beneficiaries, even when the behavior in question is irresponsible or plainly destructive. For a growing number of Americans, especially younger Americans, the very notion of "shaming" entitlement recipients for their personal behavior is regarded as completely inappropriate, if not offensive. This is a strikingly new point of view in American political culture. A "judgment-free" attitude toward the official provision of social support, one that takes personal responsibility out of the discussion, marks a fundamental break with the past on this basic American precept about civic life and civic duty.

The entitlement state appears to be degrading standards of citizenship in other ways as well. For example, mass gaming of the welfare system appears to be a fact of modern American life. The country's ballooning "disability" claims attest to this. Disability awards are a key source of financial support for non-working men now, and disability judgments also serve as a gateway to qualifying for a whole assortment of subsidiary welfare benefits. Successful claims by working-age adults against the Social Security Disability Insurance (SSDI) program rose almost six-fold between 1970 and 2012—and that number does not include claims against other major government disability programs, such as SSI. There has never been a serious official effort to audit SSDI—or, for that matter, virtually any of the country's current entitlement programs.

The late senator Daniel Patrick Moynihan once wrote, "It cannot too often be stated that the issue of welfare is not what it costs those who provide it, but what it costs those who receive it." The full tally of those costs must now include the loss of public honesty occasioned by chronic deception to extract unwarranted entitlement benefits from our government—and by the tolerance of such deception by the family members and friends of those who commit it.

Finally, there is the relation between entitlements and the middle-class mentality. An important aspect of the American national myth is that anyone who works hard and plays by the rules can gain entry to the country's middle class, regardless of their income or background. Yet while low incomes, limited educational attainment, and other material constraints manifestly have not prevented successive generations of Americans from aspiring to the middle-class or even entering it, the same cannot be said of constraints emanating from the mind. Being part of the American middle class is not just an income distinction—it is a mentality, a self-conception. To be middle class is to be hard-working and self-sufficient, with self-respect rooted in providing a good life for oneself and one's family. Can members in good standing of the American middle class really maintain that self-conception while simultaneously taking need-based government benefits that symbolically brand them and their family as wards of the state?

It is no secret that the American middle class is under great pressure these days. Most commentary and analysis on this question has focused on "structural," material reasons for this phenomenon: globalization, the faltering American jobs machine, widening economic differences in society, difficulties in keeping up the pace of mobility, and many others. Conspicuously absent from this discussion have been the consequences of enrolling a sizable and still-growing share of the populace in welfare programs intended for the helpless and needy. With more than 35% of America receiving means-tested benefits, should it really be surprising that over a third of the country no longer considers itself "middle class"?

The End of Exceptionalism

The worldwide spread and growth of the social-welfare state seems strongly to suggest that there is a universal demand today for such services and guarantees in affluent, democratic societies. Given the disproportionate growth almost everywhere of entitlements in relation to increases in national income, it would seem that voters in modern democracies the world over regard such benefits as "luxury goods." In one sense, we might therefore say there is nothing particularly special about the recent American experience with the entitlement state. But as we have also seen, there is good reason to think that the entitlement state may be especially poorly suited for a nation with America's particular political culture, sensibilities, and tradition.

The qualities celebrated under the banner of "American exceptionalism" are perhaps in poorer repair than at any time in our nation's history. There can be little doubt (to return to our medical metaphor) that the grafting of a social-welfare system onto our body public is in no small part responsible for this state of affairs.

And there is little reason to believe that the transplant will be rejected any time soon. To date the American voter's appetite for entitlement transfers appears to be scarcely less insatiable than those of voters anywhere else. Our political leadership, for its part, has no stomach for taking the lead in weaning the nation from entitlement dependence. Despite tactical, rhetorical opposition to further expansion of the entitlement state by many voices in Washington, and firm resistance by an honorable and principled few, collusive bipartisan support for an ever larger welfare state is the central fact of politics in our nation's capital today, as it has been for decades. Until and unless America undergoes some sort of awakening that turns the public against its blandishments, or some sort of forcing financial crisis that suddenly restricts the resources available to it, continued growth of the entitlement state looks very likely in the years immediately ahead. And in at least that respect, America today does not look exceptional at all.

Afterword

Arthur C. Brooks

The essays and writings amassed in this volume have pushed the boundaries of demography, challenged conventional wisdom, and indirectly impacted the lives of many people by changing how leaders and intellectuals saw the world. For those of us who join Nick Eberstadt in the pursuit of social science research, his work lays out a tremendously high standard.

But this anthology does more than remind us of Eberstadt's prescience and virtuosity. It lays out the formula for future scholars seeking to improve policy and culture. This formula has four parts.

First, *never stop striving for complete analytical rigor*. In these pages, Eberstadt shows us that great social scientists don't merely coast on the familiar techniques and datasets they learned about in graduate school. Rather, they stay hungry and curious, continually refining their techniques and honing their craft throughout their careers. Just look, for example, at the quantitative approach laid out in "Mortality and the Fate of Communist States." In order to advance his then-novel arguments about the USSR, Eberstadt had to unearth new data on death rates, cause of death, and schedules of mortality in the Soviet Bloc. Or look at "The Mismeasure of Poverty," in which Eberstadt methodically ties together data on health care, nutrition housing, income variance, and consumption to pick apart conventional wisdom about the poverty rate.

In each case, Eberstadt was able to make a new and persuasive argument because he was willing to use and synthesize unconventional data. This kind of scholarly entrepreneurship has been a defining feature of Eberstadt's career.

The second key lesson is to *question convention*. The scholar's job is to identify gaps in the current state of knowledge and, when necessary, correct the failings of our predecessors. Unfortunately, many talented thinkers fall short of their potential when they fail to interrogate the premises and constraints that silently limit the scope of their inquiry. Whether the limiting assumptions come from one's own thinking, from academic consensus, or even from broader society, the best scholars stay keenly aware of them and are quick to question anything presented as "given."

In the late twentieth century, for example, many intellectuals felt sure that rapid population growth was a massive liability for low-income countries. Their position was fundamentally Malthusian—growth would outpace innovation, and so whole countries were on course to exceed their carrying capacity. Eberstadt trained his sights squarely on this consensus—and debunked it. Instead of simply crunching numbers within the prevailing consensus, he dared to ask whether burgeoning populations were a liability at all. As Eberstadt persuasively argues in "Population Change and National Security," a growing population is better understood as a valuable renewable resource, a vital source of precious and transformative human capital.

Another fascinating example of Eberstadt exploding traditional thinking is his work on hunger. At the beginning of his career, almost every scholar thought that the cause of hunger was obvious—a shortage of food. The upshot was that factors such as weather, geography, and bad agricultural luck, taken together, explained most of why some starved while others had plenty. But in pieces such as "Hunger and Ideology," Eberstadt clearly shows why this line of thinking was dead wrong: by the 1970s, there was more than enough food on the planet to feed everyone comfortably. Hunger wasn't a supply problem. Rather, it was a problem of distribution. Manmade social hierarchies and institutions were to blame. This subversive conclusion was both realistic and optimistic: it showed that a grave problem was our responsibility to fix, but it suggested that mankind had the technological tools to conquer it.

This brings us to the third lesson—*focus on the people behind the data*. This point seems obvious, but the pressures of academic life are immense. The never-ending search for more theoretically impressive arguments or more dazzlingly abstract mathematical models can be vital for getting published. In my experience, every year in the ivory tower makes it a little easier to lose sight of the humanity behind our research questions.

Eberstadt's writings show why rigorous analysis must not be detached from a concern for people. Examples are numerous, but look especially at "Too Many People?" Eberstadt persuasively points out why technocrats' efforts to contain population growth in low-income countries had failed: they woefully neglected the fact that, so long as fertility was a voluntary choice, procreation would occur. People are human, they respond dynamically to incentives, and they make independent choices. (And they rarely care what a peer-reviewed paper says is "optimal.")

Sometimes, Eberstadt devotes an entire work to simply spotlighting the human story. In "Bring Them Home," he paints a vivid portrait of North Korean refugees, reminding the global political class that the debate over North Korean defectors went beyond just the grim statistics. The refugees were escaping the worst tyranny and poverty we could imagine. Eberstadt's arguments reminded us that people are not cogs in a machine, but storehouses of human dignity.

The fourth and most important lesson flows from the third—*social scientists can see their work as a moral mission to help people build better lives.* Eberstadt's entire research agenda embodies his commitment not merely to observing people, but also to helping them—especially the vulnerable.

Sometimes this is obvious; his essays about hunger and the poverty rate are clearly aimed at the helping society lift up the poor. But the link isn't always so clear. It's not necessarily obvious, prima facie, that academic debates about population forecasts have a tangible impact on people's lives. But Eberstadt's work shows us over and over again that they do matter. We have to understand demography to grasp the profound social and political forces that shape society. And only once a scholar understands those immense forces can he or she progress to crafting impactful policy.

This last lesson helps explain why Eberstadt's thinking has exerted so much influence on policymakers and in the public square, in addition to the halls of academia. The profound sense of purpose that underlies his efforts—the why of his work—is evident in every essay.

Index

Abortion. *See* Sex-selective abortion
Advantages of backwardness, 209
AEI. *See* American Enterprise
    Institute
AFDC. *See* Aid to Families with
    Dependent Children
Affordable Care Act, 329
Afghanistan, 37, 87, 100, 160,
    208–9
    Africa, 17
    agriculture and, 105
    food in, 83
    malnutrition in, 79
    See also Sub-Saharan Africa;
    specific countries
African Americans, 258–60, 263–64,
    266–69, 278, 293, 314, 328
Age of Exploration, 12
Age/sex/education pyramids, 175–77
Age-specific death rates, 127,
    132–34, 142, 149, 170–71,
    302–3
Age-standardized mortality, 138–41
    CVD and, 134
    in East Germany, 147, 151
    in Eastern Europe, 150
    in Hungary, 133, 149
    in Ireland, 148
    for women, 303

Aging. *See* Population aging
Agreed Framework, 189–91
Agriculture, 82, 85, 91, 105–6, 119,
    122
    in China, 167
    See also Food and Agriculture
    Organization; US Department
    of Agriculture
Ahlburg, Dennis, 26
AHS. *See* American Housing Survey
Aid to Families with Dependent
    Children (AFDC), 266–67,
    332–33
AIDS, 10
Albania, 231
Almond, Douglas, 231–32
American demographic exceptional-
    ism, 252, 310
    in fertility, 311–18
    future of, 321–24
    in immigration patterns, 318–20
American Enterprise Institute (AEI),
    xvi
American exceptionalism, 251–52,
    310, 326–28
    American revolution and, 328–30
    end of, 338
    entitlements and, 336–38
    moral fabric and, 334–36

road to welfare and, 330–34
American Housing Survey (AHS),
        100, 300
American identity, 13
American infant mortality rate, 251,
        253, 303–4
    biological and behavioral factors
        of, 258–60
    historical perspectives on,
        254–55
    illegitimacy and, 260–62
    local-level data on, 265–66
    parental practices and infant
        health and, 262–65
    policy interventions and, 266–70
    poverty and medical care and,
        156–58
    reliability of data and, 255–56
American mythos, 328, 335
Anglo Americans, 214, 279, 314–16
Annan, Kofi, 215
Anthropometric tests, 78–79
Anti-natalism, 20, 34, 39, 46, 143
Anti-poverty programs, 272,
        282–84, 307, 332, 334
Arable land, 23–25
Arabs, 8, 324n10
"Area Handbooks," 215
Argentina, 11, 83, 144
Aristide, Jean-Bertrand, 217
Armed Forces Coordinating
        Committee (Dergue), 99–100
Armenia, 36–37, 231
Asian Americans, 314
Aussiedlung, 12
Australia, 69, 256–57, 318–19

Austria, 37, 55, 67, 76, 151, 161,
        231–32

Baby booms, 69, 312
Baby bust, 312
Bahrain, 22
Bangladesh, 74, 172, 212, 231
    death rates in, 78
    economic growth in, 4
    education in, 107
    fertility in, 37
    infant mortality in, 37
    manpower growth in, 54
    nutrition in, 93n2
    as overcrowded, 21–22
    per capita output of, 204
    political stability and, 204
Barbados, 78
Bare Branches: The Security Impli-
        cations of Asia's Surplus Male
        Population, 236
Barro, Robert J., 177–78, 202
Bauer, Peter, 122, 206, 210
BEA. See Bureau of Economic
        Analysis
Becker, Gary, 235
Belgium, 78
Bennett, Merrill K., 114
Bergson, Abram, 135
Berlin Wall, 127
Bermuda, 22, 116
"Beveridge Report," 328
Bhat, Mari, 173–74, 182
Biogas converters, 91
Birth rates
    in Brazil, 160–61

in former Yugoslavia, 34
lowering, 35
raising, 17
in Russia, 19
in Turkey, 160–61
world population stabilization and, 21
BLS. *See* Bureau of Labor Statistics
Bolivia, 105, 212
Bongaarts, John, 76
Bosnia-Herzegovina, 34, 49n37
The Bottom Billion, 207
Bowley, Arthur, 77
Boyd-Orr, Lord, 77, 112–14
Brain damage, 76
Brazil, 4, 58, 162, 180, 203
birth rates in, 160–61
fertility in, 38
population control and, 70
Brecht, Bertolt, 120
British Viceregency, 119
Brunei Darussalam, 231
Buddhism, 231
Buffet, Warren, 19
Bulgaria, 37, 130–34, 140–41, 149, 150
Bundy, McGeorge, 86
Burden sharing, 249
Bureau of Economic Analysis (BEA), 280, 330
Bureau of Labor Statistics (BLS), 257, 269, 271, 275, 286–87, 291
Bureau of the Budget, 272, 276
Burma (Myanmar), xv, 83
Burundi, 83
Bush, George H. W., 127

Cairo Conference on Population and Development, 18
Caloric availability, per capita, 43
Caloric deficits, 76, 114
Cambodia, 58, 81, 87, 89, 93, 99, 120
Canada, 15, 117, 256
immigration rates in, 318–19
TFRs in, 313–14
Capital assets, 156n13
Capitalism, 75, 86, 89–90, 99, 128, 280
Cardiovascular disease (CVD), 134
Carter, Jimmy, 80
Cassen, Robert, 26
Catch-up growth, 78
Catholicism, 35
Cause-of-death data, 127, 133, 148, 340
CDC. *See* Centers for Disease Control and Prevention
Ceauéescu regime, 16
Census Bureau, US, 11, 14, 24, 52, 60, 227
on entitlement payments, 331–32
on health differential, 265
on migration, 318
on per capita income, 280
on poverty, 285
on Russia, 58, 172
sub-replacement fertility and, 53
on sub-Saharan Africa, 201
on TFRs, 321
on United States, 62
Centers for Disease Control and

Prevention (CDC), 260, 299
Central Intelligence Agency (CIA), 127, 135–36, 139–41, 211
CES. *See* Consumer Expenditure Surveys
Chai Bin Park, 230
Chen, Lincoln, 78
Child-bearing patterns, 35, 52, 68
Chile, 11, 136, 151
China, xiv
  agriculture in, 167
  banking in, 179
  death rates in, 119
  earthquakes in, 97
  economic growth in, 4
  education in, 167–68
  famine in, 98, 119
  fertility in, xvii, 184n7
  food-grain, 83
  GDP in, 55–56, 164–65
  gender imbalance in, 224
  graying population of, 169
  Great Leap Forward in, 89, 98, 143
  human capital in, 167
  life expectancy in, 80, 142
  living standards in, 88
  manpower growth in, 54–55
  marriage squeeze in, 57
  missing girls of, 228, 234
  One Child Policy in, 52, 57, 223–24, 227
  pension system of, 165–66
  per capita income, 228
  population aging in, 56, 161, 163–69
  population control in, 7, 70
  population explosion in, 56
  population structure of, 164
  refugees and, 196, 240, 242, 245–46, 248
  reproductive choice and, 38–39
  sex ratio in, 225
  son deficit in, 166
  sub-replacement fertility in, 52, 56
  Three Lean Years in, 89, 98
  triple bind of, 163–69
Cholera Research Laboratory, 78
Christianity, 7, 231, 245, 317
Chung, Woojin, 237
CIA. *See* Central Intelligence Agency
Cirrhosis, 133
Cities
  charter, 209
  death rates in, 68
  hunger in, 80
  villages compared to, 85
Civilizing missions, 208
Clinton, Bill, 332
Closed populations, 6
Coefficient of variance, 295
Cold War, 15, 128, 135, 137
Coleman, David, 231
Collapse—How Societies Choose to Fail or Succeed, 20–21
Collier, Paul, 207, 209
Commercial lending, 103
Commerciogenic malnutrition, 92
Commodity price index, 31–33
Communism, xvi, 73, 86, 89–90, 218

life expectancy and, 143
  mortality and, xvii, 126–51
Compassion fatigue, 116
Comte, Auguste, 125
Confucianism, 207, 231
Consumer Expenditure Surveys
    (CES), 257, 269, 270, 286–89,
    297–99, 301
  changes in methods of, 290–91
Consumer Price Index (CPI), 48,
    276, 285
Contraceptives, 37
Convention, questioning of, 340–41
Corn, 82
Corruption Perceptions Index, 204
Costa Rica, 78
Coups, 144–45, 204, 209
CPI. See Consumer Price Index
Croatia, 34, 49n37
Cuba, 86, 87–88, 142, 200, 231
Culture, poverty and, 206–10
Cummings, Ralph, 83
CVD. See Cardiovascular disease
Czechoslovakia, 128, 130–33, 136,
    140, 141, 149, 150

Danziger, Sheldon, 297–98
Das Gupta, Monica, 237
Dawson, Deborah, 262
Death rates, 80, 127, 149, 302
  in Bangladesh, 78
  in China, 119
  in cities, 68
  compared to height and weight,
    78
  in Hungary, 133

in India, 88
  reducing, 27
  in Russia, 19, 57–58, 170–71,
    185n12, 185n15
  in Soviet bloc, 127, 132–33, 340
  in Soviet Union, 10
  in United States, 312
  in Warsaw Pact, 132
  WHO on standardized, 11
  See also Age-specific death rates
Debt crisis, 104, 106
Deforestation, 21
Democratic People's Republic of
    Korea (DPRK), 189, 191
Democratic Republic of the Congo,
    37, 106
Demographic trends, 125
  exception in, 61–63
  health and fewer babies, 51–53
  knowledge production and
    technological innovation,
    63–64
  in manpower growth, 53–55
  in population aging, 55–61
Demography, xiv, xvi–xviii, 14,
    233–34, 340
  demographic change, 2, 26, 64,
    65
  demographic dividend, 59,
    180–82
  demographic shocks, 313
  explanatory, xv
  historical, 128
Demography, 223
Den Boer, Andrea M., 236
Deng Xiaoping, 56, 97

Denmark, 105
Dental health, 304–5
Department of Commerce, US, 287–88
Department of Energy, US, 300
Department of Health and Human Services, US, 253
Dependency ratio, 59, 116, 180–82
Depression (1930s), 77, 329
Dergue (Armed Forces Coordinating Committee), 99–100
Deserving poor, 33
Desiderata, 36
Determinism, 144
Developing market economies, 83, 161–62
Development assistance, 102–3, 107, 205–6, 219
Development Research Center, at OECD, 4
Development theory, 207
Developmental priority, 196
Diamond, Jared, xiii, 20–21, 25, 38
Direct private investment, 102–3
Dirigiste dogma, 122
Disability awards, 337
Disability-free life expectancy, 168
Dominican Republic, 204, 216
DPRK. *See* Democratic People's Republic of Korea
Drinking, 134
Dubuc, Sylvie, 233
Duvalier, François "Papa Doc," 217–18
Dyson, Tim, 174

Earth in the Balance, 20, 24, 36
Earthquakes, 96–97, 198–99
East Germany, 136, 151
    age-specific death rates in, 149
    employment strategy in, 137–38
    mortality and, 147–49
    stock of capital in, 156n13
    vacationers of, 144
East Timor, 37, 93, 99
Eastern Europe, 10–11, 17, 126–29, 149–51, 160, 184n5
Eberstadt, Nick, xii–xviii, 340–42
EC. *See* European Community
Ecological fallacy, 318
Economic development, 12–14
Economic freedom, 146
Economic growth, xiii–xvii, 15, 55–64, 85, 178–82, 197, 209
The Economist, 31
Economy food plan, 274–75
Ecuador, 105
Edlund, Lena, 231
Education, 55, 56
    in Bangladesh, 107
    in China, 167–68
    explosion, 67
    in Haiti, 218
    in India, 59–60
    in sub-Saharan Africa, 202
    in Third World, 63
    in United States, 62, 281
    World Bank on, 67
    See also Literacy
Egypt, 9, 24, 203
El Salvador, 231
Emerging markets, 55, 158, 160–63,

169, 180, 182
End of history, 198
End of the world population growth,
  43
Energy products, 49n35
Engel, Ernst, 274
Engel coefficient, 275
England, 35, 233, 312
Entitlements
  benefits, 332
  dependence, 331, 336, 339
  entitlement state, 329–30, 336
  exceptionalism and, 336–38
  means-tested, 332, 335
  middle class and, 338
  need-based, 334
  payments, 331–32
Environment, global, 5–6
Eritrea, 58
"Essay on the Principle of Popula-
  tion," 66
Ethiopia, 15, 99–100, 208, 239
European Community (EC),
  137–38, 148
European Model, 11, 138
Explanatory demography, xv
Extension training, 91

Fabian policies, 89
Failed states, 208
Fallacy of composition, 26
Family planning, 38
Family size, 38, 52, 69, 71, 118
Family-poverty rate, 262, 265–66
Famine
  acts of government and, 88–89,

94n7, 240
  in China, 98, 119
  conquering of, 111
  foreign aid and, 95–110
  ideology and, 112
  India and, 88, 119
  Malthusians on, 116, 119
  mass, 73
  in North Korea, 242
  preventing, 120–21
  Sahelian, 89, 105
FAO. See Food and Agriculture
  Organization
Farming, 276
Federal Reserve Board, 289
Fertility, xiv, 15, 118
  American demographic excep-
    tionalism in, 311–18
  in Bangladesh, 37
  in Brazil, 38
  in China, xvii, 184n7
  contraceptives and, 37
  desired levels of, 38
  differentials in, 8, 313
  GDP compared to, 40, 41
  implosion, 52
  income-fertility curves, 41
  in India, 59, 174
  in Japan, 60
  in Lebanon, 7
  literacy and, 36
  population aging and, 53
  population change and, 6–8
  predictors of, xviii
  secular fertility decline, 35, 69
  in Soviet Union, 9

sub-replacement, 43, 52–53, 56,
    59, 160, 173, 236
in Third World, 160
in United States, 9, 24–25
World War II and, 52
in Yugoslavia, 34
See also Secular fertility decline;
    Total fertility rate
Fertilizer, 82
Feudalism, 326–27
Finland, 76, 86, 257
Five Year Plan, 86
Flight from marriage, 71
Food, 298–99
    in Africa, 83
    availability of, 81–82
    budgets for, 274–75
    deficits, 83–85
    economy food plan, 274–75
    imports, 83
    myths on world problem, 112
    in North Korea, 243
    scarcity of, 80–82
    shortages, 21
    in United States, 83
    World Food Conference, 77
    world food crisis, 91
    World Food Surveys, 77, 113,
        115
    See also Famine; Hunger
Food and Agriculture Organization
    (FAO), 74, 77, 81, 112–15,
    122
Food-grain, 74, 81, 83–84, 98
Ford Foundation, 19
Foreign aid, xviii, 19, 218, 221

famine and, 95–110
to Haiti, 205, 219–20
OECD and, 101–3
South Korea and, 108
Taiwan and, 108
Third World and, 101–4
United States and, 95
France, 10, 15, 61
    illegitimacy in, 264
    infant mortality in, 37, 257
    secular fertility decline and, 35
    TFR in, 315
Franklin, Benjamin, 311
Fraser Institute, 204
Frazier, Mark W., 184n9
Freedom House, 204
French Revolution, 216
Friedman, Milton, 285
Frisch, Rose, 76
Fukuyama, Francis, 208

Gates, Bill, 19
Gaza, 7, 8, 36–37
GDP. *See* Gross domestic product
Genus, 235
Germany
    GNP and, 127
    refugees in, 12, 238–39
    social democracy of, 328
    voluntary depopulation in, 70
    See also East Germany; West
        Germany
Gerschenkron, Alexander, 209
Ghana, 85
GHESKIO, 213, 215, 219
Global 2000, 80

Global environment, 5–6
Global Marshall Plan, 39
Global order, 109
Global security, 16
GNP. *See* Gross national product
Goodkind, Daniel M., 223
Gorbachev, Mikhail, 144
Gore, Al, xiii, 19, 25, 30
    on Global Marshall Plan, 39
    on literacy, 36
    on overpopulation, 20, 24
    on population specialists, 21
Gottschalk, Peter, 294–95
Goujon, Anne, 175, 177–78
Grain insurance, 91–92
Grain trade, 30–31
Grand Apartheid, 8
Graying populations, xvii, 63, 71
    of China, 169
    of Russia, 158, 169–73
    of Third World, 158
    See also Population aging
Great Leap Forward, 89, 98, 143
Great Society, 329
Greece, 87, 105
Green Book, 219
Grilli, Enzo, 31–32
Gross domestic product (GDP), 62
    arable land compared to, 24
    BEA on, 330
    in China, 55–56, 164–65
    commodity prices compared to, 33
    estimated global, 31
    fertility rates compared to, 40, 41
    in Haiti, 199, 215, 219

in India, 55, 58
in Japan, 55
Maddison on, 29–30, 117–18, 215
per PPP, population density compared to, 23
population aging and, 161
population density compared to, 22
in Russia, 55
TFR compared to, 42
of United States, 329
Gross national product (GNP)
    agriculture in, 105
    CIA on, 127, 139, 140, 141
    commodity prices compared to, 33
    in Cuba, 87–88
    Germany and, 127
    in Jamaica, 106
    in Japan, 106
    World Bank on, 104, 144
Groth, Hans, 62
Group of 77, 118
Guatemala, 78
Guest workers, 13
Guilmoto, Christophe Z., 226
Guyana, 78

Hacker, Jacob S., 294
Haines, Michael, 24–25
Haiti, 21, 22, 195–96
    crime in, 213–16
    earthquakes in, 199
    education in, 218
    foreign aid to, 205, 219–20

GDP in, 199, 215, 219
government in, 216–18
health in, 212–13
illiteracy in, 218
life expectancy in, 58, 215
per capita income in, 206,
    211–12
population density in, 49n38
poverty in, 198–201, 211–14
United States and, 219–20
voodoo in, 217–18
World Bank and, 215
WTO on, 215–16, 219
Have nots, 3
Haves, 3
Health, xiii–xiv
dental, 304
determining, 114
fewer babies and, 51–53
in Haiti, 212–13
of infants, 262–65
progress, 5
prosperity and, 46
revolution, 9–10
in Soviet Union, 94n7
in Third World, 115
in Warsaw Pact, 144
See also Public health
Health care. See Medical care
Health crisis
in Russia, 58, 171–72, 185n12,
    185n16
in Soviet bloc, 133
in Soviet Union, 125
Health explosion, 29, 52, 65, 66, 67
Hesketh, Therese, 234

Hewlett Foundation, 19
Hinduism, 231
Hispanic Americans, 279, 293,
    314–15
Hispaniola, 204, 216
Historical demography, 128
Historical materialism, 144
"Historical Population Studies," 128
HIV/AIDS, 27, 201–3, 213–14,
    219–20
Ho Chi Minh, 84
Hong Kong, 69, 76, 89, 114, 229,
    253
Hoover, Herbert, 329
House Select Committee on Chil-
    dren, Youth, and Families,
    253–54
Household appliances, 300–301
Housing, 300–301
Hudson, Valerie M., 235–36
Human capital, 5, 46, 68, 107–8,
    137
in China, 167
investment in, 172
stock, 155n10
transformative, 341
Human Mortality Database, 171
Human resources, 1
in India, 180
population explosion and, 67–68
in United States, 62
world population stabilization
    and, 44–47
Human rights, 16
Human Rights Commission, 247
Human security, 195

Humanitarian aid, 95, 189
Hungary, 87, 130, 133, 144, 149,
    151
Hunger, xiii, 73–74
    in cities, 80
    in countryside, 79–80
    distribution and, 341
    food deficits and, 83–85
    improvement in, 80
    political morality and, 120–21
    scarcity and, 80–82
    socialism and, 86–93
    in Third World, 77, 113
    widespread and growing, 75–80
    World Bank on, 75
    See also Famine; Malnutrition
Huntington, Samuel, 204
Hvistendahl, Mara, 235

ICE. See International Collaborative
    Effort on Perinatal and Infant
    Mortality
Ideology, famine and, 112
IIASA. See International Institute for
    Applied Systems Analysis
Illegitimacy, 260–62, 264–65
Illiteracy
    in Haiti, 218
    in India, 178
    rates of, 44
    TFR compared to, 42
    UNESCO on, 67
    of women, 40–41
    World Bank on, 40–41
Immigration, xv
    American demographic

exceptionalism and, 318–20
    Canada and, 318–19
    Israel and, 12–13
    Third World and, 311, 319
    United States and, 319–20
    See also Migration
Immigration Act (1924), 320
Income
    absolute annual variability of,
        297
    growth, 197
    instability, 295
    life cycle income hypothesis, 285
    living standards and, 289
    maintenance, 329
    permanent income hypothesis,
        285, 292
    population explosion and, 67
    poverty level, 274
    transitory, 286, 294–97, 308n8
    underreporting of, 291
    year-to-year variability of, 292,
        294–95
    See also Per capita income
Income-fertility curves, 41
Index of Economic Freedom, 204
India, 21, 22
    age and education pyramid in,
        107
    age/sex/education pyramids for,
        175–77
    agriculture in, 85, 105
    child sex ratio in, 230
    death rates in, 88
    economic growth in, 4
    education in, 59–60

famine and, 88, 119
fertility in, 59, 174
GDP in, 55, 58
human resources in, 180
illiteracy in, 178
malnutrition in, 83
manpower growth in, 54
meals in, 77
missing girls of, 234
per capita income in, 203
Planning Commission, 58
population aging in, 59, 63,
    173–78
Indonesia, 4
Industrial democracies
Japan and, 14–15, 193
population trends in, 14–15
United States and, 14, 310–11
Industrial Revolution, 2
Industrialization, 93n5
Infant foods, 92
Infant health, 262–65
Infant mortality, xvi, 4, 87, 115
in Bangladesh, 37
in Cuba, 142
in East Germany, 147
estimated, 28
in France, 37, 257
in Italy, 257
in Japan, 256
in Netherlands, 255
in Russia, 28
in Soviet Union, 129–30
Switzerland and, 254–55
in United States, 251
UNPD and, 36, 128

WHO on, 236–37, 255–56
worldwide drop in, 27–28
See also American infant mortal-
    ity rate
Innovation, 82
International Collaborative Effort on
    Perinatal and Infant Mortality
    (ICE), 258
International Food Policy Research
    Institute, 83
International Institute for Applied
    Systems Analysis (IIASA), 43,
    55
International Monetary Fund, 92,
    109
International population activities, 19
International Programs Center
    (IPC), 233–34
Iran, 15, 36, 70
Iraq War, 208
Ireland, 13, 148, 257
Islam, 53, 160, 231
Israel, 7–8
    immigration and, 12–13
    refugees and, 12, 239
Italy, 15, 60, 87, 185n15, 231, 311
    agriculture and, 105
    illegitimacy in, 264
    infant mortality in, 257
Ivory Coast, 85, 90

Jamaica, 78, 89, 106
Japan
    civilizing missions and, 208
    current order in, 17
    earthquakes in, 96

fertility in, 60
GDP in, 55
GNP in, 106
industrial democracies and, 14–15, 193
infant mortality in, 256
Korean reunification and, 192–93
life expectancy in, 10
manpower growth in, 54
marriage in, 71
perinatal mortality in, 258
population aging in, 60, 62, 161
population decline in, 47n5
public health in, 60
rural industry and, 90
sub-replacement fertility in, 53
TFRs and, 69, 313
trade surpluses in, 7
voluntary depopulation in, 70
World Bank and, 193
World War II and, 10, 60
Jefferson, Thomas, 25
Jelliffe, Derrick, 92
Jencks, Christopher, 290–91
Johnson, Lyndon B., 271, 329
Jordan, 37

Kazakh Republic, 87
Kennedy, John F., 329
Kenya, 24, 36
Khmer Rouge, 93, 99, 120
Kim Dae Jung, 245, 248
Kim Jong-il, 200, 215, 240, 243, 248
Kirgizia, 94n7
Kitchen talk, 320

Knowledge production, 63–64
Korea. See North Korea; South Korea
Korean reunification, 250
Japan and, 192–93
North Korea and, 187–93
South Korea and, 191–93
weapons ledger and, 188–89
widening gulf and, 187–88
Korean War, 245
Kornai, Janos, 146, 155n13
Kyrgyzstan, 231

Labedz, Leopold, 154n1
Labor force participation, 14, 55, 61, 139, 156n14, 172, 281
Labor markets, 166
Laissez-faire capitalism, 89
Lal, Deepak, 122
Laos, 87
Law of equal cheating, 135
Lebanon, 4–5, 7, 139, 231
refugees in, 12
Lee, Jong-Wha, 177–78, 202
Lee Young Soon, 241
Liberated areas, 87, 100, 101
Liberia, 37, 106, 208
Libya, 231
Life chances, 66–67
Life cycle income hypothesis, 285
Life expectancy, 9, 118
in China, 80, 142
Communism and, 143
in Cuba, 142
disability-free, 168
doubling of, 27

estimated, 28
global, 48n27
in Haiti, 58, 215
infant mortality and, 27–28
in Japan, 10
in North Korea, 142
officially claimed or independently reconstructed
   changes in, 143
in Poland, 130–34
in Russia, 28, 170
in Soviet bloc, 128
in Soviet Union, 10–11, 130,
   132
in sub-Saharan Africa, 27, 201
UNDP and, 27, 66, 203
in United States, 129
Warsaw Pact and, 131, 142
in West Germany, 129
WHO on, 104
of women, 66, 183n3, 203
"Linked Birth and Infant Death
   Files" (NCHS), 262
Lipset, Seymour Martin, 210
Lipton, Michael, 85
Literacy, 36, 67, 107–8
   See also Illiteracy
Little Dragons, 29–230
   See also Hong Kong; Singapore;
   South Korea; Taiwan
Living standards, 20, 29, 272
   in central Asia, 9
   in China, 88
   forced reductions in, 82
   improvements in, 3, 5, 46, 104,
      198, 307

income and, 289
in Korea, 188
limits to, 67
mortality and, 136
population growth and, 33
rise in, 88, 205
in Soviet bloc, 127
in United States, 274
well-being and, 147
Lobbying, 92–93
London School of Economics, 174
Longevity, xiv, xvii
Los Angeles Times, 176
Low middle income economies, 203
Low-birth-weight babies, 259–60,
   304
Low-income economies, 3–6, 84,
   106, 203
Luxembourg, 69

MacArthur Foundation, 19
Macedonia, 34, 49n37
Macroeconomic performance, 63
Madagascar, 15
Maddison, Angus, 201, 204, 206
   on GDP, 29–30, 117–18, 215
   on per capita income, 67, 202–3,
      211–12
   on per capita output, 197, 199
Malawi, 36, 85, 90
Malnutrition, 3, 74–76, 112–15
   in Africa, 79
   commerciogenic, 92
   in India, 83
   World Bank on, 78–79
Malthus, Thomas Robert, 66, 311

Malthusian doctrine, 32, 341
  on agricultural production, 81–82
  on famine, 116, 119
  on overpopulation, 116–19
Malthusian specter, 112, 116
Manley, Michael, 89
Manpower growth, 53–55
Mao Zedong, 119
Marine Corps, 220
Market failure, 122
Marriage, 57, 71, 235
Marriage squeeze, 57, 235
Marshall, Alex, 39
Marshall Plan, 206
Marx, Karl, 218
Marxism-Leninism, 87, 94, 121,
    142, 147, 151
Maternal age, 263
Mauritania, 106
Mayas, 21
McNamara, Robert, 75–76
McNay, Kirsty, 175, 177–78
MDG. See Millennium Development
    Goals
Means-tested entitlements, 332, 335
Medicaid, 269, 329, 333
Medical care, xv, 237, 251, 263,
    267, 269, 282
  access or availability of, 306
  American infant mortality rate
    and, 156–58
  death and, 76
  mortality and, 302–7
  trends in, 305
  in United States, 256–58
Medicare, 329, 332

Medium variant projections, 43–44,
    57, 70–71, 321
Mexican Americans, 314, 320
Mexican immigrants, 320
Mexico, 4, 11, 37–38, 105, 160,
    203
  US border and, 320
Mezzogiorno, 87
Middle class, 295, 338
Middle-income economies, 84, 104,
    106, 180, 203
Migration, 6, 8, 11
  Census Bureau on, 318
  economic development and,
    12–14
  Soviet Union and, 13–14
  Third World and, 12
  as voluntary, 12
Military aid, 95
Millennium Development Goals
    (MDG), 205–6
MINUSTAH, 214–15, 217
Missing girls, 228, 234
MMWR. See Morbidity and Mortal-
    ity Weekly Report
Modern state apparatuses, 84
Modernization model, 35
Modernization theory, 312
Modigliani, Franco, 285
Moffitt, Robert A., 294–95, 309n15
Monaco, 22
Mongolia, 86
Montenegro, 231
Monthly Vital Statistics Report
    (MVSR), 263–64
Moral fabric, 334–36

Moral pressure, 93
Morbidity and Mortality Weekly
    Report (MMWR), 260
Mormons, xv
Mortality
    Communism and, xvii, 126–51
    East Germany and, 147–49
    living standards and, 136
    medical care and, 302–7
    perinatal, 257–58
    population change and, 6
    population explosion and,
        117–18
    rates, 115
    in Russia, 170–72
    in Soviet bloc, 340
    in Soviet Union, 10–11
    in United States, 133
    in Warsaw Pact, 145–47
    West Germany and, 148
    WHO on, 133
    of women, 133–34
    See also Age-standardized mortal-
        ity; Infant mortality
Mother Teresa Missionaries of Char-
    ity, 219
Moynihan, Daniel Patrick, 337
Mugabe, Robert, 200
Muslims, 7, 14, 324n10
    Soviet Union and, 8–9
    in Turkey, 9
MVSR. See Monthly Vital Statistics
    Report
Myanmar (Burma), 52–53, 70

Nam-Hoon Cho, 230

National Assembly, 248
National Center for Health Statistics
    (NCHS), 259–60, 262–63,
    268, 299, 302, 304
National elites, 84
National Family and Health Survey,
    236
National Health Interview Survey on
    Child Health, 262
National Income and Product
    Accounts, 280
National Pact, 7
National Pediatric Surveillance Sys-
    tem, 299
National pension systems, 165, 179
Native Americans, 314
Nativism, 320
Natural disasters, 89, 96–97, 199
Natural resources, 14, 30, 33–46
Nature, 43
NCHS. See National Center for
    Health Statistics
Neaderland, Benjamin, 248
Need-based entitlements, 334
Neo-Malthusian ideology, 1, 73
Neo-Marxism, 73, 280
Nepal, 15
Net replacement rate (NRR),
    312–13
Netherlands, 22, 105, 133, 139,
    203
    infant mortality in, 255
New Deal, 329
New Federal States, 127
New growth theory, 209
New York Stock Exchange, 103

New Zealand, 66, 69, 203, 318
Nigeria, 15, 24, 99, 105, 119–20
Nonproliferation Treaty, 190–91
North Korea, xiii, 87, 215
  economic decline in, 200
  famine in, 242
  food in, 243
  life expectancy in, 142
  living standards in, 188
  nuclear weapons and, 189–91
  refugees and, 196, 239–50, 342
  reunification and, 187–93
  strong states regimes of, 207
North Korean Human Rights Act,
  249
Norway, 253–54, 257–58, 313
NRR. *See* Net replacement rate
Nuclear weapons, 189–91
Nutrition, 77–78, 93n2, 114–15,
  298–99

Obesity, 299, 306, 309n18
OECD. *See* Organization for Eco-
  nomic Cooperation and
  Development
Office of Economic Opportunity
  (OEO), 272
Official poverty rate (OPR), 272–73,
  276–80, 282–84, 297–98,
  306–7, 334
Oliveau, Sébastien, 226
Oman, 160
One Child Policy, 52, 57, 223–24,
  227
OPR. *See* Official poverty rate
Organization for Economic

Cooperation and Develop-
  ment (OECD), 4, 6, 29, 54,
  58, 61–63, 157
  figures from, 205
  foreign aid and, 101–3
  members, 255–56, 311, 313,
  316
Orshansky, Mollie, 273–77, 285,
  288, 298, 306
Oster, Emily, 226
Overcrowding
  in Bangladesh, 21–22
  in households, 300
  images of, 25
  population density and, 21–22
Overpopulation
  Diamond on, 20–21
  Gore on, 20, 24
  Malthusians on, 116–19
  as misdefined, 21–26, 117
Overspending, 289, 290

Packard Foundation, 19
Pakistan, 4, 12, 13, 54, 97, 172
  agriculture and, 105
  refugee camps in, 100
Palestine, 13, 36
Pan American Health Organization,
  78
Panama, 78, 144
Panel Series on Income Dynamics
  (PSID), 294–97
Pape, Jean William, 213–14
Papua New Guinea, 231
Paraguay, 200
Parental practices, 262–65

Parental preferences, 38
Passel, Jeffrey, 319
Pauperism, 327
Pensions, xv, 165–66, 178–79, 329
People's Daily, 97
People's Republic of the Congo, 106
Per capita consumption, 136–38,
    141, 308n9
Per capita income, 67, 136, 200,
    202–3, 282–84
  Census Bureau on, 280
  in China, 228
  in Haiti, 206, 211–12
Per capita output, 4, 106, 118,
    136–39, 141, 160–61, 254
  of Bangladesh, 204
  Maddison on, 197, 199
Perinatal mortality, 257–58
Permanent income hypothesis, 285,
    292
Permanent poor, 292–93
Permanent variance, 294
Peru, 105, 144
Pesticides, 82
Pfaffenzeller, Stephan, 31–32
Philippines, 85, 203, 231–32
Planned Parenthood, xiii, 18, 21
PNAS. *See* Proceedings of the
    National Academy of Sciences
Poland, 140, 141, 149, 150, 163,
    239
  elections, 144
  life expectancy in, 130–34
Political instability, 26, 49, 204, 207
Political morality, 120–21
Political stability, 20–21

Bangladesh and, 204
  world population stabilization
    and, 26–34
Pollution, xv, 21
Poor-friendly era, 202–6
Population aging, 157–58
  in China, 56, 161, 163–69
  demographic dividend and,
    180–82
  demographic trends in, 55–61
  in developing market economies,
    161, 162
  dynamics and dimensions of,
    159–60
  emerging markets and, 160–63
  fertility and, 53
  GDP and, 161
  global implications of, 182–83
  in India, 59, 173–78
  in Japan, 60, 62, 161
  macroeconomic performance
    and, 63
  public debt and, 62–63
  in Russia, 169–73
  solutions for, 178–80
  in sub-Saharan Africa, 160
  in United States, 61–63, 161–63
Population and Development Review,
    233
Population balance, 7, 65
Population change
  fertility and, 6–8
  migration and, 6, 8
  mortality and, 6
Population control, 1, 7, 70
Population density

GDP compared to, 22
GDP per PPP compared to, 23
in Haiti, 49n38
overcrowding and, 21–22
Population explosion, xvii
 below replacement, 68–70
 characteristics of, 65–66
 in China, 56
 as health explosion, 29, 52, 66
 human resources and, 67–68
 income and, 67
 life chances and, 66–67
 mortality rates and, 117–18
 paradoxical prospects, 70–71
 reasons for, 27
 scope of, 3–4
Population growth, xvii
 end of the world, 43
 living standards and, 33
 in low-income countries, 3–6
 in sub-Saharan Africa, 5, 23–24
 in Third World, 3–4, 202
 trends in, 2
 in United States, 322–23
 world population stabilization
  and, 26–34
Population size, xiv–xv
Population specialists, 21, 35, 56
Population stabilization. See World
  population stabilization
Population support ratio (PSR), 169,
  170
Population targets, 38–39
Portugal, 231
Posner, Richard, 235
Poverty, xiii, 26, 271–72

American infant mortality rate
  and, 256–58
anti-poverty programs, 272,
  282–84, 307, 332, 334
biases and flaws, 307
Census Bureau on, 285
culture and, 206–10
estimates of, 277–80
family-poverty rate, 262, 265–66
global paradox of, 197–210
governance and, 206–10
in Haiti, 198–201, 211–14
history of calculation of, 273–77
improvements in, 297–307
long-term probability of staying
  in, 293
major discrepancy of, 284–88
neo-Malthusian ideology and, 1
other measures of, 280–84
poor-friendly era and, 202–6
as population problem, 26
in sub-Saharan Africa, 201–2
temporary, 289–97
in Third World, 40
United States and, 90, 257
Poverty guideline, 272
Poverty household, 273
Poverty line, 257, 273–76, 292–93,
  297, 334
Poverty rate. See Official poverty
  rate
Poverty threshold, 271–77, 285,
  288, 292, 306, 308n3, 332
PPP. See Purchasing power parity
Presidential Commission on World
  Hunger, US, 113

Préval, René, 217, 220
Pritchett, Lant, xviii
Privatization, 146
Proceedings of the National Academy of Sciences (PNAS), 231–32
Pronatalism, 16
Prosperity explosion, 29
PSID. *See* Panel Series on Income Dynamics
PSR. *See* Population support ratio
Public debt, 62–63
Public health, 146, 170, 203, 2993
    care programs, 267
    in Japan, 60
    in Russia, 57–58, 179–80
    in Soviet bloc, 129
    in Soviet Union, 11
    specialists, 260
    United States and, 172, 253
Puerto Rico, 231
Purchasing power parity (PPP), 23, 25, 163
Puritanism, 327
Pygmies, 78
Pyongyang, 187, 189–92, 242–43, 247, 249

Rape, 214, 240
RECS. *See* Residential Energy Consumption Survey
Red Army Socialism, 129
Reference weight, 78
Refugees, 7, 86
    China and, 196, 240, 242, 245–46, 248
    in Germany, 12, 238–39
    Israel and, 12, 239
    North Korea and, 196, 239–50, 342
    in Pakistan, 100
    South Korea and, 244–47
    United States and, 249
Religiosity, 317
Reproductive choice, 38–39
Republic of Korea (ROK), 188, 241–47
Residential Energy Consumption Survey (RECS), 300
Resource availability, 21–22, 66–67
Resource scarcity, 26, 32, 33
Retirement age population, 157
Reutlinger-Selowsky malnutrition methodology, 76–77
Revelle, Roger, 127–28
Revenue sharing, 272
Rice, 91
Rockefeller Foundation, 19, 82
Roh Moo Hyun, 245, 246, 248
ROK. *See* Republic of Korea
Romania, 16, 130–32, 141
Romer, Paul, 209
Roosevelt, Franklin D., 101, 329
Rosen, Sherwin, 147
Rotoweeders, 90
Rural industry, 90–91
Russia, xvii
    birth rates in, 19
    Census Bureau on, 58, 172
    death rates in, 19, 57–58, 170–71, 185n12, 185n15
    Five Year Plan, 86

GDP in, 55

graying population of, 158, 169–73

health crisis in, 58, 171–72, 185n12, 185n16

infant mortality in, 28

life expectancy in, 28, 170

male survival schedule in, 170

mortality in, 170–72

pension plan in, 179

population aging in, 169–73

population structure, 172

public health in, 57–58, 179–80

See also Soviet bloc; Soviet Union

Russian Federation, 19

Rwanda, 21

Sachs, Jeffrey, xiii, 205–6

Sahelian famine, 89, 105

Saudi Arabia, 13

Scalapino, Robert, 242

Scandinavia, 12–13

Scarcity, of food, 80–82

SCF. *See* Survey of Consumer Finance

Schweitzer, Albert, 213

Scientific advances, 203

Scientific population policies, 34–39

Seckler, David, 78

Second-order overspending hypothesis, 290

Secular fertility decline, 35, 69

Selassie, Haile, 99

Self-reliance, 327

Self-rule, 208

Sen, Amartya, 120

Serbia, 49n37, 231, 232

Sex ratio at birth (SRB), 223–37

Sex-selective abortion, 196

considerations for future, 237

demographic effect of, 233–34

drivers of imbalance and, 228

imbalance worldwide, 231, 233

initial signal of, 222–26

in Little Dragons, 229–30

parity-specific imbalance and, 226–28

social implications of, 234–37

in Vietnam, 229–30

Sex-selective feticide, 222, 228, 235, 236, 237

Sierra Club, 18

Sierra Leone, 208

Simon, Julian, 82

Singapore, 229, 253

SIPP. *See* Survey on Income and Program Participation

Six Day War of 1967, 7

Slesnick, Daniel, 290–91

Slovenia, 34, 49n37

Slow growers, 139

Smoking, 11, 58, 134, 260

SNAP. *See* Supplemental Nutrition Assistance Program

Social appeasement, 220

Social democracy, 328

Social insurance, 329

Social safety net, 144

Social Security, 332, 335

Social Security Act, 329, 332

Social Security Administration, 273

Social Security Disability Insurance

(SSDI), 337
Socialism, 86–93, 129, 155n12
SOGEBANK, 219–20
Somalia, 120, 208
Son deficit, 166
Sorokin, Pitirim, 317
South Africa, 8
South Korea, 10, 85, 86, 87, 229,
    237
  foreign aid and, 108
  living standards in, 188
  nutrition in, 93n2
  refugees and, 244–47
  reunification and, 191–93
  rural industry and, 90
  under siege, 242
  state-building and, 208
Soviet bloc, xvii
  as aggressive, 16
  collapse of, 126, 144
  death rates in, 127, 132–33, 340
  health crisis in, 133
  life expectancy in, 128
  living standards in, 127
  mortality in, 340
  public health in, 129
Soviet Union
  death rates in, 10
  fertility in, 9
  health in, 94n7
  infant mortality in, 129–30
  life expectancy in, 10–11, 130,
    132
  migration and, 13–14
  mortality in, 10–11
  Muslim population and, 8–9

  public health in, 11
Spain, 10, 87, 231
Spending down, 290
SRB. See Sex ratio at birth
Sri Lanka, 78, 89, 137
SSDI. See Social Security Disability
    Insurance
Stalin, Joseph, 119
Starvation, 21, 98, 238
  death from, 75, 79
  by design, 89, 99–100
  episodic, 10
  specter of, 73
  World Food Summit and,
    111–23
  See also Famine
State-building, 208–9
Sterilization programs, 82–83
Stress, 134
Strong states, 207
Sub-replacement fertility, 43, 52–53,
    56, 59, 160, 173, 236
Sub-Saharan Africa, xiv, 212, 237
  Census Bureau on, 201
  disasters in, 96
  education in, 202
  industrialization in, xvi
  infant mortality rates in, 28
  life expectancy in, 27, 201
  manpower growth in, 54
  population aging in, 160
  population growth in, 5, 23–24
  poverty in, 201–2
  UNDP and, 23–24
  See also Third World; specific
    countries

Sudan, 120
Sukarno, 84
Supplemental Nutrition Assistance Program (SNAP), 333
Supplemental Social Security Insurance, 329
Survey of Consumer Finance (SCF), 289–90, 308n10
Survey on Income and Program Participation (SIPP), 289, 293, 296, 308n10
Süssmilch, Johann Peter, 222–23
Sweden, 94, 129, 133, 254, 256
    illegitimacy in, 264–65
    social democracy of, 328
Switzerland, 129, 139–40, 171, 264–65, 313
    infant mortality and, 254–55
    male survival schedule in, 170
Syria, 15

Tadzhikistan, 14
Taiwan, 76, 83, 85, 87, 197, 229
    foreign aid and, 108
    rural industry and, 90
TANF. See Temporary Aid to Needy Families
Tanzania, 85
Technical advances, 203
Technological innovation, 63–64
Téléjiol, 214
Tempo effect, 324n7
Temporary Aid to Needy Families (TANF), 333
Temporary poverty, 289–97
TFR. See Total fertility rate

Thailand, 12, 53, 70, 87, 161–63
Third World, 17, 38, 95
    agriculture in, 106
    Argentina and, 83
    coups in, 209
    economic growth in, 15
    education in, 63
    fertility in, 160
    foreign aid and, 101–4
    graying of, 158
    health in, 115
    hunger in, 77, 113
    immigration, 311, 319
    migration and, 12
    population growth in, 3–4, 202
    poverty in, 40
    world population stabilization and, 20
Thomas, Lewis, 76
Three Lean Years, in China, 89, 98
Thrifty food plan, 274
Tilly, Charles, 35–36
To Feed This World, 83
Tocqueville, Alexis de, 310, 327, 328
Total fertility rate (TFR), 40–42, 69–70, 184, 312–16, 321, 324n7
Totalitarianism, xvii, 88
TOURISTAH, 214–15
Trade reform, 92
Tragedy of the commons, 236
Transaction costs, 121
Transitory income, 286, 294–97, 308n8
Transitory variance, 294

Transparency International, 216
Transportation, 97, 298, 301–2
Triggering event, 320
Triple bind, 163–69
Trujillo, Rafael, 204
Turkey, 86, 162, 180, 203, 231, 316
    birth rates in, 160–61
    Muslims in, 9
Turkmenia, 14, 87
Turner, Ted, 19

Ukraine, 119, 129, 151
Ultimate resource, 82
UN. *See* United Nations
UNCTAD. *See* United Nations
    Conference on Trade and
    Development
Undeserving poor, 33
UNEP. *See* United Nations Environ-
    mental Program
UNESCO. *See* United Nations Edu-
    cation, Scientific, and Cultural
    Organization
UNFPA. *See* United Nations Popula-
    tion Fund
UNICEF. *See* United Nations Chil-
    dren's Fund
United Kingdom, 77, 139, 231,
    233, 264
United Nations (UN), xiii, 15, 18,
    109, 159, 162
United Nations' Charter, 101
United Nations Children's Fund
    (UNICEF), 18
United Nations Conference on
    Trade and Development

(UNCTAD), 118
United Nations Convention Against
    Torture, 248
United Nations Convention and
    Protocol on Refugees, 248
United Nations Education, Scien-
    tific, and Cultural Organiza-
    tion (UNESCO), 42, 67
United Nations Environmental Pro-
    gram (UNEP), 18
United Nations Population Division
    (UNPD), 52, 58
    Bosnia-Herzegovina and, 39
    infant mortality and, 36, 128
    life expectancy and, 27, 66, 203
    medium variant projections,
        70–71
    sub-replacement fertility and,
        43, 53
    sub-Saharan Africa and, 23–24
United Nations Population Fund
    (UNFPA), 10, 18
United Nations Relief and Rehabili-
    tation Agency (UNRRA), 100
United States (US)
    death rates in, 312
    earthquakes in, 96
    education in, 62, 281
    fertility in, 9, 24–25
    food in, 83
    foreign aid and, 95
    GDP of, 329
    global order and, 109
    Haiti and, 219–20
    human resources in, 62
    immigration and, 12–13, 319–20

industrial democracies and, 14, 310–11
life expectancy in, 129
living standards in, 274
medical care in, 256–58
Mexico border and, 320
military aid by, 95
mortality in, 133
population aging in, 61–63, 161–63
population growth in, 322–23
population structure in, 321–23
poverty and, 90, 257
pronatalism of, 16
public health and, 253
refugees and, 249
slavery in, 216
See also American demographic exceptionalism; American exceptionalism; American infant mortality rate
United States Agency for International Development (USAID), 19, 219
Universal Declaration of Human Rights, 101
Unmarried mothers, 262–64, 266
Unnatural Selection, 235
UNPD. *See* United Nations Population Division
UNRRA. *See* United Nations Relief and Rehabilitation Agency
Urban bias, 85
Urban centers, 58–59, 173, 319
Urban Institute, 319
Urbanization, 14

Uruguay, 136
US. *See* United States
US Department of Agriculture (USDA), 74, 81, 274–75, 277
USAID. *See* United States Agency for International Development
USDA. *See* US Department of Agriculture
Usher, Dan, 147
Uzbekistan, 87

Venezuela, 11, 136, 141, 144, 200
Vertriebene, 238–39, 241
Vienna Conventions on Diplomatic and Consular Relations, 248
Vienna Institute of Demography, 55, 175
Vietnam, 53, 87, 93, 142, 143, 229–30
Voluntary depopulation, 70–71
Voodoo, 217–18

Wales, 35, 233
Wall Street Journal, 247
War on Poverty, 271–72, 280, 297, 306, 329, 335
Warsaw Pact, 11, 126–27, 129–30, 139
age-standardized mortality in, 140, 141
death rates in, 132
health in, 144
life expectancy and, 131, 142
mortality in, 145–47
Waves of democratization, 204
WDI. *See* World Development

Indicators
Weak states, 207–8
Wealth, xvii, 29, 62, 80, 103, 269
Weapons ledger, 188–89
Weapons of mass destruction
    (WMD), 189–90, 247
Welfare
    disability awards, 337
    reform, 282
    road to, 330–34
    state, 326, 329, 335
West Bank, 7–8, 36–37
West Germany, 10, 144, 238–39
    Aussiedlung and, 12
    death rates in, 147–48
    illegitimacy in, 264
    life expectancy in, 129
    mortality and, 148
    per capita output of, 136
    stock of capital in, 156n13
    workers in, 138
Western alliance, 15
Western values, xviii, 16–17, 100
Wheat, 82, 91
WHO. *See* World Health
    Organization
Williamson, Jeffrey G., 320
Winiecki, Jan, 135, 146
Winthrop, John, 310
WMD. *See* Weapons of mass
    destruction
Women
    age-standardized mortality for,
      303
    illiteracy of, 40–41
    life expectancy of, 66, 183n3,

      203
    mortality of, 133–34
    social empowerment of, 36
Working age, 12, 53–61, 148, 157,
    179–81, 281, 335–37
World Bank, 22, 92, 107, 109
    on caloric deficits, 114
    on contraceptives, 37
    on education, 67
    on GNP, 104, 144
    Haiti and, 215
    on hunger, 75
    on illiteracy, 40–41
    Japan and, 193
    literacy and, 36
    on malnutrition, 78–79
    on per capital personal income,
      200
    reliability of, 105
    Reutlinger-Selowsky malnutrition
      methodology of, 76–77
World Development Indicators
    (WDI), 22, 36, 204
World Food Conference, 77
World Food Council, 113
World food crisis, 91
World Food Summit, 111–23
World Food Surveys, 77, 113, 115
World Health Organization (WHO),
    11, 58, 138, 139
    on infant mortality, 236–37,
      255–56
    on life expectancy, 104
    on mortality, 133
World population crisis, 20, 25, 26,
    34

World Population Prospects (UNPD),
    43–44
World population stabilization,
    18–19
    birth rates and, 21
    human resources and, 44–47
    natural resources and, 33–46
    overpopulation as misdefined
        and, 21–26
    political stability and, 26–34
    population growth and, 26–34
    premises of, 20–21
    prospects for, 39–44
    through scientific population
        policies, 34–39
    Third World and, 20
World Trade Organization (WTO),
    200, 201

on Haiti, 215–16, 219
World War I, 65, 203, 320
World War II, 2, 84, 87, 286
    fertility and, 52
    global order of, 109
    Japan and, 10, 60
    liberated areas, 101
Wortman, Sterling, 83
WTO. *See* World Trade Organization

Yang, Maw Cheng, 31–32
Yemen, 37, 87, 160, 239
Yugoslavia, 34, 49n38, 231

Zaire, 108
Zeng Yi, 235
Zhu Wei Xing, 234
Zimbabwe, 200

Acknowledgments

The studies and essays in this book owe to the generosity, support, and encouragement of many more people than I can thank on a page. But it is easy to identify and salute the smaller number of people who helped me bring this particular volume into being.

First are Christopher DeMuth and Arthur Brooks, authors of the foreword and afterword of this collection, respectively. By serendipity, they were also the presidents of AEI during my tour of duty here these past 30 years. This spare acknowledgment barely begins to scratch the surface of my deeper debts of gratitude to them both.

Next is Tod Lindberg of the Hoover Institution, a dear and trusted friend who is also one of America's finest editors. Tod spared me the agony of having to make my own choices about the chapters to appear in this volume—a task I would doubtless still be dithering over absent his acute and decisive counsel.

Then there is Alex Coblin, the latest member of the "Team Eberstadt" lineup at AEI. I have been graced to work with an extraordinary roster of talented young people during my time here, and Alex has continued this all-star tradition. His superb research assistance contributed to a number of the studies in this volume. No less important, he somehow, without my quite knowing how, managed to take care of everything else required to make this volume materialize.

Finally, of course, there is Mary. This was actually her idea. As indeed most of the good things in my life have been. Darling: thank you, once again.

About the Author

Nicholas Eberstadt was born in 1955 and, in 1985, began working at the American Enterprise Institute, where he now holds the Henry Wendt Chair in Political Economy. He is also currently a senior adviser at the National Bureau of Asian Research, and has been a visiting fellow at the Rockefeller Foundation, Harvard University Population Center, and American Academy in Berlin. A political economist by training, he has authored hundreds of articles and over 20 books and monographs on issues in demography, economic development, and international security. In 2012 he was awarded the Bradley Prize. He earned his AB, MPA, and PhD at Harvard and his MSc at the London School of Economics. Mr. Eberstadt is married to the public intellectual Mary Eberstadt; they have four children.

Made in the USA
Columbia, SC
27 October 2023

25081320R00215